The Imaginative Claims
of the Artist
in Willa Cather's Fiction

Willa Cather
Willa Cather Pioneer Memorial Collection. Nebraska State Historical Society.

The Imaginative Claims
of the Artist
in Willa Cather's Fiction

"Possession Granted by
a Different Lease"

by Demaree C. Peck

SUP

Selinsgrove: Susquehanna University Press
London: Associated University Presses

Associated University Presses
440 Forsgate Drive
Cranbury, NJ 08512

Associated University Presses
16 Barter Street
London WC1A 2AH, England

Associated University Presses
P.O. Box 338, Port Credit
Mississauga, Ontario
Canada L5G 4L8

The paper used in this publication meets the requirements
of the American National Standard for Permanence of Paper
for Printed Library Materials Z39.48–1984.

Library of Congress Cataloging-in-Publication Data

Peck, Demaree C., 1959-
   The imaginative claims of the artist in Willa Cather's fiction : "possession granted
by a different lease" / by Demaree C. Peck.
      p. cm.
   Includes bibliographical references and index.
   ISBN 0-945636–87–3 (alk. paper)
   1. Cather, Willa, 1873–1947 -- Characters -- Artists 2. Art and literature -- United
States -- History -- 20th century. 3. Artists in literature. 4. Imagination. I. Title.
   PS3505.A87Z756   1996
   813'.52 -- dc20   95-40624
                                                                               CIP

PRINTED IN THE UNITED STATES OF AMERICA

To my father, Russell Peck, the professor,
and to my mother, Ruth Demaree, the pianist —
artists both — who gave me the keys
to the kingdom of the soul.

Contents

Acknowledgments

There are many people I would like to thank for helping me to write this book. I am most grateful to my advisor and mentor at the University of Virginia, Stephen Railton, who first encouraged me to investigate Willa Cather's literary inheritance from Ralph Waldo Emerson. Steve fostered many of the ideas in this book and made brilliant suggestions for structural and stylistic revisions and additions. He helped me to keep faith in the project from its beginning to its end.

I give warm thanks to Edgar and Eleanor Shannon for providing me with familial support and a room of my own in their home during my years in graduate school when I wrote my dissertation, which provided the groundwork for the book. Edgar Shannon gave me shrewd and thorough editorial comments on papers I prepared for Cather conferences.

I acknowledge those colleagues at Washington and Lee, both inside and outside the English Department, who took an interest in my work. Jim Warren read my manuscript and provided useful suggestions.

Mary Wall, special friend, fellow graduate student, and stimulating colleague at Washington and Lee, gave me invaluable moral support and new perspectives as she read drafts of the manuscript in its early stages. Thanks, Mary, for your companionship during the many runs we took together, breathlessly discussing Willa Cather.

I could not have done the important primary research for the book without institutional support. The English Department at the University of Virginia provided a generous research grant that enabled me to fly to California to read Cather's letters at the Henry E. Huntington Library. A dissertation-year fellowship enabled me to travel to Nebraska, Illinois, and Vermont in my quest to read Cather's widely dispersed letters, and to focus on my writing without other obligations. Two summer Glenn Grants and a year's unpaid leave from Washington and Lee University further helped to support my research and writing and made possible a trip to Duke University to read Cather's letters.

8

I wish to acknowledge the following libraries and historical societies for assisting me in reading Willa Cather's letters and for granting me permission to incorporate material from these letters into my book: the Willa Cather Collection (#6494), University of Virginia Library; the Nebraska State Historical Society; the University of Nebraska Library; the Bailey/Howe Library, University of Vermont; the Beineke Rare book and Manuscript Library, Yale University; the Houghton Library, Harvard University; the Henry E. Huntington Library; the Newberry Library; the Department of Rare Books and Special Collections, Princeton University Libraries; the William R. Perkins Library, Duke University; and Special Collections, Colby College Library. Special thanks to Joan Crane, former curator of rare books at the University of Virginia, for sharing her extensive knowledge of Cather's bibliography and for her words of inspiration and encouragement; to Joseph Svoboda, former rare books curator at the University of Nebraska, Lincoln, for showing me the uncatalogued Bernice Slote collection of letters and for kindly offering me accommodations in Lincoln; and to Pat Phillips, director of the Willa Cather Pioneer Memorial, for her hospitality during my visit to Red Cloud in the summer of 1986, and especially for her loan of a canoe for an inspirational trip down the Republican River with my fellow Cather aficionado, Jane Barnes.

A community of Cather scholars provided helpful suggestions for revision. In particular, I would like to thank John Swift, Ann Fisher-Wirth, and Merrill Maguire Skaggs for their thoughtful readings and constructive criticism of my book. I have enjoyed engaging in a dialogue with these and other Cather critics over the years.

In addition, I am indebted to the managing, copy, and production editors at Associated University Presses — Michael Koy, Arri Sendzimir, and Evelyn Apgar — who have efficiently and wisely assisted the book through the production process.

I thank my family, especially my husband, Ken, for their sustaining love, support, and patience. For the romantic afternoons of brandy, cheese, and crackers in your office while we printed my dissertation, for the countless hours of child care that you assumed so that I could write and revise, for your remorseless grammar checking, and for your good-humored prodding to finish the job — thank you, Ken.

Finally, I give thanks to my three beautiful children, Caleb Russell, Catherine Jeanne, and Savannah Ruth, for their gifts of love and joy.

Abbreviations

The following abbreviations are used throughout the text to refer to frequently cited works by and about Willa Cather. The edition quoted from is the most recent edition, unless noted otherwise.

Editions of Books by Willa Cather Cited in the Text

AT
: *April Twilights (1903),* ed. Bernice Slote (Boston: Richard G. Badger, 1903; repr., Lincoln: University of Nebraska Press, 1968).

ATOP
: *April Twilights and Other Poems* (New York: Alfred A. Knopf, 1923; repr., 1962).

AB
: *Alexander's Bridge* (Boston: Houghton Mifflin, 1912; revised ed., with a preface, 1922; repr., Lincoln: University of Nebraska Press, Bison ed., 1977). References to the preface to *Alexander's Bridge*, 1922 edition, are cited in the text as "Pref. AB."

OP
: *O Pioneers!* (Boston: Houghton Mifflin, 1913).

SL
: *The Song of the Lark* (Boston: Houghton Mifflin, 1915; repr. 1926; revised ed., with a preface, 1932).

MA
: *My Àntonia* (Boston: Houghton Mifflin, 1918, with original introduction; Boston: Houghton Mifflin, 1926; with revised introduction, Sentry ed., 1954).

LL
: *A Lost Lady* (New York: Alfred A. Knopf, 1923; repr., New York: Vintage, 1972).

PH
: *The Professor's House* (New York: Alfred A. Knopf, 1925; repr., New York: Vintage, 1973).

MME
: *My Mortal Enemy* (New York: Alfred A. Knopf, 1926; repr., New York: Vintage, 1961).

DCA
: *Death Comes for the Archbishop* (New York: Alfred A. Knopf, 1927; repr., New York: Vintage, 1971).

SSG	*Sapphira and the Slave Girl* (New York: Alfred A. Knopf, 1940).
NUF	*Not Under Forty* (New York: Alfred A. Knopf, 1936).
OW	*Willa Cather on Writing* (New York: Alfred A. Knopf, 1949).

Edited Collections of Willa Cather's Works

KA	*The Kingdom of Art: Willa Cather's First Principles and Critical Statements: 1893–1896,* ed. Bernice Slote (Lincoln: University of Nebraska Press, 1966).
CSF	*Willa Cather's Collected Short Fiction: 1892–1912*, ed. Virginia Faulkner (Lincoln: University of Nebraska Press, 1965; rev. ed., 1970).
WP	*The World and the Parish: Willa Cather's Articles and Reviews: 1893–1902*, ed. William M. Curtin, 2 vols. (Lincoln: University of Nebraska Press, 1970).
WCP	*Willa Cather in Person: Interviews, Speeches, and Letters*, ed. L. Brent Bohlke (Lincoln: University of Nebraska Press, 1986).

Collections of Willa Cather's Letters and Other Archival Materials

Special Collections, Colby College Library, Waterville, Maine.

Louise Pound Papers, Letters from Willa Cather to Louise Pound, Special Collections Library, Duke University, Durham, North Carolina.

Houghton Mifflin Archive (bMS Am 1925 [341]), Manuscript Department, The Houghton Library, Harvard University, Cambridge, Massachusetts.

Department of Manuscripts, The Henry E. Huntington Library, San Marino, California.

Willa Cather Collection, Gere Family Collection, Nebraska State Historical Society, Lincoln, Nebraska.

Bernice Slote Collection, University of Nebraska, Lincoln, Nebraska.

Cather/Weisz Collection, The Newberry Library, Chicago, Illinois.

Whitney Darrow Collection, Manuscripts Division, Department of Rare Books and Special Collections, Princeton University Libraries, Princeton, New Jersey.

Special Collections, Bailey / Howe Library, The University of Vermont, Burlington, Vermont.

Willa Cather Collection (#6494), Clifton Waller Barrett Library, Special Collections Department, University of Virginia Library, Charlottesville, Virginia.

Willa Cather Collection, Willa Cather Pioneer Memorial and Educational Foundation, Red Cloud, Nebraska.

Yale Collection of American Literature, Beineke Rare Book and Manuscript Library, Yale University, New Haven, Connecticut.

Books about Willa Cather

WCL   Edith Lewis, *Willa Cather Living: A Personal Record* (New York: Alfred A. Knopf, 1953; repr. Athens: Ohio University Press, 1989).

WWC   Mildred Bennett, *The World of Willa Cather*, rev. ed. (Lincoln: University of Nebraska Press, 1961).

WC: AM   Elizabeth Shepley Sergeant, *Willa Cather: A Memoir* (Philadelphia: J. B. Lippincott, 1953).

1

The Explicable Presence of "The Thing Not Named"

In recent years, feminist critics have sought to challenge the politics of canon formation by calling attention to the ways in which women writers have been excluded from the conventional portrait of mainstream British and American literature. In an effort to expand the canon, they have questioned the privileging of those literary forms and genres that represent a predominantly male tradition, so as to acknowledge the merit of other traditions established by women writers. If women writers could be viewed within the context of a literature of their own, it has been argued, they could be better appreciated and understood. Sandra Gilbert and Susan Gubar were among the first to try to place women writers in a "different literary subculture from that inhabited by male writers."[1] For Gilbert and Gubar, Elaine Showalter, and others, the woman can develop her full powers as a writer only by finding a female predecessor. In their view, a female mentor is necessary in order to legitimize the woman writer's authority which is subversively assumed in rebellion against the patriarchal order. As Gilbert and Gubar claim, the female writer "can begin such a struggle [for survival] only by actively seeking a *female* precursor who, far from representing a threatening force to be denied or killed, proves by example that a revolt against patriarchal literary authority is possible."[2] Gilbert and Gubar have suggested that "the separateness of this female subculture has been exhilarating for women,"[3] and perhaps we could say the same thing about many of the female critics who write about them; as pioneers who have created a "subculture" of scholarship outside the mainstream of literary criticism, they enjoy a liberating and exciting independence. The burgeoning enterprise of creating new anthologies of women writers carries with it important emotional rewards. Once the canon is redefined as a lineage of women writers, the feminist critic can command authority over a new literary territory, whereas not long ago, she was largely excluded from the profession.

As fostering as the theory of female literary inheritance can be to the woman writer and critic, it raises some problematic issues. The eagerness to align women with other women writers may lead to a search for singleness that both imposes a female lineage and diminishes the importance of other equally or more significant male influences. If a woman writer adopts male forebears, that appropriation is sometimes automatically deemed suspect, evidence of a misguided and unrewarding apprenticeship. But to fail to consider the full significance of a woman writer's male identifications, and to insist on placing her within a female tradition instead, risks distorting the values in her art. That the woman writer must define herself as "female" before she can discover an authentic creative voice is an assumption that needs reexamination. We need to ask whether identification with "male" models is necessarily debilitating to the female writer, or whether it can be empowering. How does the female author's quest for identity elide the categories of gender that we impose on her texts? Can the woman writer confirm her strengths through other strategies as well?

Although one would think that the placement of a woman writer in a female tradition would enhance her reputation and clarify her art, it can actually do her a disservice. Such is the case with Willa Cather. Although I am indebted to feminist scholarship and sympathetic with it, I believe that, ironically, some feminist critics, in their attempts to write Willa Cather back *into* the canon, have written her *out* of the literary tradition in which she properly belongs. Sharon O'Brien, in her book, *Willa Cather: The Emerging Voice*, has largely defined for our generation the critical ground on Cather, and so I wish to begin by positioning my argument in relation to hers. Focusing her study on the literary inheritance that enabled Cather to write her first two novels, O'Brien, in the tradition of Gilbert and Gubar, asserts as her thesis that "as long as Cather denied her womanhood she was unable to speak authentically and powerfully as a writer."[4] Accordingly, O'Brien exhaustively acknowledges the male and female models of the artist that Cather admired in her capacity as an art critic in the 1890s and in her early career as a novelist, but then disqualifies the male influences in favor of the female in confirmation of the feminist theory that a woman writer must adopt her sense of artistic identity and calling from female forebears. O'Brien poses as her central question, How did Cather manage to move from male to female identification?[5] without establishing that Cather did, in fact, wish to make such a transference.

Although O'Brien does not disenfranchise Cather from a male literary tradition,[6] she gives priority to Cather's female literary influences simply because they are female. Assuming that Cather's early "male-authored narratives" provided her with "an unpromising point of departure for a woman writer,"[7] O'Brien imagines that Cather's career had its real beginning only when she met Sarah Orne Jewett in 1908. Appointing Jewett as the female literary mentor whom Cather needed before she could create a viable art as a woman, O'Brien argues that Cather's literary aesthetic changed dramatically between her writing of her first novel, *Alexander's Bridge,* and her second novel, *O Pioneers!* In O'Brien's view, Cather's dedication of *O Pioneers!* to Sarah Orne Jewett signaled her movement away from a "masculine" aesthetics of power or "force" to embrace a "feminine" aesthetics of love and "sympathy." As O'Brien says, Jewett had the "gift of sympathy" to give herself "absolutely to her material.... This is the alternative pattern of creativity Cather ... opposed to the athletic force Kipling represented ... the self-transcending imaginative power that was not, if conventional definitions of gender were applied, 'manly.'"[8] According to the story that O'Brien tells, Cather came into her own as a writer when she recognized her true inheritance in a female model of creativity based on selflessness. Unlike the male-identified artist, the female-identified artist had the "ability to abandon the ego rather than to impose it upon her subject."[9] Writing became important to Cather, O'Brien contends, as an experience of "self-abandonment to a powerful force and joyous loss of self."[10] Similarly, O'Brien argues that the achievements of Cather's strong heroines like Thea Kronborg or Alexandra Bergson, who can be seen as versions of the female artist, arise from their capacity to "[lose] the self in something larger, from self-abnegation."[11] As O'Brien's sees them, Cather and her characters are motivated by a self-effacing quest to "dispense with self and ego."[12]

I would like to reconsider Cather's aesthetics. O'Brien's argument that Willa Cather's art was valuable to her as a negation of her own ego strikes me as inconsistent with Cather's strong sense of her vocation. As Cather's 1890s reviews of artists reveal, she repudiated nineteenth-century sentimental and domestic women's writing because it affirmed the conventional pieties and gender roles of the day. Foremost among these socialized gender roles was that of the good woman as selfless, submissive, and sacrificing her own interests to those of others.[13] This model of womanhood Cather rejected as "contemptible feminine weakness" (KA, 408). In Cather's view, the norm of selfless womanhood was incompatible with the role of the artist, which demanded a bold assertion of self. Writers such as Elizabeth Stuart Phelps, in *The Story of Avis,* and Kate Chopin, in *The Awakening* — in the literary tradition of nineteenth-

century American women writers who wrote about the female artist —
had emphasized that "woman" and "artist" were irreconcilable because
of the social pressure upon women to be selflessly devoted to the needs
of others.[14] Later feminist writers, from Virginia Woolf to Carol
Gilligan, would try to redeem traditional female selflessness by seeing it
as noble, nurturing, and connecting.[15] But Willa Cather is not in this
tradition of feminists. For her, the nineteenth-century ideal of the selfless
woman was too threatening and restricting to be celebrated. It would be
unlikely for Cather to have embraced a literary creed of self-abnegation
when the pressure to conform to a similar social role had disempowered
many would-be female artists before her. Willa Cather's novel *The Song
of the Lark* is the first *kunstlerroman* by an American woman in which
the artist heroine is not defeated by the claims of family, society, or
death, and in which, as we shall see, its heroine, Thea Kronborg,
triumphs, as did Willa Cather, because she knows that artistic success
depends on a selfish instinct of self-preservation. In contrast to Sharon
O'Brien, I argue that Willa Cather embraced the creative process not as
an abandonment of the ego but as an aggrandizement of such. Her
essential belief was not in her need for selflessness or self-effacement but
in her own inner integrity.

My argument rests on the premise that Willa Cather believed that a
woman could write productively within a male literary tradition, and that
she self-consciously set out to do so. Her sense of art was male-identified
and especially rooted in the male American romantic tradition. The
differences between my study of Cather and Sharon O'Brien's suggest
that our placement of a writer in a literary tradition can greatly influence
the way we read that writer. Viewed in the context of female domestic
realism, according to O'Brien's thesis, Cather emerges as a writer who
values sympathetic communities of women and selfless networks of
kinship, such as we find in Jewett's *The Country of the Pointed Firs*.[16]
Viewed in the context of American romanticism, however, Cather
emerges as a writer who exalts the individual's glorious egotism. In my
view, the paradigm of the female artist as self-abnegating, communal,
and receptive fails to fit Cather's heroic characters who invariably strive
to recover a self that is sovereign, unitary, and self-begotten. Whereas
Jewett writes about women's relationships with other women, exalting
"that highest gift of heaven, a perfect self-forgetfulness,"[17] Cather writes,
above all, about the individual's relationship with herself, exalting a
perfect self-restoration. One of the significant contributions that I hope to
make in this book is to take Willa Cather back from the appropriations
made by feminist critics and restore her to her rightful place in our
literary history. Cather belongs not in the tradition of female domestic

realism but in the male tradition of romance that celebrates the escape of the antinomian self away from society and back to its most primordial origins. To borrow the vocabulary of Quentin Anderson and Richard Poirier, we can best understand Cather's protagonists as twentieth-century versions of the "imperial self"[18] who takes a "visionary possession"[19] of America. Willa Cather is, I would argue, unique for being a woman in this tradition. In Cather's quest for autonomy and power, Ralph Waldo Emerson became a critically important literary forebear. Emerson emerges, in Cather's 1890s reviews, as the avatar of her version of the romantic artist. As I shall explore more fully in my discussion of *O Pioneers!,* Cather shares important romantic affinities of mind with Emerson. Like Emerson, Willa Cather wrote in order to recreate and affirm a romantic and original sense of self. While I do not intend my book to be a study of Emerson's literary influence on Cather, or a study of romanticism generally, placing Cather in the context of Emersonian romanticism can give us a fruitful way to talk about her. The powers that Emerson accorded the poet in nature provided Cather with the essential terms of the fairy tale that she would tell in her novels. The real power of Cather's novels lies above all in fantasies of return to primal wholeness.

O'Brien's theory that Cather drew her sense of identity from "female" values of selflessness and self-abnegation imposes on Cather essentialist assumptions about intrinsically different gendered traits. O'Brien divides Cather's early reviews of artists according to a polarity between egoistic masculine "force" and selfless feminine "sympathy." This categorization, however, seems arbitrary, since for Cather these qualities are not gender-specific. Long before Cather discovered Sarah Orne Jewett, for example, she praised Shakespeare for his "supreme love" (KA, 434) and Carlyle for his "love and sympathy for humanity" (KA, 422), qualities that O'Brien wishes to associate with the feminine. Conversely, Cather admired female artists such as Sarah Bernhardt and Mrs. Fiske for possessing "power" (KA, 118) and "force" (WP, 662), qualities that O'Brien ascribes to the masculine. The distinction that O'Brien sees between "force" and "sympathy" is itself a false one; for Cather, these terms are not antithetical but related.

Both "force" and "sympathy" are essential assets of the authentic artist whose power and force of personality command admiration regardless of gender. Cather uses the term "force" not to signify aggressive male action and the will to subdue through virile potency, as O'Brien maintains, but to evoke the artist's personality that could electrify an audience, as if by a physical charge. As she wrote in an early review, the true artist is "possessed of power, and force is force, it tells, it moves, it commands irrespective of morality, just as electricity does" (WP, 662). Cather meant to write with force, meaning artistic energy, power, passion, and wide appeal.

According to the standard reading, perhaps best exemplified by Edward and Lillian Bloom, Cather possesses a selfless gift of sympathy for others.[20] Critics' misunderstanding of Cather's "sympathy" derives from an overly literal reading of a statement that Cather made in her essay on Sarah Orne Jewett:

> If [the artist] achieves anything noble, anything enduring, it must be by giving himself absolutely to his material. And this gift of sympathy is his great gift; it is the fine thing in him that alone can make his work fine. He fades away into the land and people of his heart, he dies of love only to be born again. (OW, 51)

On the surface, Cather's artist who "fades away" into his subject, "giving himself absolutely to his material," seems to abandon himself to his art. Yet, his relationship with his art leads not to self-effacement but to self-creation. The artist "dies of love" only so that he can more profoundly be "born again." As usual when describing the universal artist, Cather pointedly uses the male pronoun, suggesting not feminine submissiveness but masculine self-assertiveness. Cather once said in an interview that the artist's "sole duty is to put *himself* on paper, [though] he may be absent of mind or suffering of body" (WCP, 163). In hopes that the artist could overcome his fatigued or wounded self, the self that muddles through daily life, Cather insisted that he ought to recreate in art his truest, most essential ego. In her preface to *The Song of the Lark*, Cather makes an important distinction between the artist's actual life, which is inevitably full of compromising and disappointing experiences, and his ideal imaginative life in art. In reality, she says, "the harassed, susceptible human creature comes and goes, subject to colds, brokers, dressmakers, managers."[21] Only this vulnerable and fallible being fades away in the artist's passion for his art, whereas a potent, indestructible self is memorialized. As Cather says of her heroine, the opera singer Thea Kronborg, "Her artistic life is the only one in which she is happy, or free, or even very real." Far from obliterating herself in art, the artist becomes ennobled as the "free creature" who "retains her youth and beauty and warm imagination" as eternal and "imperishable" possessions. Although the artist crucifies her frail workaday ego, she finds in art that "you cannot kill ... that heavenly birthright, that kingly dower which makes men akin to the angels and to see the visions of paradise" (KA, 392). That awesome "resurrection" is what Cather worshipped in great artists whose performances reminded her that "nothing can destroy or entirely disintegrate a personality so unique, so dominating, so pregnant with power" (WP, 663).

Cather's "gift of sympathy" has led critics to regard her values as selfless and communal, yet it implies a sympathetic identification not with others but with her own art in what is fundamentally a self-involved and egoistic relationship; the artist "[gives] himself absolutely to his material" and "fades away into the land and people" of his own heartfelt memories. He who "forgets 'self' in his passion" does so because he is "so in love with his subject."[22] We can see the artist's sympathetic engagement with her material as a kind of self-projection. Cather projected her own self-love into her creation of a story. In an early review, Cather equates the act of writing with the ability of the artist to "project his personality" (WP, 131). The artist's challenge was to seek the "full expression of the essential qualities of his being" (WCP, 151). The reason why Cather so despised mass-produced commercial art while recognizing the authenticity of ordinary crafts like carpentry and bread-baking was because she believed that the original craftsman "put self into it — and that is what makes the artist of the novel" (WCP, 162). Likening the writer's imaginative engagement with the text to an almost literal transference of self, Cather once wrote that "I think a writer ought to get into his copy as he really is" (WCP, 8).

We might better understand the "gift" that Cather's artist gives the audience as a gift of self rather than a gift of sympathy. She felt that the nature writer Ernest Seton-Thompson had "given a new thing to the world" when he "added something to the subject from his own personality" (WP, 824). The composer Ethelbert Nevin bequeathed to his audience a precious legacy when he imparted "that rare grace and distinction" of his own inimitable personality, itself the token of "a breath from some world better and brighter than ours" (WP, 633). In a speech at Bowdoin College, Cather reportedly cautioned readers to ignore the technical faults of books and instead "read them for the depiction of the spiritual, mental, soulful life of the great genius that wrote them." Books could awaken the reader as long as they "but breathed the force and beauty of the artist" (WCP, 165). She recommended Du Maurier's *Trilby* because, "Always you feel behind the book the strong, tender personality of [the] man.... That is the great charm of the book, the wise, gentle, sympathetic man, whom every sentence brings you closer to" (WP, 132–33). Similarly, she felt that the reader of the poet Richard Realf got his greatest reward by finding in his work "always the unmistakable stamp of power, always a line or two to serve as an autograph of the poet in him" (WP, 602). Cather regarded her own books as such personal autographs given to the reader. In a 1943 letter, she confesses that she is puzzled to have had a request for an autographed copy of one of her books when the signature that mattered was on every page.[23]

Cather in her early career was drawn to singers and actors above all other artists because the performer on stage could most readily impress herself upon her audience. When she went to the theater, she saw the artist in the very act of projecting his or her aura beyond the footlights. Sarah Bernhardt was such a "primitive" and "mighty force" on stage that Cather felt sure "that her greatness will not die with her, that generations unborn will feel the thrill of her presence, the magic of her power, just as we feel Cleopatra's" (KA, 118). Bernhardt's own overpowering presence was her gift of sympathy to her audience. Like the opera singer Marie Tempest, whose "powerful and moving" face, according to Cather, "has something in it that goes straight to one's sympathies" (WP, 170), the best performers were those whose personalities were sufficiently magnetic as to draw the sympathies of the audience. The artist's "gift of sympathy" was a gift for impressing his or her personality upon the audience and in turn, for inviting empathy and sympathetic homage; in reality, Cather wished not to give a gift of sympathy but to receive it from her audience. She celebrated primitive force and passionate energy as qualities that enabled the artist, male or female, to win sympathetic applause from the audience, and thus to transcend commonplace realities.

In her essay "The Novel Démeublé," Cather puts forth a theory of stylistic economy in which atmosphere is created with a minimum of "furniture," or detail. As she says,

> Whatever is felt upon the page without being specifically named there — that, one might say, is created. It is the inexplicable presence of the thing not named, of the overtone divined by the ear but not heard by it, the verbal mood, the emotional aura of the fact or the thing or the deed, that gives high quality to the novel or the drama, as well as to poetry itself. (OW, 41–42)

Cather attributes the power of her suggestive style to an ineffable presence. This "thing not named" has indeed proven elusive, for despite the attempts of Cather's critics to name it, its mysterious origin has remained unsuspected. Assuming that Cather's unspeakable muse is embodied by some "other," critics have misinterpreted it in two ways. First, critics have argued that Cather abandons conscious control and submits herself to a sublime muse, or awesome force of inspiration that transcends the self. In her seminal essay "The Kingdom of Art," Bernice Slote suggests that the unwritten essence evoked by Cather's fiction is "a thing beyond, something more than men" (KA, 45); "neither the kind, form, substance, nor principles of art would matter if there were not the 'other' — the high, rare, splendid ideal that justifies the quest and the devotion" (KA, 59). Similarly, David Stouck proposes that Cather patterned her style upon symbolist poetry so as to intimate "something that partakes of the mysterious and infinite."[24] Second, critics have followed the lead of Sharon O'Brien, who argues that Cather refrained from naming her muse in order to suppress an "unnatural" or illicit passion for other women. Speculating that Cather "is the lesbian writer forced to disguise or to conceal the unnameable emotional source of her fiction,"[25] O'Brien fills the space in the text by rewriting it as lesbian love.[26]

Gilbert and Gubar have tried to revise Harold Bloom's patriarchal model of literary history in which the male poet metaphorically defines the poetic process as a sexual encounter between a male poet and his female muse. They ask how the female poet fits into this paradigm.[27] Whether the female writer has a muse, and if so, of what sex, is an important question in the study of Willa Cather. By putting Cather in a female tradition, Sharon O'Brien implies that women must identify with and love other women. Because O'Brien wishes to regard Cather in significant relation to other women aesthetically, it is perhaps inevitable that she find lesbianism — a principle of woman-woman attraction — at the heart of Cather's fiction. However, Adrienne Rich, in her essay, "The Lesbian in Us," describes lesbianism in terms of women's imaginative, rather than sexual, attraction to each other:

> I believe it is the lesbian in every woman who is compelled by female energy, who gravitates toward strong women, who seeks a literature that will express that energy and strength. It is the lesbian in us who drives us to feel imaginatively, render in language, grasp, the full connection between woman and woman. It is the lesbian in us who is creative, for the dutiful daughter of the fathers in us is only a hack.[28]

In the absence of evidence, there is no way to prove that Willa Cather was a lesbian in a literal, physical sense — someone who formed a sexual relationship with another woman. Cather's deep ambivalence about sexuality in her fiction suggests that she never would have admitted a sexual attraction to another woman at a conscious level. According to Rich's use of the word, however, we might say that Willa Cather was a lesbian. For Rich, it is the "lesbian" in women that teaches them to talk to and identify with each other. Defined as an impulse to forge imaginative "connection[s] between woman and woman," lesbianism, in Rich's sense of the term, describes not only Willa Cather, whose most ardent emotional attachments were to other women, but many of her female critics, who regard authentic female creativity as a breaking away from the literary "fathers." To see Cather as a writer who acquired her sense of identity and inspiration from female energy and strength affirms the enterprise of the feminist critic, similarly committed to a compelling vision of female relatedness and lineage. The "lesbianism" that we see in Willa Cather may tell us a lot about ourselves as female readers and critics who feel empowered by literature as a mirror of our own "female" values and sympathies.

But however female-identified Cather's human relationships were in her life, this is not to say that "*the* thing not named" in her fiction is lesbianism. The evocative secret of Cather's art lies neither so far beyond nor so guiltily hidden within the self as critics have thought. "The inexplicable presence of the thing not named" *is* explicable — as the artist's original, primal soul. Cather's muse was not some romantic "other" but her own romantic ego. So important was this undivided ego to Willa Cather that she made her recovery of it the central quest of her characters as well.

Cather was motivated not by the fear that the indiscreet dare speak its name, but rather by the faith that "the highest cannot be spoken" (KA, 267). She wished to celebrate an innate endowment that was too elemental, too inimitable, and too integral to be socially constructed or divided by language. In her essays on Sarah Orne Jewett and Katherine Mansfield, she more precisely defines the intangible quality of her *novel démeublé* as the tantalizing aura of the writer's own personality. In Jewett's stories, the "quality that one can remember without the volume at hand ... but can never absolutely define" in the lines of text is to be found in a residual "quality of voice that is exclusively the writer's own, individual, unique" (OW, 50). Mansfield's stories also convey an overtone too rare and precious for the printing press; the reader who tries to recall the distinctive essence of her art will find that "the text is not there — but something was there, all the same — is there, though no typesetter will ever set it" (OW, 110): the vivid impression of her own exceptionally gifted nature.

In her 1890s reviews, Cather repeatedly draws attention to the inadequacy of language to capture the artist's compelling personality. Recognizing that Sarah Bernhardt possessed the one unaccountable thing in the world — original genius — she praised her for "[having] something else beside, for which language has no name" (KA, 120). As if she were trying to get beyond language's restrictive classifications, Cather describes the hallmark of the true artist as "soul," regretting, however, that "it's too bad we have no word but that to express a man's innermost ego" (KA, 416). Making a similar apology, she writes of the singer, Emma Calvé, that her "astonishing popularity is due neither to her voice nor to her art, wonderful as they are, but to a third element which, for lack of a better term, one must call her individuality — her personality" (WP, 408). A force that is self-begotten and divine, the artist's essential ego is untranslatable using conventional discourse or terms common to everyday experience. Drawing upon an inner source of wholeness and unity, the artist projects a strength that is greater than the sum of its verbal analogies. Cather chose to evoke, rather than define, the elements of the artist's greatness, for only faith could begin to apprehend the artist's holy powers of incarnation. As she wrote in a review of the actress Clara Morris, "Art and science may make a creation perfect in symmetry and form, but it is only the genius which forever evades analysis that can breathe into it a living soul and make it great" (KA, 263).

If Cather's discovery of her genuine voice were dependent on her finding a female role model like Sarah Orne Jewett, then we would expect her voice in her early reviews to be uncertain. But, though Cather was an inexperienced writer when she wrote these reviews during her years in Pittsburgh in the 1890s, she was already so sure of the criteria by which to judge artistic achievement that she wrote a series of letters of advice to various artists, and indeed, all her reviews read as authoritative letters. Their message can be summed up in the advice that she gave aspiring writers while working at *McClure's*: "Unless you have something in you so fierce that it simply pours itself out in a torrent, heedless of rules or bounds — then do not bother to write anything at all" (WCP, 123). Cather consistently argues that only those who "have something" of true genius have the authority to create original and authentic art. As she wrote of Verdi's *Falstaff*, if "there is something especially wonderful and sacred" about a work of art, then it is because "something of the very personality of the composer seems to cling to it" (WP, 178–79). There are only two kinds of artists whom Cather discusses in her reviews: those who possess a special "something" all their own, and those who do not. In her dogmatic role as critic dividing the haves from the have nots, Cather resembles a god separating the faithful from the heathen. The artist's possession of his or her soul becomes the standard of measure. On one hand, Bernhardt has "something else" (KA, 120) and the singer Madame Von Doenhoff "has something higher" (KA, 132) that raises them above mediocrity. On the other hand, the actor Steele MacKaye falls short because the gods "left something out, the indefinable something which is the difference between a genius and a jester, a poet and a buffoon" (WP, 42). Similarly, the art of the actress Mary Anderson lacks "the indescribable thrill" — the thing not named — because she "never had the art to draw the soul out of herself" (KA, 157). Whereas the actress Mrs. Fiske succeeds because she "is a woman possessed of power, and force" (WP, 662), the actor Mr. James fails because "somehow his individuality is not large and powerful enough" (KA, 299). In Cather's eyes, those artists who possess the power of their own extraordinary egos are indomitable, while those who do not are second-rate imitations.

Cather found inspiration for her own recovery of a heavenly birthright in the writings of Ralph Waldo Emerson. Empowered with the gift "to mean more than he said, and to make his readers feel it," Emerson, as Cather wrote in 1898, "made the most spiritually suggestive language ever written" (WP, 583). O'Brien opposes the male "aesthetics of force" with the female "aesthetics of suggestion,"[29] but, as we see in the example of Emerson, the great artist for Cather exemplifies both aesthetics, using a suggestive language to evoke the unnamed "force" or power of his or her own primordial ego. At the heart of his sentences Cather was moved by "something that they never say, like an inarticulate cry" — the "cry of the over-soul" (WP, 584). She imagined that Emerson worshipped in his prose an "awful majesty of ... force" (WP, 583) that in turn dumbfounded the reader as the sheer presence of his divine personality. Cather's admiration for Emerson's "language apart from words" (WP, 583) anticipates her later description of her own style in her novel démeublé. Wanting to create an "overtone divined by the ear but not heard by it," she more deeply sounded a note that echoed the "overtone of the soul" that she had first heard in Emerson's prose and recognized as "the highest of all poetry ... the life and power of English art" (WP, 584). Finding ample scope for the imagination in her own integral ego, Cather aspired to create an art like Emerson's that could express "the poetry of the over-soul" (WP, 582).

Cather revered this "overtone of the soul" as a power that was unfallen into sexuality or the fragmenting responsibilities and compromises of adulthood. Cather's quest for self-definition elides the categories of sex. Gilbert and Gubar have imagined that male literary models represent patriarchal authority that undermines the woman writer's creativity and autonomous sense of self, but they have not considered the influence or inspiration to be offered by a romantic male writer like Emerson who wished to cast off fragmenting social or sexual roles. In the American tradition exemplified by Emerson, the figure in the landscape is a lonely self with an aboriginal, presexual identity. The self that Emerson celebrates is sufficiently generic to have encouraged Cather's participation as a female reader. By identifying with a male precursor who exalted an undivided asexual ego, Cather could gain a vicarious power and authority without experiencing a conflicted sense of her own sexual identity. She would not have to "redefine the terms of her socialization"[30] according to her male mentor's reading of her as "female" because sexual politics are avoided in Emerson's primal fantasy. When imaginatively residing in the unpeopled landscapes of Emerson, Cather could feel unhandicapped by the debilitating burdens of sexuality or gender. In fact, Cather may have wanted to celebrate an asexual ego in order to avoid her own problematic sexual identity.[31]

Cather dedicated herself to art as a narcissistic means to attaining power. She preferred romantic literature for its fairy-tale illusion of sovereignty. Looking back to the beginning of the nineteenth century, she exclaims, "Dear me, what fine times those must have been to live in! The times of Byron and Moore and Campbell and Shelley and Keats, of Murat and Ney and Napoleon himself; when empires were lost and won in a day, when one man controlled the world and made the world's history, moving kings and queens about hither and thither like chessmen" (WP, 353). Like Napoleon and Byron, Cather's ideal artist could exert an incontestable authority in his organization of a fictional world. Not making gender distinctions, Cather celebrated both male and female conquerors in her early reviews; from the beginning, she found strong mentors in the female artists whom she observed on the stage. Admiring "the unvanquished" Bernhardt in her role as Cleopatra, Cather rhapsodizes, "O yes, art is a great thing when it is great, it has the elements of power and conquest in it, it's like the Roman army, it subdues a world, a world that is proud to be conquered when it is by Rome" (KA, 120). Cather imagines that Bernhardt selfishly wins love and power from her audience as the spoils of her art. Empowered by the same magic as Cleopatra, who can "pour out her wine and make men what she wills," Bernhardt gets to enjoy the fantasy that she can conform the world to her will, and that the world will be "proud" to pay her homage. For Cather, the great artist was always a "conqueror" by the sheer force of his or her imperious personality.

Cather thought of the arena of art as a "kingdom." In her early reviews of the theater, she drew a rigid line between the world of fact and the kingdom of the stage, writing that "the dress circle, the parquet, the orchestra chairs — that is all the dead world of fact, but right beyond that line of lights are the tropics, the kingdom of the unattainable, where the grand passions die not and the great forces still work" (KA, 282). In her novels, Cather would similarly draw a dividing line between the deadening world of fact and the empowering territory of the imagination within which the great force of artistic genius could still "work" to displace reality. On "the stage [that was] the kingdom of the emotions and the imagination" (KA, 217) the artist could dominate the world by projecting his essential self without interference. Like the pianist Ethelbert Nevin, he could be a "monarch" who "[came] into his kingdom" merely by growing "completely into his greatest self" (WP, 627). That stage that Cather admired in her reviews as a "world in itself" eventually became the model for her own art. In "The Novel Démeublé," she locates her art on a "bare ... stage":

> How wonderful it would be if we could throw all the furniture out of the window; and along with it, all the meaningless reiterations concerning physical sensations, all the tiresome old patterns, and leave the room as bare as the stage of a Greek theatre, or as that house into which the glory of Pentecost descended; leave the scene bare for the play of emotions, great and little — for the nursery tale, no less than the tragedy, is killed by tasteless amplitude. The elder Dumas enunciated a great principle when he said that to make a drama, a man needed one passion, and four walls. (OW, 42–43)

Cather makes an aesthetic case against the "tasteless amplitude" of realism. Appealing to the writer to "throw all the furniture out of the window," she advocates getting rid of all the social and political facts that Balzac and other realists had included in the novel in order to give an accurate picture of modern life. With sweeping disdain for the material, she would exclude "the actual city of Paris," with its houses, factories, shops, hospitals, schools, banks, crowds, and the entire realm of "physical sensations," as having no "proper place in imaginative art." As Lionel Trilling noted in his 1937 essay, Cather's "technical method is not merely a literary manner but the expression of a point of view."[32] Clearly, Cather's desire to excise the details of material, physical life from the novel reveals an agenda that is not simply aesthetic. But whereas Trilling suggests that Cather tried to create an abstract and impersonal "order" that devitalized her art of energy and emotion, I would suggest that she hoped to enshrine the artist's single "passion" as itself the ordering principle of art.

In the guise of throwing "the furniture" out of the novel démeublé, Cather wished to discard from her imaginative space not only a surplus of factual detail but the principle underlying literary realism that art should reflect life as it is. In Cather's view, the conditions of reality, though inescapable in life, should not be allowed to dictate the world of art. In her defense of Alexandre Dumas and "romance whose possibilities are ... high and limitless," she expresses her disgust for "the prisons and alleys, the hospitals and lazarettos whither realism has dragged us" (KA, 325). Her objection to the multitude of literal detail reveals a deeper reluctance to see "the ugly skeleton of things" that realism exposes. Psychologically, Cather's method of simplification is a strategy designed to subordinate the world to the artist's own dominating ego. In her view, the spiritual life could not support the intrusion of life's crude and brutal details. As she wrote bitterly in an 1895 review, "We want one thing, desire one thing, demand one thing, and that life kills" (KA, 71). Despite man's universal desire to possess his innermost ego or soul, Cather warns, life is the antagonist that destroys it. To say that "the nursery tale, no less than the tragedy, is killed by tasteless amplitude" is to say that life, with its overwhelming and alien multiplicity, kills the illusion created in nursery tales of an invincible self in control of the world. Cather here implicitly acknowledges that the artist's ego idealized in her art as the thing most powerful was also the thing most vulnerable. As a defensive gesture, she *had* to throw the material furnishings of life out of the novel. Only by leaving her fictional space "as bare as the stage of a Greek theatre" could Cather enable her artist "to lift himself into the clear firmament of creation where the world is not" (KA, 407). She wanted to believe that nothing could touch the artist who inhabited that high firmament.

Regarding the artist as a holy spirit who descended like "the glory of Pentecost," Cather had to discard from the sacred "house" of art not only the material furniture of reality but "physical sensations" as well. The pianist Teresa Carreno and the actress Eleanora Duse were two of the many artists whom Cather admired for suppressing all details of their physical, mortal, and personal lives. She thought Carreno wore "the face of a conqueror" because she "had subdued within herself everything but what is greatest and noblest — the things that death itself cannot kill" (WP, 397–98). Between Carreno and "that self-conquered kingdom" of the keyboard, Cather felt, "there is absolutely nothing, everything that may ever have come between them she has buried too deep for memory. Out of her life she has taken everything but art" (WP, 399). So too, Cather appreciated Duse for having excluded from her art all but the highest of her passions. Duse was able to attain the "divine perfection of creation" because she knew "how completely [art] should absorb and drown and hide a life, how it should exclude all trivialities, all phantoms of a day" and "the tears and failures and human weakness out of which it is wrought" (KA, 154). Above all, Cather wanted to ban sexuality from her kingdom of art.[33] Throughout her reviews, she repeatedly berates artists like Rudyard Kipling for getting married, as if marriage abased the soul and compromised artistic genius.[34] Criticizing the actor Robert Mantell for having a love affair, Cather writes, "It does not matter much in what way, whether it is through whisky or frivolity, the yoke of social bondage, general indolence or Charlotte Behrens, it all amounts to the same thing.... In some undiscernible way the elusive quality of value goes and what was precious becomes common clay" (KA, 152). Cather severely implies that all common physical appetites and needs —

whether for alcohol, game playing, society, sleep, or women — merely spoil the precious substance that constitutes creative power. According to Cather's Platonic scheme, that "peculiar balance of the vital forces, this unison of all one's powers into one lambent flame which men call genius, is such an exceedingly delicate thing" (KA, 152) that involvement in the physical world would taint and divide its essence.

Cather left the fictional stage bare for "the play of emotions," but especially for the play of "one passion." She had to exclude elaborate scenery, costumes, stage effects, and, most importantly, all other centers of consciousness. Whereas to describe "the actual city of Paris" would be to describe its innumerable competing consciousnesses, Cather wanted to create her art as the playhouse of a single personality of genius. All of her conquering artists are privileged to rule their kingdoms by special election as the "chosen ones." Nevin's supreme reward in art is that he gets to be "the only man" (WP, 633) who can enter the kingdom and control an inviolate imaginative space. As queen of the stage, Bernhardt is the "only one" who could inspire the audience's "irresistible enthusiasm" (KA, 120); as emperors of their kingdoms, Byron and Napoleon remind Cather of the days we once dreamed of in childhood "when one man controlled the world" (WP, 353). In her eagerness that "one spiritual force, one great imagination may rise to snatch for us the blue from heaven and the fire from the sun" (KA, 117), Cather apotheosized the artist as the Promethean oracle or prophet who alone could steal the secrets of the gods.

Cather objected to the realism of writers like Émile Zola because she felt that superfluous clutter of factual details left no room for "the impress of a human soul" (KA, 371). As she elaborated, "You may heap the details of beauty together forever, but they are not beauty until one human soul feels and knows. That is what Zola's books lack from first to last, the awakening of the spirit." In reality, Cather objected to Zola not for including "details of beauty" — for only those details that were infused with the human spirit were beautiful — but for including "repulsive odors" of "the butcher shop" (KA, 370) and sordid pictures of "aching poverty" (KA, 369). In her eyes, Zola heaped up the ugly facts of experience at great cost to his own soul. Her challenge to him was: "What shall it profit a man if he gain the whole world and lose his own soul?" (KA, 371). Cather's biblical diction equating profit and loss is revealing, for in her view, one could have either the world or the soul, but not both. In her efforts to create an art that was the antithesis of realism, Cather tried to make good Zola's loss: by losing the whole world, she would gain her own soul. Though in life Cather knew that men "don't get" that desirable "one thing above all things" (KA, 71), in art, her characters could repossess the glory and power of their own egos as an imperishable gift.

While Cather's romanticism has its historical origin in American transcendentalism, its psychological origin derives from the mythic domain of childhood. For Cather, "an artist is a child always" (KA, 149). By modeling her artist on the child, she could best give priority to the make-believe world of fantasy and imagination over the mundane world of actual experience. As she wrote in a letter,

> The stage is a world in itself, a world apart ... a world which awakens only when the humdrum world of the everyday is asleep ... which is every night born anew out of dreamland, like the cloud palaces of the Fata Morgana. And this world has an atmosphere, a perspective ... distinctively its own, with which one can best familiarize himself in childhood. (WP, 682)

In her early story "The Treasure of Far Island," Cather most explicitly links artist and child: the "child's normal attitude toward the world is that of the artist," and the artist, as he idealizes the child within himself, is "a case of arrested development."[35] What they share is an attitude of "power" (CSF, 273) over a world that they can transform in imagination. As the artist looks back to himself as a child, he recalls that "we were artists in those days ... building empires that set with the sun" (CSF, 280) and planning "the conquest of the world.... as they used to do it in the fairy tales" (CSF, 273). Like those bygone heroes, the child-artist seems to outwit fate without encumbering himself by experience, for he creates a new reality merely by exerting his imaginative desire. The novels operate according to the laws of wish fulfillment.[36] The primal fantasy underlying Cather's works is a quest for the recovery of a world once known in childhood, surrounding the ego with a gratifying sense of its own importance. Ideally, the artist-figure in Cather's novels gets to live out the fantasy of the egoistic child who always occupies center stage, turning all eyes and advantages towards himself. As adults, Cather acknowledges that we are "kings in exile" (CSF, 281) from childhood, "the happy land we used to rule" (CSF, 281), but that the great artist could reenter the kingdom and exert an indisputable rule once more.

In exploring this childhood fairy tale in Cather's novels, I acknowledge my greatest critical debt to Quentin Anderson's 1965 article "Willa Cather: Her Masquerade," in which he suggests that the novels put us in "imaginative possession" of the world as a fostering scene.[37] The best paradigm for this impulse towards "imaginative possession" is, as he suggests, the moment when the adult seeks to imaginatively embrace the world as a child so as to repossess his recollected original union with the cosmos. The novels offer a series of ingenious masquerades beneath whose plots lurk variations of a single story that was simultaneously Willa Cather's: the artist's quest to achieve imaginative possession of the world in order to recover the dominion of her soul. By "imaginative possession" I mean an imaginative act by which Cather's protagonists, serving as her surrogates, lay claim to the world as their own mental property. Although these spiritually acquisitive characters appear in various disguises, clad as pioneers, lawyers, or priests, they are all incarnations of the artist who appropriates people and places as parts of consciousness. Cather envisioned the artist as a conqueror who garners the imaginative spoils of the world, valuing nature only insofar as it intensifies his or her inner life. Such an imaginative investment may be symbolized by a warranty deed to a literal piece of property, as in *O Pioneers!*, or, more covertly, through a possessive stake in another person or landscape, as in *My Antonia* or *Death Comes for the Archbishop*. But, however Cather's characters seek to reserve for their imaginative gain a "peculiar part and possessions"[38] in the material world, they attempt to assimilate only those things which minister to their sense of the ideal, or which heighten their awareness of their own passionate vitality. As Cather maintains in *Alexander's Bridge*, the "possession of that unstultified survival" — the consciousness of an original and undivided self — was the "only thing that had an absolute value for each individual" (AB, 39–40). Thus, while appearing to incorporate multiple values and experiences, Cather's imaginative claimants invariably seek to appropriate the world as a reflection of the self. Carrying all essentials within themselves, they embrace only those people and places that mirror back to them something of their own egos. Paradoxically, their acquisitions affirm an innate inheritance that cannot be gained from experience or external authorities; most deeply, the novels celebrate the primordial soul as the artist's most precious possession.

After the ground-breaking essays of Bernice Slote and the work of Susan Rosowski, Cather has come to be commonly recognized as a romantic.[39] But whereas Rosowski places Cather in a tradition of British romanticism, I place her in a distinctively American tradition of romanticism. Seen by Rosowski in the tradition of Keats, Cather's characters experience in nature a "negation of the ego" and "transcendence of the physical self" as they move towards impersonal and universal ideals of "beauty and truth."[40] In my view, however, Cather's artist does not seek divine or ultimate truths so that he "escapes the limitations of his own ego";[41] rather, he seeks images that reflect and incarnate the self. The imaginative movement is fundamentally different: whereas according to Rosowski's British paradigm, Cather's romantic extends himself towards unattainable otherness, the romantic character in Cather's novels is self-absorbing and narcissistic, centering the world in his own breast. Rosowski argues that Cather preferred the British brand of romanticism in which, in her view, natural objects assume a more specific, concrete, and sensuous physical presence (she cites Keats's "Grecian Urn," or the nightingale's song). For Cather, Rosowski believes, "the imagination must provide an anchor in the real world."[42] But I believe that Cather valued a different relationship between nature and the poetic mind. Although Cather believed that the artist must anchor her art in her felt emotional life and in the lives of others,[43] she did not wish to ground it too solidly in the nature of reality itself. As we shall see, Cather loved Emerson for dissolving the world of reality into the world of consciousness; he lifted his gaze above the disagreeable particulars of nature towards the infinite space of his own soul. Cather found Whitman less satisfying because he indiscriminately celebrated all of creation in its undeniable physical and material reality.[44] If, as Henry James once wrote, a "grasping consciousness" is what the American writer must have, then Willa Cather must be seen as a particularly adamant member of the "American" literary tradition that includes Emerson, Whitman, and James. For her, such a grasping habit of mind became a strategy to escape the hard realities of life by converting them into the materials of consciousness itself. Like their nineteenth-century predecessors, Cather's characters absorb the world in order to recreate an imperial self. Emerson provided Cather with the best model for her peculiarly American ideal of imaginative possession; her characters enjoy a special inheritance according to the same laws that govern Emerson's imaginative assimilation of nature as an extension of the self. As I shall explore in more detail in chapter 3, Cather first adopted Emerson's poet landlord as the model for her own artist-claimant when she wrote her second novel, *O Pioneers!* Emerson had promised the poet who exerted an integrating vision an inviolate imaginative property to which "warranty-deeds give no title"; similarly, Cather bequeaths her characters an incontestable "possession ... granted by a different lease"[45] in reward for their romantic sensibilities.

I have let my theoretical argument emerge from the conspicuous vocabulary in Cather's novels, letters, reviews, and essays. The terminology of "possession" and "dispossession" that I draw on is Willa Cather's own. Like Tom Outland in his solitary epiphany on the mesa in *The Professor's House*, Cather's characters become most psychically complete when they experience the unalloyed happiness of "possession" (PH, 251). Through her characters' attempts to possess the world, Cather seems, in part, to be dramatizing her own artistic necessity to assimilate her literary material. She felt that her talent as a writer lay in her capacity to absorb or "accumulate"[46] impressions of people and places in consciousness or memory until she had transformed them into an inextricable part of her own being. She once wrote that assimilating her material was the most tiring part of writing since it involved transforming hard realities into her inner life.[47] Yet what Cather most desired to possess through her art was not the world but the self. As she wrote to Dorothy Canfield Fisher, the imaginative appropriations enacted in her writing restored her inner sense of unity so that she enjoyed a feeling of possession that was complete happiness.[48]

Aesthetically, Cather's art is best understood as an art of self-expression; psychologically, however, it is best understood as an art of self-recovery. Throughout her reviews of the 1890s, Cather suggests that the artist wins from his art the salvation, or possession, of his own soul. She thought, for example, that *Anna Karenina* would "do more toward saving its author's soul" (WP, 292) than would all Tolstoi's philanthropic enterprises. Whereas she typically criticizes those "prodigal" artists who "waste" and "spend" their precious powers in the process of living, she commends those who properly channel their energies into art so as to win "salvation and immortality" (KA, 152). By "salvation," Cather implies not a religious transcendence but a spiritual restoration that comes from within, as the artist draws upon his or her inner force and preserves it in art. Cather's admiration for those artists who find salvation in their work reveals aspirations of her own. She wrote to H. L. Mencken in 1922 that her soul's redemption depended on the success of her current novel, *One of Ours*.[49] In fact, as her letter to Will Owen Jones in 1927 suggests, she looked back on her whole writing career as a process of working towards her soul's salvation.[50] Even before she had written her first novel, Cather looked forward to writing as a vehicle towards self-possession. In an important letter to Sarah Orne Jewett of December 1908, written while she was managing editor of *McClure's* magazine, she laments feeling bereft and dispossessed of her essential self. She expresses a wish to write full-time so as to save her soul.[51]

Drawing upon previously undiscussed material from Cather's letters, reviews, and other archival sources, I suggest how her novels were largely dictated by her own literary and biographical imperatives. Dorothy Van Ghent has recognized in Cather's fiction

the theme of a "self" at once more generic and more individual than the self allowed to live by the constrictions of American adulthood. It is as if the aridities of her girlhood, and the drudgery that followed, had left her with a haunting sense of a "self" that had been effaced and that tormented her for realization. She was to search for it in elusive ways all her life, and sometimes, in her greatest novels, when she left off searching for it she found it.[52]

Cather's novels progress as a search for a missing self, and, as Van Ghent implies, they are motivated by Cather's own need to find compensation for personal diminishment. Cather did not become a full-time writer until she was nearly forty years old; by then she had accumulated a series of "dispossessions." As I shall explore, Cather continually felt robbed of her soul by various antagonistic forces: the Nebraska landscape, her job at *McClure's*, the compromises of family life and human relationships, the problem of sexuality, and finally, as she once expressed it in a letter, the nuts and bolts of life itself[53] — people, her own frequent illnesses, and the daily round of routine activities. In a 1941 letter, Cather praised the writer Sigrid Undset for seeming to triumph over the ruins of her life so as to possess all that she had lost.[54] Similarly, Cather made it her aim in art to repossess the heightened consciousness of self that she had lost in life. By studying the relation between Cather's art and life, I wish to show how she used her imaginative claimants as surrogates through whom she hoped to restore the integrity of her own ego.

I align myself with Leon Edel, who approaches Cather with the idea that "the work is a kind of supreme biography of the artist: it is by his work that the artist asserts himself, and writes his name, his voice, his style — his and no one else's — into the memory of men."[55] Even truer to Cather's impulse to write is Edel's belief that "writers do their work out of profound inner dictates" and thus "are engaged in creating parables about themselves."[56] Cather's own philosophy of art encourages us to consider her fiction as a working out of her psychic needs. As she wrote in a poetry review, "Every expression of the human soul through the medium of art is valuable either as art, or a documentary evidence upon life itself, as psychological data" (WP, 601). Moreover, she contends that "it is impossible to judge [poetry] purely as an art product. It is rather a man's heart's blood spilled out on paper" (WP, 602). As she understood poetry, so we can best understand Cather's fiction not as an impersonal "art product," nor even as a reflection of history or culture, but as a revelation of her own passionate desires and preoccupations. Of course, in her desire to retain an exclusive possession of her kingdom of art, Cather made her biographer's task a difficult one by destroying most of her letters and forbidding in her will their direct quotation.[57] It is likely that Cather tried to erase the traces of her personal life not because she thought that an artist's life ought to be irrelevant to her art, but because she wanted to exclude from her art the ordinary details of her everyday life so as to preserve her highest self as her most important legacy to her readers. Provided that we read Cather's search for self-recovery out of the novels and not into them, we can see the novels as the best available spiritual autobiography of their author. And yet finally, I am more interested in the novels as works of art than as documents in Cather's biography. Thus my focus is on the conspicuous pattern of imaginative possession in the individual novels themselves.

Critics generally have emphasized in Cather's career a variety of fictional interests and techniques.[58] I would suggest, however, that Cather's artistic creed and aims were firmly established at the beginning of her career and remained remarkably consistent. Cather seemed to become more identified as a "woman" writer when she dropped her male costume and name, "William Cather, M.D.," but she continued her pose in her fiction, adopting male personas and imagining "male" fantasies of power.[59] Cast in different plots and widely ranging settings, the underlying childhood fantasy of power, won through an imaginative possession of the world, provides a coherence for Cather's art and career as a whole.[60] Laura Winters has most clearly discussed "possession" as a pervasive issue in Willa Cather's work. She insightfully writes that "all her novels fundamentally concern possession. Each work presents a different version of the key question: What is it legitimate to possess?"[61] Winters interestingly suggests that novels such as *My Àntonia*, *One of Ours*, and *My Mortal Enemy,* with possessive pronouns in their titles, ask the primary question, Who owns a person's story? *The Song of the Lark*, in her view, asks whether one can ever possess one's own talent. *O Pioneers!* and *Death Comes for the Archbishop* ask, Who can possess the landscape? *The Professor's House* asks many questions, such as What can be possessed of houses, of one's family happiness, of the artifacts of a bygone civilization?[62] and so on. All of these questions are important and central to the novels. In my study, I would like to elaborate on Winters's scheme to explore how these questions are answered. Despite the seeming variety of the novels' thematic concerns, the answer to the fundamental questions of ownership — What can be possessed? and Who can possess it? — is always the same. Winters concludes that Professor St. Peter "reawaken[s] ... to a new understanding finally of what one can possess: one's own life."[63] This is the final revelation of all of Cather's protagonists: the essential thing that one needs to possess is one's own soul, and the person of artistic sensibilities is best equipped to possess it. Seeking to lay claim to other people, landscapes, or houses, the central characters, according to Cather's masquerade, really lay claim to their own inner lives, so that the crucial question becomes not *What* can be possessed?

but *How* can "it" be possessed? By examining eight of Cather's major novels in chronological order, I hope to reveal a development of various strategies that Cather used to reenact her central mission. I begin by looking back to Cather's first two novels, *Alexander's Bridge* and *O Pioneers!*, that together recount the story that Cather later celebrated in *The Song of the Lark* of how she came to claim the literary material and voice that were authentically her "own." Although critics have usually dismissed *Alexander's Bridge* because of its imitative and artificial style, I devote a proportionally large amount of the book to it in order to show how its hero's divided loyalties reflect Cather's own dilemma between claiming the world and claiming the self as the goal of her art. I argue that towards the end of the novel Cather gives priority to the life of the soul and thus points the way towards her first truly original novel, *O Pioneers!* In this book, Cather uses her pioneer heroine to stake out her own new literary territory, a territory that was not merely regional but symbolic of the more deeply grounded domain of consciousness itself. In Cather's third novel, *The Song of the Lark*, the pattern of imaginative possession characteristic of the novels as a whole is most nakedly exposed. Its heroine, the opera singer Thea Kronborg, can be seen as the exemplar of the artist as an imaginative claimant who comes "into full possession of things" (SL, 477). The secret "something" (SL, 209) that Thea recognizes everywhere as her "second self" is an incarnation of that "indefinable something" (WP, 42) that Cather herself wanted to evoke and recover through her art as the artist's essential romantic ego; less obviously, Cather's other imaginative claimants also seek to recover from the world a special "something" in token of their individuality. Thea is also the paradigmatic character in Cather's fiction in the way that she reorganizes the world around the self; her efforts to reject all threateningly "other" facts of life so as to stand within an imaginative sphere ruled solely by her own ego dramatize Cather's ambition to empower the artist within her novel démeublé made bare of all competing elements. As Cather's most explicitly autobiographical novel, *The Song of the Lark* helps us to understand Cather's own artistic development as a process of coming into full "possession" of her powers.

If Cather's novels vary in tone or dramatic oppositions, that is because Cather carries out the fantasy of imaginative possession with varying degrees of success at different points in her career. The relative fulfillment of the quest accounts for the varying degrees of optimism among the novels and gives shape to Cather's career. In the book's fifth chapter, I analyze *My Àntonia* as a transitional novel between the celebratory novels of Cather's early career and the bitter novels of her midcareer. Whereas the pioneer Alexandra Bergson had laid claim to a landscape, her descendant Jim Burden lays claim to a person — his childhood friend, Àntonia — as a cherished memory. Although his imaginative possession is triumphant, his vicarious dependence on another betrays Cather's feelings of diminishing vitality. In chapters 6 and 7, I explore *A Lost Lady* and *The Professor's House* as representative of Cather's darker middle phase. I suggest that we can see the narrator of *A Lost Lady* or the Professor in *The Professor's House* as frustrated figures of the artist whose imaginative claims upon the world have been thwarted by rival commercial philistines. Whereas the early novels enact the process by which Cather erected the boundaries of her kingdom of the soul, these novels enact her indignant efforts to defend the artist's imaginative property against the threatening usurpations of others. By making the central drama in these novels the struggle between two kinds of ownership — a material possession and an imaginative appropriation of nature — Cather herself was desperately trying to maintain her imaginative foothold in the world. In chapter 8, I examine how *Death Comes for the Archbishop* brings Cather's career full circle to its affirmative third phase. Through her Archbishop, who rids the Southwest of its corrupt priests, ostensibly on behalf of the Catholic Church, Cather reclaimed her imaginative territory in the name of what she considered that true God: the self. Finally, I consider how Cather's last completed novel, *Sapphira and the Slave Girl*, recapitulates her childhood fantasy of power in provocative and disturbing ways.

2

Alexander's Bridge:
Cather's Bridge to the Soul

Looking back on her career through the opera singer Thea Kronborg, her autobiographical heroine in *The Song of the Lark*, Willa Cather imagined that she had contained an essential self from the beginning. But in her zealous self-affirmation, she oversimplified and idealized her artistic development. In reality, Cather had begun her career beset by self-doubts. We can best understand the story of how Cather herself came "into full possession of things" (SL, 477) by examining her first two novels, *Alexander's Bridge* and *O Pioneers!* Cather used the vocabulary of possession to describe her achievement in writing *O Pioneers!* In that novel, she first laid claim to the subject matter that was "truly [her] own" (Pref. AB, vi). By contrast, she retrospectively disparaged her first novel, *Alexander's Bridge,* as an "external story" that had been composed from materials acquired from "outside [her] deepest experience" (Pref. AB, vi and v–vi). Ever since David Daiches overlooked *Alexander's Bridge* as "a mere literary exercise,"[1] most critics have similarly taken Cather at her word and disregarded the novel as a false start. But in Cather's efforts to distance herself from *Alexander's Bridge* and to celebrate her more original work in *O Pioneers!*, she exaggerated the differences between them. For, despite its artificiality, *Alexander's Bridge* profoundly reveals Cather's desires and dilemmas as a struggling writer at the outset of her career. Cather created her hero, Bartley Alexander, as a surrogate so as to measure her own potential strengths and limitations as an artist. More specifically, she used him to evaluate the qualities of the vital personality or ego that she thought necessary to project into art. Far from expressing the confidence of a Thea Kronborg, however, Cather reveals an ambivalent attitude towards the imperial self.

37

In her 1922 preface to *Alexander's Bridge,* Cather makes two implicit
analogies between herself and Bartley that suggest that she envisioned
him as a figure of the artist who projected her own desires. In hindsight,
after writing *O Pioneers!,* she claims that "after [a writer] has once or
twice done a story that formed itself, inevitably, in his mind, he will not
often turn back to the building of external stories again" (Pref. AB, vi).
By describing her composition of *Alexander's Bridge* as the "building"
of an "external" story, Cather draws a parallel between her construction
of the novel and Alexander's "building" of his bridge. Indeed, both
Alexander and Cather can be seen as artists who design their works of art
according to the most recent fashion: Alexander builds his bridge according to "the latest practice in bridge structure" (37) while Cather models
her novel on what she later called "the most conventional pattern" (OW,
91). Bartley's anxiety that the plan for his bridge seems "all very well on
paper, but it remains to be seen whether it can be done in practice" (122),
reminds us that Cather too was largely drawing her artistic inspiration
from written blueprints. Feeling that her own experience was not important enough for serious literature, she had reached far beyond herself to
imitate the literary precedent of the esteemed novels of Henry James. As
she admitted in her 1931 essay, "My First Novels [There Were Two],"
she had wanted to make a respectable literary debut and so was mindful
of the fact that "the drawing-room was considered the proper setting for a
novel, and the only characters worth reading about were smart people or
clever people" (OW, 93). In its superficial trappings, *Alexander's Bridge*
does contain recognizably Jamesian elements: an international setting
laid in Boston and London, a cast of refined characters who converse in
elegant parlors, and even a ficelle who comments on the enigmatic hero.

In her preface, Cather makes a second analogy between herself and
Bartley. Looking back on herself as "the young writer [who] must have
his affair with the external material he covets" (Pref. AB, viii), Cather
uses the word "affair" to suggest that Bartley's romantic "affair" with the
London actress Hilda Burgoyne mirrors her own literary flirtation with
the theater world of London. Bartley's visits to the theater in hopes of
finding diversion during his business trips can be seen to enact Cather's
business trips to London while on assignment for *McClure's* magazine in
1909. As Bernice Slote has documented, the novel's portrait of the theater world of London owes something to Cather's excursions to the
Abbey theater, where she saw Irish plays by Yeats and Synge.[2] Cather
later disparaged her incorporation in the novel of the "interesting
material" and "interesting people" (OW, 91) she had sought out in her
capacity as journalist, as if she had been under the naive assumption that
"knowledge is something [the writer] can get by going out to look for it,

as one goes to a theatre" (Pref. AB, vii). Such gathered impressions she came to view as novel and new, but ultimately "shallow."

Bartley Alexander enacts Cather's public ambitions to appropriate more than fashionable literary forms and subject matter. As an engineer who ultimately reconstructs Willa Cather's own professional and social gains, Bartley Alexander builds an "external" story that was more related to his author than she was later willing to admit. As I hope to show, we can see Bartley as the builder of an external story not just by the way that he uses external formulas to construct his art, but by the way that he makes various appropriations to construct his life — and, simultaneously, Willa Cather's. By way of apology for the superficial quality of *Alexander's Bridge*, Cather wrote in her preface that "it is not always easy for the inexperienced writer to distinguish between his own material and that which he would like to make his own" (Pref. AB, v). This statement suggests that Cather's aims in the novel were conflicted — that she wanted not simply to appropriate material from her worldly experience but to claim her "own material" as well. Her problem was that she could not "distinguish" between the two. In fact, I would argue that we can best understand *Alexander's Bridge* as an enactment of Cather's dilemma between two kinds of literary subject matter: the things of the world she wanted to "make her own" and the inner life of consciousness that had always been her "own." Simultaneously, we can understand the central struggle of the novel's hero, Bartley Alexander, as a dramatization of Cather's psychic conflict between the claims of a public ego and an essential self.

Cather claimed that she based the collapse of her hero's bridge upon a real news event: the collapse of the Quebec bridge into the St. Lawrence on 29 August 1907.[3] More deeply, however, Cather chose to make Bartley Alexander a builder of bridges in order to construct imaginative connections of her own. As Cather's engineer, Bartley most profoundly builds figurative bridges in opposite directions: he builds both a bridge to the world, and, as Cather described art in an early short story, "a bridge into the kingdom of the soul" (CSF, 361). Bartley's continuing self-division suggests that Cather herself remained divided throughout most of the novel between the competing claims of life as lived in the world of others and life as lived in consciousness. At the novel's end, however, she finally decided to privilege Bartley's primordial self over his public identity. Though Cather's biographer James Woodress has written that *Alexander's Bridge* "marks the end of [Cather's] beginning rather than the beginning of her end,"[4] *Alexander's Bridge* can best be seen as a transitional work that marks the beginning of her major literary quest — a novel that we might best think of as *Cather's Bridge* to the soul.

In a 1912 interview, Cather pointed out that *Alexander's Bridge* was really a psychological novel:

> This is not the story of a bridge and how it was built, but of a man who built bridges. The bridge builder with whom this story is concerned began life a pagan, crude force, with little respect for anything but youth and work and power. He married a woman of much more discriminating taste and much more clearly defined standards. He admires and believes in the social order of which she is really a part, though he has been only a participant. (WCP, 6)

Introducing Bartley as "a pagan, crude force" who marries a woman of refined and genteel tastes, Cather suggests that he builds one of his most important figurative bridges by forming a connection with high society. Before the novel opens, Bartley builds a suspension bridge that literally connects to the hill where his wife's worldly Aunt Eleanor lives. As his old professor later congratulates him, it was by meeting Aunt Eleanor "that your luck began, Bartley" (11), for Aunt Eleanor introduces him to her niece, the elegant and distinguished Winifred Pemberton, who repre-sents the monied aristocracy of old Boston. Completing his bridge just before he marries Winifred, Bartley more significantly forms a social bridge with a destination at the top of society's most exclusive hierar-chies.[5] Like Bartley, Cather felt that she herself was building a "bridge" into the high society of the East by writing the novel. In a letter she wrote to H. L. Mencken in 1922, she attributed the contrived and conventional form of her first novel to her ambitions as a young writer to enter well-to-do society in the proper company.[6] In reality, Cather had made her debut in the good society of Boston in 1907 and 1908 when she was on assignment for *McClure's*. As if to reaffirm her connections with that sophisticated society, she recreates them in the novel. Through Wilson's admiring view of Chestnut Street, "with its worn paving" and "its irregu-lar, gravely colored houses," Cather recollects her own "pleasant" (WCP, 2) memories of living on that time-worn and stately street.[7] But the house that Cather most nostalgically recalls in *Alexander's Bridge* is the home of Annie Fields, widow of the famous publisher of Ticknor and Fields, at 148 Charles Street.[8] In her description of Bartley's "long brown" (5) library, "where the wide back windows looked out upon the garden and the sunset and a fine stretch of silver-colored river" (4), Cather recreates her memory of Annie Fields's "long drawing-room" overlooking a gar-den, the sunset, and the "silvery"[9] Charles river. She could imagine that Bartley appropriates his wife's milieu so that "it all seemed to glow like [his] inevitable background" (10) because she herself had come away from her visits to the elegant parlors of Annie Fields with jubilant feeling of imaginative possession.[10] As she rejoiced in a letter to Sarah Orne Jewett in 1908, she felt that she had suddenly inherited the rarefied atmosphere of a nobler era as if it were all her own.[11] In its recreation as the room presided over by Winifred Pemberton, "an assembler" of "treasures," 148 Charles Street was a sanctum that offered Cather priceless aesthetic treasures: the impression of "costly privileges and fine spaces" (3) and "a rich and amply guarded quiet" (5). By having Wilson, himself a "man of taste" (1), approve of Bartley's acquisition of the Bostonian world, Cather seems to reassure herself that she, too, "is not out of place there" (10). Moreover, Cather confirms her place within the cultural establishment of Annie Fields through Bartley's liaison with Aunt Eleanor. As if to recreate the days when she had taken breaks from her magazine work to visit Annie Fields, she has Bartley "go up from the works to have tea with [Aunt Eleanor], and sit talking to her for hours" (11). Indeed, Aunt Eleanor, "little and fragile," with a "splendid head," "a lace scarf on her hair," and "such a flavor of life about her" (11), is largely a portrait of Annie Fields as Cather describes her in her essay "148 Charles Street" (NUF, 52–75). Bartley recalls that Aunt Eleanor, who "had known Gordon and Livingstone and Beaconsfield when she was young, ... was the first woman of that sort I'd ever known" (11). Similarly, Annie Fields was one of the first women of that sort that Cather — herself a naive westerner at the time — had ever known. Having entertained the great writers of her day in her literary salon in much the same impressive way that Aunt Eleanor had kept company with great explorers and political figures, Annie Fields gave to Cather the feeling of belonging to a prestigious intellectual tradition. Celebrating her newfound connection to "the Golden Age of American Literature," Cather exclaimed to Elizabeth Shepley Sergeant, "Think ... what it is to know someone who invited to her table Emerson, Holmes, Hawthorne, Howells, James Russell Lowell — and who remembers and quotes what they said there!" (WC: AM, 41). Also meeting the honorable lady,[12] Sarah Orne Jewett, at 148 Charles Street, Cather felt an even stronger link to a genteel literary past.

Bartley's Allway bridge also symbolizes his professional advances. As Winifred recalls, "You have only to look at it to feel that it meant the beginning of a great career" (18). By the time the novel opens, Bartley has earned a "popular" (36) reputation as the world's greatest builder of bridges. Looking "as a tamer of rivers ought to look" (9), his picture is always the one the newspaper men demand. In his rugged, powerful virility, Alexander has the epic stature of the greatest of nature's conquerors, as if he were, indeed, worthy of his namesake, Alexander the Great. Even the Emperor of Japan applauds his exceptional accomplishments, inviting him, as the world's authority on bridge building, to give a series of lectures at the Imperial University. When Hilda later congratulates Bartley for having been decorated by the emperor as the "Commander of the Order of the Rising Sun" (43), she hails him as if he had been crowned the emperor of the universe. Now, as Bartley builds his most spectacular bridge ever, he has the satisfaction of knowing that "he would probably always be known as the engineer who designed the great Moorlock Bridge, the longest cantilever in existence" (37).

Bartley's distinguished career is, at its deepest level, Willa Cather's. Cather pictured herself as a westerner of vague origins who had come east to make her way in the world and who had eventually risen to the top of her profession as a self-made "man." Just as Bartley as a youth felt social pressure to "do something extraordinary" (7), so Cather, as she revealed in a letter to Mariel Gere of May 1896, came east with the awareness that others back home hoped that she would accomplish something exceptional with her talents.[13] Though gratifying, such self-consciousness to perform increased Cather's anxieties about herself. She confided to Mariel that she was afraid that she could not live up to others' great expectations because she was too inexperienced, untraveled, and superficially educated in worldly matters. But Cather's hard work paid off when she, like Bartley, won many "genial honors and substantial comforts" (38). Working her way up from her jobs as a journalist and school teacher in Pittsburgh to become the respected managing editor of *McClure's*, Cather felt that she, like Bartley, had satisfied the worldly standards of success.

So far, I have suggested that Bartley Alexander builds a figurative bridge that extends his public self, connecting him to high society and a successful career, and that this bridge parallels the one that Cather herself had recently built in her own life. But, as Cather told Sergeant, she had written a story about "a bridge-builder, with a double nature" (WC: AM, 62), and as such, Bartley builds another mental bridge that connects him to his own original ego. To understand how Bartley's bridge to the soul similarly completes a bridge for his author, we first need to explore how he exhibits her desire to escape from burdensome social and professional restraints. Despite all of his outstanding worldly gains, Bartley complains to Wilson in the beginning of the novel, "Your life keeps going for things you don't want, and all the while you are being built alive into a social structure you don't care a rap about" (12–13). Bartley most obviously feels "buried alive" (38) by his work. Though he had thought that by gaining "genial honors and substantial comforts" he could increase his freedom and power, he finds that such acquisitions bring "only power that was in itself another kind of restraint" (38). No longer the unfettered conqueror, Alexander chafes at the enslaving demands on his time and energy that popular success has inflicted on him: lecturing in foreign countries, supervising engineering reforms, and chairing various boards and committees devoted to civic development and public welfare. Ironically, he is "tied up" (12) by the very details he had sought to control, so as to present a pathetic image of greatness enchained. Despite his desire to preserve a larger identity apart from his official duties, he finds himself reduced to "a part of a professional movement, a cautious board member, a Nestor *de pontibus"* (38). His professional label as "a public man" (38) inevitably imposes on him a series of partial identities that fragment his inner wholeness. As a "mind that society had come to regard as a powerful and reliable machine, dedicated to its service" (131), Bartley forfeits his autonomy and authority and becomes an automated tool for the exploitation of the parasitic society that conspires against his private needs.

Bartley implies to Wilson that he is as incarcerated by the "social structure" of his domestic life as by his job. Though he first exerts a dominating presence in the household so as to transform it into his "inevitable background," he soon seems obscured by its oppressive foreground. Cather shows Bartley's true nature concealed behind a series of enveloping social layers. Wilson's impression of "Bartley's profile ... still wreathed in cigar smoke that curled up more and more slowly" (15) reveals a parody of the genteel tradition whereby men retire after dinner; rather than help Bartley to "achieve a decent impersonality" (13), the smoke is just one of society's many artificial smokescreens that cloud his distinctive fresh-air vigor and vitality. The wreath of smoke insidiously ties itself around him like a noose as a symbol of strangling social conventions. At the same time, Bartley appears "sunk deep in the cushions" (15), as if he were a man drowning in domestic comforts. The one hand that "hung large and passive over the arm of his chair" seems to belong to a helpless puppet rather than to the most invincible of conquerors. He similarly disappears in the "purple velvet smoking-coat" that his wife has bought for him to wear. Though she thinks that its plush royal purple will accentuate his "fine color," it only fades his inner "glow" to give him a look of "dulling weariness" (16). As Wilson says, only the "color" (16) of Bartley's youthful force can truly illuminate his personality. Such conventional wrappings as the smoking coat are really straightjackets that cut off his inner circulation.

It is no wonder that Cather, as she wrote to her Aunt Franc, had an unusual empathy [14] for Bartley, for in him we meet her at the current stage of her career. Temperamentally unsuited to her work, Cather felt dehumanized by its onerous responsibilities. Like Bartley, she felt that she

was "being buried alive" (38) and mentally deadened when she was inundated with poor work to edit.[15] Just as Bartley is weighed down by the
"dead load" of his responsibilities, so Cather complained in a letter to
Zoë Akins that she felt crushed by the weight of her office work.[16] The
office grind was like being put through the mill until there was nothing
left.[17] If Bartley squirms under the demands made on his time by committees of public welfare and reform, Cather was equally impatient with
giving up her life and liberty for the sake of official civic duties, policies,
and social causes that she looked down on as common and vulgar.[18]
Bartley's foreman, who tells him that he can't quit now, "when there is
such competition" (123), resembles S. S. McClure, who similarly pres-
sured Cather to stay at her job to help keep the journal competitive.
Though, like Bartley, Cather had wanted to keep her personal freedom at
all costs, she found that in her office bondage, her time and energy were
not her own.[19] Most upsetting of all, she did not even have time for her
own writing, for she belonged to her boss, other committees, hundreds of
reporters, and the reading public.

Like Bartley, who "had never put more into his work than he had done
in the last few years" (37), Cather had never worked harder than in the
summer of 1911, when she wrote the novel while running *McClure's* on
her own.[20] But the effort she spent had a diminishing return. Bartley's
complaint that "he had never got so little out of it" (37) echoes nearly
exactly Cather's complaint to Jewett in a 1908 letter about her unsatisfy-
ing job at *McClure's*. She felt that though she could get on, she could not
get, or absorb into her deepest consciousness, anything of value from
such superficial and literal journalistic work.[21] In Bartley's "existence
[that] was becoming a network of great and little details" (38) we can see
a reflection of Cather's dissatisfaction as the reporter and editor who
lamented to Jewett that her mind was not meant to have to deal with
excessive information. She felt that the work devoted to acquiring the
kind of material Mr. McClure wanted, while educational, gave her only a
superficial conversance with things. Moreover, Cather felt that she
lacked the reportorial mind that could absorb such a diversity of unmediated hard facts, especially of the muckraking kind for which
McClure's was famous. Considering her later condemnation of the
realists who tried "to get returns on every situation that suggested itself"
(OW, 102), we can imagine why Cather would have disliked the seemingly indiscriminate attention that journalism paid to everything — to the
sordid as well as the beautiful. Indeed, Cather's subsequent creed of
condensation and simplification in art seems in large part a reaction
against such honest and brutal rendering of photographic detail of the
kind she had encountered in her career as a journalist. Journalism that she

viewed as too cut and dry in its unembellished facts resisted Cather's desire to mentally appropriate and idealize things. Most disturbingly to Cather, her mind, which she had come to regard as a card catalogue of details, had no room in it for her own soul.

The picture of Bartley at work as "a powerful machine" under whose activities "the person who ... he felt to be himself, was fading and dying" (39), scarcely conceals Willa Cather, who similarly felt that her real self was dying beneath her mechanical duties in the office. In Bartley's division between a public and private self, Cather projects her own schizophrenic state of mind, as she diagnosed it to Jewett, of a new psychological disorder known as split personality. As she recounts in her 1908 letter to Jewett, she had become estranged from her working personality; out making deadlines and contacts all day with the frenzy of a trapeze artist, her public mind returned to her at the end of the day such a stranger that she could not embrace it as her real self. If Cather absorbed nothing meaningful from her magazine work, then it was above all because she failed to get back the most important return of all: her soul. As she strikingly expressed it to Jewett, she felt continuously bereft and dispossessed of her self. Having lost that most important of possessions, she would have agreed with Bartley that "none of the things [she] had gained in the least compensated" (36). But interestingly, Cather's letter to Jewett reveals that she looked forward to one thing that might compensate her for her loss of self. Vowing that she would write for her own satisfaction in order to save her soul, Cather conceived of her art as a vehicle towards self-recovery. Though her work at *McClure's* had not paid off because it cost her her soul, her own writing might amply reward her if it could help her to regain it. That Cather was approaching forty years old when she wrote *Alexander's Bridge* added to the urgency with which she turned to her writing. Even more than his exhaustion from work, Bartley's disillusionment in middle age reveals Cather's own fears. As she comments, "Overwork had not exhausted him; but this dead calm of middle life which confronted him, — of that he was afraid" (38).

We can imagine that Cather found vicarious compensation for her depletion of vitality when Bartley reunites with his youthful self. Whereas she had felt dispossessed of her best self while working at *McClure's*, Bartley gets to come into imaginative "possession" (39) of the true soul hidden beneath his professional persona. During his first business trip to England, he realizes that more than he had ever wanted to possess external honors or beautiful things, "the one thing he had really wanted all his life was to be free; and there was still something unconquered in him, something besides the strong work-horse that his profession had made of him. He felt rich to-night in the possession of that unstultified survival"

(38–39) — the vestige of an original ego. By finding this inner unnamable "something," Bartley Alexander is the first of Cather's characters to discover that "the inexplicable presence of the thing not named" accompanies him as his own living soul. He creates a second imaginative bridge in the novel, one that takes him back through time:

> He remembered how, when he was a little boy and his father called him in the morning, he used to leap from his bed into the full consciousness of himself. That consciousness was Life itself. Whatever took its place, action, reflection, the power of concentrated thought, were only functions of a mechanism useful to society; things that could be bought in the market. There was only one thing that had an absolute value for each individual, and it was just that original impulse, that internal heat, that feeling of one's self in one's own breast. (39–40)

Of all passages in Willa Cather's fiction, this one most clearly reveals the primal fantasy that again and again stirs the imaginations of her central characters. Significantly, Cather defines "Life itself" not as the external world but as the inner life of consciousness. Bartley leaps into an intensified consciousness of himself, according to a narcissistic impulse. Bartley's fantasy best illustrates Quentin Anderson's argument that Cather's novels "turn on the moment of consciousness in which the child — often the child at the instant of waking — seizes on his world entire, undivided by sex, by possessions, by caste. The world is a fostering scene which sanctions his impulse to conquer, to be a large somebody."[22] Empowered by the exultant swells of his own heart's "original impulse," Alexander the conqueror outreaches possibility to embrace the cosmos as an extension of the self. In an uncompromising equation, Cather upholds "that feeling of one's self in one's breast" as the "only thing" in the world that has an irreplaceable, "absolute value," representing neither the sum of one's experiences nor the remainder of the division wrought by social relationships, or even thought.

Whereas Cather had complained to her friend Zoë Akins of being tremendously exhausted while working at *McClure's*,[23] she vicariously renewed herself when Bartley awakens in the morning with boundless energy. She had admitted to Jewett that she could not take in her mind when it returned to her after a hard day's work, but she imagined that Bartley's primitive self eagerly rushes to embrace him. Though Cather felt that she was being "split up into too many different currents" (WCL, 70), she found herself reunited through the single current of Bartley's "continuous identity" (39). In reality, Cather felt "swallowed up"[24] by innumerable details and obligations, but she imagines that Bartley's hungry ego consumes all experience. She had found, in the impact of new personalities and excitement at *McClure's*, that the world was "too big" (WCL, 70), but Bartley's colossal ego becomes a world unto itself. Finally, despite the fact that her buying and selling articles for the journal made Cather feel as if she herself had become a marketable commodity, she imagines that Bartley inherits an inner confidence far more priceless than any of those "things that could be bought in the market."

Bartley Alexander's victorious repossession of his youthful ego provides the paradigmatic scene that Cather was later to reenact as the climactic moment in most of her mature novels; indeed, many of her sub-sequent novels, such as *The Song of the Lark,* were to move towards such a scene as a conclusion. And yet, Cather doesn't allow this scene to provide the resolution to the novel. With the exception of *The Professor's House, Alexander's Bridge* is the most conflicted of Cather's novels because of her equivocal attitude towards the original self. Though Bartley fears that his public life will kill the life of his soul, he equally fears that his inner life will spoil his public life; as he reflects, "this youth was the most dangerous of companions" (41). For Bartley — as for Cather — the unpeopled, unexplored, and limitless realm of the self was both an exhilarating and frightening prospect. Though not technically flawless, *Alexander's Bridge* is thematically the richer for its uncertainties and divided allegiances. It is important in Cather's canon for suggesting Cather's initial reluctance to embrace a self that threatened to deprive her of the world.

It was not until three years after Cather wrote her 1908 letter of complaint to Jewett that she was able to imagine a vicarious self-recovery in the novel which in turn gave her the strength to leave *McClure's* soon after to devote herself full-time to her freelance writing. Though her prolonged stay at her job despite her unhappiness has puzzled her biographers, her portrayal of Bartley Alexander's divided loyalties helps to explain it. Before Cather could muster the courage to leave *McClure's*, she would have to psychoanalyze her split personality as projected through Bartley to decide if the recovery of the private self would be worth the risks. In the guise of Wilson, who comes to Boston to attend a conference of psychologists, only to find that his most disturbing subject is his old friend, Bartley Alexander, Cather was able to pose as her own psychologist. We might even see her creation of these two westerners in the novel — the sophisticated Wilson and the primitive Bartley — as another recapitulation of her own divided self.

Wilson's prophesy at the beginning of the novel about Bartley's precarious future foreshadows the danger that Bartley's soul poses to his public life. Wilson tells Bartley that despite his great abilities and promise as a youth, he "always used to feel that there was a weak spot where some day strain would tell.... The more dazzling the front you presented, the higher your facade rose, the more I expected to see a big crack zigzagging from top to bottom ... then a crash and clouds of dust" (12). Wilson predicts that Bartley's impressive climb up the social and professional ladder of success will be destroyed by a mysterious point of vulnerability. This "weak spot" is caused not by a moral flaw, as most critics have assumed, but by the unaccountable pressure exerted by Bartley's amoral, pagan ego. When Wilson dismisses his old premonition because, as he tells Bartley, "You've changed. You have decided to leave some birds in the bushes" (12), he implies that Bartley's security depends upon his contentedness with his social and professional acquisitions. Wilson is right to think that Bartley would be out of danger if, indeed, he had chosen to devote himself unreservedly to his work, his marriage, and his social duties. But of course, Wilson mistakes the peace and harmony of Bartley's Bostonian home for the peace and harmony of Bartley's spirit. In reality, as Bartley himself is quick to point out, he hasn't "forgotten that there are birds in the bushes" (13). Unhappily built alive into his public image, he wonders "what sort of chap I'd have been if I hadn't been this sort; I want to go and live out his potentialities, too." Even as he speaks, Bartley tries to live out the potentialities of another sort of personality. "Frowning into the fire, his shoulders thrust forward as if he were about to spring at something," he tries to grasp "something" of his former unfettered and uncivilized self. As Wilson predicts, the "unreasoning and unreasonable activities going on in [him]" do seem to endanger the security of his public facade, for he seems transformed into a sullen and desperate predatory beast, hardly the man to grace Winifred's decorous table or to command the world's most advanced engineering projects. Wilson's fears seem confirmed by Cather's statement in her 1912 *New York Evening Sun* interview that "just so long as [Alexander's] ever-kindling energy exhibits itself only in his work everything goes well; but he runs the risk of encountering new emotional as well as new intellectual stimuli" (WCP, 6). Responding to the stimulus of a primitive impulse, Bartley runs the risk of bringing all his worldly achievements to ruin.

At the end of her life, as Cather looked back over the years, she took a kind of inventory of the things she had acquired and rejected, writing to Zoë Akins that she had gotten most of the things she had wanted. More importantly, she had avoided the things she adamantly had not wanted: too much money, publicity, and burdensome social introductions. Although she recalled that when she was editor of *McClure's* she had enjoyed getting to meet many people in America and in England, she had grown tired of it. She had decided that she wanted something much more enjoyable: her absolute freedom.[25] Although in hindsight of her successful career as a novelist, Cather discounted the assets of her life at *McClure's*, in 1911 she could not underestimate the cost of giving up those advantages to follow the enthusiasm of her soul. Like Wilson, she saw in her career a "weak spot": the power of an unwanted self threatened to destroy her hard-won appearance of social and professional success. For, though she was coming to appreciate her private soul as the "one thing that had an absolute value," she had, over the past few years, put a greater value on her recognition by the world. As she had triumphantly written to Will Owen Jones, her former editor at the *Nebraska State Journal*, S. S. McClure's first acceptance of her short stories had increased her sense of self-worth. Encouraged by McClure's belief in her, she found herself taking much more care in crossing the street, as if suddenly she had become worth preserving.[26] By quitting the job that had enabled her to win such approval and esteem, Cather shared Bartley's fear that if he abandoned the world for the self, "he would lose the thing he valued most in the world" (113). Moreover, though in her fatigue she suffered from the cost of "genial honors and substantial comforts," she had, nonetheless, worked hard to attain such honors and comforts and was not willing to give them up easily. As a small-town westerner trying to make good in the big city of the East, she was understandably tempted by "magazine success" and "the lure of big money rewards" (WC: AM, 62). As she pointedly told Sergeant while leaving the French restaurant Delmonico's, "one must have simple tastes — to give up a good salary" (WC: AM, 53).

Above all, Cather doubted her future success as a serious writer. Since she had begun work at the magazine in 1906, she had published only a handful of stories, and many of those had been written during her earlier years in Pittsburgh. If she had had any leisure time at home, she had usually had to spend it editing others' stories, not her own. In addition to her lack of recent writing experience, McClure's professed lack of faith in her artistic ability undermined her confidence. In her 1908 letter to Jewett, she recounted that McClure valued her abilities as an executive but not as a writer of stories. Cather herself doubted her skills as a writer, feeling every time she tried to write a story as vulnerable and inexperienced as a newborn baby. She wondered whether a pursuit at which she seemed so incompetent could possibly be her destiny.[27] Though she looked forward to escaping her hectic and overwhelming schedule at *McClure's*, Cather recognized that such a schedule had at least given her life a definite direction and focus, without which her newfound freedom might simply be futile aimlessness. Undoubtedly, she worried that for her, as for Bartley, "there would be nothing ... afterward" but "a restless existence ... getting up in the morning with a great bustle and splashing of water, to begin a day that had no purpose and no meaning" (113–14).

Just as Cather was afraid that she might be exposed as a naked baby beneath her professional accomplishments, so she suggests that Bartley, despite his veneer of worldly success, may conceal an inner emptiness. Bartley secretly feels that beneath his impressive social and professional facade, he is a fraud. When Wilson compliments him on his success in the world, Bartley protests that he has merely appropriated the cultural polish of his wife: "Nonsense! It's not I you feel sure of; it's Winifred" (12). Wilson, too, feels that apart from the sophistication that Bartley has assumed as Winifred's husband, he remains an inchoate personality, "a natural force, certainly, but beyond that, ... not anything very really or for very long at a time" (15). Because Bartley has failed to define his identity, Wilson concludes that "however much one admired him, one had to admit that he simply wouldn't square." As if she were taking stock of Bartley's development in order to reassess her own growth as an artist, Cather betrays an anxiety that, despite her early promise, she, too, may not have amounted to much after all. Like Bartley, she may have possessed an extraordinary amount of energy and an intense drive to succeed, but as yet, she had not been able to bring that energy to artistic fruition. Staking all on the unknown quantity of the self that might prove unsustaining and unproductive, Cather was terrified of the prospect of writing novels. If her own soul failed her, she would lose everything — both her solid reputation as a successful professional woman of the world and her chance to be a great writer. Most of all, she would lose her self-esteem.[28]

Cather's decision to leave *McClure's* was no doubt made more difficult by the mutually exclusive alternatives that she posed for herself. Bartley's paralyzing knowledge that "each life spoils the other" (82) expresses Cather's own reluctance to choose either the life of her public self or the life of her private self, if choosing one were to mean giving up the benefits of the other. In a conversation with Sergeant in 1911, when the unsettling prospect of leaving *McClure's* was uppermost in her mind, Cather expressed her dilemma in its broadest terms when she said that "to write life itself ... one must have the power to refuse most of the rest of life" (WC: AM, 63). Cather's seeming paradox is explicable if we consider that as she saw it, "to write life itself" was not to write about life — not to record it or to be involved in it as she had been as a journalist — but to incarnate a sense of felt life in her characters from the depths of her own soul. To do this, she felt that she would have to give her first priority to art and her second priority to human relationships. She would have "nothing to do with marriage and children" (WC: AM, 63). Throughout her early reviews of the 1890s, Cather had hailed the artist as a kind of voluntary exile or priest who had to renounce the world to give all to art. As she wrote in 1894, "An author's only safe course is to cling close to the skirts of his art, forsaking all others, and keep unto her as long as they two shall live" (KA, 407). And yet, when actually faced with taking that vow, she doubted her capacity to abandon everything for this solitary pursuit. As she importunately asked Sergeant, "Could *you* do it — give yourself, dedicate yourself to your art, you who love life and find human beings so fascinating?" (WC: AM, 63). Imagining her choice as one between single-minded devotion to her calling and involvement with "fascinating human beings," Cather seems to have particularly regretted the prospect of forsaking the stimulating people she had met and impressed while working at *McClure's*.[29] Paradoxically, the exacting strictness of Cather's creed that art should be all or nothing initially prevented even her from unreservedly following it.

Bartley's fear that "there would be no going back" (113) once he surrendered himself to the life of his antinomian soul seems to reflect Cather's fear that such a commitment would be irrevocable. At one level, Cather may have hesitated to burn her bridges back to her worldly contacts; more deeply, the novel suggests that she feared being completely absorbed by the needs of her own soul. In his letter to Hilda, Bartley expresses his concern that his primitive self, who "is fighting for his life at the cost of mine," is growing so "strong," that "eventually ... he will absorb me altogether" (102). Indeed, the more that his inner self absorbs him, the more he finds to his dismay that he "can't get at [the world] anymore" (82). Bartley fears that he must either completely deny the existence of his pagan ego or totally give himself over to it, as if its hunger for attention were too demanding and all-consuming to admit of any other desires. In fact, Bartley is divided not so much between irreconcilable rewards as between contrary threats — between a public ego that is gratifying but ultimately restricting, and an original self that is vital but insatiable.

Thus, in self-defense, Bartley builds his external bridges to the world in order to escape the threat of a destructive primal self; conversely, he builds his internal bridges to the soul in order to escape the threat of a burdensome public role. When, during one of his evening walks on deck as he sails across the Atlantic, he "started back and tore his coat open as if something warm were actually clinging to him beneath it" (75), he experiences an instant of startling self-recognition. As he stares in fascination at the life concealed within his own breast, he resembles the child who becomes mesmerized when he first sees his own reflection in a mirror. Yet, he seems terrified by his own narcissism. As if spooked by a primal hunger that threatens to consume him altogether, Bartley rushes into the saloon to find security in the company of others. As he "threw himself upon" (75) the other guests — playing accompaniments for them on the piano, entertaining them in conversation, or winning a reputation at cards — he almost literally clings to them so as to escape the pagan soul that is "clinging" to him, luring him away from the world to a point of no return. He fears that unless he hides from himself, his grasping self-ishness will preclude strong social relationships.

Playing "bridge until two o'clock in the morning," Bartley does more than play cards; he emblematically builds a social "bridge" between himself and others so as to escape the terror of self-confrontation. But he plays the game halfheartedly, managing "to lose a considerable sum of money without really noticing that he was doing so" (75), for symbolically, he devalues himself in his social role. Part of him still wants to build a bridge towards his private self. His constant pacing back and forth across the deck over the next few days traces the pattern of his conflicting goals. Finally, by letting go his conscious will, he finds that "more and more often, when he first wakened in the morning or when he stepped into a warm place after being chilled on the deck, he felt a sudden painful delight at being nearer another shore" (76). Though we assume that Bartley looks forward to meeting his lover, Hilda, on the shores of England, he more keenly anticipates another reunion when he "leaps into an overwhelming consciousness of himself" (76–77). Bartley seemingly makes a journey out that is really a "marvelous return" (77) to an inner shore that cannot be located on any map. For all his joy in nearing this inner destination, however, Bartley experiences a "painful delight," for ultimately, he still remains uncertain about which shore he seeks. His constant traveling back and forth between his mistress in London and his wife in Boston further reflects this continuing ambivalence. In one direction, by visiting his old lover Hilda, who reminds him of "some one vastly dearer to him than she had ever been — his own young self" (40), Bartley builds a bridge that leads back to his lost youth. In the opposite direction, by returning to his wife, Winifred, he builds a bridge that leads to his successful social identity.

We again see Bartley tortured by contradictory impulses in the scene in which he helps his wife prepare for their Christmas Eve party. At first, he seems to rebel against the household cage. While Winifred graciously decorates the house and receives the guests, he quickly loses interest in his duties. He tires of having "to twist the tough stems of the holly into the framework of the chandelier" (62), as if he were having to twist some tough wild stock of his own nature into a contrived and constraining social framework. Overcome by a sudden depression "as he was cutting off a length of string" (63), he sighs in the realization that he is "cutting off" an integral part of his own being by measuring himself against a social ruler. He quits his drudgery in the awakening belief that he is more than the man who must dress for dinner or offer his guests hors-d'oeuvres. In a characteristic gesture, he "kept clasping and unclasping his big hands as if he were trying to realize something," for, like his counterpart Thea Kronborg, he hopes to grasp the elusive root of his own nature. "Holding himself away from his surroundings, from the room, and from the very chair in which he sat," he tries to escape all the external furnishings of a social life so as to recreate a scene furnished of nothing but his own consciousness. Withdrawing from all but "the wild eddies of snow above the river on which his eyes were fixed with feverish intentness, as if he were trying to project himself thither" (63–64), he hopes to return to a scene that embodies the wild freedom and unrestrained energy that he has lost. He realizes that his primitive force is too resistless, amoral, asexual, and anarchic to be contained within civilized spaces. And yet, at the ominous prospect of the snowstorm that "began to thicken and darken turbidly," Bartley feels a mixture of "apprehension and suspense," as if by unleashing his primitive powers in a delirious mania, he might lose, rather than find himself. But before he makes that dangerous mental leap into the asocial abyss, Wilson enters the room. Just as Bartley had rushed into the ship's saloon for reassuring company, so he "sprang eagerly to his feet and hurried to meet his old instructor," thus once again creating a social bridge to escape a threatening self. Exclaiming to Wilson, "What luck," he breathes a sigh of relief that he has been saved from committing himself to his own isolate soul that admits of no other company. Initially impatient of domestic restraints, Bartley longs to project himself into the beyond; but, becoming apprehensive of his own lawless energies, he longs to regain his ballast in the household once more.

Despite Cather's self-doubts, her desire to replenish her diminishing vitality finally prompted her to give priority to the original ego over the public self at the end of the novel. We can begin by considering Bartley's final train ride to the construction site of the Moorlock bridge. On his way, he meditates on two very different bridges: the bridge he views through the train window that symbolically leads towards his primitive self and the past, and the bridge he subsequently crosses that symbolically leads towards others and the future. This second bridge is the one he has built at Allway. The most progressive of his bridges, the Allway bridge is, as Winifred recalls, "a bridge into the future" (18); Wilson concurs that it is such a bridge "over which the feet of every one of us will go" (17). The name "Allway" suggests that it is, indeed, the way of all — all who live in time — and that therefore it must be crossed. As Cather puns, Bartley "had always to pass through Allway" (116) — literally, so as to get to his new bridge, and symbolically, so as to move onward to new experiences and forward in time. But this is precisely what Bartley does not want to do. Though he builds the bridges into the future, his own feet refuse to cross them. Whereas up until this scene, Bartley had been unable to decide which bridge to build, he now regrets having to cross this bridge into the world, reflecting that "he did not like coming and going across that bridge, or remembering the man who built it" (117). As we have seen, the man who built this bridge into the future was a man about to embark on "the beginning of a great career" (18) and the beginning of an impressive marriage. Bartley's rejection of that former self reveals his reluctance to make the necessary transition from the innocence and freedom of childhood into the sexuality and responsibility of adulthood. Though Winifred has always admired the bridge for its beautiful "bridal look" (17), Bartley comes to hate it as the reminder of "the ugliness he had brought into the world" (119) simply by forging connections between himself and others. Loathing the company of those who cross the bridge with him, he sees the Allway bridge as a symbol of nothing less than his unfortunate passage into involvement with the human race. Because such passages have become precarious and insupportable to him, he is relieved to have crossed the bridge with its "hollow sound" and to feel himself "on the solid roadbed again" (117).

As the engineer who builds bridges into the future, Bartley seems meant to appear as the popular symbol of twentieth-century American progress.[30] But Bartley's desires are finally more regressive than progressive. As he reluctantly crosses the Allway bridge, he wishes that "he could go back" (116) to the scene of another bridge which he has just glimpsed in the distance. The memory of this bridge in turn leads him back further to a memory of his own childhood. Overarching a group of boys sitting around their campfire, this bridge "took his mind back a long way, to a campfire on a sandbar in a Western river." Though it is old, the boys' "weather-stained wooden bridge" is far more supportive to Bartley's imagination than the modern one he builds, for theirs was a bridge that did not have to be crossed into a threatening future — it had only to be hidden under as a comfortable "shelter" that protected their timeless dreams. The scene recalls Bartley to a state of being that is more powerfully felt than directly described. Yet we, too, can see "exactly how the world had looked then" if we look back at the early poem, "Dedicatory," that opens Cather's first volume of poetry, *April Twilights*. In that poem, as in a couple of her early short stories, Cather makes a wish similar to

Bartley's to return to "an island in a western river" (AT, 3) where she and her brothers had played as children. From the point of view of the three children who "lay and planned at moonrise ... the conquest of the world together," the world had looked like a land of "enchantment" where every adventure was an "odyssey" promising the "brigandage" of priceless imaginative possessions. The most valuable booty of all the children gained not from the "sack of cities" but from their pride in themselves as the world's unvanquished conquerors. By contrast to the Allway bridge, the boys' bridge appeals to Bartley for its isolation; with the exception of an old farmer, "there was not another living creature to be seen" (116). Back in the days when he, too, sat on an island, planning the conquest of the world, his imaginative space was his own. He did not have to share it with a wife or with committees. When Bartley imaginatively reconstructs a bridge back to this "vanished kingdom," he seems, once again, to cross that "bridge into the kingdom of the soul" where he alone is sovereign, as if, for a brief instant, he really were the world's greatest builder of bridges.

As Cather recovers her own memory of a childhood fantasy world in a faraway Western setting, she speaks with a greater intensity of feeling than in any other passage in the novel.[31] In response to this scene, Edith Lewis writes that "it is as if [Cather's] true voice; submerged before in conventional speech, had broken through, and were speaking in irrepressible accents of passion and authority" (WCL, 78). This newfound authority would lead Cather to recreate this imaginative childhood scene in later works like *My Àntonia*. But, though Bartley's childhood memory anticipates Cather's later novels, it more immediately predetermines the ending of *Alexander's Bridge,* for we can best understand Bartley's death, after his Moorlock bridge collapses, as the means by which Cather enables him to return to his longed-for primordial wholeness. By the time Bartley's train arrives at the Moorlock bridge, the tension between his desire to move backwards across bridges of time and the necessity to move forwards across them has reached a climax. When the bridge finally breaks in two, as if in response to these two incompatible directions of force, Bartley is granted a reprieve from having to make the transitions across life's bridges. Though society views his drowning as the end of a mind "bent upon its own destruction" (131), he finds in death the only means to his salvation. Earlier in the novel, Cather had reflected that Bartley "had always meant to keep his personal liberty at all costs, as old MacKeller, his first chief, had done" (38). In order to free himself from the burdensome task of building the Moorlock bridge, MacKeller had paid the ultimate price by dying. Similarly keeping his liberty at all costs, Bartley finds in death his most blessed release. Dreaming in his last moment of consciousness that his wife "let him go" (127), Bartley disengages himself once and for all from his wife, his lover, his coworkers, and the "messy ... patchwork" (70) of life itself.

When Bartley had been on the ship to England, happy to be "submerged in the vast impersonal grayness about him" (73), he had merged with the ocean as the symbolic extension of the "ebbing and flowing ... pulse" within him; again, at the novel's conclusion, water proves the element most sympathetic to him. In the first serialized version of the novel, "Alexander's Masquerade," Cather had written that "there was a persistent strain of doubt in him, a strain of opposition to his own will. Some treacherous current in the midwaters of the Atlantic had caught him and was dragging him with it."[32] Though Bartley initially tries to exert his will against this primordial current, he ultimately longs to let himself go with it in order to reunite with the wild current of his own original nature. Only by merging in death with the current whose rushing power incarnates his own life force could Bartley seem to be continuously carried by his surging passions while staying arrested in time.

The collapse of the bridge at the end of the novel seems literally to fulfill Wilson's prophesy that a "weak spot" in Bartley's nature would cause his social facade to "crack" and fall with "a crash and clouds of dust." Cather's foreshadowing of Bartley's doom has bothered Dorothy Van Ghent and other critics as "finger-pointing symbolism."[33] On the surface, Wilson's prediction seems mechanically realized when Bartley's bridge cracks apart, as if to imply that Bartley is doomed by his own "flawed moral nature."[34] Yet the end of the novel establishes a radical sympathy towards Bartley that is very different from Wilson's disapproval from a conventional standpoint. Despite Wilson's initial skepticism, Cather paradoxically portrays the breaking point of the bridge as the revelation of Bartley's strongest and most integral center. The "crack" in Bartley's nature really signifies his tragic self-diminishment under the strain of his public obligations. By pulling down Bartley's bridge, Cather suggests that she no longer gives her allegiance to her hero's social facade by which he has externally constructed his life. Although initially Cather valued the bridge as symbolic of the dazzling front that Bartley must preserve in order to keep the world's admiration, now she views it as symbolic of the imprisoning social structure that his vital self must escape in order to live. The zigzagging crack signals the birth pangs of Bartley's truest self as it breaks free from its public confinements. Cather engineers the collapse of the bridge so as to confirm and empower Bartley's original ego.

Bartley Alexander's problem is not that he imposes his will on nature but that others have imposed their will on him, preventing him from shaping his bridge as the expression of an innate power.[35] His bridge falls apart because he fails to integrate his regressive desires into his creativity so as to structure his art around the cohesive center of his selfish ego. Bartley's physical resemblance to a bridge implies that the strongest art would be one that conforms itself to the invincible vitality of the artist. When Bartley first appears in the novel, "his shoulders look[ing] strong enough in themselves to support a span of any one of his ten great bridges" (9), he presents the figure of an Atlas, capable of shouldering an infinite weight. Cather's analogy between Bartley's broad shoulders and the span of his bridge suggests that he himself symbolically provides the central support for his bridge. Had he been able to project into his art a primal virility, his bridge would have been, like his own physique, "as hard and powerful as a catapult." Had he been able to sustain his art with his own youthful energy, his bridge, like his desire, would have "cut its name" as it "put a girdle round the earth ... from New York to Moorlock" (115). Cather uses the fate of the bridge's central support to mirror Bartley's fate within the constricting frameworks of his life and art. Under the burden of his many obligatory social and professional relationships, even his indomitable shoulders buckle in a collapse that is completed symbolically by the anthropomorphized bridge when its "lower chord of the cantilever arm [gave] a little, like an elbow bending" (124). Feeling "crowded" (65) and "cramped in every way by a niggardly commission" (37), Bartley is forced to build his bridge according to "a scale that was perfectly safe for an ordinary bridge" but not for "anything of such length" (122). That Bartley has to squeeze his original large plans for the bridge into the smaller patterns prescribed by narrow-minded officials is more broadly symbolic of his having to crowd his original "big" (8) personality into society's restricting blueprints; he is unable to adjust the realities of his life to a scale colossal enough to accommodate his own ego. Bartley's wish that he could "have thrown up the job when they crowded me" (122–23) finally comes true when the bridge bursts apart so as to throw him free of its confines. Having long felt the "vibration of an unnatural excitement" (68) whenever his second self visited him, Bartley again feels the tremor of that irrepressible inner force as it shakes itself free from the foundations of his bridge. When "something had broken loose in him" (68) during the Christmas Eve party, Bartley had struggled to keep his public identity intact, but when that anarchic spirit reappears as that "something [that] was out of line in the lower chord" (124) of the bridge, Cather is resolved to let him surrender to it. Symbolically, that deviating "something" that breaks loose from the bridge to leave behind only an "iron carcass" (127) incarnates Bartley's own soul as it abandons the lifeless remains of his public life.

Cather exonerates Bartley and blames the fall of the bridge on others. As Horton (Bartley's assistant) assures Winifred after the disaster, "Nobody blames him, Mrs. Alexander. If any one is to blame, I'm afraid it's I" (128). Horton blames himself for not stopping the work and getting the workers off the bridge in time. Indeed, those workers, even more than Horton, are to blame for Bartley's fate. Cather makes the point that Bartley could have swum to safety were it not for the hoards of drowning men who fall on top of him, "clutching at him and at each other," until "one caught him about the neck, another gripped him about the middle, and they went down together" (126). Bartley's strangulation by his own crew seems to suggest Cather's fear that a communal space of creativity, or art, is bound to be claustrophobic and suffocating. When Bartley miscalculates "the dead load" (123) of steel that overburdens his bridge, he symbolically underestimates the weight of all those fellow workers and public responsibilities that drag him to his death.

In the unstable construction of Bartley's bridge, Cather betrays an authorial anxiety about the structural soundness of her own novel, which she similarly viewed as an artificial "external" structure that lacked the organic integrity of her inner consciousness or "life line" (Pref. AB, vi). Thus by extension, when Cather destroys Bartley's bridge, she symbolically tears down the scaffolding of the novel. And yet, just as she blames others for the collapse of Bartley's bridge, so she implicitly blames others for the failure of her narrative form. Like Bartley, who is the victim of committees who twist his plan for the bridge to suit their own, Cather seems to have felt constrained by formulaic expectations of her art. Bartley's resentment at having to keep up with his "competition" by conforming his bridge to "the latest practice[s]" mirrors Cather's dissatisfaction at having to make her novel popular according to the conventions of the Jamesian novel or "the conventional editorial point of view" (OW, 92) of her journalism. Bartley is not the only one forced to build his art out of unsuitably light-weight materials, for Cather felt that the material of journalism was "cheap" (WC: AM, 62). Writing to satisfy public taste and make money, she felt that she, like Bartley, was committed to a false art of "public utility" (38). So, too, she shared Bartley's frustration at having to "crowd" his work within the ordinary scale required for it. In a letter to Sergeant, she recalls how she hated having to make cuts in her work at *McClure's*. [36] Just as Bartley tries to build his bridge on a longer scale than he has ever used before, so Cather was in the process of writing her first novel that was longer than any of her previous poems, short stories, or articles for the magazine.[37] Yet, like her hero, she had to cramp her work into a smaller mold when *McClure's* published *Alexander's Bridge* in three serial parts.

Bartley's bridge can be seen as an emblem not only of the external materials and limiting forms of Cather's art but also of her unsuitable working environment at *McClure's*. As a public and utilitarian enterprise, the Moorlock bridge resembles the world within which Cather worked at the magazine, a world that was equally claustrophobic and hectic. Just as Bartley has only a nominal control over the construction of his bridge, which is impeded by the inefficient direction of committees, so at *McClure's*, Cather was forced to share her authority over her work and be answerable to others. If she felt "crushed" by her office work, it was no doubt in part because she felt that scores of coworkers were dragging her, as they drag Bartley, to her death. By pulling Bartley's bridge down, however, Cather psychologically prepared herself to sever her ties with *McClure's*. Just two or three months after she finished writing the novel, she would abandon the editorial desk and head for the Southwest. Though up until the end of the novel the prospect of leaving behind a successful career had filled Cather with fear and self-doubt, she ultimately justifies her decision, just as she takes pains to clear Bartley of all blame. Asserting that "when a great man dies in his prime there is no surgeon who can say whether he did well; whether or not the future was his, as it seemed to be" (131), Cather seems, at a deeper level, to defy anyone to question her motives for leaving her position at *McClure's*.

When Bartley's reunion with Hilda towards the end of the novel prevents him from receiving the warning telegram about the bridge in time, Cather engineers the plot so as to imply that his liaison with her is to blame for the bridge's destruction. But the way that Bartley's affair with Hilda determines the crash of the bridge has been misunderstood. Some critics have regarded the final sequence of events as arbitrary; others have interpreted the ending as a moral punishment of Bartley for his marital infidelity.[38] By contrast, I would argue that Bartley's bridge is destroyed as a symbolic retribution for his choice of Hilda, but without conventional moral implications. Cather presents Bartley's decision to renew ties with Hilda as a betrayal not of a social or moral ethic but, rather, of his own childhood ego that demands his unwavering allegiance.

By agreeing to prolong the affair with Hilda, Bartley disloyally forsakes the company of himself. Earlier, when Bartley writes his letter of renunciation to Hilda, he recognizes that he must give her up if he is to preserve his integrity. Since he has attached himself to her, Bartley confesses, he has come to feel exiled from the imaginative garden of "life and power and freedom," where he used to be able to walk when he "had a single purpose and a single heart" (101). As he puts it, the "window" to that garden is closed to him now — and Hilda, by implication, is to blame. We recall that when he had taken Hilda, instead of his own young self, in his arms, his gesture was a divided one: "Alexander unclenched the two hands at his sides. With one he threw down the window and with the other — still standing behind her — he drew her back against him" (58–59). By closing the window, Bartley had brought Hilda nearer but shut himself out of that beautiful garden where he had cherished an inner unity and power. In his letter of renunciation, Bartley further implies that he cannot unite with Hilda without losing his soul. As he strikingly puts it, "Now I know that no one can build his security upon the nobleness of another person. Two people, when they love each other, grow alike in their tastes and habits and pride, but their moral natures (whatever we may mean by that canting expression) are never welded" (100–101). Instead of regretting that their differences cannot be overcome, Bartley narcissistically guards his separate self against inevitable diminishment in any kind of "welding" human relationship.

Despite his better judgment, Bartley decides to see Hilda one last time before he visits his bridge under construction, and in this decision, he metaphorically builds his most tenuous bridge in the novel. Bartley's prolonged affair with Hilda proves that such attempts at social "welding" are self-destructive. As the engineering metaphors in Bartley's letter suggest, Cather envisions the faulty construction of his bridge as a paradigm for the faulty construction of intimate human relationships. By the time Bartley arrives at the bridge, he has already set in motion its imminent collapse. As "the tension work began to pull asunder" (125), it vividly illustrates the hazardous result of his false job of social welding. No less than Bartley's coworkers or wife, Hilda hampers him in a social mold objectified in the bridge. No more than the bridge's "integral part could bear for an instant the enormous strain loosed upon it" can Bartley's inner integrity withstand the strain of his relationship with Hilda.

Perhaps we can best sum up how *Alexander's Bridge* helped Cather to develop her later artistic creed if we consider a statement she made about the novel's form in a 1933 speech to the Friends of the Princeton University Library, in New York. Using the metaphors of *Alexander's Bridge* as if she were speaking from her experience in writing that novel, Cather forewarns aspiring writers,

> When we learn to give our purpose the form that exactly clothes it and no more; when we make a form for every story instead of trying to crowd it into one of the stock moulds on the shelf, then we shall be on the right road at least. We all start with something true, and then in the effort to make it bigger than it really is, we try to weld something false onto it; something delightful, usually, but that was not in the original impulse. Electrical engineers haven't yet produced a device that will do that kind of welding.[39]

Read in the context of this passage, *Alexander's Bridge* can be seen as an allegory about Bartley Alexander's abortive attempt to create an art with an organic form. Though he "start[s] with something true" within himself in his conception for his bridge, he fails to let his art shape itself to that "original impulse." By letting commissions dictate the conventional structure of his bridge, he mistakenly tries "to crowd [his original purpose] into ...stock moulds"; by having an affair with the external materials of life, like Hilda, he vainly tries "to weld something false onto it." We can even see the collapse of Bartley's bridge as a vivid illustration of Cather's point that "engineers haven't yet produced a device that will do that kind of welding"; despite Bartley's attempt to unite his inner genius with the external forms and materials he acquires, he finds that they refuse to be reconciled.

This passage helps us to understand *Alexander's Bridge* as an allegory about an artist's failed attempt to create an organic form; *Alexander's Bridge*, in turn, helps to illuminate Cather's organic form as an attempt to preserve the artist's soul, for Bartley Alexander's story reveals that the determining principle of Cather's art — what she here calls that "something true," or that "original impulse" — has a psychological origin in the artist's romantic ego. That the fate of the bridge rests on Bartley's mental and emotional condition suggests that Cather conceived of art as an embodiment of the artist's psychological life. In the context of the novel, Cather's call for the preservation of an "original impulse" is more than an artistic choice; it is a profound psychic necessity. The subject of the novel is not simply the integration of Alexander's art but the reintegration of his own consciousness. If we take the novel as an illustration of Cather's idea that the artist must forsake all "that was not in the original impulse," then she seems to be saying that the great artist must forsake life itself in order to protect his soul. He must detach himself not only from conventional literary forms but more importantly, from stifling professional roles and social and sexual human relationships.

By destroying Bartley's bridge, Cather opens new creative possibilities for herself. Imagining that for Bartley "there was nothing to do but pull the whole structure down and begin over again" (122), she must have felt that there was something cathartic about pulling the external structure of her own art and life to ruins, for out of those ruins, she too could "begin over again" to build a new bridge. Indeed, in the epilogue to the novel, Cather seems to anticipate the nature of her future art as a bridge to the kingdom of the soul. When, even in Bartley's absence, Winifred and Wilson can't help "feeling that he must be up in his study" (135), he exerts a power that is analogous to the felt presence of the artist in Cather's novel démeublé. At one point, Wilson comments that "he left an echo. The ripples go on in all of us. He belonged to the people who make the play" (138). If we take Wilson as a spokesman for Cather, the one who has ultimately "[made] the play," then she seems to be claiming Bartley's spirit as the essence of the novel. Like Wilson, she invokes Bartley not in his social or worldly identity, but rather, in his primitive and inexplicable being, celebrating him for "his deviations ... where he didn't square" (137). Apparently, while Bartley's efforts to connect him-self to the world fail to produce a sound art, his narcissistic desire to con-nect himself to his original soul transforms him into the suggestive ani-mating impulse at the heart of Cather's new "play."

The epilogue brought compensating rewards to Willa Cather. Though during her frenetic years at *McClure's*, she regretted that she belonged to many others, now she seems assured that she belongs to herself in the way that the primitive Bartley "belong[s]" to Wilson. Through Wilson, who now claims that "I liked him just as he was" (137), Cather seems to give herself a vote of self-approval. At the same time, she does not imagine that her self-possession will cost her the good opinion of the world. Though she had feared that by leaving the public world, she would lose her popular reputation, she reassures herself that she, like Bartley, will leave behind her an appreciated presence. She manages to "have her cake and eat it too" after all, when she imagines that Bartley both unites with his soul in death and yet continues to live on in the minds of his friends. Agreeing that "nothing can happen to one after Bartley" (138), the remaining characters find that Bartley alone has given meaning to their lives. Moreover, Cather even enlists these worldly char-acters as Bartley's advocates in his struggle against the world: Winifred guards her memory of Bartley as if theirs had been a "happiness ... against [the world]" (137), and Wilson protects the preciousness of his friend's soul against the "brutal and stupid world" (138). Such inconsis-tencies suggest that Cather uses the epilogue to justify her decision to renounce the world so as to become a solitary artist dedicated to the life of the soul.

Even as Cather was completing the novel, she seems to have looked forward to her hero's future redemption. Before Bartley dies, he feels that he will live "to recover all he had lost" (126), and even after his death, his survivors believe that "had he lived, he would have retrieved himself" (131). In fact, insofar as Bartley Alexander does live on through his successive reincarnations in the novels, he — like his author — re-turns to recover himself as his most precious possession. When Cather left *McClure's* in the fall of 1911 to begin work on her second novel, *O Pioneers!*, she began to find a new source for her art; she would no longer conform her stories to artificial models but would let them take organic shape from her own reintegrated personality. Her recreation of her art as self-expression would become simultaneously her artistic and psychic salvation. In *O Pioneers!*, she would dramatically revise her story in *Alexander's Bridge*. As the similarity in their names suggests, Alexander and Alexandra are close kin. By turning Alexander into Alexandra, Cather created an artist-conqueror who successfully integrates the romantic ego into her nature and her art.

3

A Pioneer in Art: Staking Out the Claim
to Consciousness in *O Pioneers!*

In a 1921 interview, Cather said that before she wrote *O Pioneers!*, "I had been trying to sing a song that did not lie in my voice."[1] By contrast, in her third novel, *The Song of the Lark,* Cather, like her opera-singer heroine, came to sing a song that lay in her voice once she infused her art with her own individuality. Though, as a covert autobiography, *The Song of the Lark* incorporates material that Cather had been accumulating since childhood, it more specifically owes its genesis to her second novel, *O Pioneers!,* for it was in *O Pioneers!* that Cather first found her voice as a writer; in *The Song of the Lark,* she retrospectively celebrated that discovery. Thea Kronborg's imaginative possession of "her own land" (SL, 219) and "her kind" (SL, 240) reenacts Cather's literary claim in *O Pioneers!* Rather than write about sophisticated people of high society in eastern drawing rooms, Cather had decided to turn back to the land and people she had known while growing up in Nebraska. Though in the beginning of her career Cather had rejected Nebraska as a harsh environment that stifled the artist, her trip to the Southwest in the spring of 1912 seemed to transform her attitude. Just as Thea Kronborg returns home on the train from Chicago to hear "a new song in that blue air which had never been sung in the world before" (SL, 220), so Cather had returned to Nebraska from the Southwest in 1912 to hear in the prairie a new note.[2] Thea Kronborg had found in Panther Canyon a new "song" that welled up from within her own body like a "spring" (SL, 299). Similarly, I would suggest, Cather came to hear in the Western prairie another note once she imagined that landscape, like the Southwest, as one that could be made to sing a song of herself. This new note in the prairie inspired Cather to write a new kind of novel in *O Pioneers!,* which she turned to soon after her return to the East in the autumn of 1912. Like many of Cather's novels that self-reflexively reveal the process of their own composition, *O Pioneers!* tells the story of Cather's imaginative revision of the landscape.

"Possession Granted by a Different Lease": Alexandra Bergson's Imaginative Conquest of Cather's Nebraska

Ever since *O Pioneers!* was first reviewed in 1913 as "a study of the struggles and privations of the foreign emigrant in the herculean task of subduing the untamed prairie land of the Far West,"[3] it has become enshrined in our literature as a national epic. Yet, ironically, Cather omits the actual chronicle of the pioneer's taming of the wild frontier in a sixteen-year hiatus in the plot. Moreover, she never directly portrays her heroine, Alexandra Bergson, physically working the land. Although Alexandra has typically been seen as a representative of the early pioneers who settled the prairie, she can be better understood as a representative of Cather, herself a pioneer breaking new ground in art — ground that, as we shall see, lay not, finally, in Nebraska but in consciousness. The real pioneers whose footsteps marked the way for Alexandra's imaginative conquest of Cather's Nebraska are Emerson and his fellow transcendentalists Thoreau and Whitman.[4]

By naming *O Pioneers!* after Whitman's poem, Willa Cather was making a bold bid for a place in the literary tradition of the American transcendentalists. John Murphy has insightfully drawn parallels between Alexandra's spiritual communion with the Genius of the Divide and "the intercourse between poet and soul" in Whitman's "Song of Myself."[5] Yet, while the line of influence from Whitman to Cather is direct and clear, it has its source in Ralph Waldo Emerson. Cather explicitly upheld Emerson as her model of the artist in the short story that laid the groundwork for her novel. Written in 1902, "The Treasure of Far Island" was the first story in which Cather idealized Nebraska; it thus can be seen as a rehearsal for her extended celebration of the prairie in *O Pioneers!* Although Cather was fond of looking back on *O Pioneers!* as the novel in which she discovered the material "that [was] truly [her] own" (Pref. AB, vii), she had first claimed ownership of Nebraska when she wrote "Far Island." Ostensibly about two children who play on an island in a Nebraska river as its "original ... claimants" (CSF, 265), "Far Island" is more profoundly about Cather's own original claim upon her regional subject matter. Cather legitimates the children's rule by invoking Emerson: as she insists, the "empire" of Far Island "seemed particularly to belong to the two children ... because they were of that favored race whom a New England sage called the true land-lords and sea-lords of the world" (CSF, 265). Emerson had granted the poet a figurative possession of nature in reward for his imaginative possession, or incorporation, of beauty when he promised him, "Thou shalt have the whole land for thy park and manor, the sea for thy bath and navigation, without tax and without envy; the woods and the rivers thou shalt own, and thou shalt possess that wherein others are only tenants and boarders. Thou true land-lord! sea-lord! air-lord!"[6] Similarly, Cather favors her children with exclusive ownership of the island because they value it as a stimulus "to the intensity of their inner life" (CSF, 276). By arguing that the children's superior imaginative investment in nature qualifies them to claim it as natural "artist[s]" (CSF, 275) akin to Emerson's poet, Cather was able to justify her own acquisition of Nebraska for her art. When she next attempted to celebrate Nebraska in *O Pioneers!*, she would more subtly enact her imaginative appropriation of the landscape through a surrogate "claimant" in the fiction. Although disguised as a Swedish immigrant farmer, Alexandra Bergson is really a noble descendant of Emerson's poet landlord, through whom Cather vicariously staked out a territory within her own imagination as the real site of the novel.

At one level, Cather modeled her claimants upon Emerson's poet landlord in order to put herself and her readers in possession of the continent by a means that was not tainted by greed. Struggling to gain an imaginative foothold in the land of opportunity, whose opportunism she abhorred, Cather, like Emerson, sought a way to privilege the claims of the artist over those of the materialist. To justify the property rights of her child-artist in "Far Island," she argues that "his peculiar part and possessions in the material objects around him are so different from those of his elders, that it may be said his rights are granted by a different lease" (CSF, 275–76); as Emerson put it at the beginning of *Nature*, the poet is the only true landlord because he has an imaginative property to which "warranty-deeds give no title."[7] Although Emerson acknowledged that "Miller owns this field, Locke that, and Manning the woodland beyond," he nonetheless asserted that "none of them owns the landscape. There is a property in the horizon which no man has but he whose eye can integrate all the parts, that is, the poet".[8] Emerson's distinction between materialistic ownership and imaginative appropriation of nature can similarly help us to understand the priority that Cather gives to Alexandra's property rights over those of her brothers. Like Emerson's practical farmers Miller and Locke, Lou and Oscar desire to parcel out nature into its economic units. By adding up the landscape in dollars and cents, they merely divide its integrity. Although their hard labor in the fields writes the actual history of Western settlement, they disinherit themselves from the "best part" of the landscape by failing to assimilate its beauty. By contrast, Cather makes it clear that Alexandra alone deserves to claim the Nebraska Divide because she has the poet landlord's capacity to incorporate the beauty of the soil in which her brothers can only rub their hands. Cather ennobles Alexandra in a series of contemplative poses to suggest that she, like Emerson's poet landlord, possesses the "eye [that] can integrate all the parts." Exempted from all physical work by her father, as if in reward for her transcendental inheritance, Alexandra exerts her superior claim upon the land by simply looking at it. Instead of taming the land by the sweat of her brow, "Her body [is] in an attitude of perfect repose" (OP, 61). Sitting in her rocking chair, "looking thoughtfully away at the point where the upland road disappeared over the rim of the prairie," Alexandra recognizes in the horizon that special Emersonian property that is as invisible and indivisible as her own exaltation.

When Lou and Oscar dispute the legitimacy of Alexandra's title to her lands, they ironically fail to see that her legal lease symbolically ensures her a sovereign and inviolate possession of a region located in consciousness itself. In the last scene of the novel, Alexandra herself comments on the vanity of her brothers' materialistic claims to the land in a way that is reminiscent of Emerson. Alexandra reflects that she cannot "will" her land to her brothers because mere "names on the county clerk's plat" (307) give no title to that imaginative property she sees before her in the sunset. Cather frames this last scene carefully: we see the sky only as reflected by Alexandra when "the level rays of the sinking sun shone in her clear eyes" (308), as if to imply that the sunset's transcendent essence really originates within her own radiant nature. Emerson had said that "in the tranquil landscape, and especially in the distant line of the horizon, man beholds somewhat as beautiful as his own nature."[9] For Alexandra, too, her own nature proves to be her most valuable acquisition from the horizon. By recognizing in the sunset an inner light, Alexandra imaginatively claims the Divide as her Unity and, in coming home to it, comes home to herself.

Cather would make the competition between material ownership and imaginative appropriation of nature the central dramatic conflict in such later novels as *The Professor's House*. Her main interest in "The Treasure of Far Island" and *O Pioneers!*, however, was not to attack the materialism of her day but rather, as I have suggested, to assert her own authorial claim upon Nebraska. Cather had to overcome an even greater antagonist than the twentieth-century materialist such as Lou or Oscar;

ultimately, that greatest enemy was the reality of the land itself. The children who recreate the island as their "Wonderland" (CSF, 276) or "Ultima Thule" (CSF, 266) aptly name it "Far Island," for Cather's initial affirmation of Nebraska's beauty likewise depended upon her ability to remove it far away from geographical reality. When she had tried to portray the prairie with an unsparing realism in previous stories, such as "Peter" (1892) and "On the Divide" (1896), she had found that she could not forgive the land for its hostile conditions. In these first bitter stories, she had protested against the immigrants' hardships during the drought of the 1890s in order to vent her own resentment against the prairie that she felt had starved her imagination.[10] But in the guise of the adult Douglass of "Far Island," who returns to the scene of his childhood after making his career as a playwright, Cather herself mentally returned to her Nebraska home in order to view it in a new light after launching her career as a writer. Expressing a homesickness that is not for the real Nebraska but rather for "that happy land we used to rule" (CSF, 281) as children, Cather reminds us that her own appropriation of Nebraska began as a child when she and her brothers, like the children of Far Island, played on an island in the Republican River (WCL, 23). In her poem of dedication to her brothers in *April Twilights*, she would again recall that primal scene as one of imaginative possession or "conquest of the world" (AT, 3). As she reconstructs her search for imaginative spoils in "Far Island," the island's real buried "treasure" lies not in its sandhills or cottonwood groves but in her own youthful "sense of power" (CSF, 273). Like the naked white beach of the island that has no vegetation but is "full of possibilities for the imagination" (CSF, 265), the Nebraska landscape that Cather wanted to possess in "Far Island" was important not as local color but as the backdrop upon which she could recreate the world as a reflection of the spirit. Above all, "Far Island" suggests that before Cather could claim Nebraska for her "own," she had to take it off the regional map and place it in consciousness.

Most literally, of course, Cather took possession of her "own material" (Pref. AB, v) in *O Pioneers!* when she abandoned the artificial Jamesian formulas of her first novel, *Alexander's Bridge*, and embraced her "own" past experience in Nebraska. As she later assessed her accomplishment, "A painter or writer must learn to distinguish what is his *own* from that which he admires. I never abandoned trying to make a compromise between the kind of matter that my experience had given me and the manner of writing which I admired, until I began my second novel, 'O Pioneers!'" (WCP, 21). Yet the material that Cather claimed for her "own" in *O Pioneers!* lay most firmly rooted not in her native soil but in her own native soul. Although she had been ambivalent about claiming "the full consciousness of [her]self" that was "life itself" in *Alexander's Bridge* (AB, 39), she unreservedly made that affirmation when she wrote *O Pioneers!* Claiming as her "own" those "things [that] ... lie at the bottom of [the writer's] consciousness" (Pref. AB, vi) as "life itself" (ix), Cather was really claiming an innate psychological material that she believed had always been her own. Ultimately, the ideas that Cather possessed in writing *O Pioneers!* and that "continue[d] to feed [her]" (vi) were so deeply embedded in her psyche that they fed both her personality and her art inextricably. As she said, "There is a time in a writer's development when his 'life line' and the line of his personal endeavor meet.... After he has once or twice done a story that formed itself, inevitably, in his mind, he will not often turn back to the building of external stories again" (vi). Portraying her literary evolution as effortless, Cather suggests that once she let *O Pioneers!* shape itself according to her deepest impulses, she no longer needed to return to such artificial "external stories" as *Alexander's Bridge.* By infusing her new art with a "life line" of vitality — a kind of spiritual umbilical chord — she gave birth to it as an organic expression of the soul.

To understand how Alexandra's Emersonian appropriation of the land mirrors Cather's literary claim upon the life of consciousness, we can begin with Cather's need to revise her own traumatic experience of the prairie. As she later recalled her childhood move with her family in 1883 from Virginia to Nebraska, she first experienced the prairie as a devastating loss:

We drove out from Red Cloud to my grandfather's homestead one day in April. I was sitting on the hay in the bottom of a Studebaker wagon, holding on to the side of the wagon box to steady myself — the roads were mostly faint trails over the bunch grass in those days. The land was open range and there was almost no fencing. As we drove further and further out into the country, I felt a good deal as if we had come to the end of everything — it was a kind of erasure of personality.

I would not know how much of a child's life is bound up in the woods and hills and meadows around it, if I had not been jerked away from all these and thrown out into a country as bare as a piece of sheet iron. I had heard my father say you had to show grit in a new country, and I would have got on pretty well during that ride if it had not been for the larks. Every now and then one flew up and sang a few splendid notes and dropped down into the grass again. That reminded me of something — I don't know what, but my one purpose in life just then was not to cry, and every time they did it, I thought I should go under. (KA, 448)

For the nine-year-old girl, the uprooting from the enfolding and reassuring hills of Virginia to the sheet-iron flatness of Nebraska signified not merely a loss of home but a more painful loss of identity. If, in that bleak and lonely Nebraska landscape, the larks sounded the only familiar note, that was because they evoked the memory of a lost "something" that Cather imagined having once possessed in some idyllic youth. Fearing that she, too, would "go under" each time the larks disappeared in the grass, Cather took them as an emblem of her own psychological burial or death. As if she had looked into a mirror and found nothing there, Cather suffered "an erasure of personality." At forty as at nine, Cather again found in the prairie only a missing sense of self. As she confessed in a letter to Elizabeth Shepley Sergeant just before she wrote *O Pioneers!*, she could not write about Nebraska because of a paralyzing childhood fear that she would lose something. [11] Yet Cather's choice of the word "erasure" to describe her childhood crisis implicitly asserts writing as a possible defense against such a negation or submergence of personality. Indeed, as early as 1908, when she wrote to Sarah Orne Jewett that she looked forward to devoting all her time to writing so as to save her soul, [12] Cather cherished the happiness of self-possession as the greatest personal reward of her art. But if she were to write about her own country and save her soul besides, she knew that she would first have to rewrite the nature of the landscape that had robbed her of her self as a girl.

In order to recover herself through an imaginative possession of the landscape, Cather not surprisingly turned to Emerson. Cather had grown up with Emerson in the family library as with a best friend and had even listed him as her favorite prose writer in 1888, when she was fifteen (WWC, 112). In a letter to Mariel Gere of 1 August 1893, she had described going to a meeting of a country literary society given by her aunt Franc on the topic of Emerson. Her condescending description of the other guests as country bumpkins who understood transcendentalism about as well as most university students suggests that she considered herself, at age twenty, an expert on Emerson. [13] In her art reviews and essays of the 1890s, Cather had referred and deferred to Emerson as much as to any other writer. She was clearly most fond of the landlord passage from "The Poet." As a writer who was hoping to idealize Nebraska, in spite of its "distinctly déclassé" (OW, 94) status as a literary subject, Cather found an important precedent in Emerson's romantic celebration of the sublime in the familiar and the low rather than in the remote and the exotic. But her need for Emerson's inspiration was finally more personal. For Cather, the greatest importance of Emerson lay in his authority to sanction her possession of an ideal landscape; from his trope of the poet landlord, she drew the moral that "a poet's consummation and crown is that the ideal shall be real to him" (WP, 42). In an early book review, she asserts that Emerson's faith in the poet landlord's ability to compensate himself for harsh experience is his "highest dignity" (WP, 354). As she reminds her readers, Emerson had promised the poet that "there is Beauty, plenteous as rain, shed for thee, and though thou shouldst walk the world over, thou shalt not be able to find one condition inopportune or ignoble" (WP, 353). Emerson's faith in the ideal reassured Cather that she could turn even the Nebraska prairie — the most inopportune condition of all — to her advantage. She had written to Witter Bynner on 7 June 1905 that, by contrast to the beautiful Shenandoah Valley, one could not imagine anything so bleak and desolate as a Nebraska ranch in the 1880s. There were no trees to alleviate the barren flatness, and even the miserable sluggish stream eighteen miles away was no more than a series of mudholes in the summer.[14] But if Emerson could stand in snow puddles on a bare common to be transported to a "perfect exhilaration" as a "transparent eye-ball,"[15] then surely Cather felt that she could escape the banks of her muddy stream in transcendental rapture. Emerson gave her faith that no matter how appalling the ugliness of the prairie, nature could be made to wear the beautiful colors of the spirit. The prairie might have depressed her as an indifferent blank, as "naked as the back of your hand,"[16] but Emerson's belief that "the blank that we see when we look at nature is in our own eye"[17] helped her to believe that she could restore nature's beauty merely by repairing her own vision. By perceiving the true animating spirit beneath nature's seeming indifference, she could endow a featureless landscape with her own superior attributes. Although Cather recalled that she felt "little and homesick and lonely"[18] when she first came to the prairie, Emerson's faith in the kinship between nature and man through a common "oversoul" meant that she would not be "alone and unacknowledged"[19] after all. She had resented being in exile on the prairie,[20] but Emerson had said that every man is "a god in ruins,"[21] a "banished king," who could nonetheless "vault at once into his throne"[22] by appropriating nature under the dominion of his spirit.

Emerson's *Nature* as the literary prototype of *O Pioneers*! also provides the best model for the psychological causes of its composition. Shortly after the death of his first wife, Ellen, in 1831, Emerson wrote in his journal that he would "let my bark head its own way toward the law of laws, toward the compensation or action and reaction of the Moral Universe."[23] He came to believe that compensation offers a gain for every loss. By the time he wrote *Nature* five years later, he was even more desperate to steer his course by this compensating "law of laws," for he had just lost his favorite brother, Charles, as well as his brother Edward two years earlier, to tuberculosis. Emerson's grief seems revealed in the conspicuous pattern of references to death in *Nature,* and yet surprisingly, Emerson uses these to affirm man's omnipotence. He could rejoice that "even the corpse has its own beauty"[24] because he was determined that his faith in his own unifying vision would be able to recover what his several bereavements had taken away. Whereas Emerson had suffered the actual deaths of his beloved family, Cather had suffered the psychological death of her childhood identity. No less than Emerson, Cather looked for consolation according to the authorial law of compensation when she set out to write about Nebraska in *O Pioneers!*

Indeed, with Emerson's help, Cather found in writing *O Pioneers* that even the agoraphobic nightmare of the Nebraska prairie could be turned into a fostering dwelling place for the spirit. Although in a letter to Sergeant she admits that she always feels little and diminished by Nebraska's endless space, she nonetheless asserts that bigness is to be the subject of her new story.[25] As we shall see, Cather would not reconcile the antagonism between the dwarfed self and the giant land, but she would simply change the terms of the opposition. In the realistic opening chapters of the novel, Alexandra feels threatened, as Cather was, by the bigness of the land "which seemed to overwhelm the little beginnings of human society that struggled in its sombre wastes" (15). Yet, as if Cather had derived consolation from Emerson's conviction that the "magnitude of material things is relative, and all objects shrink and expand to serve the passion of the poet,"[26] she lets Alexandra reverse this disproportion between the self and the prairie by projecting upon it her own "big" (64) ego.

Critics have unanimously agreed that Alexandra successfully tames the land by devoting herself to something greater, more impersonal, and more universal than the self personified in "the Genius of the Divide."[27] But though deceptively self-effacing, Alexandra's look of "love and yearning" has seduced her critics, for the "Genius" she worships in the land is the self. Far from selflessly abandoning herself to some "other," Alexandra self-centeredly embraces the land as an incarnation of her own romantic ego.

The two scenes that best organize the transcendental terms of Alexandra's relationship to the land are those involving the storm and the garden; whereas the storm scene operates according to the laws of reality, the garden scene operates according to the new law of Alexandra's desire. As if to challenge herself to make over her first depressing view of the country that threatened to erase her, Cather sets the opening scenes of the novel in a landscape where "the roads were but faint tracks in the grass, and the fields were scarcely noticeable" (19). Remembering her own invisibility as a child within the void, she imagines that the inability of men "to make any mark" (15) on the barren ground gives it its most frightening aspect. Moreover, when the snowstorm, like a huge eraser, sweeps away all human landmarks in its path so that even the town of Hanover, "anchored on a windy Nebraska tableland, was trying not to be blown away" (3), Cather recreates the obliterating landscape of her entry into Nebraska with the warning that only those who cling to an inner anchor of stability will survive. Cather insists that humans can't afford to give up the self to a landscape that threatens to blot out their identity. In *Nature,* Emerson writes that "the reason why the world lacks unity, and lies broken and in heaps, is because man is disunited with himself" (55); to recover a harmonious unity between himself and the world, he must practice "a continual self-recovery" (51). As if she were following Emerson's advice, Alexandra brings order out of the novel's initial chaos simply by recovering her own vitality and inner sense of unity. As in the first scene, when she "looked fixedly up the bleak street as if she were gathering her strength to face something" (10), Alexandra appears in a series of tableaux to marshal her energies in defense against an annihilating wasteland. [28] Whereas Carl is immediately erased from the scene when he recklessly sets out into the blizzard, Alexandra alone manages to blaze a trail across the darkness "as a moving point of light" because she garners her luminous vitality as "firmly" (18) as she holds her lantern. In fact, her vow throughout "The Wild Land" is to "hold on" (59, 64).

Alexandra most clearly transforms nature through her own Emersonian self-recovery in the garden scene. Although in reality the endless winds blowing across the prairie had overwhelmed Cather with a fear that she would be lulled forever to sleep,[29] Alexandra nonchalantly drowses in the garden because she stands protected within the spell of her own consciousness. "Standing perfectly still, with that serious ease so characteristic of her" (49), she detaches herself from her surroundings in an impenetrable calm as if she were exhibiting what Cather admired as Emerson's "lofty repose and magnificent tranquility" (WP 274). She is too "lost in thought" (48) to heed Carl's approach. Nor is she disturbed by the drought or heat as she tosses her sunbonnet aside in her careless enjoyment of an inner equilibrium. "Leaning upon her pitchfork" (48) with "serious ease" (49), Alexandra most obviously imitates Whitman's imperturbable and self-contained stance at the beginning of "Song of Myself" when he leans and loafs at his ease, contemplating a spear of summer grass. Like Whitman, Alexandra forgets her labor in an effort to concentrate, rather than squander, her vital force. She, too, exerts a power over the scene that lies in her unruffled omnipotence rather than in her actions. As self-absorbed and self-absorbing as Whitman, Alexandra seems to incorporate nature as effortlessly as she soaks in the sunshine. When "her thick, reddish braids, twisted about her head, fairly burned in the sunlight," she seems to have consumed so much of the sun's energy as to become herself the generative life force in the garden. Yet, as for Whitman and all the transcendentalists, that resplendent glow about Alexandra's head ultimately signifies the power of her own exceptional being, a power she recovers through nature. Just as Thoreau used to wonder at the halo of light around his shadow and fancy himself one of the "elect,"[30] so Alexandra radiates a natural halo that reveals her as the privileged divinity who overshadows the mundane world around her.

Once Alexandra recovers her soul, she is ready to complete her restoration of the garden by projecting upon it a superior new vision. Emerson had been confident that nothing could befall him in life — "no disgrace, no calamity (leaving me my eyes), which nature cannot repair"[31] because his eyes alone enabled him to recreate nature as a reassuring scene. He affirmed that "the eye is the best of artists,"[32] for the eye could recompose the scene in the transfiguring light of its owner's nature. Although her father had consulted her about the problem that "no one understood how to farm it properly" (22), Alexandra successfully improves the land when she, like Emerson, realizes that the crucial question is not how to farm it but, rather, how to perceive it. Indeed, when Carl returns to see Alexandra's farm, reflecting that "I would never have believed it could be done. I'm disappointed in my own eye, in my imagination" (108), he attributes her triumph to her imaginative eye. Thus, though Alexandra's pitchfork stands idle in the garden, it serves as the icon for another kind of cultivation of the soil. As Alexandra does nothing but steadfastly gaze out over the land, she makes the cultivating eye of the Emersonian poet, rather than the pitchfork or plow, the crucial tool that allows her to justify her claim. Alexandra leans on her pitchfork as Thoreau leans on his hoe: to cultivate thoughts rather than vegetables. Whereas John Bergson and his materialistic sons have "the Old-World belief that land, in itself, is desirable" (21), Alexandra adopts Emerson's New-World belief in "new lands, new men, [and] new thoughts."[33] Bergson, who values the land "in itself," reminds us of Emerson's "sensual man [who] conforms thoughts to things," but Alexandra, who values "the idea of things more than the things themselves" (48), recalls Emerson's poet who "conforms things to his thoughts."[34] She is the analogist who more radically reads nature as a text that corresponds to her own mind. John Bergson's story teaches the moral of Cather's early realistic stories that the land inevitably defeats those who defer to its inescapable presence as "the great fact" (15). His battle against the land as a material reality is a self-fulfilling prophecy that leaves him with nothing at the end of his life but the indifferent prospect of "the same land, the same lead-colored miles" (20). Despite all his efforts to improve the land, he fails to change its implacable reality, and so remains a victim to its droughts, blizzards, and plagues. Whereas her literal-minded father and brothers "were meant to follow in paths already marked out for them," Alexandra is able "to break trails in a new country" (48) as she makes inroads into consciousness itself. Her perceptual challenge in "The Wild Land" is to transform the land from its initially objective reality as "the great fact" into the great metaphor.

Although Alexandra has become eulogized as a heroic tamer of the frontier, she does not tame the wild land at all but rather, appropriates its wildness as a metaphor for her own primordial soul. Her triumphant metamorphosis of the land is evident at the end of the garden scene, when even Carl "felt something strong and young and wild come out of it, that laughed at care" (49). Although this elusive "something" appears to come organically out of the earth, it bears little resemblance to the actual nature of the garden. Whereas the garden itself is cultivated, the spirit that Alexandra summons from it is "wild." Moreover, while the garden contains only "drying vines" and tough withered stalks, this new spirit is "strong and young." Were this impoverished and "barren" ground to speak for itself, it would hardly laugh at care. But just as Emerson said that "the beauty of nature re-forms itself in the mind, and not for barren contemplation, but for new creation,"[35] so the barren garden flushes into a new vernal and blithe existence in its seeming eagerness to incarnate Alexandra's engendering spirit. Alexandra herself, still haloed by the wonderful "youth and strength" (25) that her father worshipped, is the only strong, young, wild thing in the scene. Although critics have imagined that Alexandra gives herself up to "something larger" than the self, she recognizes in her garden the same "something" that her successor, Thea Kronborg, more explicitly recognizes as her "second self," and that her author, Willa Cather, recognized as the artist's romantic ego. When, during the harvest, "something frank and joyous and young in the open face of the country" (76) again issues from it, the land most unabashedly reveals its origins in a human countenance, for the soil produces its most valuable and instantaneous crop when it yields back to Alexandra her own smiling reflection. Simultaneously, the prairie becomes a mirror for Willa Cather that reflects back to her a token of that youthful "something" that she had lost as a child.

At the end of part 1, when Alexandra appears "leaning against the frame of the mill" (70) as she had leaned against her pitchfork in the garden, she watches the stars in another peculiarly Emersonian pose. Her awe of the stars' "vastness and distance, and ... ordered march" has led critics to assume that she worships the harmonious design of a supernal will.[36] But just as Emerson at the beginning of *Nature* stands reverently before the stars that beckon him to "let his thoughts be of equal scope,"[37] so Alexandra stands before a celestial "vastness" that invites her soul to expand to its gigantic occasion. And so it does, for though she appears to pay homage to a divine order, she contemplates that order as a fluid process, "an ordered march," that suggests the unfolding of an animating consciousness. We might say that she conducts the stars' "ordered march" with the same authority that enables Emerson's poet to "[turn] the world to glass, and [show] us all things in their right series and pro-cession"[38] once he transforms them into a mirror of his own thought. If, indeed, "the law [that lay] behind [the stars]" (70–71) has its precedent in Emerson's "higher law"[39] that guaranteed the origin of natural facts in the mind, then it is no wonder that Alexandra feels such "a sense of per-sonal security" (71). To exercise that "higher law," she need not open her arms to receive divine inspiration; rather, as she "drew her shawl closer about her" (70), she need simply hug to her breast the original impulse within her. Although in the opening snowstorm Alexandra had wrapped her coat about herself in her vulnerability, she now repeats the gesture as a sign of the imaginative strength that can transform brutal elements into reaffirming tokens of the soul.

Alexandra's ability to substitute the higher law of her will for the law of nature gives her triumph over the land the miraculous power of a fairy tale. Rosowski has drawn our attention to the fantasy at work beneath the novel's ostensible historical realism when she writes, "Like the heroine of a fairy tale who must find the key to transformation, Alexandra must learn the secret that will release the land from darkness."[40] I would like to extend Rosowski's reading of the book as a fairy tale. Although Alexandra learns many facts about farming from her father, she finds such secondhand knowledge proves as useless as did her father, when, for all his constant experimentation, he fails to solve the "enigma" (22) of the land. Cather's paradoxical point is that, while John Bergson wastes his life trying to solve the land's enigma, Alexandra succeeds by not even trying. In fact, *O Pioneers!* begins where fairy tales usually end: when Alexandra's father crowns her queen of the Divide in reward for her superior "strength of will" (24). Her magical inheritance from her father follows the psychological laws of wish fulfillment. She gets to eclipse her rival brothers when her father dies, grateful in his knowledge that "there was one among his children to whom he could entrust the future of his family and the possibilities of his hard-won land" (24). Alexandra "must not work in the fields" (27) but merely rule the farm as its "one head" (26–27). Like God reversing the judgment on Adam and Eve in a new creation story in which the child rules preeminent, Bergson exempts his daughter from both toil and subservience and flatly decrees, "That is good" (27).

Rather than have to go out to "find the key to transformation," then, Alexandra need merely realize that she has possessed it within herself all along. In the way that Emerson's child-poet learns the "secret" to nature when he discovers "that he can reduce under his will ... whole series of events, and so conform all facts to his character,"[41] so Alexandra solves the land's "enigma" (22) by putting her faith in her own powerful desire. When she returns to the Divide, stubbornly determined "to hold on harder than ever" (64), she instantaneously puts herself in imaginative possession of the land as her own dowry and estate. Although the cause of Alexandra's happiness as she looks out over the Divide is meant to elude her brother Emil, it becomes apparent if we consider her Emersonian pedigree. As Cather says,

> Her face was so radiant that he felt shy about asking her. For the first time, perhaps, since that land emerged from the waters of geologic ages, a human face was set toward it with love and yearning. It seemed beautiful to her, rich and strong and glorious. Her eyes drank in the breadth of it, until her tears blinded her. Then the Genius of the Divide, the great, free spirit which breathes across it, must have bent lower than it ever bent to a human will before. The history of every country begins in the heart of a man or a woman. (65)

Alexandra may not be able to will the land to her brothers, but this climactic scene reveals that she can will it to herself. As if in fulfillment of Emerson's prediction that "in proportion to the energy of his thought and will, [the poet] takes up the world into himself,"[42] Alexandra takes up the entire prairie into herself when "her eyes drank in the breadth of it, until her tears blinded her" (65). Hardly self-abnegating as critics have claimed, Alexandra swallows the prairie whole in an appetitive gesture of self-aggrandizement. She is no more selfless than is her Emersonian counterpart in Cather's poem "Macon Prairie" (1923), whose "burning eyes ... took possession / Of the red waste" as an act of "self-restitution" (ATOP, 58–59). With her drinking eyes, Alexandra, too, takes imaginative possession of the Nebraska plains so as to reconstitute her own soul. "Bent lower than it ever bent to a human will before," the "great, free spirit" of the Divide is no longer so great and no longer so free. As if as an emblem of Emerson's faith that nature "is made to serve,"[43] the Genius of the Divide abdicates its free reign to bow humbly before its new mistress. Instead of having any longer to appease the land's Genius, Alexandra simply wills it to minister to the imperious needs of her own, and so usurps the role of the Divide's governing anima. Above all, the land's subservience, as it bends lower than it has ever bent to a human will before, serves to flatter Alexandra as the strongest personality in all history.

Cather is careful to make the personality of her heroine, rather than the landscape itself, the focus of the scene. As we watch Alexandra's rapt face through the eyes of Emil, we are clearly meant to share his awe for her. Moreover, when Cather juxtaposes the land to Alexandra so that "for the first time, perhaps, since that land emerged from the waters of the geologic ages, a human face was set toward it with love and yearning," she magnifies Alexandra's face to a colossal size so that it dwarfs even the prairie's infinite space and history. Enlarged by Cather's zoom lens, Alexandra's countenance assumes such visual and syntactic dominance in this scene that even she seems to respond to it. When Cather writes, "It seemed beautiful to her, rich and strong and glorious," she deliberately exploits the ambiguity of the indefinite pronoun "it." Although we might assume that "it" refers to the land, Cather allows us to read its real antecedent as Alexandra's own "human face." At a symbolic level, the two sentences are most profoundly linked by Alexandra as their mutual subject, for what really "seemed beautiful" to Alexandra, Cather implies, is her own inexpressible soul as it unites with the Genius of the land as a kindred spirit. Soon, Alexandra sees nothing but this reflection of herself. In an important causal sequence, Cather tells us that Alexandra's "eyes drank in the breadth of it, until her tears blinded her," and "then the Genius of the Divide" bent before her. After Alexandra's tears blind her to the objective scene before her — and only then — is the metamorphosis of the land into self possible. When we first saw Alexandra, her "eyes ... fixed intently on the distance, without seeming to see anything, as if she were in trouble" (6), she had looked at a real landscape only to see nothing. Ultimately, it is only when she sees a subjective landscape embodying the self that she sees something. Thus, she solves her "trouble" just as Emerson solves his at the end of *Nature*. As if assured by Emerson's faith that all reality's disagreeable appearances will disappear once man conforms nature to the beauty of his mind's "pure idea,"[44] Alexandra exerts a prophetic vision before which bleak wastes vanish and the world becomes "a realized will, — the double of the man."[45] The "stern frozen ... bosom" (15) of the country in its cold reality gives way to the humanized "swells of the Divide" (65) that "breathe" with Alexandra's own passions and reflect back into her drinking eyes the currents of her own being.

But surely the most miraculous transformation implicit in Alexandra's narcissistic reunion with the self is that of Cather's own experience. Although Cather had feared that she "would go under" upon that first ride into the prairie, she imagines that Alexandra gets to lean over the Genius of the Divide as it bows under her. Cather had feared that the West was too gigantic and engulfing,[46] but as Alexandra's magnificent face overshadows the horizon, she overwhelms it. Although, when actually in Nebraska, Cather had "an unreasoning fear of being swallowed by the distances" (WC: AM, 79) and of being drunk up by desert sands,[47] she gets vicarious satisfaction when Alexandra drinks in the land with her insatiable eyes. Cather takes her greatest revenge upon the landscape that had erased her as a child by figuratively erasing, or foreshortening, its entire history between the "geologic ages" (65) and the moment when her alter ego, Alexandra, chooses to turn her adoring face towards it. To say that "the history of every country begins in the heart of a man or a woman" suggests that its history begins only when someone with enough personality like Alexandra leaves a heartfelt impression upon it. Hovering over the Divide as if its millions of years of history were no longer than her own shadow, Alexandra is not the victim of history, as was the nine-year-old Willa, nor is she even a part of it. Rather, she is the deity who creates the land anew. In Genesis, God created man on the sixth day; correspondingly, Alexandra takes her ride back to the Divide "on the sixth day" (64) to recreate the land in her image. With the sublime light of a god over a new creation, Alexandra's "radiant" face shapes the land out of the primordial "waters" of chaos into a new country founded in her own begetting consciousness.[48] Sanctioned by the "different lease" that Emerson granted the poet over his material, Alexandra is allowed to project her passions upon the same landscape that had originally obliterated her author. Finally, Alexandra's imaginative claim upon the land most profoundly celebrates Willa Cather herself as the new "Genius" of the Divide.

Letting the Land "Work Itself": Cather's Writing of *O Pioneers!*

So far, I have argued that Cather enacted her acquisition of her "own material" in consciousness through Alexandra Bergson's imaginative appropriation of the prairie. I would like to extend this argument to show how Cather used Alexandra's story further to dramatize her discovery of her literary material, her artistic method, and even the very process of her writing.

So self-conscious was Cather in working out her artistic choices in the novel that she envisioned all the other major characters as types of the artist as well; in various ways, Carl, John Bergson, and the lovers, Marie and Emil, all provide foils to Alexandra and, implicitly, to Willa Cather, enabling her to distance herself from previous roles and temptations so as to confirm her new artistic identity. As they stand together in the storm in the opening scene of the novel, Alexandra and Carl form a pair that suggests Cather's dual vision of herself as an artist: in Alexandra, "who seemed to be looking with such anguished perplexity into the future," we can see Cather's forward-looking persona as the artist-to-be, as yet untested and uncertain, whereas in "the sombre" Carl, "who seemed already to be looking into the past" (14), we can see her backwards-looking persona as the inexperienced writer who had failed. Carl plays the role that Cather retrospectively cast for herself as the writer of *Alexander's Bridge*; as an ineffectual engraver of other men's pictures, he is as imitative as Cather felt she had been in her attempts to copy pictures already made by James and Wharton. When Carl first appears in the drugstore "turning over a portfolio of chromo 'studies' which the druggist sold to the Hanover women who did china-painting" (9), he conforms his art to popular patterns much as Cather felt that she had adhered to conventional academic standards in her "studio picture" (OW, 91). In addition, Cather had figuratively engraved other men's pictures when she had edited newspaper articles; indeed, she implies analogies between Carl's experience as an artist and her own as a journalist. Complaining to Alexandra that "everything's cheap metal work nowadays, touching up miserable photographs, forcing up poor drawings" (122), Carl echoes Cather's complaints as the magazine editor who had to touch up "cheap work" (WC: AM, 62). As we see him "dreaming over an illustrated paper" (31), Carl betrays "the conventional editorial point of view" from which Cather felt glad to have "recovered" (OW, 92) in *O Pioneers!* As if he, like Cather, had been deceived by the false assumption that "the new [was] more exciting than the familiar," he peruses the paper for evidence of sensational, "interesting material" (OW, 91). Traveling to St. Louis, Chicago, and Alaska in search of external sources of artistic inspiration, Carl commits what Cather later regretted as her own error in thinking that she could acquire her material "by going out to look for it" (Pref. AB, vii). Finally, Carl's "fortune-hunt[ing]" (107) for gold in Alaska seems to dramatize Cather's temptation while at *McClure's* to succumb to "the lure of big money rewards" (WC: AM, 62).

Yet, as if Carl had learned Cather's lesson in writing *O Pioneers!* that "the young writer must ... imitate and strive to follow the masters he most admires, until he finds he is starving for reality and cannot make this go any longer" (Pref. AB, viii), he tires of his apprenticeship to others and returns home after sixteen years to find that Alexandra has created a more authentic art from the "reality" of her immediate experience. As Carl testifies to Alexandra's success, acknowledging that, "I've been away engraving other men's pictures, and you've stayed at home and made your own" (116), he explicitly draws attention to her role as the most successful artist in the novel. While Carl has acquired his art secondhand from distant experiences and other models, Alexandra has created her pictures from her "own" regional experience, and more deeply, from her "own" personality. The land provides her an artistic medium of self-expression; as Cather says, "You feel that, properly, Alexandra's house is the big out-of-doors, and that it is in the soil that she expresses herself best" (84). Ultimately, Alexandra makes pictures by transforming the landscape into her own self-portrait. Though her predecessor, Bartley Alexander, had failed to find a plan for his bridge that could accommodate an original "something," Alexandra molds the land into the very expression of her soul so that "there was something individual about the great farm" (83). Whereas Carl, as a derivative engraver, cannot even sign his name to his art, Alexandra leaves a memorable personal signature on the land that stamps it as hers and nobody else's so that "anyone thereabouts would have told you that this was one of the richest farms on the Divide, and that the farmer was a woman, Alexandra Bergson" (83). Ironically, while Carl seeks a fortune in gold by traveling all the way to Alaska, Alexandra is the one who becomes "rich" simply by enriching her art with her precious inner life.

Alexandra commits herself to the Divide only after she, like Carl, takes a journey away from home. Going to the river valley to satisfy her curiosity about "what they've got down there" (62), Alexandra travels in search of novelty, as had Cather when she visited places like London for her material. Hoping to learn about other, more-popular farming techniques, Alexandra reenacts Cather's efforts to adopt the fashionable "literary devices" and techniques of writers like James. As if she, too, were experimenting with new ideas during a kind of training period, Alexandra spends a day with "one young farmer who had been away at school, and who was experimenting with a new kind of clover hay" (64). As had Cather, she "learn[s] a great deal" from her exposure to the greater world of knowledge. But finally, when Alexandra returns to the Divide, she has Cather's revelation that "when a writer once begins to work with his own material, he realizes that, no matter what his literary excursions may have been, he has been working with it from the beginning — by living it" (Pref. AB, viii). Telling Emil that "they can always scrape along down there, but they can never do anything big" (64), she realizes that the endless space of the Divide, unlike the narrow valley, is the only creative medium large enough to contain her expansive spirit. Alexandra's aspirations towards bigness reflect her author's newfound freedom to express herself as she wanted. In a celebratory mood, Cather wrote to Sergeant that, for the first time, she had been able to give a story a big subject since she had not had to pare down its essential substance.[49] No longer had she to confine her soul within restrictive literary plots and forms as she had in *Alexander's Bridge*.

We can see Alexandra's trip to the river valley and back as a veiled enactment not only of Cather's career but also of her process of writing the novel. In her essay "My First Novels," Cather maintains that writing *O Pioneers!* was like "taking a ride through a familiar country on a horse that knew the way, on a fine morning when you felt like riding" (OW, 92–93). Cather's metaphor of horseback riding suggests a comparison between Alexandra's riding home to the Divide on her horse and Cather's writing the novel. The idea of the artist as a traveler on horseback echoes Emerson's trope in "The Poet." Just "as the traveler who has lost his way throws his reins on his horse's neck and trusts to the instinct of the animal to find his road," Emerson says, "so must we do with the divine animal who carries us through this world."[50] Like Emerson's traveler, Alexandra first appears in the snowstorm as a "traveler, who [has] lost [her] way" (10–11). But when she "urge[s] Brigham forward" (64), throwing her reins on her horse's neck, she emblematically finds her proper direction by trusting to the divine instinct she carries within her. Once the indifferent landscape suddenly becomes the familiar and easily traveled road of consciousness, Alexandra, like Emerson's traveler, finds that "the metamorphosis is possible."[51]

Through Alexandra, Cather thus enacts the fantasy that she can write with sureness and power merely by trusting the guidance of her own unconscious instincts. As she more fully elaborates in her preface to *Alexander's Bridge*,

> In working with [his own] material [the writer] finds that he need have little to do with literary devices; he comes to depend more and more on something else — the thing by which our feet find the road home on a dark night, accounting of themselves for roots and stones which he had never noticed by day. This guide is not always with him, of course. He loses it and wanders. But when it is with him it corresponds to what Mr. Bergson calls the wisdom of intuition as opposed to that of intellect. With this to shape his course, a writer contrives and connives only as regards mechanical details, and questions of effective presentation, always debatable. About the essential matter

of his story he cannot argue this way or that; he has seen it, has been enlight-
ened about it in flashes that are as unreasoning, often as unreasonable, as life
itself. (Pref. AB, viii–ix)

Cather felt that her writing took her on "the road home" to a point of
origins in consciousness. To travel faultlessly through this "dark" subjective landscape, Cather depended not on any external literary devices
but on "something else": an internal "guide" of "intuition." When Lou
challenges Alexandra shortly after her return, to explain how she suddenly "*know[s]*" that the land will make them all rich, she can only say,
"I can't explain that, Lou. You'll have to take my word for it. I *know*,
that's all. When you drive about over the country you can feel it coming"
(67). No more than Cather could "argue this way or that" about the
"essential matter" of her story, can Alexandra give a rational explanation
for her mystical revelation about the land. Sensing only that an unnamed
presence — some "it" — is coming, she, like Cather, experiences a flash
of enlightenment about "life itself" — that inner vitality that can be
known only by faith.

In this passage Cather upholds the philosopher Henri Bergson as an
inspiration for her writing of *O Pioneers!*, and, I would suggest, for
Alexandra Bergson's creative apprehension of the prairie. Bergson, as
well as Emerson, is a model for Alexandra Bergson, and what's more, he
may well be her namesake. As Sergeant notes, Cather "was a reader of
Henri Bergson"; "Mind and invention were not her tools; the decisive
element was intuitive, poetical, almost mystical perception" (WC: AM,
203). Cather's distinction between Bergson's "wisdom of intuition" and
intellectual analysis recalls the distinction that Bergson makes in *An
Introduction to Metaphysics*, a book published in 1903 with which she
was most likely familiar. Cather's letters reveal that while she was writing *O Pioneers*, she was avidly reading Bergson's *Creative Evolution*,
first published in English in 1911.[52] Loretta Wasserman and Tom Quirk
have explored the influence of Bergson on Cather.[53] Quirk sees Alexandra as a "Bergsonian heroine, one who has a mysterious intuition of the
great operations of nature."[54] Emphasizing the novel's Bergsonian ideal
of nature as a vital organic force, Quirk suggests that Alexandra's intuition enables her to gain insight into a greater whole, a continuum in
space and time. In addition, I would like to suggest that Bergson's philosophy of intuition provided Cather not simply with a mystical conduit
of knowledge into nature but with a metaphysical means of transforming
the currents of the world into the currents of consciousness. In a letter to
Sergeant in 1912, Cather imagines that to read Bergson at sea is to grasp
something waiting especially for her on the water.[55] Bergson's concept

of intuition provided her with another model whereby she could appropriate the world, be it the Atlantic Ocean or the Nebraska Divide. Analysis, Bergson writes, is an inevitably incomplete way of knowing because it conceives of nature as a series of contingent functions or approximate and partial points of view. By contrast, "intuition," a kind of *sympathie intellectuelle*[56] (intellectual empathy) allows one to place oneself within an object so as to know it in its entirety, undivided from one's own inner nature. Whereas analysis allows one to translate the object into other impersonal symbols, intuition allows one to dispense with intermediary symbols so as to translate the object into an extension of one's own fluid and unified consciousness. As Bergson writes:

> S'il existe un moyen de posséder une réalité absolument au lieu de la connâitre relativement, de se placer en elle au lieu d'adopter des points de vue sur elle, d'en avoir l'intuition au lieu d'en faire l'analyse, enfin de la saisir en dehors de toute expression, traduction ou représentation symbolique, la métaphysique est cela même.[57]

> [If there exists any means of having absolute possession of a reality rather than a relative knowledge of it, of placing oneself inside it rather than adopting perspectives on it, of intuiting it rather than analyzing it, of finally seizing it apart from all expression, translation, or symbolic representation, metaphysics is that means.]

Bergson's vocabulary of possession would have appealed to Cather. As Alexandra looks lovingly at the Divide, she, too, exerts an empathic intuition to "possess" or "seize" reality as part of her own totality of being. For Bergson, as for Cather, intuition most importantly ensured the individual an imaginative possession of his own personality. As he would have reassured her, "Il y a une réalité au moins que nous saisissons tous du dedans, par intuition et non par simple analyse. C'est notre propre personne dans son écoulement à travers le temps. C'est notre moi que dure. Nous pouvons ne sympathiser intellectuellement avec aucune autre chose. Mais nous sympathisons sûrement avec nous-mêmes."[58] [There is one reality, at least, that we all seize from within, by intuition and not by mere analysis. It is our own personality in its flowing through time. It is our ego which endures. We may sympathize intellectually with nothing else. But we surely sympathize with our own selves.]

As if she had undergone a complete metamorphosis as the writer who had come into her own in *O Pioneers!,* Cather wrote in her 1922 preface that

> With this material he is another writer. He has less and less power of choice about the moulding of it. It seems to be there of itself, already moulded. If he

tries to meddle with its vague outline, to twist it into some categorical shape, above all if he tries to adapt or modify its mood, he destroys its value. (Pref. AB, viii)

Just as Carl can be seen to represent the false artist as imitative follower, so John Bergson can be seen to represent the false artist as conscious controller. He illustrates Cather's warning that the artist who "tries to meddle with [his material's] vague outline, to twist it into some categorical shape, above all ... to adapt or modify its mood, ... destroys its value." By dividing the prairie into corrals and cultivated fields, Bergson may improve its literal value as farmland, but he ironically destroys its symbolic artistic value, which lies in its undivided integrity. By contrast, Alexandra returns to the Divide to discover that the land, like Cather's literary material, was "there of itself, already moulded." Unlike her father, Alexandra realizes that meddling with the land's "vague outline" would be going against nature — her own nature. In a letter to Sergeant, Cather wrote that she had not tried to give the novel a sharp structure because the country itself lacked a definite outline; like the fluid, rich soil, her novel was soft and formless.[59] Interestingly, Cather suggests that she saw the organic soil as a metaphor for the organic material and form of her art. The land, like Cather's novel, lacks a definite contour because it takes its "vague outline" from the indistinct shape of consciousness itself. Moreover, Cather's description in her letter of the soil running through her fingers suggests an analogy between the earth (her literal subject matter) and her own lifeblood. Of course, though Cather claimed that her material in *O Pioneers!* was "already moulded" and that she did not interfere, she had taken great pains to remold it in her own image. She wrote to Sergeant that the country was the real hero of the story[60] because she had recreated it in the heroic image of the self.

As we have seen, Cather does not ever show her heroine actually toiling in the fields. As Alexandra assures her brothers, she knows "an easier way" (70). All they need do, she tells them, is "hold on" (59) to the land and let it take care of itself. At one level, Alexandra's determination "to hold on" to the high ground of the Divide seems to reflect Cather's desire to hold on to the high level of her artistic aspirations. Jewett, to whom Cather dedicated the novel, had encouraged her to recognize the "higher" quality of her work and to know that "it is to that level you must hold."[61] Moreover, Alexandra's desire "to hold on" to her land suggests Cather's belief that she needed fully to assimilate her creative material before she could write. Edith Lewis recalls that in writing *O Pioneers!*, Cather felt that "there was something there which she did not wish to waste by inadequate presentation. If she held it for a while, she might get

some new light on it" (WCL, 83). It is during that "fallow" period when
Alexandra is not physically working the land but merely holding on to it
as a part of her own being that she makes the soil most fertile. As Cather
says, "There were certain days in her life, outwardly uneventful, which
Alexandra remembered as peculiarly happy; days when she was close to
the flat, fallow world about her, and felt, as it were, in her own body the
joyous germination in the soil" (203–4). Just as Alexandra enriches her
land most when she is not working it, so Cather claimed that she enriched
her art most when she was not writing. As she said in a 1921 interview,
"most of the basic material a writer works with is acquired before the age
of fifteen. That's the important period: when one's not writing. Those
years determine whether one's work will be poor and thin or rich and
fine" (WCP, 20). Cather here implies that she thought of her literary
material as a "rich and fine" soil that she could cultivate merely by
plowing it under in consciousness as a part of her fertile memories.

As if to justify her own long "fallow" period as the writer making her
debut at forty, Cather has the fields finally yield their bountiful harvest
after they have symbolically lain for sixteen years in Alexandra's subconscious. When, after his long absence, Carl asks Alexandra how she
did it, she replies,

> We hadn't any of us much to do with it, Carl. The land did it. It had its little
> joke. It pretended to be poor because nobody knew how to work it right; and
> then, all at once, it worked itself. It woke up out of its sleep and stretched
> itself, and it was so big, so rich, that we suddenly found we were rich, just
> from sitting still. (116)

The "little joke" of this passage is that despite Alexandra's apparent
passivity, she is central and dominating, for her effortless working of the
land parallels Cather's effortless writing of the novel.[62] By having
Alexandra's land seem "all at once" to "work itself," Cather indulged in
a fantasy that her own novel had seemed spontaneously to write itself. As
she said in her 1921 *Bookman* interview, "From the first chapter, I
decided not to 'write' at all," but "simply to give myself up to [deepest
impulses and memories]" (WCP, 21). She liked to think that she had let
the story take its own shape so that it "formed itself, inevitably, in [her]
mind" (Pref. AB, vi). Through Alexandra, Cather reminds herself that
she, too, would become emotionally "rich, just from sitting still," while
composing the novel.

In the famous harvest scene, the desolate prairie seems, after sixteen
years, to be suddenly and radically humanized:

The rich soil yields heavy harvests; the dry, bracing climate and the smoothness of the land make labor easy for men and beasts. There are few scenes more gratifying than a spring plowing in that country, where the furrows of a single field often lie a mile in length, and the brown earth, with such a strong, clean smell, and such a power of growth and fertility in it, yields itself eagerly to the plow; rolls away from the shear, not even dimming the brightness of the metal, with a soft, deep sigh of happiness.... The grain is so heavy that it bends toward the blade and cuts like velvet.

There is something frank and joyous and young in the open face of the country. It gives itself ungrudgingly to the moods of the season, holding nothing back. Like the plains of Lombardy, it seems to rise a little to meet the sun. The air and the earth are curiously mated and intermingled, as if the one were the breath of the other. You feel in the atmosphere the same tonic, puissant quality that is in the tilth, the same strength and resoluteness. (76–77)

Once again, Cather conveys a romanticized version of her own "gratifying" relationship with her artistic material. We can read the harvest that "make[s] labor easy for men and beasts" as an analogy to Cather's tranquil task[63] when "her pen, of its own volition" (WC: AM, 89), began to write the novel. "Yield[ing] itself eagerly to the plow, roll[ing] away from the shear," the earth resembles Cather's written words that seemed readily to roll off her pen.[64] We can even see the earth's "soft, deep sigh of happiness" (76) at being cultivated as an expression of Cather's own "perfect joy and happiness"[65] while writing. Recounting that she did not revise or fuss over her compositions, but simply "let life flow along the pages," she seemed to write as continuously along the lines of her paper as the spring plowing continues uninterrupted along "furrows of ... a mile in length" (76).

"The air and the earth" are indeed "curiously mated and intermingled, as if the one were the breath of the other" (77), for they can be seen to represent the fusion between Cather's literary material and her creative inspiration. Breathing the new life of her spirit into her art, Cather, like Emerson, lets faith make its own forms. The earth that "mate[s]" with the air expresses Cather's feeling in writing *O Pioneers!* that she had found the "two things — strong enough to mate together without either killing the other," — a subject and a "birthright."[66] She goes on to say that a writer must have more than a good technique; above all, he "must know his subject with an understanding that passes understanding — like the babe knows its own mother's breast." Cather's analogy suggests that her bond with her material was as emotional, intuitive, and intimate as the baby's symbiotic relationship with his mother. The babe doesn't "know" its mother's breast, except instinctively. Though the breast gives him life, he has the illusion that he himself has created it through his own narcissistic desire, and so, we have seen, did Cather create the loving "swells" of the Divide in her own image.

Cather imagines that the land is grateful to the "atmosphere" around it in the same way that she imagines that the artist's material becomes enlivened only through "the atmosphere" of her passions. As she wrote in an early review, "What is a play but a wraith, an inanimate thing into which some man or woman must pour his or her heart's blood, a thing born of the passion of some great brain, and which lives only in the atmosphere of the passions, as certain sea mosses, which have lain shrunken and brown upon the rocks many a summer, expand and grow green again when they feel their native element about them?" (WP, 449). Cather's analogy perhaps provides the best gloss for the harvest scene. Though "shrunken and brown" like the withered sea mosses, Alexandra's garden — a metaphor for Cather's novel — gradually "expand[s] and grow[s] green again" in its "native element" once it feels renewed by the "tonic, puissant quality" (77) of its creator's spirit.

The Tragedy of the Lovers in *O Pioneers!*: Cather's Defense of her Self-Conservation for Art

Of course, Alexandra's story doesn't end with her triumphant taming of the land. Although, as originally written in 1911, her story stood alone as "Alexandra," Cather decided to write a "two-part pastoral" (WC: AM, 86) by combining it with "The White Mulberry Tree," the tragic tale written a year later of the young lovers Marie and Emil, who are killed by Marie's jealous husband while making love in the orchard. Cather brought these two stories together in the fall of 1912 to try to resolve her conflicting allegiances between the self and others that had plagued her in *Alexander's Bridge*. In her essay on Katherine Mansfield, Cather wrote that "human relationships are the tragic necessity of human life.... they can never be wholly satisfactory, [for] every ego is half the time greedily seeking them, and half the time pulling away from them" (OW, 109). As Sharon O'Brien suggests, Alexandra, who pulls away from human relationships, and the lovers Marie and Emil, who greedily seek them, "suggest the two halves of a divided self. They may embody the division within Willa Cather herself, who for years struggled to reconcile her need for human relationships with the austere demands of Art."[67] O'Brien insightfully argues that "in sympathizing with Marie's spontaneity and passionate openness, Willa Cather was acknowledging her own emotional needs, those 'tragic necessities' of life; in ultimately repudiating Marie's choice and giving her deepest admiration to the emotionally guarded but productive Alexandra, she was endorsing the part of herself that wanted to channel passion into artistic expression."[68] As O'Brien correctly perceives, Cather gives her greatest allegiance to Alexandra, as a figure of the artist. In O'Brien's view, the lovers' story records the dangers of "narcissistic self-involvement,"[69] while Alexandra's story celebrates the rewards of directing passion towards an impersonal goal beyond the self. I would like to reconsider the two stories of *O Pioneers!* as contrasting parables about the role of passion in art and life. By contrast to O'Brien, I see Alexandra's story as a parable about the successful artist's narcissistic conservation of her passion for her art, and the lovers' story as a parable about the fatal expenditure of passion in human relationships. By dooming the lovers to a tragic end, Cather confirmed her highest devotion to the self, which she hoped to repossess inviolate through her art. The lovers meet disaster because they are so selflessly involved with each other; Alexandra triumphs because she is so selfishly absorbed in herself. By projecting herself into the land, as the artist consecrates herself to a single purpose, Alexandra not only creates a fruitful art, manifest in her abundant harvest, but preserves her own soul. By contrast, when the lovers impulsively commit themselves to each other, they not only fail to become artists but lose their essential force and, indeed, their very lives.

Alexandra's social ties mask a deeper narcissism. When Carl strolls through the Bergson pasture, he recalls that "it was just there that he and Alexandra used to do their milking together, he on his side of the fence, she on hers" (126). Alexandra keeps even her prospective lover on the other side of the fence that surrounds her imperturbable composure. Having staked out an imaginative territory all her own in the first section of the novel "The Wild Land," she makes it her mission in "Neighboring Fields" to erect literal and figurative fences that put a "safe" (308) protective distance between herself and others. She is oblivious to the feelings of Emil and Marie because they are "different from her own" (284), whereas she is most attuned to the sympathies of her friend Carl because he reminds her of the happy times they had as children, who "liked the same things and ... liked them together" (52). Alexandra rejects otherness and most deeply embraces those who sustain her memory of the egoistic confidence of childhood. Clearly, she has a more passionate relationship with the land than with any human lover, and, as I have argued, she gives herself up to it only after she has recognized its Genius as her own.

The desire for autonomy that informs the novel is perhaps best illustrated by Alexandra's favorite memory of the wild duck on the pond. Alexandra shares the memory of the duck with her younger brother Emil, and yet, far from signifying social companionship, the duck comes to symbolize for Alexandra the single consciousness that she wishes to possess with others. No living thing — not even her closest friend — had ever seemed to Alexandra as beautiful as that "single wild duck" (204) because she invests it with the freedom and antinomian power of her own primordial ego. Far from being communal or selfless, the solitary duck that does nothing but "take its pleasure ... all by herself" (205) makes self-indulgence, like Freud's "pleasure principle," the cardinal rule of its existence. As "a kind of enchanted bird that did not know age or change" (205), the duck fosters Alexandra's illusion that she, too, can remain unconquered and uncompromised by an alien world. In fact, we might best think of the pond as a metaphor for the insular medium of consciousness that provides the artist with an impermeable refuge against time, change, and all the disruptive experiences of actual life. In her tribute to the composer Ethelbert Nevin, Cather described the artist's inner life as a "vacuum in which the soul is held free from atmospheric disturbances and the contraction and expansion of a changing temperature," a "sort of non-conducting medium between the world and [the self], [a] sort of protection to break the jar of things" (WP, 638). The duck's little inlet, so tranquil that it seems "to sleep in the sun" (204), seems an apt emblem of such an ideal psychic space in which the artist's "soul is held free" from life's extreme temperatures and jarring circumstances.

Like the pond, Alexandra's sanctuary of consciousness is most conspicuous for what it leaves out. In a 1913 interview, Cather said that in writing *O Pioneers!*, she discovered that art became "a process of simplifying all the time — of sacrificing many things that were in themselves interesting and pleasing, and all the time getting closer to the one thing — It" (KA, 447). Cather's idea that her art should exclude all but "the one thing" — the unnamed presence of the artist's romantic ego — seems well illustrated by the solitary duck that presides undisturbed over the pond. In fact, Cather's analogy between Alexandra's mind and "a white book" (205) suggests that we can take Alexandra's memory of the duck as a paradigm for the imaginative space of the novel. In that uncluttered page of Alexandra's mental book and in that unadulterated surface of the pond we recognize variations of Cather's novel démeublé that reserved the territory of art for the artist's dominion. That Alexandra's mind, rather than her life, "was a white book" suggests that Alexandra, like her author, creates her art from the innate materials of consciousness itself. In order to maintain this undisputed authority at the center of her mind's pond, Alexandra must reject those things in life that threaten to usurp the primacy of the self. One of those threats is sexuality, and so in *O Pioneers!*, the lovers must die.[70]

Cather foreshadows Emil and Marie's deaths in the scene in which they go duck hunting. By contrast to Alexandra's self-contained duck, the lovers' ducks embody their uncontainable ecstasy in being together. When, holding the blood-drenched birds in her hands, Marie laments that they were "too happy.... [and] didn't really think anything could hurt them" (128), she unwittingly predicts the cause of her own downfall with Emil. As a final explanation for the tragedy, Carl says, "I've seen it before. There are women who spread ruin around them through no fault of theirs, just by being too beautiful, too full of life and love" (304). Despite Carl's sympathetic allowance that Marie cannot help the way she is, Cather nonetheless does "fault" Marie's bountiful nature as the catalyst of the tragedy. Pronouncing as some universal axiom that women are the instruments of ruin, Carl voices Cather's profound uneasiness with the expression of sexual vitality. Cather implies that if Marie brings about her own bloody destruction, that is merely because she, like the ducks, is "too happy" and careless of pain in the beloved company of another. By the same reasoning, Cather faults Emil, whose heart is "too much alive" (257). Although undoubtedly Cather admires the lovers' ardent intensity, she nonetheless warns against the instability of such unrestrained excess that entails its own depletion. Had the lovers emulated Alexandra's duck, immolating themselves within the bounds of the pond so as to take their pleasure, rather than give it, they might have lived. Ultimately, then, couples of lovers, no less surely than couples of ducks, doom themselves simply by being two and not one; Carl, who witnesses the entire duck-hunting scene, feels "unreasonably mournful to find two young things abroad in the pasture" (129), as if the mere presence of two augured an inevitable loss. Indeed, by a kind of terrifying mathematics, and an even stranger biology, Cather suggests that one duck equals eternity, while two ducks equal death.

When Cather kills off even the happily married Amédée for no other reason than that he, too, seems to be "too happy," she reveals that she is punishing the lovers' adultery not as an immoral transgression but merely as a reckless unleashing of sexual energy. A swaggering new father, Amédée is overheated in his impulsive desire to have twenty more children "right off!" (214) "With a new baby in the cradle and a new header in the field" (242), he wants to "come to a head" too rashly. Cather shows that, whether he be harvesting his wheat or inseminating his sex-

ual seed, Amédée fails to know his own limits. Although he seemingly
dies from an attack of appendicitis while working in the field, in Cather's
view, his appendicitis is symptomatic of a more deadly affliction. Like
the wheat that is so "full [of] berries" and "so ripe it will begin to shatter
next week" (245), Amédée himself is so over-ripe with sexual vitality
that he literally shatters open when his appendix splits.

Although Alexandra's indifference to the emotions of others signifies
a limitation of her imagination, Cather nonetheless confirms her heroine's "blind side" (203) as an essential condition of her creativity. As she
says,

> Her training had all been toward the end of making her proficient in what she
> had undertaken to do. Her personal life, her own realization of herself, was
> almost a subconscious existence; like an underground river that came to the
> surface only here and there, at intervals months apart, and then sank again to
> flow on under her own fields. Nevertheless, the underground stream was
> there, and it was because she had so much personality to put into her enter-
> prises and succeeded in putting it into them so completely, that her affairs
> prospered better than those of her neighbors. (203)

By channeling the "underground river" of her personality away from
human relationships and into the land, as if by a kind of sublimation,
Alexandra resembles Cather's exemplary artist who must conserve her
entire personality for her self-expression through art. Alexandra nour-
ishes the land with everything in her personality in the same way that
Cather believed that "we feed our art with everything in our lives" (WP,
662). For Cather, the true artist knew that "the work is all, or it is nothing" (WP, 662), and so also, Alexandra knows that she must train herself
towards the single "end" of investing herself in the land. The artist could
not, Cather felt, "feed two flames so consuming" (WP, 602–3) by feeding
both her art and her life with her passions; she had to choose to devote
herself exclusively either to the life of consciousness as lived in art, or to
life as lived in the world of others. Cather's insistence that Alexandra
keep the "river" of her passions safely beneath "the surface" of her conscious life betrays a fear that social or sexual relationships might drain it.
As if personality were a quantifiable, and hence expendable, asset,
Cather suggests that Alexandra "had so much" only because she cautiously saves rather than heedlessly spends it. Only within the refuge of
her art can she possess her soul against the threat of life's dispossessing
human relationships.

Alexandra most resembles her author in her desire to conserve her
vitality. Believing that "a book is made with one's own flesh and blood

of years. It is cremated youth. It is all yours — no one gave it to you,"[71] Cather valued her inherent youth as her exclusive and most precious possession — and the very source of her art. Yet since she felt that the process of writing "cremated" or burned up her valuable store of youthful energy, she felt the constant need to replenish that energy by getting more out of life to infuse into herself and her work. She despaired that she had little youthful energy left to fuel the flames of art when she prepared to write *O Pioneers!*. As we have seen, she was, in the fall of 1911, still trying to recuperate from her exhausting job as managing editor of *McClure's* magazine. Physically and emotionally diminished, she had written to Jewett in 1908 that she was "spent quite bankrupt."[72] Her frenetic schedule and the burdensome demands of others gave her no peace in which to "hoard" (WC: AM, 62) her energies. Thirty-nine when she wrote *O Pioneers!*, Cather was paying the additional toll of her advancing years. Heeding Jewett's admonition that "when one's first working power has spent itself nothing ever brings it back just the same,"[73] Cather feared that "one's powers do not last forever" (WC: AM, 53). As she wrote in a 1913 play review, "Youth is the only really valuable thing in the world, ... because it is force, potency, a physiological fact.... The individual possesses this power for only a little while, a few years. He is sent into the world charged with it, but he can't keep it a day beyond its allotted time."[74] Dreading the inevitable loss of her youth, her most valuable asset as a writer, Cather felt all the more desperately determined to follow Jewett's advice to "keep and guard ... [her] force"[75] solely for her art. The desire to conserve and augment what she regarded as essentially a static supply of youthful vitality is perhaps the best psychological explanation for Cather's efforts to appropriate life for her art. Alexandra Bergson's desire to "put" herself solely into her creative enterprise in the land reflects Cather's decision upon leaving her worldly ties at *McClure's* to "refuse most of the rest of life" (WC: AM, 63) so as to devote herself exclusively to art as the thing that "*was* all in all" (WC: AM, 115). She would try to disentangle herself from her social duties and ties so as "to use the stuff of intense personal human experience for art only" (WC: AM, 115). Although she regarded writing as "the result of a surplus of vitality" (WC: AM, 123), there were days when, as she wrote to Sergeant in 1913, the draining experiences of life made it difficult to get the lifeblood she needed to infuse into her work.[76] Yet Cather tried to regain that precious store through the very process of writing. Hoping, as she wrote to Jewett in her letter of 1908, to write so as to save her soul,[77] Cather vowed to make her own self-possession the supreme goal of her art. Three years later, in 1911, when she finally left *McClure's* to become a full-time writer, Cather celebrated in *O Pioneers!* her commitment to art as a means of restoring her soul. When Alexandra projects the "underground stream" of her vitality into the land, she reenacts Cather's writing of *O Pioneers!,* in which she drew upon an inner "life line" "at the bottom of [her] consciousness" (Pref. AB, vi) so as to recreate the novel as an organic form that could preserve her passions.

Cather asserts that because Alexandra conserves all of herself for her creative expression in the land, "her affairs prospered better than those of her neighbors"; as if to prove the point, she portrays the love "affair" between Alexandra's neighbors Marie and Emil as tragic. Ultimately, their "affair" fails because they give themselves to life instead of art. By contrast to Alexandra, Marie is outgoing and giving. Cather continually makes the point that Marie is full of such impassioned ardor that unlike the placid Alexandra, she is constitutionally unable to repress herself. In the picture the pair makes in the garden, "the Swedish woman so white and gold, kindly and amused, but armored in calm, and the alert brown one, her full lips parted, points of yellow light dancing in her eyes as she laughed and chattered" (135), Alexandra defensively guards her inner serenity against external mischances, while Marie spontaneously effervesces with high spirits. Even Alexandra recognizes that it is Marie who "could give her whole heart" (180). From the very first scene, in fact, when Marie gives her candy to Emil, she is constantly giving to others, until finally she can give only the sweeter treasure of herself. As Cather puts it, "They had spent the last penny of their small change; there was nothing left but gold. The day of love-tokens was past. They had now only their hearts to give each other" (249).

After the lovers have been shot, Alexandra wonders, "Was there, then, something wrong in being warm-hearted and impulsive like that" (296). The implicit answer seems to be yes. Although the novel gives no convincing explanation why Alexandra should blame Marie, we might understand Cather's own judgment of her as an attempt to justify the self-conservation of her surrogate. Unlike Alexandra, Marie resembles those artists whom Cather chastised for letting "the fever of living [consume] the flower of [their] strength" (WP, 602). As she said in her review of the actress Clara Morris, "The artist proper cultivates method to save himself, he ... learns to cherish and guard his emotional force" (WP, 700). But because Morris let too much of her violent emotion "escape" her, Cather said, "she burned the wick; and she burned it out quickly." Marie, who kindles "with a fierce little flame," her eyes "like the sparks from a forge" (136), and Emil with his "violent ... feelings" (117), similarly burn the wick of their fiery emotions only to burn out their emotional force. Like Gaston Cleric in *My Àntonia*, Marie and Emil miss being great artists because they "squandered too much in the heat of personal communication" (MA, 260). When the lovers pour out their feelings for each other only to get shot in the orchard by Marie's husband, Frank, Cather seems to apply to life her conviction that "the spontaneous untu-tored outpouring of personal feeling does not go very far in art" (OW, 117).

The fate of the lovers suggests that the "outpouring of personal feeling" drains not only their resources as potential artists but their very lifeblood — as if to suggest that the artist's self-conservation were necessary not simply for his self-expression but for his survival. Repeatedly in her fiction, Cather presents a youthful character with the prospect of the dead to dramatize her preoccupation with the evanescence of youth. We recall that by setting Bartley Alexander in the mummy room of the British Museum, "where all the dead things in the world were assembled to make one's hour of youth the more precious" (33), she impresses upon him the fearful brevity of time. Though looking back as an adult on his youth, Bartley imagines that he "had enough and to spare" (55), Cather emphasizes in this scene that even in his youth, he could not afford to spare such a rare gift. Far from freely giving up the "flaming liquor" (34), Bartley tries to preserve it, "trembl[ing] lest before he got out it might somehow escape him, lest he might drop the glass from over-eagerness and see it shivered on the stone floor at his feet" (33). As if all the dead were conspiring to steal his vitality, Bartley strikes a defensive pose: "How one hid his youth under his coat and hugged it" (33). Once he escapes from the imagined enemy in the vault into the sunshine, he sighs in relief "to know that the warm and vital thing within him was still there and had not been snatched away to flush Caesar's lean cheek or to feed the veins of some bearded Assyrian king" (33–34). Though Bartley's own mortality still plots to "snatch" that *élan vital* from him, he enjoys the illusion of being the one king who can keep his youth — that greatest of spoils — forever. Bartley's covetous guard-ing of his youthful force against the specter of the dead provides an ex-emplary attitude in Cather's fiction.

Critics have discussed the story of the lovers against the background of literary antecedents as far-reaching as Ovid, Shakespeare, Keats, and Dante.[78] But, in my view, we can best understand why Cather kills off the lovers in *O Pioneers!* if we consider her own early and less-con-trolled story, "The Elopement of Allen Poole" (1893). On his way through the woods to elope with his lover, Poole feels himself brimming over with a great surge of energy. He is so confident in his own inner fullness that when he passes the graveyard, he, unlike Bartley Alexander, wishes that he could impart his abundant life to the dead. As Cather says, "That night of all nights he was so rich in hope and love, lord of so much life, that he wished he could give a little of it to those poor, cold, stiff fellows shut up down there in their narrow boxes ... give a little of the warm blood that tingled through his own veins, just enough, perhaps, to make them dream of love" (CSF, 576). Ironically, however, Allen's desire to share his life's warm blood proves to be a costly delusion; rather than enliven the dead, he needlessly forfeits his life to join them. The abrupt turning point comes when Allen's "heart went out to the heart of the night, and he broke out into such a passion of music as made [the whippoorwill] in the locusts sick with melody" (CSF, 576). As if, at some level, this passionate display nauseated Cather as well as the bird in the trees, she has Allen immediately and unexpectedly shot to death. Although according to the trappings of the plot, Allen is shot by an officer of the law for being a moonshiner, at a deeper level, he is punished by Cather, who invokes a "law" of her own indicting lovers who reck-lessly squander their passions. Cather implies an ironic cause and effect when Poole fulfills the destiny suggested by his name and his desire; as if his extravagant wish to "give a little of [his] warm blood" to others were prophetically satisfied, he soon lies in pools of blood that are of his own making. The officer, whom Cather excuses as "not a bad fellow," but "only young and a little hot headed" (CSF, 577), runs away from the horrible scene in shocked disbelief, as if he had been unwillingly involved in the tragedy, for indeed, he is little more than a device whose shooting of Poole enforces the moral of the story: sexual consummation is a sacrifice of one's heart's blood. Telling his fiancée that "I'd sooner die now" (CSF, 578), Allen himself implicitly finds relief in dying securely like "a little baby" in his "mother['s]" (CSF, 577) arms, rather than later, dangerously self-abandoned in the arms of a lover. Allen's sublimation of his sexual drive as a desire to arouse the sleeping dead seems to pun on the old literary trope of a sexual "death" so as to give it an ominous literal meaning: the act of surrendering to another in love seems tantamount to resigning oneself to the grave. By hoping to awaken the dead through a kind of blood transfusion, Allen misses the lesson of the graveyard, which is meant to function as a *momento mori*, reminding him that no mortal can spare the ephemeral currents of youth.

In her tragic tale of the lovers in *O Pioneers!*, Cather retells the same parable about misdirected passion. Emil, like his predecessor Allen Poole, passes by a graveyard on his way to meet his lover. Like Allen, Emil feels himself to be so intensely alive that death seems irrelevant. Transported by a thrilling pride in his own immeasurable vitality, he imagines himself "at that height of excitement from which everything is foreshortened, from which life seems short and simple, death very near, and the soul seems to soar like an eagle.... The heart, when it is too much alive, aches for that brown earth, and ecstasy has no fear of death" (257). In his ecstatic, hallucinatory trance, Emil eulogizes death as an invitation to expand his soul to infinite proportions. But paradoxically, Cather implies that Emil precipitates his own death by overestimating the inexhaustibility of his life force. Reminiscent of Allen Poole, whose "heart went out to the heart of the night," so earlier in the novel, Emil's "spirit went out of his body and crossed the fields to Marie Shabata" (180). Now again, as Emil impetuously flies across the fields "like an arrow shot from the bow" (258), he risks overextending himself, giving out his spirit beyond the point of return. When, finally, "his life poured itself out along the road before him as he rode to the Shabata farm" (258), Cather signals that he fatally empties himself of his vitality in a kind of spiritual ejaculation. With dramatic irony, Cather says, "It was not until he had passed the graveyard that Emil realized where he was going" (257), for although he thinks that he is going to woo Marie in a climactic embrace, Cather implies that such feverish passion really courts death.

Cather suggests that Marie similarly provokes the tragedy by unreservedly pouring out her passions. Interestingly, when Frank walks to the orchard where the lovers lie, Cather says, "In the warm, breathless night air he heard a murmuring sound, perfectly inarticulate, as low as the sound of water coming from a spring, where there is no fall, and where there are no stones to fret it" (262). Although inarticulate, this sound is explicable according to a metaphor in Cather's early essay on *The Mill on the Floss*, in which she lamented that we are defeated when "we spend our lives ... in loving and unloving. We give out the precious things of our heart like water, and sell cheap that which is most dear" (WP, 363). By analogy, what Frank hears as the murmuring sound of running water is, I would suggest, the sound of Marie "giv[ing] out the precious things of [her] heart" in her love for Emil. Cather implies a sharp contrast between the flow of Marie's passions and that of Alexandra's: whereas Alexandra keeps the "underground river" of her inner life safely hidden below the surface of her consciousness, so that it can continue to feed her art, Marie lets the river of her emotions rise up to the surface, only to drain her inner wellspring. As in "The Elopement of Allen Poole," Cather follows the unthinking expression of personal passion with swift retribution when Frank fires as soon as he again hears "the murmur, like water welling out of the ground" (263). Like his earlier incarnation as the law officer in "Allen Poole," Frank fires "mechanically ... without knowing why" (263), as if his role were merely perfunctory. But although Frank doesn't know why he shoots, we do: Cather has him shoot Marie at the precise moment when he hears the flow of her heart's blood, to dramatize the wastefulness of spending human love. Alexandra does not incriminate Frank. She shares his blame. And yet, surprisingly, she places the greatest blame for the tragedy neither on her own blindness nor on Frank's murderous passion, but on the lovers' sexual passion. That is because, in Cather's view, Frank merely abets the lovers' suicidal self-sacrifice. Moreover, Cather sympathizes with Frank in the scene in which Alexandra visits him in jail as the real victim of the lovers' hot-headed passions, rather than the other way around. The misery that the lovers bring upon those around them confirms Cather's assertion in an early review that "grand passions are the most expensive things in life; so costly that two lives cannot pay for one, there must always be others who pay in blood and tears for a delight that is not theirs" (WP, 531).

We can most accurately interpret "the story of what had happened [that] was written plainly on the orchard grass, and on the white mulberries ... covered with dark stain" (268) as Cather's illustration of the tragic story that life itself writes. Those hideous "trail[s] of blood" (269) in the orchard graphically testify to what Cather protested against in an early review as "the red blood that is wasted all over the world every day, [when] health and strength ... are squandered" (WP, 663). Even Marie seems to recognize the life-threatening hazards of loving another person when, during her night walk, she reflects that there is "always the same yearning, the same pulling at the chain — until the instinct to live had torn itself and bled and weakened for the last time, until the chain secured a dead woman, who might cautiously be released.... How terrible it was to love people when you could not really share their lives!" (248). Cather's grotesque image of the dead woman, torn and bleeding in her chains, foreshadows Marie's death in the orchard. Astonishingly, Cather suggests that the seemingly healthy impulse to live and love leads to masochistic self-mutilation. Marie cannot "really share" Emil's life, Cather seems to say, not simply because she is a married woman but because she is a human being held captive by the "chain" of reality — the chain, as Cather wrote in an early review, by which we are "vexed and torn by the thankless love of life" (WP, 363). Similarly, Cather implies that if Marie bleeds to death in the orchard, it is because she has been wounded not so much by Frank's gun as by the heart-rending agony of emotional commitments. Manipulating the case against social intimacy by distorting the lovers' emotional pleasure as pain, Cather writes that "young people ... cannot feel that the heart lives at all unless it is still at the mercy of storms; unless its strings can scream to the touch of pain" (226). Even as a child, when her uncle Joe hugs her until she cries out, "Please don't, Uncle Joe! You hurt me" (13), Marie seems forced to learn the lesson that social contacts are inevitably wounding. In a novel in which hugs hurt and kisses leave blood "stains" (269), the presentation of love seems idiosyncratic.[79] That "chain," against which Marie bleeds away her life force, seems to be forged less by necessity than by Cather's own distrustful view of human relationships. It seems that Cather so feared the loss of the vitality that Marie suffers that she had to release even a dead woman from her chains "cautiously" (248).

Marie recognizes that self-involvement is her only means of psychic and emotional survival, and in this realization, she clearly wins Cather's approval. As long as she sleeps alone in the orchard, absorbed in an inner world all her own in which she can dream about "her new life of perfect love" (259), Marie knows that she will be happily nurtured. She takes proper advantage of the orchard's protective psychological space. Ever since Alexandra planted the fruit trees in order to cheer herself up for being excluded from the town circus, the orchard has offered a sanctuary that could compensate for life's disappointing experiences. But it is a haven whose fruitfulness paradoxically depends on the exclusion of sexuality. The trees grow only because Alexandra "save[s]" (138) her apricot seeds, and symbolically, her sexual seeds. Notably, as Alexandra tells Marie, "up to the time Carl went away, [the seeds] hadn't borne at all" (138). Conversely, when Emil comes back and sews his sexual seed, he violates the orchard, both as a fruitful ground for trees and as a fertile ground for the imagination. Marie's last words as Emil wakes her up, "I was dreaming this ... don't take my dream away!" (259) protest against his dispossessing her of a restorative solipsism by an actual exchange of love. The text confirms Marie's intuition that love is perfect only in dreams, for when Emil does interrupt Marie's fantasy, they are killed. The lovers' fate suggests that, for Cather, the only human relationships that were, finally, very real, were imaginative ones. Apparently, it does not figure in Cather's scheme that one might give out love to get something back.

Cather's final comment on the lovers' tragedy is that "the stained, slippery grass, the darkened mulberries, told only half the story" (270). Without explicating either half of this story, Cather concludes the tale of the lovers in "The Mulberry Tree" with two cryptic images that serve as a kind of epitaph: "Above Marie and Emil, two white butterflies from Frank's alfalfa-field were fluttering in and out among the interlacing shadows; diving and soaring, now close together, now far apart; and in the long grass by the fence the last wild roses of the year opened their pink hearts to die" (270). Illustrating the tragic side of the lovers' story, the wild roses — the flowers of passion — open their hearts only to perish. Dying from the fecundity of their own natures, the lovers suffer an ironic fate reminiscent of the actor Steele MacKaye on whom Cather pronounced: "Perhaps it was the very richness and exuberance of [his] genius which rendered it useless, like tropical plants that die of the richness of their own blossoming" (WP, 42). Yet Cather suggests another more hopeful resolution to the story; emblematically, the two white butterflies suggest that the lovers find transcendence after all. "Now close together, now far apart," the butterflies seem harmoniously united only because a strict distance between them preserves their mutual autonomy; moreover, their pure deathly whiteness betokens a void of any dangerous passion. For the lovers, this happy metamorphosis can occur only in death. As Marie, like Allen Poole, dies blissfully with "a look of ineffable content" (269), Cather suggests that even for her character, death is a welcome alternative to anguished human intercourse. Lying peacefully "as if in a day-dream or a light slumber," Marie regressively returns to the life of perfect love in solitude.

Death provided Cather with the perfect solution to the problem of the lovers; it removed their threatening bodily presence from the novel while immortalizing their youthful spirits. Paradoxically, it comes to them as both a punishment and a reward. Emil's urge to embrace death as part of the soul's expansiveness ultimately engages Cather's sympathy, for she regards his death as the necessary vehicle for his spiritual reconstitution. Cather ennobles the lovers' death according to the familiar literary convention of *liebestod* because their death makes possible the illusion of returning to one's prenatal origins. We recall that Alexandra makes peace with the lovers when her nightly vigil at their graves recalls her to a reassuring integrity before life's suffering: "Back ... into the dark, before you were born" (281). Like Alexandra, Cather herself seems to accept "the dead [as] more real than the living" (281) once she is able to imagine them as links back to that most "real" life enjoyed by an aboriginal consciousness. The lovers have to die so as to lose their threatening difference and become transformed into beautiful ideas fit for the imaginative appropriation of Alexandra and her author. Cherishing Emil as "my boy" (305), Alexandra had tried to claim him, as she had the land, for her own imaginative property. She had assumed that his consciousness was an extension of her own, and that he had lived through her favorite memories, such as seeing the duck when they were children. When Emil had grown up into a sexual and independent man, however, Alexandra discovered that she could no longer conform him to her ideal. But she reconciles herself to Emil in death, for then she can imagine him once again as she wants him to be. Only in death can the lovers incarnate all of youth's poignant beauty and passion without any of its ruinous consequences. *O Pioneers!* implies that whereas to possess another in life is to destroy the individual's sovereignty, to possess another in memory is to redeem and preserve that individual as an ideal.

Cather may have been partly enraptured with Emil's and Marie's story as well as Alexandra's. That Cather found it necessary to murder the lovers so violently, and to dwell on the gruesome details of their deaths for several pages in a kind of narrative "overkill," would seem to suggest that she was working hard to teach herself a lesson about human relationships that, despite herself, she found compelling. In *O Pioneers!*, as in most of her subsequent novels, Cather tries to determine whether one can impose the requirements and standards of the artist on ordinary people who lack the artist's temperament. Marie and Emil's compelling love affair makes us feel that even though the pursuit of art means that one must not spill the precious creative juices, to be alive is another story. But though Cather was divided between the claims of art and the claims of life, she was not prepared to admit that ambivalence when she wrote *O Pioneers!*, for this was the novel in which she was testing her resolution to become a serious writer. Whatever vicarious attraction Cather might have felt for the life of sexuality and family, she knew that the story of the lovers was not one that she could choose to live out. It is perhaps not so surprising after all that Cather upheld Frank as her most satisfying character,[80] because his murder of the lovers seemed, at any rate, to settle the score between the two competing kinds of passion in the novel: by revealing the violent results of outgoing passions like the lovers', Frank affirmed the selfishly contained passion of Alexandra as the only productive course. Striking a cheerful and carefree attitude, Cather exclaimed in a letter to Sergeant that she had spent three days killing the lovers.[81] In her seeming lack of remorse, Cather herself pulled the trigger so as to validate her own spiritual self-possession through art.

"Only it is We Who Write It": Alexandra's Triumphant Revision of Life's "Old Story"

After the lovers' death, Alexandra feels so "tired of life" that she wants "to be free" (282) of it altogether. Leaving Frank's prison, she had felt that she was merely stepping into a greater prison — as if, in the words of her old school poem, "Henceforth the world will only be / A wider prison-house to me" (298). Once she is back on the Divide, however, she tells Carl, "There is great peace here, Carl, and freedom" (307). Alexandra's final return to the Great Divide seems symbolic of her crossing a greater dividing line, one we might think of as existing between life and art, for the Divide preserves the higher, freer ground of her own consciousness. Having withstood the "storm" of the land in the opening scenes of the novel, and subsequently, the "storm" (298) of the lovers' passions, Alexandra returns to the peace of the space ruled over by her own spirit.

Alexandra has seen enough of life's brutality to know that she owes her allegiance to that lofty ground presided over by her own transcendental genius.[82] Her return to the Divide repeats her first joyful homecoming at the end of "The Wild Land," but she commits herself to her creative ground "now more than ever" (307) because now her single consciousness alone presides. As the section's title, "Alexandra," highlights, the disruptive presence of the lovers has been removed. All that seemingly remains in the last scene is Alexandra, Carl, and the land. As we have seen, Alexandra can imaginatively possess the land as her "own" (308) because its horizon reflects her own personality. So too, Alexandra can appropriate Carl because he worshipfully reflects back to her an idealized vision of herself as "a triumphant kind of person" (302). With both Carl and the landscape as her mirrors, Alexandra can maintain "her usual air of sureness and self-possession" (287).

As Alexandra looks out over the land with Carl, she muses, "You remember what you once said about the graveyard, and the old story writing itself over? Only it is we who write it, with the best we have" (307). Alexandra refers back to a conversation that she and Carl had had one day by the graveyard. Thinking of her "father and mother and those who are gone," Alexandra had reflected, "We can remember the graveyard when it was wild prairie, Carl, and now —" (118–19). Carl had philosophically finished her thought: "And now the old story has begun to write itself over there.... Isn't it queer: there are only two or three human stories, and they go on repeating themselves as fiercely as if they had never happened before; like the larks in this country, that have been singing the same five notes over for thousands of years." Carl's observation that "there are only two or three human stories" suggests that Cather is commenting on the archetypal stories within her own novel. Above all, the graveyard marks the end of the "old story" of human desire and failure. The "two or three stories" lived out by John Bergson, Marie, and Emil reveal the doomed course of youth's passions. We recall John Bergson on his deathbed, looking "at his white hands, with all the work gone out of them" (24) in his recognition of an inner waste. As if he knew the end of the old story too well to wish to live on, he decides that "he would not have had [youthful force] again if he could, not he! He knew the end too well to wish to begin again. He knew where it all went to, what it all became" (25). Cather implies that when youth is spent, life is no longer worth living; indeed, Bergson and the lovers die not so much from natural causes as from an exhaustion of their youthful force.

The old story that "writes itself" by the graveyard is the story that life writes. But as Alexandra stands back from the graveyard to cast her parents and "the young people [who] live so hard" (119) as characters in life's drama, she seems to be a detached spectator of life rather than a participant in it. Whereas John Bergson and the lovers fall victim to the story of loss that life writes for them, Alexandra seems to triumph over life's old story by writing one of her own. Her triumph is owing to a reestablishment of authorship: "Remember ... the old story writing itself over?" she asks Carl. "Only it is *we* who write it" (307; italics mine). Whereas life's story writes itself "over" through a process of unchanging repetition, Alexandra's story is one that writes life's old story "over" through a process of imaginative revision. Rewriting life's story "with the best we have," Alexandra echoes Carl's statement that Emil and Marie were "the best you had here" (305). Whereas Carl, however, had acknowledged the lovers in the past tense as dead and gone, Alexandra declares them to be present and alive. In reality — on the other side of the symbolic Divide — Alexandra had felt disheartened that without her favorite brother and her best female friend, "she had not much more left in her life" (298). After she returns to the Divide, however, she feels that once again she "has" everything that she needs, for she possesses all within her own appropriating consciousness. Moreover, Cather trans-forms the lovers from the most threatening presence in the novel into ingredients for art. Though years ago, when Carl had watched the lovers abroad hunting ducks, he had felt "unreasonably mournful" (129), now, in the last scene, he recalls the same memory of their youth with a pulse-quickening sensation. As he tells Alexandra, "My dear, it was something one felt in the air, as you feel the spring coming, or a storm in summer. I didn't *see* anything. Simply, when I was with those two young things, I felt my blood go quicker, I felt — how shall I say it? — an acceleration of life. After I got away, it was all too delicate, too intangible, to write about" (305). Cather suggests an implicit analogy between the suggestive "something" Carl "felt in the air" but could not write about, and that inef-fable "something" in her own writing that was too "intangible" to convey directly.

As if Cather had found "an acceleration of life" of her own, she ends the novel by ardently declaring: "Fortunate country, that is one day to re-ceive hearts like Alexandra's into its bosom, to give them out again in the yellow wheat, in the rustling corn, in the shining eyes of youth!" (309). At first, this passage seems self-contradictory and incongruous. How, we wonder, can the land receive a hardened heart like Alexandra's and give out "the shining eyes of youth" that Cather had always associated with the "tiger eyes" of Marie? Moreover, how does Cather reconcile her picture of Alexandra in the previous paragraph as "tired" and worn-out with her celebration of her vivacious youth? We can explain the seeming incongruity between Cather's two final images of Alexandra as her deliberate juxtaposition of Alexandra's ordinary human self with her romantic ego, expressed through her creative relationship with the land, for Cather's paean to that "fortunate country" might be read as a disguised tribute to her own art. As Alexandra gives her heart to the land that gives it out again as an evocation of youth, she expresses the artist's "gift of sympathy" for her material; as Cather put it in her essay on Jewett, the artist "fades away into the land and people of his heart, he dies of love only to be born again" (OW, 51). Presumably, Alexandra's art is "fortunate" to be animated by her personality. In turn, because Alexandra gives up her heart to the "fortunate country" of her art, rather than to the unlucky country of actual life, she does not lose her vitality, as do her father or the lovers. As an artist, she alone can "die" into "the land and people of her heart" and yet be "born again" as a stronger and more vital self — as "the very flower of [her]self and [her] genius" (OW, 51). Like Whitman, who bequeaths himself to the dirt to grow eternally from the grass under our boot soles, Alexandra bequeaths her spirit to the country of art so as to be forever reincarnated in its rustling corn and yellow wheat.

Cather once said that she wrote *O Pioneers!* because she "had searched for books telling about the beauty of the country I loved, its romance, the heroism and strength and courage of its people that had been plowed into the very furrows of its soil and I did not find them."[83] Through her art, Alexandra ceases to have a personality apart from the soil; the lovers, however, cease only in death to have a personality apart from the soil. In death, their youth and strength are figuratively plowed into the very furrows of Alexandra's and Cather's creative soil and authorial consciousness. Writing to Sergeant on 12 September 1912 that she was writing a two-part pastoral in order to recreate her heroine and lengthen her by half, Cather suggests that she conceived of the story of the lovers in order to augment the personality of Alexandra. As the woman nearing forty who felt lacking in vitality before she wrote the novel, Cather may have felt that her counterpart, Alexandra — who, significantly, is also forty — was not really as full of energy as she seems at the end of "The Wild Land." It is no wonder that when Cather combined the two stories for her two-part pastoral, she felt a "sudden inner explosion and enlightenment,"[84] for by adding the story of the lovers to the story of Alexandra, she could vicariously appropriate some of Marie's volatile spirit, and so regain that quotient of vitality that she needed for art. When Cather demands that the lovers pour their lives into the soil so as to feed her lifeline to her art, she demonstrates with a kind of parasitic zeal the truth she recognized in Henry James: "How much of life it takes to make a little art!" (WP, 601).

We can sum up Cather's accomplishment in the novel by examining the poem she includes as its prelude, "Prairie Spring." In the first half of the poem (as in the beginning of her novel), Cather realistically portrays life on the prairie in its "harshness" and monotony. "Toiling horses" and "tired men" work endlessly in the "silent" fields, beneath an "eternal, unresponsive sky." Life seems to be an endless round of drudgery against the backdrop of an indifferent nature. But in the dramatic spondaic line halfway through the poem — "Against all this, Youth" — Cather rejoices that Youth gloriously asserts itself in opposition to the hard life of the prairie. Nevertheless, she regrets that Youth "with its insupportable sweetness" cannot survive for long in its battle against life. "Flaming like the wild roses, / Singing like the larks over the plowed fields, / Flashing like a star out of the twilight," Youth is a brilliant but ephemeral force, doomed to flash itself out. At the end of the poem, however, as at the end of her novel, Cather seems to reverse life's old story so that Youth miraculously springs forth from the tomb of the earth: "Singing and singing, / Out of the lips of silence, / Out of the earthy dusk." The phrase "the lips of silence" suggests not only the grave but a human mouth. Cather seems to have transformed the silent realistic landscape of the beginning of the poem into a humanized form of joyous artistic expression. Though in real life, Youth sings a song that fades to silence in the grave, in art, Cather suggests, Youth can sing eternally without faltering or loss. In a profound way, Cather's art is a kind of compensatory replacement or antidote for the graveyard. By choosing the conditions of art over the terms of life, Alexandra — and Willa Cather — wins her greatest victory by symbolically transforming the graveyard that claims others into the birthplace of her own soul.

4

Thea Kronborg's "Song of Myself": The Artist's Imaginative Inheritance in *The Song of the Lark*

Willa Cather's third novel, *The Song of the Lark*, tells the story of an American opera singer, Thea Kronborg, from her childhood in a small town in Colorado, her musical training in Chicago, and her exploration of the Cliff Dweller ruins in Arizona, to her dazzling triumphs at the Metropolitan opera. As wide-ranging in time as in space, the story charts its heroine's development over a course of thirty years, from the time she is ten until she is in her midforties. Equally encompassing in its characters, the novel includes a large and colorful cast. Such panoramic breadth has led David Stouck to categorize the novel as a typical *kunstlerroman,* in which the artist escapes from the restrictions of the provincial hometown to broaden her experience in the larger world.[1] Yet *The Song of the Lark* resembles the realistic novel of the artist's education only in the superficial trappings of its plot. Despite its apparent scope, the novel subordinates all time, space, and characters to Thea. Although as a child dreaming at her bedroom window, Thea seems poised at the threshold of the "great big world" (139), her window exists, ironically, to frame its own insignificance; what is really "big" for Thea, Cather reminds us, is her own ardent passion, the "life [that] rushes from within, not from without" (140). Indeed, Thea goes out into the world less to encounter new and different life beyond herself than to confirm the infinite and timeless life of consciousness that she projects from within.

Cather discounted the conventional "plot" of the novel. In a 1926 speech, she insisted, "Great literature has no plot" (WCP, 163). Affirming that Shakespeare "made no plots as such," she argued that his plays have "two plots": the external "tale" or story that he took from his sources, and "the spiritual plot," which "is inside the rough plot of the tale" and uniquely his "own." She felt that "we are not interested in the tale or the plot at all" but rather, concerned with the inner spiritual life of the drama, which is revealed by character and emotion. We can understand the kind of double plot that goes on in Cather's novels according to Quentin Anderson's metaphor for them as a "masquerade which made it appear that she was accepting the conditions of adulthood while actually rejecting them."[2] The external plot belongs to the character's public, social self as it adjusts to the demands of everyday, real life — school, family, career, community. But beneath this story of action lies the poetic evocation of a state of being fulfilled by the character's primitive romantic ego — what Cather most explicitly refers to in *The Song of the Lark* as her heroine's "second self." As Anderson has noted, the real story that the characters desire to live out occurs "within, [as] the 'second self' plots its freedom ... to repossess that union of self and cosmos."[3] Although masked, this second, "spiritual plot" takes over the narrative in Cather's affirmative novels, as her characters seek to regain an original omnipotence. Thea's actions are motivated by her promise to keep "an appointment to meet the rest of herself sometime, somewhere" (216). An exile who is initially dispossessed and disinherited, but who finds her way home to herself, Thea is the paradigmatic character in Cather's fiction.

Rather than regard *The Song of the Lark* as a realistic *bildungsroman*, I would like to consider it a fairy tale, or wish fulfillment, in which Thea's desire, like Willa Cather's in writing the novel, has the magical power to reorganize the world around the self.[4] After she had completed *The Song of the Lark*, Cather wrote to Dorothy Canfield Fisher that she had enjoyed losing herself in a fairy tale of her own creating.[5] In his psychoanalytic study of the meaning of fairy tales, Bruno Bettelheim suggests that the significant difference between fairy tales and dreams is that fairy tales more openly express and satisfy the need for wish fulfillment; unlike the dream, the fairy tale "projects the relief of all pressures and not only offers ways to solve problems but promises that a 'happy' solution will be found."[6] Bettelheim aptly perceives that stories can serve as the fantasies that allow the individual to escape his burdensome life; whereas the ego, or conscious self, must meet the requirements of reality, the id, unbound to the world of common practicality, can indulge its wildest wishes in the world of the fairy tale. As the heroine in Cather's fairy tale, Thea seems exempt from the usual restrictions of life. Her vulnerability to fortune is an illusion; as Cather says in her preface, she merely "seemed wholly at the mercy of accident; but to persons of her vitality and honesty, fortunate accidents will always happen" (Pref. SL, xxxii). As we learn in the novel, only those common mortals like Ray Kennedy, who loses his flock of sheep in a blizzard, must learn the bitter lesson of experience, which inevitably teaches "how little [man] is, and how big everything else is" (123). Thea, on the other hand, miraculously makes the world conform to her overriding desire: "the one big thing" — against which, her piano teacher Wunsch prophesies, "all [else] is little" (76). Although, in reality, the child Thea is dwarfed by the larger privileges and powers of adults and the world beyond, the force of her desire reverses the actual proportion of things, until she, like Jack and the Beanstalk, climbs above the rest of humanity to unprecedented heights of glory, herself a giant among men.

The novel most nakedly enacts the power of Thea's desire in the first scene, which is characterized by all the selfish rewards of fairy tale endings. The scene opens realistically when young Thea is neglected by her parents while they prepare for Mrs. Kronborg's childbirth. Thea's pneumonia can be seen as symptomatic of the older child's heartache when suddenly the needs of younger, rival siblings threaten to usurp her own. Reality, however, soon gives way to one of Cather's "fortunate accidents" in the shape of Dr. Archie, who opportunely comes to Thea's rescue. Although bemoaning his role as midwife, Dr. Archie rejoices in his chance to indulge Thea, reflecting that "the baby would have got into the world somehow; they always do. But a nice little girl like that — she's worth the whole litter" (8). Dismissing the rest of the children as if they were dogs or cats — members of some inferior species — Dr. Archie honors his protégé with the attention that every child secretly feels the world owes her. Admiring Thea's chin as the mark where "some fairy godmother had caressed her ... and left a cryptic promise" (10), Dr. Archie dotes on her as the favored child who has been blessed with a special destiny by her real fairy godmother — Willa Cather. In the course of the novel, Thea's desire, expressed in her look of "greedy affection" (7) for Dr. Archie's devotion, conjures up a whole entourage of male well-wishers like the railroad man Ray Kennedy and her piano teacher Wunsch, who "live solely" for her. In typical fairy tales like "Cinderella," the girl is usually supplied with a fairy godmother. Cather's decision to give her heroine a series of fairy godfathers indicates a new twist in the fairy tale that implies an interesting reversal of gender conventions. Susan Rosowski has noted that Cather "gave to Thea qualities ordinarily reserved for men — fierce independence, ambition, discipline, and hard headedness. At the same time, she gave to supporting male characters roles ordinarily granted to women, of serving as instruments in the central character's advancement."[7] By having men play the role of ministering angels to Thea, Cather implies that her heroine's inner power so transcends traditional sex roles as to make even the men surrounding her seem subservient.

In the epilogue to the novel, Cather seems to defend her fairy tale before skeptical realists by vindicating the faith of Thea's aunt Tillie, who "had always insisted, against all evidence, that life was full of fairy tales, and it was!" (489). Tillie need simply read the newspaper accounts of Thea receiving a jewel from the King of England to find proof of her belief that dreams will come true — even the small-town girl can become a princess. Cather clarifies the nature of Thea's fairy tale by contrasting it with another Moonstone legend. Between Moonstone's two local triumphs — one the boy who built up a big business in Omaha and got rich, and the other Thea — people talk more often of Thea, Cather says, because "a voice has even a wider appeal than a fortune" (489); it is a "treasure of creative power" (265) that can be assessed neither in dollars and cents nor even in crown jewels. Thus, Cather distinguishes between two kinds of fairy tales: a worldly fairy tale in which the rich boy garners material possessions, and the more magical fairy tale in which the artist reaps priceless immaterial rewards. As a young woman, Thea herself sees her future as a choice between these two possible plots when she tells Dr. Archie, after her first disappointing winter in Chicago, that although she "can get along, in a little way," she does not want to live at all unless she "can get something big out of it" (242). As Thea knows, to "get along" would be to live out the realistic story of the Moonstone boy, a story of getting and spending told in another version in Theodore Dreiser's *kunstlerroman* of the same year, *The Genius*.[8] By contrast, Thea lives out a romance: only when she escapes to the Southwest, where she feels "completely released from the enslaving desire to get on in the world" (296), is she able to "get out" of life "something big" in the form of imaginative and spiritual returns.

We can best understand Thea's artistic development as a fairy tale that celebrates her imaginative possession of a valuable inheritance.[9] Thea comes into her own as an artist when, in her first great performance as Wagner's Seiglinde, "she merely came into full possession of things she had been refining and perfecting for so long" (477). Yet the composition and source of this inner "inheritance" that Thea "[lays] up" (477) is complex. Indeed, we might take Dr. Archie's musing in the first scene — "Where she ever got it from– "(8) — as the most central and often-asked question in the novel. At one level, Thea assimilates, in the course of her career, a broad cultural tradition of music, literature, and art, as well as a rich mine of memories from her Moonstone past. Cather suggests that

Thea is able to appropriate a refined cultural heritage because of her intense desire. As Wunsch assures her, "Nothing is far and nothing is near, if one desires" (75). Looking back on *The Song of the Lark* in a 1943 letter, Cather elaborates on the nature of desire as a powerful force that no circumstances can thwart. Equipped with the necessity of desire, she says, the individual can possess the treasure of the world's great music, literature, and art as his own.[10] Thea's desire to reach the cultural treasures of the world largely reflects the desire of the young Willa Cather. As a westerner from a small town, Cather felt a particularly acute desire to gain the easterner's sophisticated intellectual inheritance. In a letter to Dorothy Canfield Fisher, written 7 April 1922, Cather self-deprecatingly likened herself to an insecure hick from the West who encounters East Coast civilization only to feel as if he has been deprived of the cultural wealth of centuries just because he doesn't know how to play an instrument or speak a foreign language.[11] Cather's resentment of the uncultured West in her early stories like "A Wagner Matinée" and "The Sculptor's Funeral" she retrospectively disparaged in a 1911 letter as the fury of a young person denied the advantages and opportunities she wished to have.[12] In Thea's fiercely competitive attitude towards the easterners on the train, we can see a comically exaggerated version of Cather's own youthful impatience to possess the things of the world so as to compensate for her cultural and material deprivation. Feeling insecure next to the easterners, whose polished language and elegant clothes she "pretended to scorn and secretly admired" (219), Thea defiantly vows "to grab a few things"; unlike the other common young people in the world, however, *"she was going to get them!"* (218).

At a deeper level, however, Cather repeatedly insists that her heroine's most valuable imaginative possession is not the legacy of the world but an incomparable original endowment — something that has been neither inherited nor learned but always her "own." Just as Cather liked to think that the essential stuff of art was "all yours" and that "no one gave it to you,"[13] so Thea knows that "if one became an artist one had to be born again, and that one owed nothing to anybody" (378). Indeed, Dr. Archie's question in the first scene about the origin of Thea's gift suggests that Thea innately possesses the one unnamable thing that distinguishes her genius above all others. By setting Thea against the background of her mother in labor, Cather implies that her heroine possesses a divine birthright that her mother never brought into the world; as an artist, Thea has the superior power to make herself born. Even Thea's mother ratifies this, taking a surprising consolation on her death-bed in the fact that the photograph of the daughter who has neglected her "doesn't look like she was beholding to anybody, does she?" (406). Similarly, Thea's teachers humbly acknowledge that their instruction counts as nothing against her inherent talent. As her German teacher, Landry, attests, her most important asset is "a big personality," something you either "have ... or you haven't" (448). Thea herself, reflecting that "there was always — something" (209), intuitively possesses the secret of her own creativity from the beginning. Even after she has acquired a great deal from her musical training and worldly travels, she affirms her faith in her original self as her only meaningful belonging — the thing that was, as she says, "all I had" (211). "What else have I got?" (464).

Paradoxically, then, Thea accumulates a vast store of impressions and knowledge. Yet, at the same time, she seems to have contained all essentials within herself. This paradox is resolved, however, when we realize that Thea's desires to lay claim to the world and to her own soul are not, in reality, two different impulses but one. In a moment of anxiety before returning to Chicago to study, Thea asks Dr. Archie, "But suppose one can never get out what they've got in them?" (244). She thus states her fundamental challenge in the novel as a whole: how to appropriate the world so as to recover the self. Thea's outward-bound quest is deceptive, for in the guise of acquiring a wide range of values and experiences, she invariably repossesses her own romantic ego. [14] By examining Thea's appropriation of music, landscapes, and people, we shall see that her preoccupation with "refining and perfecting" (477) her imaginative possessions is more profoundly a process of careful selection whereby she embraces exclusively those things that she recognizes as incarnations of the self, and rejects the rest.

As if to emphasize the intrinsic source of Thea's art, Cather never includes a single one of her legitimate, formal voice lessons and entirely omits the ten years of Thea's operatic training in Germany. Her music teacher in Chicago, Madison Bowers, characterized as having the "soul of a shrimp," is more of an anti-role-model meant to show that an exacting emphasis on technical perfection without passion is mere pedantry. For all Thea's technical training, her ambition "to get at it!" (364) in her music lessons betrays a more zealous desire to get directly at her own soul. Crying to Wunsch during an early piano lesson that "difficult things are enemies ... when you have to get them" (72), Thea remains frustrated as long as she tries to get from a piano score something that only she herself can provide. Although Richard Giannone sees Thea's early lack of piano lessons as a handicap,[15] Cather deemphasizes such training because she believes that Thea must reject the external instrument so as to adopt the voice as the most unmediated, spontaneous expression of her passions. By making her heroine a singer, whose voice, "more than any other part of her, had to do with [her] ... sense of wholeness and inner well-being" (216), Cather suggests that the greatest art is one of self-projection. Moreover, Cather repeatedly insists in her music reviews that the artist's passionate soul — "the only thing which gives art a right to be" (KA, 53–54) — is not to be acquired through any external mediums, labor, discipline, or technique (KA, 71). As she announced in a letter to the opera singer Nordica, she was grateful that there remained "that one thing, at least, [which] is not to be got by conscientious endeavors" (WP, 643). Thus, Thea gets the inspiration for her art only when she stops trying to find it. Jubilantly exclaiming to her teacher, Harsanyi, "Oh, yes, I get it now!" (190), Thea ostensibly gets the idea of the "river" in the song "Die Lorelei," but more profoundly acquires a sense of her own flowing vitality that "fills her up to the eyes" (192). Again, when Thea sings Orpheus's lament for Euridice, she unconsciously recovers the essential soul that had eluded her while she sought to master the piano. Once she sings "from the bottom of herself ... [so that] the voice did not thin as it went up" (188), Thea blends not only the upper and lower reaches of her musical range but the upper and lower reaches of her personality as well, and so symbolically reverses the outcome of the Greek myth. Unlike Orpheus, who loses his Euridice in the underworld, Thea completes the voyage perilous by bringing that "something unconscious and unawakened" (96) about herself to the surface of artistic expression. Whereas Orpheus fails by looking back to Euridice in a moment of doubt, Thea rescues her lost muse because she imagines her not as some external ideal, but as her own inner power.

In the process of refining her knowledge of music, Thea rejects not only all external instruments and techniques but also all uncongenial musical themes. Although she puzzles Harsanyi as a student who is "not quick" (192), her slowness reflects not a lack of intelligence but a deliberate resistance to unfamiliar ideas. As Cather wrote of Thea's ostensible prototype, the opera singer Olive Fremstad, "She does not catch ideas or suggestions from what she sees or hears; everything comes from within herself."[16] Minimizing the struggle that real opera singers endure to master their art, Cather romanticizes Thea in the same way that she romanticizes Fremstad in her review; Thea takes a long time to learn the part of Fricka, but when, "all at once, she got her line" (448), she does so by simplifying the character down to the musical idea it's built on: her own unified and unifying being. Insisting that Wagner's conception of the fat, nagging, jealous Queen of the Gods is "not my idea. Wait till you hear my *Fricka*" (443), Thea infuses the role with the leitmotif of her own beautiful personality so that it becomes, as one listener says, "interesting because she does it" (449).

In recent years, critics have agreed that Thea is a heroine who is selflessly committed to her art and to others.[17] Certainly Thea emerges on stage as a transcendent legendary figure, one for the sake of whom she has deliberately neglected much of her personal life. We should not, however, misconstrue this transformation of identity as an abandonment of self but rather see it as a joyful and egoistic self-recovery. In a letter to Dorothy Canfield Fisher, reflecting on her own commitments as an artist, Cather herself dismissed what she viewed as the myth of a frail creature sacrificing life's joys for her art. She points out that all of her sacrifices for her art have been, paradoxically, selfish ones; all her life, she reflects, it was not at all hard to push aside less-pleasing attractions for more-satisfying, important things.[18] In the guise of self-sacrifice, Thea, like her author, leads a life of self-indulgence. Cather wrote in an 1895 review that "the secret of stage success is selfishness, to develop the ego to its highest possibilities, regardless of everything else" (WP, 227). Indeed, if Thea sacrifices "everything else" for her art, she does so willingly, out of a need for self-preservation. Just as she rejects the piano, or extraneous musical interpretations, so she gladly renounces the claims of others, and even the needs of her everyday, social self. On stage, Thea escapes her vulnerability to fatigue, illnesses, and supervisors so as to become repossessed of her romantic "Me Myself" — that imperishable original ego that, like Whitman's, remains eternally vigorous, young, and free.[19] Nowhere is this reincarnation more complete than in Thea's stunning performance as Seiglinde. "Nothing new came to [her], no enlightenment, no inspiration" (477) because she merely relaxes her inhibitions so as to gain access to her oldest and deepest unconscious self. Seiglinde's meeting with her long-lost twin brother, Seigmund, provides the perfect occasion for Thea's reunion with her long-lost alter ego. Singing "of how the thing which was truly herself, 'bright as the day, rose to the surface' when in the hostile world she for the first time beheld her Friend" (475), Thea herself meets a "friendly spirit" (79) — that "thing which was truly herself" — back in the beginning, before the hostile world had tried to separate them. Her song of herself is complete.

We can sum up the process of Thea's imaginative acquisition of music by considering her hands as a symbolic attribute. As suggested by her most characteristic gesture — an impatient "opening and shutting" (72) of her hands — Thea confronts the things of her experience with a fiercely grasping consciousness. At one point during a music lesson with Harsanyi, she complains that the sonata she is studying "isn't here unless I have it — not for me.... Only what I hold in my two hands is there for me!" (176). As if music had no objective, external reality apart from herself, Thea here maintains that the sonata can come into existence only once she incorporates it as a part of her own nature, so as to make it, figuratively speaking, an extension of her own hand. In an essay that Cather wrote for the *Red Cloud Republican* when she was just seventeen, she described the deepest learning as "a process of assimilation in which the arts and sciences are not merely a part of our duty or the school routine, but a part of ourselves, as much our own as a hand or arm."[20] Significantly, it is not in the schoolroom but in the remote Panther Canyon that Thea assimilates the essential ingredients for her art. Return- ing to a kind of primal sleep, "she could lie for half a day undistracted, holding pleasant and incomplete conceptions in her mind — almost in her hands" (299). That Thea holds ideas in her hands, and not just in her mind, suggests that her art takes a sensuous form that has nothing to do with words or rational, conscious thoughts; she derives her inspiration from innate emotions, instincts, and physical energies. Later, when Thea sings the part of Seiglinde, she discovers that "what she had so often tried to reach, lay under her hand" (478). Whereas her attempts to reach after notes and phrases left her empty-handed, she now draws upon her inner resources to bring "all that deep-rooted vitality" to the surface so that it "flowered in her voice, her face, in her very finger-tips" (478). Grasping her own vigor as if it were a tactile reality, Thea is able to bring her art to life through a process of imaginative alchemy. Having "only to touch an idea to make it live" (478), she exercises a kind of Midas touch that magically transforms all ideas into the priceless "gold quality" (448) of her own consciousness.

When Thea walks through the Chicago Art Institute, she once again gets either all or nothing out of art. Like many other paintings, the Corot is one that she "did not like or dislike; ... [but] never saw" (197) because she is seeking to recognize only one thing — a portrait of the self. She finds such a painting in Jules Breton's "The Song of the Lark," a painting which Cather also admired. That painting seems to have been destined to belong only to her, as she imagines that it "was her picture.... The flat country, the early morning light, the wet fields, the look in the girl's heavy face — well, they were all hers, anyhow, whatever was there" (197). Given the implied narrative in the painting of a peasant girl stopping on her way to work in the field to look up to listen to a lark, we might think that she, and by extension, Thea, awakens to art, symbolized by the lark's song. But Cather discouraged this reading when she wrote in her preface that "many readers take it for granted that the 'lark song' refers to the vocal accomplishments of the heroine, which is altogether a mistake. Her song was not of the skylark order" (Pref. SL, xxxi). Indeed, Thea's song is not directly inspired by the possibilities of art or even by beautiful melodies like the lark's. If she identifies with the painting, in which, appropriately, no lark appears, it is because she is drawn toward something more psychological and innate than art. In her preface, Cather said that she named the novel after this painting "to suggest a young girl's awakening to something beautiful" (Pref. SL, xxxi) — a phrase that resonates with Thea's awakening in the novel to the boundless possibilities of her own soul. As Cather's initial subtitle for the novel, "Artist's Youth," implies, both the girl in the painting and Thea devote themselves to a vision of their own youthful strength. Breton's peasant girl lets her scythe drop to her side, having forgotten her labor in the contemplation of an inner landscape. As instinctive as her "heavy" thoughts, as primitive as the earth beneath her bare feet, as radiant as the sunrise behind her, as free as the sky above her, the girl in the painting seems to remind Thea — and Willa Cather — of her own dawning consciousness. Understandably, Thea feels that the painting is "all hers," for it belongs to her as exclusively as if it were the signature of her own birthright.

Thea's self-referential vision in the gallery is paradigmatic of her selective appropriation of city life as a whole. It seems likely that Thea's response to Chicago resembles Cather's first response to New York City when she moved there in 1906. According to one of Cather's interviewers, "Out of the enormous mêlée of the city she picked and chose, as though, when she came there first from the prairies, she had known all about the city, and what was for her, and what was trash" (WCP, 92). Thea, too, relies on an inner intuition rather than experience to distinguish between what is "for her" and what is not. Ultimately, the "big, rich, appetent Western city she did not take in at all" (193) because it is full of stubbornly other consciousnesses with appetites as voracious as her own. These other consciousnesses most dramatically assault Thea when she enters the city streets after hearing the Chicago symphony. Blinded by a cloud of dust, Thea is more profoundly blinded by all the powers in the city that she does not wish to see. To her eye, "there was some power abroad in the world bent upon taking away from her that feeling with which she had come out of the concert hall. Everything seemed to sweep down on her to tear it out from under her cape. If one had that, the world became one's enemy" (201). The battle line is so uncompromisingly drawn in this scene, that it seems that the world has, indeed, as Cather would later lament, broken in two,[21] for as Thea imagines that "everything" — buildings, wagons, cars, and people — lines up to "take something" from her, she seems to fight against an antagonist that is no less formidable than life itself. We can understand the cause of Thea's defensive posture when we consider the virtual impossibility of her keeping that inner "something" beneath her breast. Having just heard Dvorak's *New World Symphony* for the first time, Thea had felt possessed anew of something old and familiar, a soul "that had dreamed something despairing, something glorious, in the dark before it was born" (199). Like Wordsworth's babe trailing clouds of glory, Thea had recovered a vestige of a prenatal integrity, a token of a more complete state of being when consciousness and the unconscious, self and nature had seemed to be one. We can see why, then, "if one had that" (a sense of one's own newborn and unbegotten soul) the world inevitably becomes one's enemy, for life (which is necessarily divided) sunders the illusion of a single continuous identity. But although life harbors powers that refuse to be conquered by the spirit, art — Thea hopes — will allow her to recreate the reality of her imagination. Vowing, as she hears the notes of the trumpets, to "have it, have it, — *it!*" (201), Thea seems, as John Randall has suggested, to consecrate herself to art as if in a scene of religious conversion.[22] But more profoundly, as Thea stands with her hands clutched against her bosom, she reveals a desire to grasp not a higher god but the ecstasy within the altar of her own breast; her conversion is no more than a turning back to regain the lost paradise of her original sovereign self.

Although Thea takes music lessons in Chicago and Germany, she looks back on the landscape of the Southwest, where, significantly, no technical musical references appear, as the place where she came to acquire her most important assets as an artist. Whereas in Chicago she "had got almost nothing" (301), in Panther Canyon she gets all she needs when everything there takes root in her unconscious self. The reason that the Southwest so readily yields itself to Thea's desire is because it conforms to her idea of her psychological origins. An ancient landscape stripped down to its bedrock essentials, the Southwest enables Thea to recapture a sense of the primordial foundation of her own most irreducible personality. Unlike the streets of Chicago, bustling with a disturbing multiplicity of life, the empty cave that Thea inhabits in Panther Canyon is filled only with the aura of her own personality. Standing in her cave as if to stand most firmly in the center of her own consciousness, she finds herself in that exemplary imaginative space that Cather reserved for the artist as "one passion, and four walls" (NUF, 51). As if dramatizing Cather's efforts to throw all the excess material furniture out of her novel démeublé, Thea discards all that clutters her mind in a kind of mental housekeeping: "Her mind was like a ragbag into which she had been frantically thrusting whatever she could grab. And here she must throw this lumber away. The things that were really hers separated themselves from the rest" (306). Ultimately, Thea sweeps away as so much dead wood all that she has acquired secondhand through her worldly experience — her social and professional roles, the brutal facts of the city, even other people. Far from acquiring anything new, she merely repossesses what has been "really hers" from the beginning. Indeed, as she lies within her womb-like cave — that most unfurnished room of all — she restores the illusion of an aboriginal ego in union with the cosmos. Just as in her childhood, Thea had felt that she *was* a sandhill, or that she *was* the vine growing by Mrs. Tellamantez's door, so once again she imagines that she shares a mystically merged identity with lizards, cicadas, and rocks. As Cather says, "The things which were for her, she saw; she experienced them physically and remembered them as if they had once been a part of herself" (301). Thea here relives the fantasy of the egoistic child who claims the world as if it were coextensive with the self. Like Whitman's child in "There was a Child Went Forth," she looks upon the objects in Panther Canyon, and those objects she becomes.[23] Having escaped not only from Chicago but more profoundly from the landscape of adulthood, inhabited by others with claims of their own, Thea imagines that she can reassemble her indivisible childhood ego before it was broken up by experience and fragmented into its social parts.

Critics have assumed that Thea gains from the Southwest a new sense of history and culture that enables her to make her art more universal and communal.[24] To be sure, Thea gains access to history among the Cliff Dweller ruins, but the point of reference is never "history" or other people, but always Thea. Whereas in Chicago the streets are full of threatening other human consciousnesses, in the "city" of Panther Canyon all others are, necessarily, dead. The extinction of the Indians, far from being a barrier, is a crucial precondition for Thea's imaginative appropriation of them. She gets ideas "out of the rocks, out of the dead people" (463), as if she were equating the two; for in the company of ghosts, as in the company of caves, Thea resurrects all feelings out of her own. Imagining that the Indians had a desire for "food, fire, water, and something else" (305), she invests them with her own desire to live for more than material things. Moreover, she projects upon the Indians her own defensive struggle against life's dispossessing forces by imagining that they, too, "must have had to endure so much for the little they got out of life" (313). Ultimately, Thea imagines that the Cliff Dwellers "got out of life" that which she herself wishes to get — a preconscious integration. Earlier in the novel, Cather notes that Thea carries herself with a look of "noble unconsciousness" such as Indian women used to have, "a large kind of look, that was not all the time being broken up and convulsed by trivial things" (121). Similarly, in her review of Thomas Mann's novel *Joseph and his Brothers*, entitled "The Birth of Personality," Cather again associates the earliest races with "an unconscious world."[25] This essay suggests that her interest in the "Ancient People" (295) of the Southwest, like her interest in the "ancient people" of Israel, was not in the birth of history or culture per se but in the birth of consciousness itself. As she says of the Israelites in Mann's novel, "Their attention is fixed upon something within themselves which they feel to be their real life, consciousness; where it came from, and what becomes of it." In the same way that Cather looks back to the Israelites as a people who were nearer than modern man to their unconscious origins, so Thea looks to the Cliff Dwellers as a link back to her own psychological beginnings, to locate that "something within herself" and where it came from.[26] Thea sees the pottery as a metaphor for art: "The stream and the broken pottery: what was any art but an effort to make a sheath, a mould in which to imprison for a moment the shining, elusive element which is life itself" (304). Although critics have taken the pottery as a symbol of the order that art imposes on the stream of outer life,[27] I would suggest that the pottery functions as the organic form or container that art provides for the artist's inner stream of vitality — that elusive life of consciousness Cather defined in *Alexander's Bridge* as "life itself" (Pref. AB, ix). The Indian women, by investing the stream with the "sovereign qualities" of their desire, held the water in their jars as a "living thing" or "loosely knit personality" (304). By making an analogy between the Indian women's pottery and the "vessel" of Thea's voice, Cather suggests that Thea similarly creates her art as the living expression of her personality; as she says, "In singing, one made a vessel of one's throat and nostrils and held it on one's breath, caught the stream in a scale of natural intervals" (304). If the stream lengthens Thea's past by providing a "continuity of life that reached back into the old time" (304), it extends itself not externally towards a point in history but internally towards the ancient, ahistorical wellspring of her own being. As Thea later reflects upon her experience in Panther Canyon, "No singing teacher can give anybody what I got down there" (463), for "down there" ultimately refers to the depths of her own psyche. Restored amidst sun and rocks to her childhood memory of "waking up every morning with the feeling that your life is your own, and your strength is your own, and your talent is your own; that you're all there" (317), Thea gains the confident feeling of self-possession that Cather celebrated as the essential ingredient of great art.

In order to appreciate the full importance of Thea's claim in Panther Canyon, we need to understand her experiences in the context of Cather's own biography. Like Thea, Cather felt "released from the enslaving desire to get on in the world" when she quit her job at *McClure's* magazine in New York in September 1911 and took a trip to the Southwest the following spring. In a letter to Jewett of December 1908, Cather wrote that she felt dispossessed and bereft of her soul while working at *McClure's*.[28] She seems to have projected this feeling of self-dispossession into Thea's bereavement when "deserted" (177) by her soul in Chicago. As the harried accompanist, Thea has something in her of Cather, the managing editor of *McClure's*, for in that role Cather also resented having to put her own work aside to assist the mediocre work of others; she, also, was exhausted by a frenetic and mechanical routine. But in Thea's jubilant self-recovery in Panther Canyon, Cather was to recall her own happiness when she first visited Arizona and New Mexico in 1912. When later, in 1920, Cather wrote to Elizabeth Shepley Sergeant in envy of her coming into possession of things in New Mexico,[29] she was really recalling her own experience there eight years earlier. Cather's letters to Sergeant in the spring of 1912 reveal her exploration of the landscape as a deliberate search for the thing most necessary to writing. On 20 April, after her visit to Albuquerque, Cather wrote to Sergeant, herself a writer, that she was sure that the experience would give her, too, precisely that unnamed something that one needs.[30] Her joyful absorption of strength reminded her of a similar acquisition in France in 1902; as she recalled in a letter of 15 June 1912, the Rhone river does give it to one.[31] But if the Valley of the Rhone infused one with the energy to write, it was nothing, she said, next to what the brilliance of New Mexico had to offer. There, it was as if a splendid stage had been set for a special purpose.[32] Cather filled that stage with her own self-creation, it seems, when she visited the Grand Canyon, of which she wrote on 30 May that it was the only place she had found where she could get all she wanted.[33] Like Thea Kronborg, Cather had finally found the life, talent, and strength that were all her "own." That Cather made five trips to the Southwest over the next fifteen years attests to the power of her initial self-possession there.

During a subsequent visit to the Southwest with Edith Lewis in 1915, Cather wrote to Sergeant that she imagined that the painter who could capture the beauty of the landscape would have to have an ego as big as the Cliff Dwellers' was.[34] In the process of writing *The Song of the Lark*, Cather surely felt that she herself was destined to be that "painter." Setting her heroine against the cliffs as a "personality that carried across big spaces and expanded among big things" (320), she identified with a romantic surrogate capable of projecting her own egotism. In reality, of course, the Cliff Dwellers, precariously clinging to the sides of cliffs, probably felt infinitesimal in comparison to the huge plains all around them. If they had had a lot of egotism, as Cather fancied, it would have had to have been in compensation for their vulnerability. Certainly, it was out of a compensatory need that Cather herself affirmed her big ego in the Southwest and then again in *The Song of the Lark*. In reality, Cather may not have felt big enough to work effectively at *McClure's*,[35] but with her "big nature" (341), Thea is large enough for any challenge. Whereas at *McClure's*, Cather couldn't get much pleasure out of her work, Thea makes the world yield constant returns for the soul, and consequently, whereas Cather felt empty, Thea feels full (192). Whereas Cather felt shallow, Thea feels a "deep-rooted vitality" (478). Having felt diluted by office work, Cather makes Thea feel "concentrated" (339) and "all-compact" (407). If Cather felt weakened, Thea feels strong. Surely more than any other section of the novel, the scenes in Panther Canyon gave Cather the delightful feeling of losing herself in her own fairy tale.

Although Cather enjoyed taking imaginative possession of congenial landscapes, she ultimately derived more satisfaction out of appropriating other people. When she wrote *The Song of the Lark*, she found it exciting to assimilate the life of the opera singer Olive Fremstad into her own biography. Writing to Sergeant in 1913 of her discovery of the wonderful Fremstad, she reflects that getting under a new human skin is a more exciting and challenging sport than reaching a new country. As Cather got older, she increasingly found solace in the memories of her past friendships, a possession she came to value as more essential than the impressions she acquired from places. While vacationing with Edith Lewis in the Azores in 1935, she wrote to her childhood friend Mary Miner that if she didn't have those deep memories of old friendships, she wouldn't be able to acquire much from exotic sunny lands.[36] As she put the emphasis in a letter to Mariel Gere, people are more important than places, are they not?[37]

Like her author, Thea gains a lot not only from her appropriation of music and landscapes but, more importantly, from her appropriation of people. As Cather wrote in a letter to Fisher, she wanted to focus on Thea's relationship to Moonstone: what she acquired from it, and what she gave back to it.[38] Most obviously, Thea accumulates recollections of a diverse range of people so as to become a living repository, "full," as Tillie says, "of all them old times!" (486). Much of what Thea gets from Moonstone is, of course, a fictional version of what Cather "accumulated"[39] from her own friends of childhood. Cather wrote to her Pittsburgh friend, Mrs. Seibel, in January 1916, that her purpose in writing the book was simply to present a group of people she had known and loved.[40] Mildred Bennett, in her book *The World of Willa Cather*, gives a vivid picture of Willa as a young girl who forgot nothing in her eager efforts to acquire impressions of other people. As a child, she "absorbed everything" (WWC, 92) that she would later turn into her life's work. According to George Seibel, she was, in those early years, "a flesh and blood dictograph — eyes in every pore" (WWC, 92). We have only to read Bennett's book to see how the characters in the novel might correspond to the real people Cather knew — Professor Wunsch seems to be modeled partly on Cather's piano teacher, Professor Shindelmeiser. Dr. Archie seems based on the Cathers' family doctor, Dr. McKeeby; Ray Kennedy on a brakeman named Tooker, whom Cather met on her first trip to the Southwest; Lily Fisher on a pretentious singer Cather once heard at a "literary"; Mrs. Livery Johnson and her set on the factions in the Red Cloud Baptist Church; and so on. But, as Cather goes on to say in her letter to Mrs. Seibel, although she incorporated into the novel Mr. Kohler's piece-picture and other memories of real people she had known, Thea was composed of larger stuff that made her exceptional.[41] Cather implies that though Thea, like herself, is in part a composite — a kind of heterogeneous patchwork quilt — made up out of the threads of her early childhood memories, her being is more tightly and brilliantly woven out of another fabric: the one big thing that constitutes the warp and woof of her fundamental nature.[42]

Far from indiscriminately absorbing impressions of others, however, Thea once again appropriates only those who give back to her a token of herself. Despite the seeming diversity of the cast, the novel more profoundly divides the characters into two camps: those whom Thea rejects as her rivals and those whom she claims as her disciples. The real reason why the novel lumps together the majority of its characters as "Stupid Faces" is that they fail to pay homage to the innate superiority of Thea's genius. The unforgivable crime of Thea's most obnoxious enemy, Mrs. Livery Johnson, is her sabotage of Thea's chance for popularity at the Moonstone Christmas church concert; similarly, the unpardonable sin of Lily Fisher, Mrs. Johnson's angel-faced favorite, is her upstaging of Thea on the program. In her egotism, Thea even lumps her brothers and sisters together under the category of "Stupid Faces": "She had done them the honor, she told herself bitterly, to believe that though they had no particular endowments, *they were of her kind,* and not of the Moonstone kind" (240). As members of the conventional "Moonstone kind," Anna, who dutifully curls her hair and attends church meetings, and Gus, who unambitiously aspires to be a grocery boy, more egregiously err by refusing to let themselves be appropriated by their sister's domineering consciousness. In her essay on Mann's *Joseph and his Brothers,* Cather accounts for the brothers' jealousy of Joseph on the grounds that "it was this 'something,' this innate superiority in the boy himself, which the brothers hated even more than they hated the father's favourite: a deeper and more galling kind of jealousy.... The natural antagonism between the sane and commonplace, and the exceptional and inventive, is never so bitter as when it occurs in a family" (NUF, 114). Like the "natural antag- onism" between Joseph and his brothers, Cather presents the "natural

enmity" between Thea and her siblings as an inevitable response of the
dull to the gifted. Whatever the validity of this as sociology, it serves to
rationalize all of Thea's familial disputes with an obvious psychological
benefit for Thea. As if she were another Joseph, Thea can imagine that
she is "the father's favorite," worshipped as the chosen one not only by
her parents but by the god she imagines to rule the world in favor of
genius.

By contrast, Thea rejoices that "she could get the most wonderful
things out of Spanish Johnny, or Wunsch, or Dr. Archie" (79) because
her exceptional "something" compels their admiration. Like Fred Ottenburg, who confesses to Thea, "You've got me in deep" (332), Thea's
friends proudly proclaim themselves to belong completely to her.
Harsanyi tells her, "When people, serious people, believe in you, they
give you some of their best, so — take care of it" (376), and the best part
of themselves that others give to Thea is, invariably, their faith in her. A
good example of Thea's uncanny ability to get something wonderful
from others is in the scene in which she attends Ray Kennedy, fatally
wounded in a railroad wreck. Rather than call for a doctor or a priest,
Ray wants only Thea. As his term of endearment, "Thee" (146), suggests,
she is the god whom he worships. At first, it seems as though Thea might
wish to grasp something of Ray's essential self when "the spark in his
eye, which is one's very self, caught the spark in hers that was herself,
and for a moment they looked into each other's natures" (148). But this
psychic exchange is as short-lived as Ray himself, for in the incandescent
glow of Thea's nature, the spark of Ray's is snuffed out; in his admiration for her, his self-expression gives way to her self-reflection, so that
she "saw in his wet eyes her own face, very small, but much prettier than
the cracked glass at home had ever shown it" (148). Thea's "broken
looking-glass" (64) in her bedroom, in which she had sorrowfully gazed
after her failure to win applause at the Christmas concert, reflects the fact
that her ego becomes shattered without others' admiration. By contrast,
Thea appears beautified when Ray's eyes, instead of providing windows
to his soul, serve as mirrors to her own. Though we expect Thea to help
Ray in his pain and suffering, Ray wants only to minister to her needs.
Protesting even with his last breath, "It's a darned shame I can't wait on
you" (146), he plays the loyal vassal to the end. More advantageous even
than the $600 that Ray leaves Thea through his life insurance policy is
his assurance that she can hold a conscious "power" (147) over others
merely through her awesome presence. Ray's death gives Thea all of the
benefits of attention without any of the consequent obligations of real
human relationships. As a dying man, Ray can praise her as "a queen"
(149) without threatening her autonomy, but had he lived to try to marry

her, he would have wanted to "keep her like a queen" (53), thus making her his property. Though Thea wants to be worshipped as a queen, she certainly does not want to be "kept" like one. Resenting Ray's "proprietary tone" (90), Thea vehemently rejects his marriage proposal, as she later does Fred Ottenburg's, so that she can belong to no other but herself. Once Ray is dead, Thea can appropriate him as *her* imaginative property. Most valuably, Ray's death graphically illustrates the fact that all of the exemplary characters in the novel are willing to lay down their lives for Thea.

Thea most unabashedly absorbs others so as to augment her sense of self when she sings to the Mexican town. Prostrate with adoration, the Mexicans

> turned themselves and all they had over to her. For the moment they cared about nothing in the world but what she was doing. Their faces confronted her, open, eager, unprotected. She felt as if all these warm-blooded people debouched into her. Mrs. Tellamantez's fateful resignation, Johnny's mad- ness, the adoration of the boy who lay still in the sand; in an instant these things seemed to be within her instead of without, as if they had come from her in the first place. (232)

Although on the surface Thea seems to incorporate *other* personalities and cultures, all other selves collapse into her insatiable ego. By project- ing her "secret self" into song, so that nobody cares about anything except what she is doing, Thea reveals the real secret of the novel: her omnipotent ego has the power to displace all other authorities so as to command the center of the stage. So fully does Thea conquer her "unprotected" audience that they helplessly relinquish to her not only their attention but their very souls. Metaphorically swallowing all other currents of life into her own, as the people suddenly "debouched into her" like a flowing river, Thea exhibits an irresistible centripetal power to match that of Whitman. Although while working at *McClure's*, Cather felt that all her energies had drained away as the power does in a broken circuit,[43] Thea's powerful hold over her audience allows her to mend that circuit of vitality. When, "in an instant these things seemed to be within her instead of without, as if they had come from her in the first place," Thea exerts a divine power to claim the world as her own instantaneous creation. Certainly, as we see her shining like a vision of paradise before the "altar-boys," who lie like devoted apostles at her feet, "one on her right and one on her left" (231), Thea assumes all the authority of a female god and thus reveals the origin of her name and her power.

At the end of the novel, when Thea appears "as much at home on the stage as ... down in Panther Canyon" (462), she seems to complete her artistic development simply by recovering the primitive strength that she had gained in the Southwest. By the novel's deepest plot, however, Thea's experience in Panther Canyon is only a rehearsal for her later performances. Although she most effortlessly reconstitutes herself when she lays claim to an unpopulated landscape, her imaginative possession of people remains her ultimate goal. The empty canyon has to give way to the full house of the theater because Thea needs others to share her consciousness and confirm her sovereignty. In reality, hers is not a nature that can find itself alone. In the canyon, Thea seems to be "all there" (317) in the full vigor of her personality, but she is not "wholly present" (442) until she can bring others into the same orbit — which is what performance can accomplish. Like a planet of strong gravitational "pull" (451), Thea irresistibly draws her admirers towards her magnetic center. Harsanyi, following his pupil's every move with his single eye "like a satellite" (474), exemplifies the single-minded devotion with which the entire audience has gratefully revolved its existence around Thea from the beginning. Thea remains as autonomous on stage as she was in her solitude in the canyon, for although she is surrounded by an audience full of living people, they surrender their selves to her as much as the "Cliff People" did. Indeed, throughout the last section of the novel, entitled "Kronborg," Thea's dominating aura as the great diva is as big as her name up in lights. Even though she herself is absent for most of these final scenes, her consciousness is nonetheless the sole informing presence during the endless discussions about her and the source of her genius. When others talk, it is essentially only to praise Thea. Finally, as if to literalize the role of adoring audience that the community has played all along, the entire cast of Thea-ologists reassemble on her Friday afternoon performance of Seiglinde. Impressed with Thea's compelling passion, Harsanyi exclaims, "At last, somebody with *enough!*" (476). As readers who have witnessed Thea's insatiable desire to appropriate the Mexicans, the Cliff Dwellers, and finally, the whole cast, we, too, ought to be convinced that "at last," Thea has "enough."

Yet paradoxically, although Cather insists that Thea innately contains the "one big thing" (76), we can see this big thing not so much as a power, or a gift, but as a hunger, or a lack — an emptiness that it takes the whole world to fill; otherwise, she doesn't exist. In the early stages of her own career, Cather had worried that she lacked the essential gift of the artist. A letter she wrote to Mariel Gere, a friend from Red Cloud, in August 1896, reveals the insecurities she felt a couple of months after she arrived in Pittsburgh to begin her work as a journalist. On one hand, she seems to have felt that she had a special nature that destined her to be one of the elect. Yet, despite her bold claim, Cather ends her letter by admitting her fear that she lacks the one necessary thing.[44] Though Cather knew that she wanted to devote herself to art, she was not sure whether she possessed the native gift that justified the quest and the devotion. Whereas she had begun her career in self-doubt, lamenting an inner deficiency, she came into her own when she wrote *The Song of the Lark*, boasting to her publisher Ferris Greenslet that she had gotten it this time.[45] Celebrating her own repossession of self, along with her heroine's, Cather seemed to have laid to rest her earlier feelings of inadequacy once and for all. Yet it was only in the process of writing that Cather was able to fill this inner void. Indeed, one reason why she got so carried away in this uncharacteristically long and detailed novel — which she later disparaged for its "full-blooded method" (OW, 96) — was that she had to work hard to satisfy herself that she was, in fact, as possessed of vitality, power, and the makings of success as she wished to be. While Cather celebrates the personality informing great art as an innate endowment, she reveals through her characters' quests for imaginative possession that, in fact, personality itself is often a painfully accumulated work of art.

Finally, as Cather said in her letter to Fisher, she wanted to portray not only what Thea "got" from Moonstone but what she "gave back to it"; indeed, she focuses much of the last book on what others "get" from Thea. As in a last judgment, all of the characters are either punished or rewarded at the end of the novel in proportion to the degree of faith that they have put in Thea.[46] In fulfillment of Wunsch's prophecy that "Desire" has the power to make all else "little" against it, Thea expands with an "augmented" (371) aura while her enemies become as small and insignificant as she had always known them to be. Mrs. Archie, who in her petty "littleness" (85) had discouraged young Thea from picking strawberries in her yard, seemingly dies as a result of her stingy housekeeping, but with even more poetic justice for having incurred Thea's wrath. Other opponents similarly pay their just dues: Jessie Darcey, the stupid singer who had dared to criticize Thea's piano playing, suffers from a cracking voice and a wrinkling face; Thea's baby brother, Thor, who had ungratefully ordered her to pull him in the wagon all over Moonstone, becomes, ironically, a chauffeur forced to drive others around; Lily Fisher, the girl who had unforgivably upstaged Thea at the Moonstone concert, turns out to be no more than a humdrum housewife, silenced to witness her children's delight in the tales told of Thea's fame at local picnics.

But what of those exemplary characters who do benefit from Thea's performances? Critics have argued that Thea's art serves a selfless end

by allowing those in her audience to fulfill their dreams. [47] I would maintain, however, that Thea's gift of sympathy selfishly disguises a deeper
gift of self. Cather once wrote, "The great enjoyment that makes the
theatre worth while is in seeing individual talent, in watching a man give
back what God put into him" (KA, 115). What Thea gives to others is
not, primarily, an increased sense of themselves but an increased awe for
her. Harsanyi comments that Thea "always gave something back" (476),
and that "something" is, unfailingly, an overwhelming appreciation of
her own exceptional nature. Harsanyi most clearly describes what he gets
from Thea when, after one of her sensational performances, he tells his
wife, "I believe in her. She will do nothing common. She is uncommon,
in a common, common world. That is what I get out of it" (212). The
humble recognition of Thea's superiority to the ordinary, commonplace
world — the world in which they themselves live — is, above all, what
Harsanyi and his fellow disciples "get" out of Thea's art. [48]

It is, finally, for the reader to identify with Thea — and thus, to get,
vicariously — the benefit of this homage. Although Thea's art cannot
help us much with the life we *must* live, it can help us to recreate the life
we once wished for and still stubbornly, unconsciously believe in. Dr.
Archie reminisces that his memories of Thea's youth "came nearer to
being tender secrets than any others he possessed. Nearer than anything
else they corresponded to what he had hoped to find in the world, and
had not found" (400–401). The idea of Thea's golden youth is not only
Dr. Archie's most valuable imaginative possession but perhaps also ours,
which explains why critics and readers alike are so *gladly* taken in by
Cather's fairy tale. Despite Rosowski's assertion that "Cather avoids ...
narcissism and a resulting view of art as a means to love and power," [49]
the emotional appeal of *The Song of the Lark* lies precisely in the way it
celebrates art as a vehicle for gaining fame and sovereignty. Above all,
Thea's art sanctions the primal fantasy of the narcissistic child who,
waking with "a burst of joy at recovering her precious self and her
precious world" (427), welcomes the world as if it were reserved for her
as a nurturing scene. In his essay "On Narcissism," Freud writes that
adults are inclined

> to renew on [the child's] behalf the claims to privileges which were long ago
> given up by themselves. The child shall have a better time than his parents; he
> shall not be subject to the necessities which they have recognized as
> paramount in life. Illness, death, renunciation of enjoyment, restrictions on
> his own will, shall not touch him; the laws of nature and of society shall be
> abrogated in his favour; he shall once more really be the centre and core of
> creation — "His Majesty the Baby," as we once fancied ourselves. [50]

Of course, real life teaches us that we are susceptible to disagreeable circumstances, burdensome adult responsibilities, dispossessing human relationships, and the ravages of time. As a wish fulfillment, however, *The Song of the Lark* sustains the illusion that we wish to preserve of our early youth — the illusion, as Freud writes, that all the laws of nature and society shall miraculously be repealed in our favor so that we can once again imaginatively conquer the world, making it vulnerable to the powers of the self. In reality, we lose the sweet confidence of childhood, but we get a return on our imaginative investment in Thea, for in the artist's undivided ego, we vicariously recover our own. Moreover, we imagine that — with the help of fairy godfathers like Dr. Archie or Ray Kennedy — we, too, can reclaim that unbounded childhood "feeling of empire" (220) where the ego reigns supreme.

5

My Àntonia:
The Imaginative Possession of Childhood

The critical debate on *My Àntonia* has centered on the reliability of the
narrator, Jim Burden, who tells the story of his childhood friend Àntonia.
In particular, feminist critics have seen Jim as an untrustworthy narrative
voice. They have argued that Jim undermines his credibility as a narrator
by conforming Àntonia to male stereotypes and myths about women.[1] In
their view, Jim's revision of the title of his manuscript from "Àntonia" to
"My Àntonia" is evidence of a suspect patriarchal authority.[2] From my
perspective, however, Cather upholds the exemplary nature of the word
"my." I believe that we can best understand *My Àntonia* not according to
a politics of sexuality but as a theology of consciousness. Jim's possessive pronoun expresses not simply a male's chauvinism but an artist's
egoism. Like his predecessors Alexandra Bergson and Thea Kronborg,
Jim can be seen as an artist who lays claim to the inner life of consciousness. Granted that "possession ... by a different lease," he rejects
Àntonia as an autonomous woman and claims her instead as a momento
treasured in his own psyche. While, from one point of view, the
exclusively imaginative value that Jim places on others makes him an
unreliable guide to life, it nonetheless makes him a reliable guide to
Cather's own needs and desires as a romantic artist. Cather created Jim
not to deconstruct social patriarchy but to construct her own fictional
mask. Cather uses Jim, as she does most all of her protagonists, as a
model of the artist who can claim the privilege of making the world
completely available as an appropriable territory for her imaginative use.
Far from undermining his authority, Jim's imaginative possession of
Àntonia as a symbol of "the country, the conditions, the whole adventure
of our childhood" (MA, introduction)[3] is essential to the mission Cather

uses him to undertake: the recovery of her inviolable and indivisible childhood self.

To understand Cather's emotional need to create Jim as her surrogate, we can begin by examining her unusual introduction to the novel. Speaking as an unidentified "I," Cather pretends to have received the manuscript from her old childhood friend, Jim Burden, whom she meets again during a train ride across the West. In the original 1918 introduction to the novel, both Cather and Jim agree to write about their memories of Àntonia. Months later, however, when he proudly delivers his manuscript to her at her New York apartment, she is forced to confess that her own account of Àntonia has "not gone beyond a few straggling notes" (1918, xiv). Since, as she says, "My own story was never written," she presents Jim's manuscript instead, "substantially as he brought it to me" (1918, xiv). Jean Schwind ingeniously argues that Cather's silence undercuts Jim's "male" narrative with a "female" story of her own, represented by the novel's pictures.[4] By contrast, I would argue that Cather's use of Jim as narrator was a crucial authorial strategy that enabled her to write the novel; far from undermining Jim's voice, Cather adopted it so as to recover her own. She presents herself in the novel as the professional writer who has lost the ability to write, and who thus can furnish only another writer's work because, in reality, she had been too emotionally incapacitated to write the novel for six months after she had conceived it. As she wrote to Dorothy Canfield Fisher in mid-March 1916, the idea for the book was there, but she felt too apathetic towards it to begin writing.[5] We can judge the cause of Cather's paralysis from the rest of the letter: her dearest friend, Isabelle McClung, had just announced her engagement to the violinist Jan Hambourg. As Cather expressed her personal anguish to Fisher, Isabelle's marriage was an overwhelming change in her life that devastated her with a sense of loss, grief, and pain. At Isabelle's news, Cather's carefully nurtured world collapsed. She knew that Isabelle's marriage would close the window on an intimate relationship that had lasted since their first meeting in 1899 in Pittsburgh.[6] Moreover, she knew that she would lose the protected peace and security she had found in the refuge of the McClung household, where she had lived continuously from 1901 to 1906, and on and off ever since. The "window" that Isabelle's news broke most devastatingly was in Cather's attic bedroom, a safe sanctuary where she had come into her own as a writer, having written *April Twilights*, *The Troll Garden*, and major parts of *O Pioneers!* and *The Song of the Lark*. In later years, Cather would look back on Isabelle as her muse, the special one friend for whom all her books had been written.[7] After sharing with Isabelle a single-minded worship of the artist's passion for her art, Cather could not

easily admit another rival passion into her imaginative world. As a divisive sexual passion, Isabelle's love for Jan was especially threatening to
Cather's sense of autonomy and power that Isabelle, in her indulgent
protection, had helped to foster.

Speaking of Isabelle McClung's marriage, the psychoanalytic critic
Leon Edel has noted, "It is from this moment that the biographer can date
a change in Willa Cather's works."[8] Edel shows how Cather's later
novel, *The Professor's House* (1925), reveals "an increasing tension and
deep uneasiness"[9] resulting from her break with Isabelle. We can apply
Edel's approach to *My Àntonia* as well. *My Àntonia*, a seemingly optimistic work, most immediately originated out of the emotional turmoil
caused by Isabelle McClung's marriage. Tellingly, Cather suggests
nothing about the source of Jim's unhappiness except that he has made
an unfortunate marriage. In her persona as the narrator of the introduction, Cather explains that she has seen little of Jim in New York because
"I do not like his wife" (MA, introduction). If the fictional Cather rejects
Jim's wife, it is, at the deepest psychological level, because his wife had,
in her mind, rejected her, for Jim's wife can be seen as a portrait of
Isabelle McClung, the woman with whom Cather herself had lived in a
kind of "Boston marriage" but from whom she, like Jim, was now
estranged. In the original 1918 version of the introduction, Cather included a full page of incriminating description of Jim's wife that points
to her preoccupation with Isabelle. "Handsome, energetic, executive, but
… unimpressionable and temperamentally incapable of enthusiasm"
(1918, x–xi), Jim's wife resembles the Isabelle whom Cather's biographers describe as handsome, stately, statuesque, dignified, and cold.
Naming Jim's wife "Genevieve Whitney," Cather further suggests that
she, like her predecessor in *Alexander's Bridge*, Winifred Pemberton,
was modeled on such an aristocratic and socially prominent woman. Just
as "Genevieve Whitney was the only daughter of a distinguished man"
(1918, x), so Isabelle McClung was the only daughter of the distinguished Judge McClung of Pittsburgh. In Bartley Alexander, Cather had
cast herself as a struggling and naive youth from the West who began his
career by marrying the sophisticated woman of society, Winifred Pemberton; similarly, she now recasts herself as Jim, "an obscure young
lawyer, struggling to make his way in New York [whose] career was
suddenly advanced by a brilliant marriage" (1918, x). As the
"roughneck" from the West who suddenly found that Isabelle's adoption
of her put her in the highest social and artistic circles of Pittsburgh,
Cather felt that she, too, had brilliantly advanced her career. Genevieve's
"marriage with young Burden was the subject of sharp comment at the
time" (1918, x); similarly, Isabelle's unconventional liaison with Cather

was initially criticized by her parents and the conservative elite of Pittsburgh. As Phyllis Robinson has said of Isabelle, she had cultivated "a reputation as something of a rebel in the staid Calvinist society in which her family moved."[10] By casting herself in the "role of patron of the arts," Isabelle found in Willa "not only a companion who delighted in the things that she did, but also an artist whose genius she might help to develop."[11] For her part, Cather enjoyed Isabelle's exclusive attention, which provided her with flattering introductions at social gatherings, as well as the privacy she needed for her work. Like Jim's wife, however, whom Cather describes as having only a "fleeting interest" (1918, x) in the various causes she espouses, so Isabelle, in Cather's view, seemed to show only a passing interest in her when she chose to give her support to the violinist Jan Hambourg instead. Cather's slighting remark of Jim's wife, "Her husband's quiet tastes irritate her, I think, and she finds it worth while to play the patroness to a group of young poets and painters of advanced ideas and mediocre ability" (1918, xi), points to her resentment of Isabelle's patronage of Jan, the artist who, in her jealousy, she might well have wanted to dismiss as second-rate. Perhaps Cather reveals her greatest cause for bitterness when she writes that Jim's wife "has her own fortune and lives her own life" (1918, xi). Since the death of Isabelle's father the previous November, she had inherited a fortune of her own that gave her the means to marry and thus to live a life of her own, apart from Cather.

After the introduction, Cather is careful to leave out any mention of Jim's personal life, as if she would gladly forget such painful memories of her own. Her reunion with her old childhood friend Jim allows her to identify with his more youthful persona. As Sergeant describes seeing Cather after her rupture with Isabelle, "All her natural exuberance [was] drained away" so that her face was "bleak" and her eyes "vacant" (WC: AM, 140). But Jim, though also "over forty now," enabled Cather to regain the vitality she had lost, for, as she says in her first introduction, "He never seems to me to grow older. His fresh color and sandy hair and quick-changing blue eyes are those of a young man" (1918, xii). By affirming that "no disappointments have been severe enough to chill his naturally romantic and ardent disposition" (1918, xi), Cather invested herself in Jim in order to get over her own disappointing relationship with Isabelle. Throughout the novel, Jim's imagination works to keep a narrative distance from threatening material so that, on the surface, a mood of serenity and happiness prevails. Cather's strategies of escape and evasion in *My Àntonia* register the painful experience from which she was trying to recover by writing.

My purpose in beginning with Cather's biography is not to read *My*

Àntonia as a *roman à clef* but to see how her emotional crisis shaped the
imaginative direction of the novel. Cather's letters and, more importantly, the novel itself, suggest that her loss of Isabelle filled her with two
overriding emotional needs: to repossess the friends of her childhood and
to repossess her own youth. More than any of Cather's previous novels,
My Àntonia reveals a new and more generous celebration of group ties.
The first person whom Jim meets on his train trip west in the opening
chapter is the conductor, whose real job in the novel is to announce the
importance of belonging to various social groups. As Cather describes
him, "He wore the rings and pins and badges of different fraternal orders
to which he belonged. Even his cuff-buttons were engraved with hiero-
glyphics, and he was more inscribed than an Egyptian obelisk" (4). As a
mark of his initiation into the new country, Jim, too, gets to wear the
badges of various "fraternal orders": at his grandparents' house in the
country, he belongs to an extended family that includes the hired hands
Jake and Otto; in town, he becomes a part of the gay evenings of entertainment at the Harlings' house and at the dancing tent; and at the end of
the novel, he gains membership into the happiest family of all when he
reunites with Àntonia and her eleven children. It is easy to understand
how Isabelle's marriage left Cather with a longing for a sympathetic
community, a longing she fulfilled in part by returning to Red Cloud in
the summer of 1916, and in part by writing the novel. By losing the
McClungs, she had lost her membership within a perfect surrogate family, one in which she had found support and a sense of belonging, and yet
had escaped the rivalries and responsibilities of a real family. Isabelle's
marriage must have made Cather feel especially lonely and abandoned,
for it vividly represented the world of sex and family that she had
renounced for her art. In a letter to Will Owen Jones in 1919, Cather
wrote that the novel's introduction had to state the facts of Jim's life: that
he is a man of worldly background, with no children to live for and not
very happy in his domestic, private life. If he were, Cather revealingly
adds, he would not need to reminisce so deeply upon his early childhood.[12] With more irony and self-knowledge than Cather usually betrays,
she seems to admit that she herself, a woman of worldly experience with
no children to plan for and an unfortunate domestic life, projected into
Jim her own desire to return to her childhood in order to affirm
communal allegiances.

 If Cather felt alone and excluded from Isabelle's new relationship with
a husband, she found consolation by imaginatively recreating exclusive
ties of her own in the novel. As Cather and Jim agree in the introduction,
"No one who had not grown up in a little prairie town could know anything about it. It was a kind of freemasonry, we said." Cather liked to

claim that *My Àntonia* was written for a few of the people who shared her early memories of the wild prairie landscape.[13] In her dedication of the novel to her childhood friends Carrie and Irene Miner, "In memory of affections old and true" (Dedication page), Cather affirmed a friendship that was presumably older and truer than Isabelle's had been; she later wrote to Carrie that she felt her friendship with her was like a family bond.[14] Although Isabelle had failed her, Cather could depend on old friends like Carrie to offer security and support for her artistic endeavor. As Cather wrote to Carrie on 10 November 1921, her old attachments were the very well-spring out of which she drew her inspiration for her best work; she felt that nothing was more empowering than having one's oldest friends participate in one's work.[15] "I still remember," "I can see them now," "They are with me still" — such retrospective lines become, as Rosowski has noted, the novel's refrain.[16] For Cather, lonely in Isabelle's absence, needed solace came from the belief that one could still keep company with the friends of the past in memory. As if to reassure herself that she had a group of her own after all, Cather based many other characters in the novel on people she had known as part of the "freemasonry" of her childhood.[17]

As her letters and interviews suggest, however, Cather wanted less to belong to the people of her past than to have them belong to her. As she wrote to "her" Bishop George Beecher, whom she addressed with the possessive pronoun, she considered old friends like him as valuable possessions, more cherished than any worldly gifts.[18] She wrote to Ferris Greenslet that no matter how absurd the world became, she took consolation in the fact that her old friends remained her most treasured possessions.[19] By putting her friends into her novels, Cather ensured her possession of them as friends in the future; as she later recalled to Carrie Miner, her dearest friends had kept in touch with her regarding her books.[20] More importantly, however, by "recapturing in memory people and places I had believed forgotten" (WCP, 21), Cather could reclaim her old friends in the very process of remembering them in her fiction. Such an imaginative possession was more complete and stimulating to Cather than any dramatic relationship in real life could be. As Cather wrote to Irene Miner in 1945, writing in *My Àntonia* about the people and places she loved brought them back to her so clearly that it was like having them again in reality; moreover, she reflects, these imagined presences seemed even more heartwarming and stirring than the actual people had been.[21] Understandably, Cather could more satisfyingly "have" people as ideal and unchanging figures in consciousness than as actual presences, for, as she knew too well, real people might disappoint or betray her.

Cather's desire to share a mutual possession of the past[22] with her early friends conceals a deeper desire to reclaim her own childhood and youth — the past that had always been most attractive to her. In an important letter to Fisher in 1922, Cather reflects that when one is old enough to cast a backwards glance upon one's own youth as a vanished glory, then the beloved figures of the past assume a new vividness, and one's mind turns and grasps at them as if one pictured them clearly for the first time. [23] Interestingly, Cather suggests that her turning back to grasp the recollected presence of early childhood friends was more deeply an effort to grasp her own elusive youth that she shared with them in memory. Adding in her letter to Fisher that she herself came to this reflective stage later in life, about four or five years ago, she sets this retrospective turning point in her vision at the time when she was writing *My Àntonia*; indeed, it seems likely that her rupture with Isabelle made her feel dispossessed of her youth as a lost thing. Cather seems to have cherished a comradeship with Isabelle that had its emotional roots in childhood. In a letter to May Willard in 1941, she looked back to the happy days in Pittsburgh when she and Isabelle, May Willard, and Ethel Litchfield seemed to recover their youthful zestfulness at folk dancing parties. [24] During an early visit with Isabelle in 1899, Cather wrote ecstatically to Dorothy Canfield Fisher that she had been having such a gay time with Isabelle, going on picnics and hearing bands play, that Isabelle had made her feel like a frivolous kid again; as she lightheartedly joked, she and Isabelle would be playing with dolls before long. [25] Though Sharon O'Brien and others have described Cather's relationship with Isabelle as "lesbian," [26] the degree to which her relationship was sexually intimate is not, and cannot, be known. We might best consider it a narcissistic bonding, such as pre-pubescent boys and girls often share with a kind of twin. [27] Though physical desire may have made itself felt in the mood of the relationship, it was not to be confronted or consummated.

By dedicating *The Song of the Lark* to Isabelle, Cather acknowledged that her friend had inspired her to believe in her own story of "Artist's Youth." Once Cather lost Isabelle, we see a major change in her novels. Isabelle's support had encouraged Cather to imagine herself the strong artist heroine in *O Pioneers!* and *The Song of the Lark*. But, as if Isabelle's defection had undermined Cather's confidence, she cast herself in *My Àntonia* and *A Lost Lady* as the unfulfilled male artist in search of a lost female muse. Though critics have argued that Cather adopted her male persona in *My Àntonia* as a mask for lesbian love, [28] Jim's revulsion for female sexuality suggests that Cather did not consciously admit to a physical attraction to women. Cather chose "male" over "female" personas in her later novels because they more easily gave her the illusion of transcending limiting biological and sexual necessities and conventions;

for her, the "male" mask was a pose of androgeny that served as a strategy for attaining autonomous power. The relation between Cather's male narrators and their female objects of desire, which critics have construed as lesbian, I wish to reconsider as a symbiotic relationship between two halves of one self. Whereas Alexandra Bergson and Thea Kronborg had triumphantly possessed an innate ego, Jim Burden and Niel Herbert must try to repossess that "something" through their imaginative appropriations of female ideals. As if to admit that she had lost the youthful second self that had once accompanied her, as it had Thea Kronborg, Cather sadly confesses in the introduction, "I had lost sight of her altogether." Through Jim, however, who "had found her again after long years," she is vicariously "made [to] see her again, feel her presence."

* * *

My Àntonia is divided into five sections, each of which takes place at a different place and time in Jim's life. As David Stouck has noted, however, book 1, recounting Jim's memories of the year he spent as a child in the country on his grandparents' farm and his friendship with the Bohemian girl Àntonia, forms the "crucial experience upon which the whole of the novel rests; books 2–5 are in essence a reexamination of that central experience from four different perspectives."[29] The first book constitutes nearly half of the novel and thematically controls all of the novel; the stories recorded in the first book dwell in Jim's memory long after he grows up and moves away from the country. In fact, the subsequent four sections of the novel can all be seen as Jim's attempts to recapture the magical "conditions" of his country of childhood. Jim himself created these "conditions," in the beginning, as a product of his "romantic disposition which ... has been one of the strongest elements in his success." Although putatively a lawyer for one of the great Western railways, Jim aims not to advance the progress of civilization and industry but to develop the country as a romantic idea. As portrayed in the opening of *O Pioneers!*, the actual "conditions" of the prairie were harsh and threatening, but in the early childhood scenes of *My Àntonia*, Jim's romantic imagination so idealizes the world that space, time, and other people cease to exist as external realities and minister solely to his sense of power and freedom. Cather's first three novels begin realistically, with the self alternately threatened by professional and social exactions, the harsh conditions of nature, and the demands of family. They then seek to recover the self through a kind of wish fulfillment. But when *My Àntonia* opens, the imaginative appropriation of the world has already been made as a precondition of Jim's childlike perspective. No doubt one reason

why *My Àntonia* continues to be such a popular novel is that the early
transcendental scenes of Jim in the prairie answer to our nostalgia for
childhood as the blessed scene of unity with a restorative world.

According to its surface plot, of course, the novel begins as a story of
disinheritance and exile, as the ten-year-old orphaned Jim is uprooted
from his comfortable home in Virginia and taken to live with his grandparents in desolate Nebraska. As a fictional version of Cather's own experience, Jim's story would seem to be traumatic. His recollection,
"There seemed to be nothing to see; no fences, no creeks or trees, no hills
or fields" (7), had filled his author with despair. But Jim turns the
prairie's blankness to his own advantage when he imagines that "there
was nothing but land: not a country at all, but the material out of which
countries are made" (7). The empty landscape loses its intimidating
aspect as it becomes the raw material for Jim's artistic recreation. Cather
once wrote to Fisher that the common thread running through her novels
was the feeling of escape she had while riding the train west,[30] and surely
Jim's first wagon ride into the prairie illustrates the greatest escape of all,
for he symbolically escapes from the world of reality into the world of
disembodied spirit. Feeling as if "the world was left behind, that we had
got over the edge of it, and were outside man's jurisdiction," Jim occupies instead "the complete dome of heaven, all there was of it" (8). In this
void that predates creation, Jim seems to be the only inhabitant. As he
recalls, "I did not believe that my dead father and mother were watching
me from up there; they would still be looking for me at the sheep-fold
down by the creek, or along the white road that led to the mountain pas-
tures" (8). Jim has traded places with his dead parents, enjoying a
"heaven" of his own that indeed makes theirs seem earthly by comparison. His "heaven" bears a resemblance not to the Christian dwelling
place for the dead in the afterlife, but to the psychological dwelling place
for the soul in its life before birth. He "did not say my prayers that
night," for he inhabits a primitive world where God does not yet rule, and
where he himself does not yet "exist"; he is an undifferentiated being
who has not yet fallen into self-awareness. Cradled in his cozy nest at the
back of the covered wagon, swaddled in a warm buffalo robe and gently
rocked through the darkness over a "slightly undulating" ground, Jim has
no cause to be homesick, for, psychologically, he returns to the security
of his first home in the womb.

Recalling on the following morning that "the glide of long railway
travel was still with me" (16), Jim carries with him the childhood feeling
of "escape" throughout the early scenes of the novel. In his grandmother's garden, he continues to live out a transcendental fantasy of getting
"over the edge of the world" (16). Just as Alexandra Bergson had forgot-

ten to hoe her potatoes in the garden while she contemplated the hawk that flew "up and up, into the blazing depths of the sky" (OP, 49), so Jim forgets to help his grandmother dig potatoes in their garden, as he reflects that "the light air about me told me that the world ended here: only the ground and sun and sky were left, and if one went a little farther there would be only sun and sky, and one would float off into them, like the tawny hawks which sailed over our heads making slow shadows on the grass" (16). Jim imagines that he could be as unfettered by the laws of nature and gravity, and by all earthly chains of responsibility, as if he, too, were a tenant of the air. Forgetting that he even "had a grandmother" (15), he returns to an earlier source than any human lineage, imagining that:

> I was something that lay under the sun and felt it, like the pumpkins, and I did not want to be anything more. I was entirely happy. Perhaps we feel like that when we die and become a part of something entire, whether it is sun and air, or goodness and knowledge. At any rate, that is happiness; to be dissolved into something complete and great. When it comes to one, it comes as naturally as sleep. (18)

Though this passage seems to celebrate Jim's self-dissolution,[31] we could also understand it as a dream of self-reconstitution. Jim becomes "dissolved into something complete and great" in the way that man, according to Emerson, was "once ... permeated and dissolved by spirit ... fill[ing] nature with his overflowing currents."[32] He "become[s] a part of something entire" for the same reason that Emerson became "part or parcel of God":[33] he gives up the "mean egotism" of his ordinary personality and becomes subsumed by the greater circumference of his own oversoul. A passive receptacle for heat and physical sensations, as was Thea Kronborg in her cave, Jim becomes reunited with the elemental stuff of his own creation. Lying still and undisturbed in the warm earth where "nothing happened" (18), Jim seems to occupy the womb and grave simultaneously. As Freud suggested in his description of the death wish as *"a need to restore an earlier state of things,"*[34] Cather illuminates the drive towards death as a desire to repeat moments of preconscious integration.

Jim's imaginative appropriation of Àntonia as part of his childhood idyll presents Cather with a narrative challenge, for, in reality, Àntonia could hardly be more different from him. Differences in ethnic background and class divide them. A Bohemian immigrant, Àntonia speaks a foreign language, is brought up to believe a foreign religion, and knows foreign customs. Whereas Jim enjoys the privilege of being an only child brought up by pious and well-to-do grandparents in an orderly household, Àntonia has to fight for her independence among three other siblings in the poverty of a sod hut. Whereas Jim gets the advantage of an education, Àntonia must support her family by working in the fields and as a hired-girl in town. While Jim, as an artist, devotes himself to the rarefied and timeless life of the mind, Àntonia "falls" into the real world of physical labor, sex, family, and cyclical time. But Cather imagines that, as children, Jim and Àntonia are not yet estranged from each other. Throughout her writings, Cather consistently idealized the bond between children, often between brother and sister, as the single social relation-ship that was always happy. Her own close relationship with her brothers, especially Douglass, provided such a paradigm in her own life. In her review of George Eliot's *The Mill on the Floss*, for example, Cather described "that strongest and most satisfactory relation of human life" as the childhood union between brother and sister, for, as she said, they "have entered into each other's lives and minds more completely than ever man or woman can again.... It is more than a tie of blood; much more" (WP, 363). O'Brien suggests that "Cather ... saw the opposite-sex sibling as embodying a part of the self."[35] Indeed, by having Jim and Àntonia arrive in the "new world" together on the same train, Cather introduces them as soul mates, or spiritual twins. As long as Jim and Àntonia remain as parts of the same self in a narcissistic bond, Jim claims her as his dearest friend without fear of forfeiting his autonomy.

Blanche Gelfant suggests that Jim's shadow, that "visible elongation of self," represents "the enduring though elusive image of his original self."[36] As a projection of his own romantic ego, Jim's shadow becomes the perfect symbolic vehicle for appropriating Àntonia. Recalling how, on those never-changing afternoons playing on the prairie with Àntonia, "always two long black shadows flitted before us or followed after, dark spots on the ruddy grass" (40), Jim imagines that the other is as undiffer-entiated from the self as his own shadow — the perfect companion who will always loyally follow his will. In a letter to Fisher, Cather wrote that when she looked back on her past, she wanted to escape herself as a real person and see, instead, the shadow that she cast. She suggests that her shadow self is not her physical self with her creaturely needs but a disembodied expression of the emotions or sensations that constitute her essential inner self. She tells Fisher that she was most contented when she was running as fast as she could — away from her real self and the real world, and towards her shadowy projection.[37] With Àntonia and her sister, who "were always ready to forget their troubles at home, and to run away with me over the prairie" (32), Jim is also happiest when he is running away from adult responsibilities. When he and Àntonia "raced

off toward Squaw Creek and did not stop until the ground itself stopped
— fell away before us so abruptly that the next step would have been out
into the tree-tops" (25), they nearly take flight from the earth into the
empyrean.

As Rosowski has observed, whether Jim and Àntonia are curled up
together in the hay wagon or burrowed down in the wavy grass of the
prairie, they characteristically share primal, womblike nests.[38] Like the
little insect that they "lured back to life by false pretences" (40) in Àntonia's curly hair, Jim and Àntonia themselves live "by false pretences" by
escaping life "so deep in the grass that we could see nothing but the blue
sky over us and the gold tree in front of us" (26). Pointing out the
comparison between Jim's "blue eyes" and the "blue sky" (26), Àntonia
serves to reinforce Jim's transcendental connection to the universe. Like
Emerson, dissolved as a "transparent eyeball"[39] to become one with all
space, Jim gazes into the blue sky so as to behold the depths of his own
clairvoyant nature.

Àntonia shares Jim's imaginative appropriation of the landscape and,
more importantly, his imaginative appropriation of people. The inset
story of how the two Russians, Peter and Pavel, had thrown a bride and
groom off a sledge to the pursuing wolves has been criticized for bearing
an "uncertain"[40] relation to the novel as a whole, and for thus marring its
structure. But the story adds to what Michael Peterman has called the
children's "mutual treasure hoard."[41] Talking of nothing for days afterward but the story of Peter and Pavel — "our Pavel and Peter!" (56), as
Jim exclaims — Jim and Àntonia appropriate the Russians as mental
possessions in a common inner drama. Stories provide Jim with a way to
make another's otherwise alien experiences appropriable. Taking on a
life of their own, stories can be transmitted so as to seem to erase the distinction between one consciousness and another. When Jim dreams about
Pavel's story, imagining that he rides the bride's sledge, not through the
snowy hills of the Ukraine but "through a country that looked something
like Nebraska and something like Virginia" (61), he vicariously lives out
the story as he has made it over according to his own experiences.
Clearly, his imaginative revision of the events has little in common with
his friends' grisly memories of shrieking and mauled wedding guests.
Despite the fact that Pavel is left a guilt-ridden skeleton and Peter a
drooling idiot, the story has only a stimulating effect upon Jim and
Àntonia, who, like the children of "Far Island," incorporate others as
"stage properties of the imagination." As if the story and its characters
belonged as imaginative property only to them, Jim recalls, "We did not
tell Pavel's secret to anyone, but guarded it jealously — as if the wolves
of the Ukraine had gathered that night long ago, and the wedding party

been sacrificed, to give us a painful and peculiar pleasure" (61). Imagining that the lives of all those people had been sacrificed just to heighten his inner life, Jim exhibits the egoistic imagination of the child. Safely removed from the horror, he experiences pain as pleasure. Indeed, regardless of how dangerous or tragic the event — be it a bitter blizzard or Mr. Shimerda's suicide — Jim appropriates it as if it were a miracle staged for his imaginative entertainment.

Jim's incorporation of Peter and Pavel as characters in his mind is paradigmatic of his appreciation for people in the novel as a whole. Like Frances Harling, Jim carries people "in [his] mind as if they were characters in a book or a play" (150). He casts the hired hands Jake and Otto as "Arctic explorers" (65), and his grandfather, with his long white beard and oracular voice, as an "Arabian sheik" (12) or a biblical prophet. In the very first scene, Jim assigns such a fictional role to Otto Fuchs, who meets him at the train station. Although Otto's savage scar and twisted mustache give him a sinister look that might well frighten a child, Jim is pleased by his appearance because he imagines that it conforms to the stereotype of the desperado in the dime novel he has been reading. As Jim rejoices when Otto appears, "He might have stepped out of the pages of 'Jesse James.' ... He looked lively and ferocious ... as if he had a history" (6). Jim never cares to find out Otto's actual history, preferring to invent one for him. Throughout the rest of Jim's childhood scenes, life seems to step right out of the pages of storybooks. Jim's sense of the exotic is enhanced by the literature he has read. By reading *Robinson Crusoe* or *The Swiss Family Robinson* — children's books about conquering inhospitable environments — Jim is able to fictionalize his own experience, as if it were a romantic narrative equally as "adventurous" (66). As soon as a novel like *Robinson Crusoe* allows Jim to conform reality to the idea in his mind, it has fulfilled its escapist purpose, and he sets it aside, secure in the illusion that life as portrayed in the novel "seemed dull compared with ours" (100).

Although, in the introduction, Jim claims that his manuscript "hasn't any form," we can see the Christmas tree that the Burdens decorate as an emblem of the novel's structure that ultimately lies within Jim's memory. Hung with popcorn and candles and the Austrian paper ornaments sent by Otto's mother, "Our tree," Jim recalls, "became the talking tree of the fairy tale; legends and stories nestled like birds in its branches. Grandmother said it reminded her of the Tree of Knowledge" (83). Though not in a religious context, the tree does signify a "tree of knowledge," for the legends and stories nestled in its branches are emblematic of Jim's own branching consciousness. Within Jim's mind, people, like the ornaments on the tree, become fixed as characters out of various stories and legends, treasured for their imaginative value. Marilyn Callander has noted that Jim "sees his past in the simple and definite forms and lines, the clear colors, the juxtaposed absolutes of a fairy tale."[42] As Jim later recollects his friends Jake and Otto "exactly as they looked" (83) about the tree, we might say that he envisions them as clearly and as simply as the cut-out hanging figures. Above all, Jim's mission in the novel is to appropriate Àntonia as a momento of the past. Cather wrote in a letter to Carrie Miner that Àntonia was no more than a figure upon which to hang other associations.[43] Less a person to be known than a figure to be imaginatively constructed, Àntonia is, like the Christmas tree itself, precious to Jim as a symbol upon which to hang his other memories of the past.

After the opening childhood idyll, in which Jim and Àntonia harmoniously coexist as one consciousness, we can plot their relationship according to a series of ruptures followed by reunions: whenever Àntonia tries to assert her own individuality apart from Jim, Jim renounces the friendship; conversely, whenever Àntonia accommodates herself to Jim's imaginative ideal, he seeks a reunion. Although Jim's attitude towards Àntonia strikes us as self-serving, Cather affirms his power in the relationship as necessary to foster his imagination.[44] In an 1893 article on a play called "Friends," Cather attacked a relationship between two of the characters on the grounds that "one man's loving another man better than himself ... is a beautiful idea, perhaps, but it does not exist outside of girls' boarding schools" (WP, 28). Denigrating selflessness as a sentimental feminine cliché, Cather boldly chooses a male model of friendship based on self-interest. "The fact is," she affirms, "we all love ourselves very much more than we do any other being on earth. We like other people as they administer to our vanity or amusement" (WP, 29). Certainly, Jim reveals that his love for Àntonia is as selfish and conditional as that which Cather describes, for he likes Àntonia only insofar as she flatters him or provides him with imaginative stimulation.

From the beginning of the novel, when Mr. Shimerda appeals to Jim to "Te-e-ach, te-e-ach my An-tonia!" (27), Jim is authorized to teach Àntonia not only how to speak English but, more importantly, how to speak the script he assigns her as a character in his imagination. Jim first disapproves of Àntonia when she begins to outgrow her designated role as his obedient pupil. "Much as I liked Àntonia," he says, "I hated a superior tone that she sometimes took with me" (43). Though as a girl four years Jim's senior and more worldly in her experience, Àntonia has a right to carry herself as his superior, Jim's imaginative investment in the relationship depends on *his* superiority. Luckily for Jim, a timely adventure properly humbles Àntonia, so that, as he recalls with relief, "Before the autumn was over, she began to treat me more like an equal and to defer

to me in other things than reading lessons." Ironically, Jim regards
Àntonia as his "equal" only when she plays the role of his deferential
subordinate.[45] He reestablishes the balance of power in his favor when he
kills a huge rattlesnake. What begins as a light-hearted exploration of the
"underground connections" (44) of the prairie-dog town ends as a nightmarish confrontation with the repressed adolescent fears "below the surface" (45) of his own unconscious. For much of my interpretation, I am
indebted to Blanche Gelfant in her seminal article "The Forgotten
Reaping-Hook: Sex in *My Àntonia*." Gelfant insightfully argues that
Jim's battle with the snake dramatizes his efforts to conquer the threat of
sexuality that might divide him from his preadolescent union with
Àntonia.[46] Indeed, as Jim says, the snake "was not merely a big snake,"
for in "his abominable muscularity, his loathsome, fluid motion, ... [and]
disgusting vitality" (45), he represents the phallic incarnation of a more
archetypal "evil." According to the novel's wish fulfillment, Jim rewrites
human history so as to keep the Garden unfallen by killing the snake. By
reflecting in retrospect that "in reality it was a mock adventure; the game
was fixed for me by chance" (49–50), Jim denies that the old snake ever
presented a threat at all and so denies all the terrifying unconscious
impulses that it embodied. Himself "fixing" the game by his own desire,
Jim transforms Àntonia into the loyal childhood friend who "never took a
supercilious air with me again" (50). Insisting that nobody in this country
had ever killed such a big snake, Àntonia flatters Jim that he is "just like
big mans" (46). Gelfant sees irony in the fact that while Àntonia pro-
claims Jim a man, she "keeps him a boy,"[47] for she validates only a
pseudo-initiation into manhood that actually disguises a return to
childhood.

The snake-killing episode is paradigmatic of Jim's future efforts to
bring Àntonia under his spiritual authority. With each successive break in
their relationship, however, Jim finds it increasingly difficult to bridge
the gap between Àntonia's consciousness and his own. Àntonia next
rebels against Jim's authority when he tries to get her to go to a good
school, an effort which masks his continuing desire to reform her in his
image. Knowing that she is needed at home to till the fields, Àntonia
asserts, "I ain't got time to learn. I can work like mans now" (123). We
admire Àntonia for maturely sacrificing her own education in order to
work for the family bread, but for Jim, such necessities as feeding a
family have no reality. He would have Àntonia cultivate only the imaginative soil of the "big and free" (48) country of childhood. As if taking a
narrative revenge against Àntonia for her betrayal of him, Jim portrays
her as increasingly vulgar and coarsened. He intolerantly recalls how
"disagreeable" it was that "Àntonia ate so noisily now, like a man, and

... yawned often at the table and kept stretching her arms over her head, as if they ached" (125). Portraying Àntonia as having "lost" all her "nice ways," Jim is angry with her not only for having lost the genteel manners of her father but for having lost a respect for his refining tutelage. His recollection of visiting her one day while she was plowing reveals the real cause of his injury: "She stopped at the end of a row to chat for a moment, then gripped her plough-handles, clucked to her team, and waded on down the furrow, making me feel that she was now grown up and had no time for me" (126). In his childish demand for exclusive attention, Jim construes Àntonia's adult responsibility as her cardinal offense: she dares to "grow up" and leave him behind.

Once again, however, the game is fixed for Jim's victory when his grandfather hires Àntonia to work for the family, thereby "sav[ing]" (147) her from life's hard work so that she can remain an unspoiled icon. As a "hired girl," Àntonia, like Jake and Otto, becomes more deeply enlisted in the service of Jim's imagination. This time, the reunion takes place when Jim and Àntonia watch the storm together from the chicken coop. In fulfillment of Jim's desire, Àntonia once again reassures him of her loyalty by declaring that she "like[s] ... all things here" (140). Her wish that her father were still living implicitly reinstates Jim's paternal authority. Pleased by her confidence in him, Jim asks her why she isn't "always nice like this." Despite his claim to appreciate her "just like this; like yourself," Jim likes Àntonia because she satisfies his expectations of her. Finally, despite Jim's desire to pattern Àntonia's feelings after his own, the scene ends with the unsettling reminder that they are destined to live different lives. Àntonia's wish that "no winter ever come again" (140) reminds us that she lives in actual, seasonal time, vulnerable to loss and disappointment. By contrast, Jim's reassurance that "it will be summer a long while yet," reminds us that he desires to live outside of time in the eternal world of memory and imagination, where he is immune to loss and change. As Àntonia wistfully prophesies, "Things will be easy for you. But they will be hard for us."

Although when the Burdens move to town, Jim seems to adapt to a new kind of community, he really stays in the same social context as on the prairie; during the festive evenings at the Harlings' house, there are simply many children, instead of just two. In the Harlings' house with its "brightly lighted" rooms and "gay pictures on the walls" (175), Jim enters a make-believe world lit by the light of illusion. Mrs. Harling, who vows to "bring something out of that girl" and teach her "new ways" (153), becomes Àntonia's new teacher. But Mrs. Harling is really just a substitute teacher for Jim. Jim fully approves of Àntonia's employ at the Harlings because there she learns not "new ways" but the old ways of

childhood. Ann Romines rightly suggests that the Harling episode is psychologically rooted in "the child's initial pre-oedipal union with the
mother."[48] Both Mrs. Harling and Àntonia serve Jim's imagination as
mother figures who are themselves just big children. Living life in a
spirit of creativity and spontaneity, "they loved children and animals and
music, and rough play and digging in the earth. They liked to prepare
rich, hearty food and see people eat it; to make up soft white beds and to
see youngsters asleep in them" (180). Far from disciplining the children,
Mrs. Harling and Àntonia want only to indulge and entertain them.
During that first winter, when "every Saturday night was like a party"
(175), the child gets to be center stage: Jim and the other children act
charades, have a costume ball, learn to dance, and listen to Mrs. Harling
play old operas for them on the piano. Most gratifying to Jim, Àntonia
becomes transformed into a kind of Wendy from "Peter Pan," a child-
mother who constantly tells the children stories and sings to them.
Whereas Àntonia had not had time for Jim while plowing in the field,
now "she was never too tired to make taffy or chocolate cookies for us"
(175–76) whenever he and the other children so desire. For Jim, the Harling household is a never-never land where he does not have to grow up
to recognize any other claims but his own.

During this middle section of the novel, "The Hired Girls," Jim is
pleased with Àntonia when "her thoughts never seemed to stray outside
that little kingdom" (204–5). Inevitably, however, Àntonia does stray
once again outside the kingdom of Jim's jurisdiction and into the world.
The turning point comes when the dancing tent comes to town and, with
it, the unleashing of Àntonia's sexuality. At first, Jim loves the tent's
carnival atmosphere. Disguised as the scene where boys and girls "are
growing up" (193), the tent really provides one more playground where
Jim and the country girls can escape the "cold light" (173) of reality.
There the country girls dance with unbounded energy and shine out with
brilliant vitality so as to allow Jim to see them as incarnations of "the
light of youth" (192). Yet Àntonia's exposure in the tent leads to her
expulsion from the Harlings' protective care. After young Harry Paine,
who is just about to get married, tries to kiss Àntonia one evening on the
porch and a scuffle breaks out, the Harlings dismiss Àntonia from their
employ, and she goes to live with the disreputable moneylender Wick
Cutter and his wife. Jim continues to champion Àntonia, but only as long
as she remains as distrustful of sexuality as he. In fulfillment of Jim's
desire, Àntonia protects him, as he protects her, from the threat of sex.
Earlier, she had tried to warn him against the snake. Now, she tries to
warn him against the seductive Norwegian Lena Lingard. When Jim
gives Àntonia a kiss like the ones he gives Lena, she gets indignant and

vows to "scratch ... out" Lena's eyes if she should be up to any of her "nonsense" (224) with him. Far from feeling rebuffed, however, Jim is "proud" (225) of Àntonia, as if she had successfully passed a test that did credit to his good training of her. Significantly, Àntonia's high-minded rejection of sex heartens Jim that he can still take imaginative possession of her as his ideal; as he gratefully exclaims, "She was, oh, she was still *my* Àntonia!" (225, italics mine). Simultaneously, Willa Cather, through a kind of unconscious displacement, may have reassured herself that her beloved friend Isabelle was still, after all, "hers." By dramatizing Àntonia's budding sexuality and then undoing or denying it, Cather may have been acknowledging her friend's sexuality in hopes of removing its threat. As if Àntonia's sexuality were a reminder of facts of life that Cather could not escape, it keeps reemerging in the text, so that Cather was not able to give herself this final reassurance until the end of the novel after a series of disillusionments and evasions.

Jim describes "his" Àntonia when he proudly compares her to the other hired girls as "Snow-White in the fairy tale ... still 'fairest of them all'" (215). Whereas, in the fairy tale, the prince's kiss arouses Snow White to love and sexuality, Jim plays the role of an antiprince whose mission it is to keep Àntonia frozen in timeless purity and perfection, so that he does not have to wake from his childhood world.[49] But Àntonia does not remain in Jim's fictional sphere as Snow White for long. In her fear of Wick Cutter's lecherous advances, Àntonia convinces Jim to sleep in her bed at the Cutters for a night and thus unwittingly lures him into danger when Cutter, mistaking Jim for Àntonia, tries to rape him. As an "insane" (248) Cutter beats and chokes Jim into "a battered object" (249), the scene takes on such exaggerated violence that it seems not so much an expression of Cutter's fury at being deceived, as a projection of Cather's terror of sex as debased and sadistic. Surprisingly, Jim blames Àntonia for his wounding experience, confessing, "I felt that I never wanted to see her again. I hated her almost as much as I hated Cutter. She had let me in for all this disgustingness" (250). It doesn't matter to Jim that Àntonia herself has had nothing to do with the incident and remains untouched by it; he is angry that she has failed in her mission as his protector and, moreover, that she has allowed her symbolic role to be tarnished by being perceived as a sexual being through lustful male eyes.

Jim says that he never wants to see Àntonia again, and his words prove almost prophetic. The third section of the novel, taking Jim to the University at Lincoln, excludes Àntonia altogether and instead focuses on Jim's flirtation with another childhood friend, Lena Lingard. During the summer after his freshman year, Lena encourages Jim to go home to visit Àntonia. Instead, he goes to Harvard to finish his undergraduate

degree. When he finally does return to visit Àntonia, it is not until two
years later, by which time, Àntonia, having been shamefully seduced and
abandoned by her fiancé Larry Donovan, is an unwed mother in social
exile, suffering physical privations as she toils in the fields for her cruel
brother Ambrosch. But even though Àntonia needs him more than ever at
this critical point in her life, Jim meets her only briefly to confess his
feelings of devotion and then to say good-bye once again. He promises to
come back to see her soon. This time, however, he stays away for twenty
years. Àntonia's disappearance has bothered the novel's critics from the
beginning.[50] But to see the absence of Àntonia as a structural flaw
assumes that the novel is about the actual Àntonia in a dramatic relationship with Jim, rather than about Jim's imaginative relationship with her.
The outburst of Àntonia's sexuality — both in the Wick Cutter episode
and in her affair with Larry Donovan — leads Jim to banish her from his
thoughts and, hence, from the novel. Although Jim apparently leaves
home to attend the University of Nebraska and then Harvard, he really
leaves, as he says, "to shut Àntonia out of my mind" (298). Once Àntonia
develops her sexuality, Jim finds that the only way that he can hope to
repossess Àntonia as "his" once again is by excluding the real person
from his mind so as to reconstruct an ideal through the selective process
of memory. In a 1925 interview, Cather commented that she made the
"structural fault[s]" of *My Àntonia* deliberately, since "that was the way I
could best get my squint at her.... Sometimes too much symmetry kills
things" (WCP, 79). To have kept a sexual Àntonia on stage for the sake
of "symmetry," Cather, like Jim, would have had to compromise her idea
of her; the best way that she could "get" her character the way she
wanted her, as a part of her own mood, was to remove her from the
action of the story.

The third section of the novel, "Lena Lingard," telling the story of
Jim's schooling at the University at Lincoln and his flirtation with Lena,
seems at first irrelevant to Jim's relationship with Àntonia. But Jim's
education serves to teach him how to reappropriate Àntonia. His great
lesson is that characters possessed in the imagination are more valuable
than people. Such a lesson functions not as an initiation into new knowledge or experience but as a confirmation of Jim's old allegiance to the
ideal over the real. The emotional value of Jim's education is apparent in
his recollection that his teacher, Gaston Cleric, "introduced me to the
world of ideas ... [where] everything else fades for a time, and all that
went before is as if it had not been" (258). He finds that his new life of
the mind is inhabited by special people of his past, like Jake and Otto and
Russian Peter, who still accompany him, he reflects, as "all I had" — as
imaginative possessions that are undeniably his "own" (262). Such peo-

ple have survived into Jim's new life only because they have been reshaped and clarified in his memory as two-dimensional "figures" that project a flawless mental image. Likening these figures that "stood out strengthened and simplified" in his memory to "the image of the plough against the sun" (262), Jim recalls a famous image in the novel that has typically been seen as a symbol of a heroic agrarian life, but is more profoundly an emblem of the artist's idealizing imagination and memory.

Jim affirms that "whenever my consciousness was quickened, all those early friends were quickened within it" (262), as if he most vividly brings his old friends into existence as functions of his own thoughts. Asserting in his most openly narcissistic statement that "they were so much alive in me that I scarcely stopped to wonder whether they were alive anywhere else, or how" (262), Jim gives his subjective idea of his old friends such priority that he disregards their external existence altogether. His exclusive allegiance to the mental figures living within himself served Cather as a strategy by which to forget, or defend herself against, the complexities and disappointments of her real human relationships.

In his study at school, Jim fashions a secure world inhabited only by his highest and purest artistic aspirations. Inspired by the evening star that hangs like the lamp on the title page of old Latin texts, he "light[s] [his] wick in answer" (263). Unlike the lecherous Wick Cutter, who, as his name suggests, burns the wick of his sexual passions only to cut off his vitality, Jim extinguishes such sexual flames so as to light the "wick" of genius. To keep that inner lantern burning with the hard and gem-like flame of art, embodied in the star, Jim emblematically shuts the window against the world's distractions. He even symbolically excludes from the room all tokens of the social facade he assumes to meet the outer world. As he recalls, his wardrobe, with all his clothes, shoes, and hats, he "had pushed out of the way, and ... considered ... non-existent, as children eliminate incongruous objects when they are playing house" (259). Within his study, Jim is, indeed, a child within his playroom, ignoring all that does not bolster his sense of self.

And yet, into this mental sanctuary walks the most incongruous object of all — the sex queen Lena Lingard. Scantily clad and voluptuous while tending her cattle on the prairie, Lena had innocently attracted the farmer Ole Benson and driven his wife, Crazy Mary, so mad with jealousy that she vowed to chase Lena through the fields with a knife to "trim some of that shape" (168) off her. Lena enters the scene as a sexual temptation that Jim must resist; through a kind of displacement, Jim's ensuing flirtation with Lena helps him to confront and diminish the problem of sexuality that was too threatening to face directly in his relationship with Àntonia. After her first visit, Lena teasingly asks, "But maybe you have

all the friends you want. Have you? ... Have you?" (270). Jim has just affirmed that he "had" all the friends he needed in his own consciousness,
and Lena comes along to test that conviction. Ultimately, the interlude
serves to prove Jim right. By valuing a seductress, Jim seems to prove
the power of his imagination to appropriate even the most menacing reality. When he has accomplished this, he is ready to meet Àntonia again.
As we shall see, Jim's relationship with Lena in book 3 establishes the
pattern of his meeting with Àntonia in book 4 and again in the
conclusion.

Terence Martin has aptly described how Jim, throughout his narrative,
"makes a deliberate — and almost total — sacrifice of immediacy in
favor of the afterglow of remembrance."[51] Certainly, Jim sacrifices the
immediacy of Lena for the afterglow of her presence, for only after she
has left his room does Jim commune with her spirit as "something warm
and friendly in the lamplight" (270). Lena helps Jim to recover youthful
memories of her and the other hired girls. As Jim reflects, "When I
closed my eyes I could hear them all laughing — the Danish laundry
girls and the three Bohemian Marys. Lena had brought them all back to
me" (270). Though Jim would reject the reality of the poor girls toiling
and sweating over hot tubs, he embraces the cheerful image of them
laughing as suitable material for his private fantasy. Finally, when Jim
realizes that his old sensuous dream about Lena coming across the
harvest field seems "like the memory of an actual experience" (271), he
once again confirms the life in consciousness as the only real life after
all.

As Gelfant has argued, Jim's conversion of Lena into an idea makes it
safe to have a brief affair with her; like the snake-killing episode, this
initiation into sexuality is really nothing but a "mock-adventure," as
devoid of real passion as a game of pretend between children.[52] Rather
than court Lena, Jim merely plays with her, recalling how "I played with
Lena and Prince, I played with the Pole, I went buggy-riding with the old
colonel" (288). Gelfant points out that they not only play together but
spend most of their time going to see actual plays, which adds to the
make-believe quality of their affair. Recalling her own love as a child for
the opera house in Red Cloud, Cather wrote that living actors "can make
us forget who we are and where we are, can make us (especially the children) actually live in the story that is going on before us, can make the
dangers of that heroine and the desperation of that hero much more
important to us, for the time much dearer to us, than our own lives" (WP,
957). Similarly, Jim and Lena enjoy a performance of the tragic love
story "Camille" in order to forget the complications of their lives in Lincoln, Nebraska, and be transported to a gay and dazzling salon in Paris.

Jim recalls that he liked watching plays with Lena, for "everything was wonderful to her, and everything was true. It was like going to revival meetings with someone who was always being converted" (271). Lena is converted to Cather's faith in the superior reality of imaginative experi-ence; as Jim puts it at the end of his play-going, the "idea," after all, "is one that no circumstances can frustrate" (278). From the first scene of the novel, when Jim hid from Àntonia's pretty brown eyes behind his book of *Jesse James*, he has used various fictions behind which to hide from sex. Now, congratulating himself during the play that "Lena was at least a woman, and I was a man" (275), Jim defines adulthood as the capacity to feel deep emotions, although ironically, he enjoys the play so much precisely because its artifice allows him to escape the reality of the woman sitting next to him, as well as his own sexuality. Seeing the pun in Gaston Cleric's name, Gelfant writes that "Cleric's function is to guide Jim to renunciation of Lena, to offer instead the example of desire subli-mated to art."[53] Indeed, Cleric's warning to Jim, "You won't recover yourself while you are playing about with this handsome Norwegian" (289), confirms the most important lesson of Jim's life: that he must ab-jure real human relationships if he is to recover his soul. Possessing Lena most deeply as a fictional character on an inner stage, Jim unregretfully bids the flesh-and-blood woman goodbye and, in his studies at Harvard, rededicates himself to himself. His farewell completes his rehearsal for his later departure from Àntonia.

In the fourth section of the novel, "The Pioneer Woman's Story," Jim and Àntonia finally meet again after the three years that Jim was away at school. Their reunion is emotionally charged. Although Jim declares his love for Àntonia, he does not propose to marry her. His reserve has dis-turbed the novel's critics. E. K. Brown, for example, observes, "At the very center of [Jim's] relation with Àntonia there is an emptiness where the strongest emotion might have been expected to gather."[54] Yet, para-doxically, it is because of this very lack of a real social relation that Jim's most powerful emotion grows. As Jim avows in his most impassioned profession of love,

> Do you know, Àntonia, since I've been away, I think of you more often than of anyone else in this part of the world. I'd have liked to have you for a sweetheart, or a wife, or my mother or my sister — anything that a woman can be to a man. The idea of you is a part of my mind; you influence my likes and dislikes, all my tastes, hundreds of times when I don't realize it. You really are a part of me. (321)

In hopes of giving his attachment to Àntonia some permanence and legitimacy, Jim casts about for a socially defined and acceptable role for

Àntonia — sweetheart, wife, mother, or sister. However, the list of possibilities reads as a kind of multiple choice to which he knows the answer is "not one of the above." As a symbol in Jim's mind, Àntonia means more than can be contained by any conventional social or familial role. Jim chooses not to regard her even as an object of desire apart from him, but as an extension of his own being. Proclaiming, "You really are a part of me," Jim announces his successful imaginative possession of Àntonia as an "idea" that forms an inseparable part of his "mind." As if she influenced his choices and tastes even when he doesn't realize it, Jim casts Àntonia in the role of his creative muse, or inner guide of intuition. Although we assume that Jim professes his love for the woman at his side, he really professes his love for his memory of her, cherished most in solitude. The whole speech is given in the past tense, as Jim confesses the feelings he recalled for Àntonia while he was away at school. He left her to "recover" himself: indeed, his professed love for Àntonia disguises a deeper love of his own integrated psyche.

Though Jim claims such intimacy in his relationship with Àntonia, there is, as Rosowski has noted, "strikingly little of Àntonia in this meeting." [55] Àntonia's erasure from the scene does not undermine Jim's perception of her as unreliable, however. As Jim's alter ego, Àntonia seems willingly and gladly to share his consciousness, which suggests that Willa Cather herself was participating in Jim's seductive fantasy. Àntonia shows that she understands the real nature of the possession Jim elusively describes when she replies, "Ain't it wonderful, Jim, how much people can mean to each other? I'm so glad we had each other when we were little" (321). Àntonia and Jim both imagine that they "had each other" most completely when they were children, for as children, they still seemed to possess their own essential souls undivided from the world and from each other. Jim enjoys with Àntonia the same gratifying feeling that Douglass, in "The Treasure of Far Island," gains from his reunion with his childhood friend Margie. As Cather describes Douglass's renewed childhood bond, it is "a case of arrested development" that is unabashedly narcissistic:

> As he talked he felt the old sense of power, lost for many years; the power of conveying himself wholly to her in speech, of awakening in her mind every tint and shadow and vague association that was in his at the moment. He quite forgot the beauty of the woman beside him in the exultant realization of comradeship, the egoistic satisfaction of being wholly understood. (CSF, 273)

Similarly, Jim so successfully awakens in Àntonia's mind every "tint and shadow" that is in his own that he forgets her beauty in the egoistic satisfaction of recovering himself in the wholeness of his original identity. As he holds her hands to his heart, he recalls: "About us it was growing darker and darker, and I had to look hard to see her face, which I meant always to carry with me; the closest, realest face, under all the shadows of women's faces, at the very bottom of my memory" (322). Just as Alexandra Bergson had taken imaginative possession of the prairie when her tears had blinded her, so Jim appropriates Àntonia when the darkness blots out her actual presence. Imagining as he leaves that "a boy and girl ran along beside me, as our shadows used to do" (323), Jim reclaims Àntonia as the shadow that he himself cast as a boy.

Despite her personal loss, Àntonia accepts Jim's leaving as an incidental fact in their relationship. Even if he were to go away for good, she says, "That don't mean I'll lose you" (320), for she will keep him in her thoughts. In fact, Àntonia implies that Jim, like her dead father, will be even more vividly present to her in his absence. As she says of her father, "He is more real to me than almost anybody else. He never goes out of my life. I talk to him and consult him all the time. The older I grow, the better I know him and the more I understand him" (320). Keeping her dearest company with a ghost, as had Jim in an earlier scene, Àntonia reveals the eerie implications of Cather's imaginative life with characters of the mind: even dead people who can become fictional constructs can be more real than the living. Indeed, as Jim and Àntonia emblematically stand on Mr. Shimerda's grave, they are, in the terms of the real world, dead to each other already. Preceded by Peter, Pavel, Jake, Otto, Mr. Shimerda, and Lena, Àntonia says good-bye to Jim as the last in a long series of characters who have to become absent before they can become wholly present in Jim's appropriating consciousness. The disappearance of all of these characters fulfills Emerson's prophesy in *Nature* that once a friend, "like skies and waters," becomes "coextensive with our idea, ... it is a sign to us that his office is closing, and he is commonly withdrawn from our sight in a short time."[56] With an Emersonian egotism, Jim similarly disregards people once he has converted them into objects of thought; having fulfilled her usefulness to Jim as a stimulus to his imagination, Àntonia is withdrawn from his sight for twenty years. Cather provides a cosmic analogy to Jim's separation from Àntonia when she describes how the sun hung in the west while the moon rose in the east, so that "the two luminaries confronted each other across the level land, resting on opposite edges of the world" (322). Cather implies that even though Jim and Àntonia, like "the two luminaries" above them, will henceforth occupy different poles of experience, they will nonetheless be together as they hang in a kind of spiritual balance in each other's thoughts.

Underneath the scene's reverential nostalgia lies a bittersweet sense of loss that may be owing to Cather's own regretful renunciation of her friend Isabelle McClung; she may have been dramatizing her hope that she and Isabelle would keep each other in their thoughts despite the new distance that would separate them. We might consider Jim's appropriation of Àntonia according to another paradigm as well: the author's possession of her character, a possession that importantly helped Cather to bear dispossessing human relationships. Jim's appropriation of Àntonia as "a part" of him reenacts Cather's creation of her characters in a process she once described as a fusion of some external figure with the writer's self.[57] At one level, Jim's appropriation of Àntonia mirrors Cather's appropriation of the real-life Annie Pavelka as a character who "became part of her soul-stuff" (WCP, 122). As a figure from Jim's past who shared his life, Àntonia becomes a part of him, just as figures from Cather's past became a part of her. As she once wrote, "Our past becomes a part of us, it is in our blood" (WP, 359). More deeply, however, Àntonia became a part of Cather's psyche because she was her own creation. Writing to Dorothy Canfield Fisher that the components that went into her characterizations were her character, her self, and an unnamed something, she implies that the deepest bond she shared with her protagonists was her own romantic ego. Recalling the stolen interviews between Thea Kronborg and her second self in *The Song of the Lark*, Cather describes her life while writing as a series of secret appointments with her central character, who would so palpably appear beside her at a tea or a concert that she could feel the strength and warmth of his or her body.[58] As Cather wrote to H. L. Mencken, she knew her character Claude Wheeler in *One of Ours* as well as she knew her own blood relatives[59] because she had infused him with her own lifeblood.[60] As if she inhabited the skins of her characters, Cather wrote that she enjoyed restoring herself in their stronger and younger bodies to become someone better than herself.[61] When, finally, Jim symbolically completes his imaginative possession of Àntonia by claiming her as "my Àntonia," he enacts Cather's own triumphant claim upon her characters as her most prized possessions. Passionately addressing in her letters her favorite characters with the personal possessive pronoun[62] — her Professor, her Bishop, her Àntonia, and so on — Cather ultimately found in them the heightened sense of her own youthful vitality that she could not always find in other people. It is no wonder, then, that Cather looked to her own characters as her best friends. Friends in whom she had invested herself so as to mirror back to her an ideal self, and who could fill the emptiness left by other people so as never to disappoint or desert her, Cather's characters gave her what she valued as the perfect happiness of true companionship.[63]

When Jim returns a second time to see Àntonia, he explains his twenty-year absence by admitting, "In the course of twenty crowded years one parts with many illusions. I did not wish to lose the early ones. Some memories are realities, and are better than anything that can ever happen to one again" (328). Jim's willingness to lose touch with Àntonia so that he can keep her as his most valuable possession in memory — unaged and unchanged — seems selfish and, as even he admits, cowardly. When he does decide to see Àntonia again, he seems, on the surface, to have gained the courage to part with his illusions and to grant the inevitable passage of time. Some have seen the ending of the novel as proof of Jim's maturity and coming of age, as an older, sadder, and wiser Jim gives up his illusions about the past and admits the moral failures of his adolescence.[64] Far from offering Jim a sobering vision of reality, however, the last section of the novel functions as a wish fulfillment that affirms his memories and dreams. Writing to Fisher in 1922 that she put her faith in those things of which she dreamed,[65] Cather had the authorial power to bring such dreams into existence. We can best understand the twenty-year hiatus between the last two sections of the novel as the equivalent of the sixteen year hiatus in *O Pioneers!* Symbolically, that was a period of gestation, in which Alexandra imaginatively assimilated the land into consciousness until it yielded itself up to her during the harvest as an incarnation of her own youthful spirit. Similarly, the elided twenty years in *My Àntonia* serve Jim as a period in which to appropriate Àntonia in his imagination. So tenaciously does Jim cling to his illusions about Àntonia during these years that they miraculously take shape as reality. Finding that Àntonia still shares his consciousness, Jim lays claim once again to their mutual stock of memories, concluding his narrative with the jubilant assertion, "Whatever we had missed, we possessed together the precious, the incommunicable past" (372).

In the final chapters of the novel, Àntonia emerges as a strong character rendered by Jim — as "his" Àntonia.[66] He affirms that "Àntonia had always been one to leave images in the mind that did not fade — that grew stronger with time" (352). In fact, all of Jim's descriptions of Àntonia in this section are designed to prove that his idea of her has persisted against time, reality, and even Àntonia herself; his greatest triumph is that "everything was as it should be" (346), according to his memory. When Jim first sees Àntonia as she walks into the kitchen, he imaginatively transforms her from a "flat-chested" and "grizzled"(331) woman, who bears little resemblance to his ideal, into the woman who "was there" after all, "in the full vigour of her personality, battered but not diminished" (331–32). When Jim rejoices that "the changes grew less apparent to me, her identity stronger" (331), he imaginatively erases the significant history written on her wrinkled brow so as to overlook her past experiences and confirm instead his cherished memory of her.

Àntonia has been rendered toothless and scarred by toil and hardship, but paradoxically, her physical bruises encourage Jim's imaginative appropriation of her, for her conspicuous lack of sexual appeal means that he can lay claim to another, more sentimental image. In reality, Jim hated to see Àntonia sweat in the fields, but now he enjoys his memory of her "coming in with her work-team along the evening sky-line" as one of a series of "pictures" that are "fixed there like the old woodcuts of one's first primer" (353). Unlike naturalistic portraits, such as those by Zola, "pictures," Cather felt, were intended to convey the writer's own point of view or mood. She believed that children most easily acquired such mental pictures. The child-artist Jim creates his most vivid mental picture of Àntonia as a woman standing in her garden. Incarnating "that something which fires the imagination" (353), Àntonia plays the role of the muse whose "inexplicable presence" inspired Cather's own creative impulse. If Àntonia lends herself to attitudes that Jim recognizes as "true," then that is ultimately because Cather recognizes her pose as one that she had created for herself before. Cather claims in Àntonia the primordial physical vitality and romantic ego that she had invested in her previous alter egos, Alexandra Bergson and Thea Kronborg. In writing *My Àntonia*, she had lost the power to project herself as the heroine who possessed a vital "something"; instead, she, like Jim, seems to be in search of a lost youth that is invested in another; Jim's imaginative idealization of Àntonia in the orchard reassures Cather that she still has the power to create strong characters through whom she can vicariously recover a sense of her own inner life.

The last section of the novel celebrates the earth-mother Àntonia,[67] but more deeply, Jim's memories of himself as a boy. Even when Àntonia takes him to see the family fruit cave, it appears that what has been best preserved there is not spiced plums or strawberry jam but the even more delicious memory of exuberant childhood, released when the children "all came running up the steps together, big and little, tow heads and gold heads and brown, and flashing little naked legs; a veritable explosion of life out of the dark cave into the sunlight" (338–39). As "a sight any man might have come far to see" (352), this display of youthful energy best embodies the goal of Jim's journey in the novel. Whereas he and Àntonia had run across the prairie as two, now her children run across the land in their image as eleven.

As Rosowski has pointed out, scenes from Jim's childhood recur: he arrives by wagon as he once had as a boy; he finds a cheerful security in

Àntonia's sunny kitchen that is reminiscent of his grandmother's; he witnesses a great explosion of youth from the fruit cellar, as he had from the Shimerda's cave; he lies in the hayloft as warm and contented as he once was in the garden; and so on.[68] In addition, the evenings of entertainment recreate the atmosphere at the Harlings' as the children "look to [Àntonia] for stories and entertainment as we used to do" (351). Àntonia tells stories as she always has in order to satisfy Jim's desire to be entertained; it is his creative authority, upheld by Cather, that dictates the program of the evening.[69] Now not only Àntonia but her whole family charm him; Yulka and Leo play the violin and Nina does a dance. To please him most of all, Àntonia brings out the family photographs. Tellingly, these are not photographs of her family, as we would expect, but of all the people in Jim's past. In her book *On Photography*, Susan Sontag writes that "photographs really are experience captured, and the camera is the ideal arm of consciousness in its acquisitive mood. To photograph is to appropriate the thing photographed."[70] Jim acts as the photographer who appropriates Àntonia as a framed image in consciousness, retouched and redeemed, against time. That Àntonia's family applauds the pictures of Jim and his old friends "as if these characters in their mother's girlhood had been remarkable people" (349) further validates the reality of the fiction of Jim's past. Although in real life people had not always conformed to the mythic roles that Jim had assigned them, now, as Àntonia's family looks back at the past through his eyes, people assume their proper characters. As the children cheer for the picture of Frances Harling in her riding costume, "one could see that Frances had come down as a heroine in the family legend" (350). Similarly, as portrayed by the photographs, Mr. Harling is passed down as an imperious lord, Jake as a comical cowboy, and Otto as a ferocious desperado. Although in the midst of the family feud, Àntonia had hated Jake, now, as she looks at his picture, she takes Jim's view that he and Otto were "good fellows" (351). Most importantly, the tintype of "an awkward-looking boy in baggy clothes" (350) allows Jim to repossess his own youth. He, too, has been reconstructed through the photographic portrait as a hero. Although in reality Jim's killing of the snake was a lucky accident, Àntonia's sons so applaud the embellished story — "sometimes mother says six feet and sometimes she says five" (351) — that they elevate Jim's status as a valiant dragon slayer.

Despite Jim's neglect of them for the past twenty years, Àntonia and the children worship him with "simple gratitude" (345). Àntonia has kept her promise to Jim that, even in his absence, he would continue to be present to her and her family. According to Jim's wish fulfillment, she has even raised her family as a kind of memorial to him and the old days.

As she says, "I declare Jim, I loved you children almost as much as I love my own. These children know all about you and Charley and Sally, like as if they'd grown up with you" (334). By returning to Àntonia, who still loves him as if he were her own little boy, Jim finds in her the absolutely good protective mother of the fairy tales that brings his journey to its happiest resolution.[71] Moreover, with her children, who remember him as one of their own playmates, Jim maintains the fantasy of being a child himself all over again as if time had stood still. Like her mischievous and frolicsome son Leo, who was born on Easter day, all of Àntonia's sons serve to celebrate a resurrection — the rebirth of Jim's boyhood ego. As Jim walks with the boys towards the sunset, he rejoices that he feels "like a boy in their company"; merging once again with his shadow, "moving along at my right, over the close-cropped grass" (345), he is more importantly restored through them to the company of his original self. After he leaves Àntonia, he dreams of all the trips he plans to take with her boys through the Bad Lands and up the Stinking Water river. In a remarkable statement, he reflects, "There were enough Cuzaks to play with for a long while yet. Even after the boys grew up, there would always be Cuzak himself!" (370). Turning even Cuzak, his potential rival for Àntonia's attention, into a preadolescent boy, Jim makes plans for the future that recapitulate the past.

When Jim moves to town, he finds the river "compensation for the lost freedom of the farming country" (145); subsequently, he continues to find various playgrounds that compensate him for the lost freedom of childhood. Jim's play can serve as a paradigm for Cather's writing of the novel. Unlike real life, the playground of the page was a space that Cather controlled according to her own rules. As she wrote to George Seibel in 1932, she liked to feel that writing was her own game, a kind of child's play as amusing as a little boy's playing Indian.[72] Exclaiming to Mr. Milton Graff what splendid fun it was to play out the play in her stories, Cather found a childlike satisfaction in working out her fictions just as she wanted them.[73] For Cather, as for Jim, the "game was fixed" so that she could win back a sense of the power she imagined that she had exerted over reality as a child; in her game of fiction, as in Jim's, the odds are against growing up. Cather's comment on Ernest Seton-Thompson that "his enthusiasm for that country is at once that of an artist and a boy" (WP, 838) equally well describes her own childlike enthusiasm for her homeland in Nebraska, as she expressed it in a 1921 interview: "I loved the country where I had been a kid, where they still called me 'Willie' Cather" (WCP, 37). By playing out the play in My Àntonia, Cather, like Jim, could become that blissful boy once more.

In the last chapter of the novel, after Jim says good-bye to Àntonia and her family, he leaves as if to face the world and the future. His day in Black Hawk is "disappointing" (369) because it returns him to the real world of time and change — old friends have died, or have moved away; strange children play in the Harlings' yard; old familiar trees have been cut down. But Jim's journey doesn't end in Black Hawk; he has a more important destination. Walking along the faint wagon trail over which he had first ridden into the wild country as a boy, Jim

> had the sense of coming home to myself, and of having found out what a little circle man's experience is. For Àntonia and for me, this had been the road of Destiny; had taken us to those early accidents of fortune which predetermined for us all that we can ever be. Now I understood that the same road was to bring us together again. Whatever we had missed, we possessed together the precious, the incommunicable past. (371–72)

Jim's phrase — "whatever we had missed" — reminds us that Jim has deliberately missed sharing most of the central events of Àntonia's life: her poverty and trials growing up on the farm, her grief over her father's death, her shame over her abortive affair and pregnancy, her marriage, her raising of her family, her growing old. Only because Jim has over-looked these differences between himself and Àntonia has he been able, in his view, to share with her a more precious and ineffable "possession" — an ideal childhood freedom and innocence. With an idealizing and selective memory, Jim imagines that both he and Àntonia "were bedded down in the straw" (371) of the wagon together as he entered the prairie country for the first time. In reality, however, only he occupied that nest. Even then, in that primordial past, Àntonia was on a different road. Àntonia alone has traveled the "road of Destiny" with its "accidents of fortune," for she has traveled the road of experience; Jim, by contrast, has traveled the road of desire. Àntonia herself is not the destination of Jim's road but a facilitating signpost towards a goal that is further back in time. Like Alexandra Bergson or Thea Kronborg, Jim most profoundly takes the road home so as to come home to his original self; once he finds that "first road" (370) where he started from, his journey is com-plete, his story over.

The ending of *My Àntonia* reminds us of "what a little circle" Cather's experience as an artist was also. In a letter to Fisher in 1922, she won-dered nostalgically whether life's endings were ever as perfect as our beginnings.[74] Though Cather could not always make a happy ending in life, she could in art. She wrote her novels as means towards their ends; as she once said, "In some books I have done more careful planning than in others, but always the end was seen from the beginning, and in each case it was the end that I set out to reach — I mean ... the feeling of the end, the mood in which I should leave my characters and in which I my-self should say good-by to them" (WCP, 171). For Cather, "the end was seen from the beginning" because the end was the beginning; while seeming to move forward in a linear temporal progression, her novels resolve with happy endings that return us to the "simple and concrete beginnings" (SL, 480) known in childhood. When, at the end of *My Àntonia,* Jim rejoices that "the feelings of that night were so near that I could reach out and touch them with my hand" (371), Cather celebrated having found the "feeling of the end" that she had "set out to reach" — the exultant feeling of self-possession that she imagined having known as a child.

6

"Strong in Attack but Weak in Defence": Defending the Usurped Territory in *A Lost Lady*

The novels Cather wrote in the middle of her career — *A Lost Lady* (1923) and *The Professor's House* (1925) — are, at one level, shrill indictments of "the ugly crest of materialism"[1] that stamped the era of the 1920s. In her portraits of Ivy Peters, the greedy land speculator in *A Lost Lady*, or of Louie Marsellus, the gaudy consumer in *The Professor's House*, Cather created a new breed of character — the commercial villain — who seemed to reflect the vulgar prosperity of the times. Cather herself tried to account for the bitter, querulous tone of these novels as her response to the decadence of the current age when she wrote in the Prefatory Note to *Not Under Forty*, "The world broke in two in 1922 or thereabouts" (NUF, v). In her essay "Nebraska: The End of the First Cycle," she explains her view of this seeming watershed in history as the decay of values between two generations of pioneers who settled the West: the idealistic first generation, which quested for freedom, romance, beauty, and sentiment; and the corrupt second generation, which sought only material comfort and snug success.[2] In her novels of this period, the world similarly seems to break in two between the noble ideals of the older generation and the crass ambitions of the younger; indeed, *A Lost Lady*, the tale of how Captain Forrester, the courageous pioneer who homesteaded the land, is displaced by Ivy Peters, the unscrupulous pioneer of the next generation, seems meant to epitomize a larger historical drama. In fact, the novel has been traditionally read as a chronicle of the decline of the West.[3] Taken as real history, however, Cather's discussion of the two generations of pioneers in her "Nebraska" essay and *A*

Lost Lady must strike us as faulty and naive. Despite her contempt for those in the second generation for playing "the game of getting on in the world,"[4] it was only by playing such a high-risk game — called survival — that men and women were able to domesticate the wilderness. I do not believe, however, that Cather is talking about actual history in these works. Her chronology is her own fiction. Cather's approval in her "Nebraska" essay of the first pioneers who valued "poetry" rather than the "market-report"[5] makes not a historical but an aesthetic distinction. She indicts all those who concern themselves with the practical, utilitarian ends of this world rather than with the beauty of the life of the imagination. In her division between the first and second generation of pioneers, Cather historicizes an ahistorical distinction between idealists, who live for the sake of the spirit, and materialists, who live for the sake of the world. Cather's condemnation of a second generation of pioneers allows her to uphold the fantasy that once upon a time people inhabited an unfallen paradise of imaginative ideals, invulnerable to the terms of the real world that she wanted to deny.

Cather's novels of the 1920s are similarly divided between two groups of characters: the superior artists and the common philistines, who assert competing claims for possession of the world. If these novels can be said to have any "plots," they take shape as dramatic conflicts between two kinds of ownership: an imaginative appropriation and a material possession of nature. Thus, in *A Lost Lady*, the narrator, Niel Herbert, vies with the corrupt Ivy Peters for "possession" of the estate at Sweet Water and its mistress, the lovely Marian Forrester; in *The Professor's House*, Professor St. Peter contends with his grasping family for "possession" of the memory and fortune of the young westerner, Tom Outland; in the novel's inset story, Tom Outland, in turn, argues with his friend, Roddy Blake, over the value of the Mesa and its artifacts; and so on. In a letter to Sergeant, describing how news of World War I had broken in on her vacation in the Southwest in 1914, Cather lamented that the powers of the world seemed motivated by a greedy desire for possession of material things.[6] If, in real life, it seemed to Cather that possession was determined by the power to take, in her fiction she redefined possession as the power to be. But, whereas in Cather's earlier works like *O Pioneers!*, imaginative possession of people and places was made incontestable by the sheer force of the claimant's personality, in these novels of Cather's middle period, the contest for possession is not so easily won. Niel Herbert and Professor St. Peter can be seen as disillusioned artists who try to appropriate an ideal figure or place only to be defeated by the stronger worldly claims of others.

Cather herself is waging the fiercest battle in these novels in order to preserve the threatened borderlands of her imagination. By the 1920s, the boundaries of Cather's art no longer seemed to surround the self so invulnerably as they once had. Though, as many of her letters and her war novel *One of Ours* suggests, Cather was disenchanted by World War I and the garish prosperity that followed it, she felt more deeply alienated by difficulties in her own life. She was nearing fifty, and, as is evident in *The Professor's House,* which she began writing in 1923, she was suffering from a kind of midlife crisis or "menopausal depression."[7] As James Woodress and Merrill Skaggs have discussed, Cather's dissatisfaction can in part be explained by the poor critical reception in 1922 of *One of Ours*, a novel that was attacked for sentimentalizing warfare.[8] Cather's friends in Nebraska were outraged at her satiric presentation of her home state. Considering Cather's high standards for herself, her competitiveness, and her desire for public approval, we can see how she may have overreacted to the bad reviews. As Skaggs insightfully reasons, Cather would have "lost the energizing belief that the universe is just, and that her own best efforts would be rewarded. She also lost her illusions that she could control her own relations to her public, her work, and her artistic achievements."[9] In addition to her disappointment in her career, Cather suffered a more personal disappointment: her resentment against an unjust universe in 1922 dated back to the marriage of Isabelle McClung in 1916. For all of these reasons, Cather's assertion that "the world broke in two" is, as a generalization about history, misleading, but as a reference to her own view of her life and art as she projected it upon history, it is revealing. Cather's spatial metaphor is suggestive of another spatial metaphor — the aesthetic world of her novel démeublé. Somehow, the four walls safely surrounding the artist's single passion had crumbled, leaving her disunited and exposed to external forces. From the beginning of her career, Cather had conceived of the world in transcendental terms as a dichotomy between the "me" and the "not me." At its most fulfilling, the experience of writing had always allowed Cather the sense of escaping to a world unified around her own ego. Yet, after she finished *One of Ours* in 1922, she suffered from a new sense of vulnerability. She wrote to Dorothy Canfield Fisher that she detested the interval between books, when she no longer had an insulating buffer between herself and the irritations of the world.[10] As suggested by the Wordsworthian refrain of her letters that the world was too much with her,[11] Cather's world increasingly broke in two when she could no longer effectively exclude life itself from her sovereign kingdom of art. Ultimately, the division Cather registers is not between a real historical past and a present, a before and an after, but between her sense of inner and outer life.

In her novels of the 1920s, Cather is forced to concede once again that life is a two-term affair, divided between the self and the world of others, but whereas she had clung to this realization in her first novel, *Alexander's Bridge*, for its saving sense of perspective, she now defies it as a moral outrage to the soul. We can largely explain the hostile and pessimistic tone of these novels as the expression of an artist who found it increasingly difficult to make the world yield itself to her as the raw material for her imaginative consumption. Harold Bloom has insightfully remarked of Cather's nostalgic vision that "her essential imaginative knowledge was of loss, which she interpreted temporally, though her loss was aboriginal, in the Romantic mode of Wordsworth, Emerson, and all their varied descendants. The glory that had passed away belonged not to the pioneers but to her own transparent eyeball, her own original relation to the universe." [12] Cather's nostalgia for the more romantic and heroic "pioneer era" of the past conceals a deeper nostalgia for another era with which it corresponded: the era of her own youth. Cather found in history an analogy to her own experience because she felt "she belonged to the earlier half" (WC: AM, 159) of her own career when her imaginative world still seemed dominated by the self. In the guise of attacking the materialistic villains of the 1920s who usurp possession of the world and degrade an ideal historic past, Cather is more profoundly attacking all of the forces that have robbed her of her claim to the imaginative territory of her art, dedicated to the bygone ideals of childhood.

Cather's critics have defined the conflict in *A Lost Lady* and *The Professor's House* as one between selfless idealists and selfish material-ists. [13] In my view, however, this distinction oversimplifies the nature of Cather's characters and the issues over which they struggle. Cather's artist-claimants themselves have a stake in the world, and in many ways they appear as self-interested as their materialistic antagonists. Though portrayed in a negative light, the materialistic claimant at least provides for the financial, physical, and social needs of other people, whereas the imaginative claimant often disregards the material needs of others in his or her exclusive allegiance to the needs of his or her own imagination. Whereas the commercial degenerate is portrayed as wanting to hoard material or physical things — land, houses, jewelry, a woman's body — the artist-claimant greedily tries to appropriate the very genius of the land or the very consciousness of other people as a mirror to the self.

At a psychological level, the rival's claims are dictated by the selfish desires of the imaginative claimant who enacts the artist figure's fears of being displaced. We can best understand the origin of this fear in Cather's early story "The Enchanted Bluff" (1909). Written long before the commercial villains appeared in her fiction, this story suggests that the competitive struggle for possession in the later novels dramatizes Cather's own frustrated childhood fantasies. "The Enchanted Bluff" fore-shadows the plots of both *A Lost Lady* and *The Professor's House*. The boy narrator longs for an "undisputed possession" (CSF, 69) of the Enchanted Bluff, to be recreated most obviously in *The Professor's House*. One night, however, when the boy had gone to sleep, he "dreamed about a race for the Bluff," and "awoke in a kind of fear that other people were getting ahead of me and that I was losing my chance" (CSF, 76). The boy's paranoia of being supplanted by others is inspired by his own intense need to be the sole ruler of the bluff. Similarly, I would argue that the fear of displacement enacted in her later fiction reveals Cather's emotional need to be the single proprietor of her imaginative estate, a need that became more desperate as she grew older. Although the boy's fear of being dispossessed turns out to be only a bad dream, it proves to be a nightmarish reality for the protagonists of Cather's middle phase. In a sense, twenty years after "The Enchanted Bluff," Cather imagines that the rivals have gotten to the prized place first, and so she must find ways to triumph over them. We might say that through her degrading characterizations of the artists' antagonists, Cather exacts a sort of narrative revenge. The odious portraits of Ivy Peters and Louie Marsellus are owing not to their materialism per se but to their threatening roles as competitors for the imaginative kingdom. We might even say that Cather portrays them as materialistic precisely because they are usurpers — usurpers whom she imagines to have an inferior claim. Most deeply, Cather invents her materialistic villains as scapegoats on whom she can blame the failure of her dreams of imaginative possession. The real enemy Cather's protagonists must combat in these novels is not materialistic others but the inescapable laws of material reality.

As the first novel Cather wrote after her "world broke in two," *A Lost Lady* reveals the psychological impulses behind her fictionalized struggle for "possession." Most of the novel concerns the efforts of the central consciousness, Niel Herbert, to appropriate Marian Forrester, the charming woman who had filled his childhood with beauty, romance, and social distinction. But to understand Niel's efforts to recover his lost lady, we first need to understand how the career of his mentor, Captain Forrester, sanctions his claims. Niel wishes to preserve Marian as a member of "the pioneer period to which she belonged" (169), a period personified by her husband, the Captain, whom the novel more deeply appoints as its moral custodian. Cather wrote in a letter to Zoë Akins that the integral core of the book lay in the character of Captain Forrester.[14] As the great pioneer conqueror of the first generation, the Captain is himself a kind of surrogate for Cather, resembling her "first generation" of pioneering protagonists who took imaginative possession of the world for the self. The Captain's story offers an analogy to Cather's fiction and career up until this time: it not only rehearses the successes of her former imaginative claimants but foretells their downfall, as other materialistic claimants displace them. As herself the literary creator of that lineage of early pioneers, who formed "a courteous brotherhood, strong in attack but weak in defence" (106), Cather admits that she has entered a less triumphant phase in her career, in which she is forced to defend her imaginative territory in a losing battle. As embodied in the invalid Captain, her former role in the fiction as the founding artist seems outworn and ineffective.

Like Cather's own story, the story of how the Captain came to found his imaginative property has already occurred; in a sense, it ended in the distant, idealized past before the novel opens. The Captain's relation of "his narrative" (52) during a dinner party suggests that we should consider his past as a story or invention. As implied by Marian's introductory remarks — even "if some of us have heard it, we can hear it again" (54) — we, as readers, are asked to listen indulgently to a story that we have repeatedly heard before, beginning with *O Pioneers!* A story that began as "an ideal life for a young man" (52), it shares with Cather's previous novels the benefits of a wish fulfillment. As the young man journeyed west across an endless sea of grass, feeling that "one day was like another," he felt no vulnerability nor sense of tedium, as historical reality and Cather's own biography would have made likely, but only the glorious freedom and inexhaustible abundance offered him in "good hunting, plenty of antelope and buffalo, boundless sunny sky, boundless plains of waving grass" (52). As if he were a pioneer with a mission as noble and a vision as prophetic as Alexandra Bergson's on her ride home to the Divide, the Captain instantly recognized the beautiful hill where the willows grew as the promised land for his estate. Like his forbear, the Captain subdued the wild prairie through a simple act of will when he "drove the stake into the ground to mark the spot where he wished to build" (52–53). A precursor to another theologist of the will, Jay Gatsby, who conforms his life to the "Platonic conception of himself,"[15] the Captain reflects in later years, "I had planned it in my mind, pretty much as it is today" (53). For all his sympathy with Gatsby, Fitzgerald ironically exposes the naiveté and delusiveness of Gatsby's self-created fictions whereas, by contrast, Cather nostalgically participates in the Captain's vanished dreams as a splendid reality.

The Captain claimed his "property" at Sweet Water, as Alexandra Bergson had claimed the Divide, for its imaginative and aesthetic, rather than its material or practical, value. The reason he selected the site for his house was simply "because it looked beautiful to him, and he happened to like the way the creek wound through his pasture" (11). Although the house, "stripped of its vines and denuded of its shrubbery" (10–11), presented a stark bareness, the Captain was an idealist dedicated to cultivating the illusions that disguise the ugliness of everyday facts. Long before he could return to build his house, he inhabited its paradisal groves and gardens in his dreams, claiming it as a sanctuary from the sickness and responsibilities of his real life. Ultimately, the beauty of the Captain's property, like the beauty of Alexandra's farm, reflects the heroic grandeur of his own genius. Through Niel's eyes, "The Forrester place, as every one called it, was not at all remarkable; the people who lived there made it seem much larger and finer than it was" (10). Within such an estate, life could be transformed to contain the magical possibilities enjoyed only in fairy tales. As a boy, Niel likes seeing the Captain survey the extent of his kingdom, as if his look seemed to say, "A man's house is his castle" (73). But to protect this "private" (11) castle at this stage in her career, Cather needed to surround it with not one moat but two.

The escapist fantasy underlying Captain Forrester's claim to his land becomes most clear in his lofty conclusion:

> "Well, then, my philosophy is that what you think of and plan for day by day, in spite of yourself, so to speak — you will get. You will get it more or less. That is, unless you are one of the people who get nothing in this world. There are such people. I have lived too much in mining works and construction camps not to know that." He paused as if, though this was too dark a chapter to be gone into, it must have its place, its moment of silent recognition. "If you are not one of those, Constance and Niel, you will accomplish what you dream of most."

> "And why? That's the interesting part of it," his wife prompted him.

> "Because," he roused himself from his abstraction and looked about at the company, "because a thing that is dreamed of in the way I mean, is already an accomplished fact. All our great West has been developed from such dreams; the homesteader's and the prospector's and the contractor's. We dreamed the railroads across the mountains, just as I dreamed my place on the Sweet Water. All these things will be everyday facts to the coming generation, but to us — " Captain Forrester ended with a sort of grunt. Something forbidding had come into his voice, the lonely, defiant note that is so often heard in the voices of old Indians. (54–55)

Although this speech seems to express the Captain's "philosophy of life" (54), by which real people can live, we might more accurately read it as an expression of Cather's "philosophy" of art, by which only her characters can live so as to enact her and her reader's fantasies. The Captain, like Cather, tries to legitimate his philosophy by grounding it in the hard realities of experience — mining works and construction camps; yet, he must brush such things aside as "too dark a chapter to be gone into" in order to preserve the bright optimism of his faith. In his view, circumstance and chance ought to play no role in human fortunes; ultimately, the only determining factor should be the power of the individual personality. In the Captain's philosophy that divides people into the elite who "get all" and the commoners who "get nothing," we recognize Cather's own all-or-nothing philosophy by which she justifies the great destinies of her surrogates in the novels. Above all, we recognize the Captain's faith in the capacity of the idealist to "get" whatever he dreams of as the faith that inspired Cather's own first generation of pioneers — Alexandra Bergson, Thea Kronborg, and Jim Burden — to take possession of the world as an imaginative reality through the sheer force of their desires. The real logic of his faith hinges on the premise that "in spite of" reality, dreams will come true by way of compensation. Yet, as the Captain breaks off the end of his speech with an inconclusive "grunt," he seems forced to acknowledge that he doubts his faith in his dreams. Though he blames the materialistic new generation for the cheapening of his ideals, the real reason why he cannot finish his story is that in reality, fairy tales rarely come true.

In fact, even before the advent of the new generation, the Captain has been silenced, his story already come to a sad end. At the end of the first chapter, we are told that "after the Captain's terrible fall with his horse in the mountains, which broke him so that he could no longer build railroads, he and his wife retired to the house on the hill. He grew old there, — and even she, alas! grew older" (13). The Captain's fall carries with it all the penalties of that first fall from an Adamic paradise; he falls from innocence into experience and time, from the child's world of illusions of beauty, freedom, power, and perpetual youth into the adult's world of ugly facts, constraints, vulnerability, suffering, and aging. The Captain is a crippled version of Cather's earlier imaginative claimants. "Broken," so that he can no longer build railroads, he, like his author, has symbolically lost the power to lay personal claim to the world. Those avenues of escape that were still open to his predecessor, the railroad man Jim Burden, are forever closed to him.

The "forbidding" note of warning in the Captain's voice ushers in a new "dark chapter" in Cather's novels. Cather gives the Captain the voice of "the lonely, defiant ... old Indian" in order to foreshadow the future contest between him and the land shark Ivy Peters, who eventually buys up his property and, in a symbolic parallel, "cheat[s] Indians" (124) in shady business deals. Mumbling violent, incoherent threats under his breath, the Captain brings to mind a twentieth-century version of the disgruntled Chingachgook in Cooper's *The Pioneers*.[16] Like Chingachgook, the Captain is meant to be admired as the noble hero of a better past, now unjustly dispossessed of his rightful and original claim to the land by the immoral opportunists who advance civilization in the name of "progress." Yet Ivy Peters is no more guilty of robbing the Indians of their inheritance than is the Captain, who invaded the Indians' territory when he chose to build his house on the very site where he "found an Indian encampment" (52).

These inconsistencies are perhaps not surprising, since Cather was interested not in recording real history, and its various dispossessions, but in defending her own history, itself a story of dispossession.[17] As if Cather herself were longing to hang on to the "inscriptions" in her own earlier writings, she affirms that "something in the way [the Captain] uttered his unornamented phrases gave them the impressiveness of inscriptions cut in stone" (54). But even stone tablets don't seem to be able to resist the crumbling of Cather's faith in her own art. Masquerading as Captain Forrester, she herself is the old and defiant Indian who protests against a new, more materialistic generation, as if she, too, could conveniently blame the corruptions of others for silencing her ability to finish her story the way she wanted to. Beneath the story of Ivy Peters's usurpation of the Forrester Estate resonates a deeper story of Cather's own loss of her creative powers. When Ivy drains the Forresters' marsh, the fertile scene that had fostered Niel's boyhood imagination, he drains far more than a few acres of land. He had drained the land, Cather says, "of something he hated, though he could not name it, and had asserted his power over the people who had loved those unproductive meadows for their idleness and silvery beauty" (106). Ivy's draining the land of its beautiful spirit, that "something ... he could not name," dramatizes Cather's own feelings of being drained of the wellspring of her creative vitality. Although when Cather wrote *O Pioneers!*, she had confidently imagined the whole prairie as a metaphor for her art, now she seems unable to retain even a few acres of marshland as inviolate mental property. In her own life in Red Cloud, a similar marshland at the house of the Silas Garbers, the prototypes for the Forresters, had provided her with sanctuary for childhood play. In later years, she would return to it in her mind as a metaphor for the territory that fostered her creativity; as she once said, to write well she needed to be as carefree as if she were thirteen and going for a picnic in Garber's grove.[18] But when Ivy Peters drains the marsh so as to "drink up the mirage" (106), Cather seems bitterly to concede that the world she had imagined as a beautiful reflection of the self in earlier novels was only an ephemeral illusion after all.

Like the Captain, Cather passes on the mantle of her authority to Niel, a younger surrogate. Niel's mission in the novel is to guard the boundaries of Cather's own artistic property, symbolized by the Sweet Water estate, that she had won but could no longer hold. He tries to retain this territory by keeping an imaginative grip on Marian Forrester, the Captain's beautiful wife, who had always made his property "attractive" (53) to him, as if she were a kind of muse. The main conflict of the novel develops as Niel tries to assert his superior imaginative claim to Marian over the inferior claims of the "coarse worldlings" (85), Frank Ellinger and Ivy Peters. Although they become Niel's antagonists when they exert "an air or proprietorship" (118) over Marian, he himself is her most possessive and jealous guardian. As the adoring child who relegates Marian to his own fantasy world of ideal beauty and power, Niel prides himself on being her first and worthiest claimant. Reflecting towards the end of the novel that "the right man could save her, even now" (166), Niel never relinquishes his desire to be that savior. Following Marian into church so as to worship her, the boy Niel "was proud now that at the first moment he had recognized her as belonging to a different world from any he had ever known" (42). The central issue of dispute between Niel and his rivals involves this question of territory: should Marian, the prize of the contest, be appropriated for Niel's "different world" of imaginative romance, or for others' ordinary world of prosaic reality?

As in *My Àntonia*, the central critical issue in *A Lost Lady* has become the reliability of the point of view of the celibate male who idealizes the female heroine. Feminist critics have seen Niel as an untrustworthy narrator who imposes his patriarchal values on Marian. Hoping to recover a lost lady from Niel's limiting perception of her so as to restore her to the narrative in her own right, they have contended that there exists an ironic distance between Cather and Niel.[19] But, although Niel does attempt to deny Marian's autonomy and difference from himself, the standard by which he judges her is not gender-coded phallic power but the presexual integrity of childhood. While Niel's preadolescent idealism may make him seem unreliable to the reader, Cather does not make him the target of *her* irony. Niel's response to Marian and her story is the author's own. The resemblance between the narrative perspectives of Niel and Jim Burden, Cather's more clearly autobiographical narrator, suggests that she regarded Niel, also, as her "male" alter ego. No more than *My Àntonia* is *A Lost Lady* meant to be about the actual woman of the title as subject, but about her status as object evoked through her male admirer's appropriating gaze. As a story of loss, rather than recovery, *A Lost Lady* is a bitter and ironic reworking of *My Àntonia*, reflecting similar needs and desires of its author.

In a 1925 interview, Cather diminished Niel's importance as a character with a distinct identity; as she put it, "He isn't a character at all; he is just a peephole into that world.... [I]n reality he is only a point of view" (WCP, 77). Cather deemphasized Niel's individuality because she regarded him as a lens through which she could look back on her own childhood world. As she recalled, "*A Lost Lady* was a woman I loved very much in my childhood" (WCP, 77) — Mrs. Silas Garber, the elegant wife of the former governor of Nebraska and socially prominent lady of the town when Cather was growing up. Recalling that "I wasn't interested in her character when I was little, but in her lovely hair and her laugh which made me happy clear down to my toes," Cather suggests that her interest lay not in detailing Mrs. Garber's actual character, as in a "character study," but in recalling the pleasant effect that she had had on Cather as a little girl. As she discussed her composition of the novel in a letter to Irene Miner Weisz, her subject was not really another person but the strong personal feeling of her own heart — the thing most rare and most essential for writing.[20] To find, or recover, this feeling was Cather's goal in writing the novel. In fact, she describes her authorial challenge in terms that align her point of view with Niel's; just as Niel wishes to take an imaginative possession of Marian as an ideal memory, so, for Cather, "the problem was to *get* her"; as she elaborates, "There was no fun in it unless I could *get* her just as I remembered her and produce the effect she had on me" (WCP, 77, italics mine). Cather's imaginative claim of her lost lady as an ideal in consciousness was made easy by Mrs. Garber's death. When Cather read Mrs. Garber's obituary, an event she looked back on as the epiphany which produced the novel, she did not experience a loss but was reminded of a presence that had long kept her company. Cather once likened her brain to a kind of "limbo, full of ghosts, for which [the writer] has always tried to find bodies" (WCP, 79). By writing about Mrs. Forrester, Cather merely gave bodily expression to her own emotions. As she recalls,

A Lost Lady was a beautiful ghost in my mind for twenty years before it came together as a possible subject for presentation. All the lovely emotions that one has had some day appear with bodies, and it isn't as if one found ideas suddenly. Before this the memories of these experiences and emotions have been like perfumes. It is the difference between a remembered face and having that friend one day come in through the door. She is really no more yours then than she has been right along in your memory. (WCP, 79)

Because "a lost lady" returned to Cather as a ghost and not as an actual person walking through her door, she belonged to her author in a way that no real person could. As Cather says, those who exist in "your memory" are "yours." Mrs. Garber returned to Cather as a feeling that Cather had possessed all along. Through her "peephole," Niel, Cather has more difficulty "getting" her lost lady just right, for her surrogate must deal with a real woman. Yet, as we shall see, Niel most satisfyingly recovers his lost lady when she, too, is transformed into a ghost at the end of the novel.

Niel's story, beginning in chapter 2, promises to be a happy reversal of the Captain's fall at the end of chapter 1. As if hoping to transform the novel into a fairy tale with a "Once upon a time" (164) beginning, Cather starts the novel all over again: "But we will begin this story with a summer morning long ago, when Mrs. Forrester was still a young woman, and Sweet Water was a town of which great things were expected" (14). Even though Niel himself has a fall in this chapter when he climbs a tree to save the bird cruelly wounded by Ivy Peters, it proves to be a fortunate fall, for it returns him to the unfallen paradise of childhood in Mrs. Forrester's bedroom. It makes no difference that the Doctor cannot arrive until later, for Mrs. Forrester is the nurse who provides for Niel's real needs, which are not physical, but emotional and aesthetic. As the "lovely lady" bathes Niel's forehead in sweet cologne water, she emblematically fulfills her function as the mistress of "Sweet Water" who can sweeten and purify the conditions of his existence. Although Niel wakens to see Marian's cleavage — her "white throat rising and falling so quickly" (28) — Cather takes pains to diffuse the scene's inadmissible eroticism even as she evokes it. As if in modest response to Niel's fascinated stare, Mrs. Forrester immediately "got up to take off her glittering rings" and so symbolically transforms herself from an attached married woman into the virginal mother of Niel's dreams, devoted only to him.[21] The white ruffles of her maternal bosom and the ruffled white pillows beneath his head further emphasize the sexual innocence that Niel and Cather wish — at a conscious level — to embrace.

By contrast to the Forresters' sumptuous, well-to-do mansion with its heavy curtains and polished silver, Niel's own house he disdains for its lack of social distinction and its unpleasant disorder of unmade beds, soaking linen, and washing on the line. By escaping to the Forresters', he adopts new parents and a new home that seem better than the ones he has in reality. As Diane Cousineau and John Swift have discussed, Niel's adulation of the Forresters resembles the male childhood fantasy that

Freud called the "family romance."[22] According to Freud, the child substitutes "exalted personages" for his humbler, unimpressive parents out of his "longing for the happy, vanished days when his father seemed to him the noblest and strongest of men and his mother the dearest and loveliest of women.... His phantasy is no more than the expression of a regret that those happy days are gone."[23] As Swift has noted, Freud's language "uncannily echoes Cather's vocabulary of nostalgic desire" in *A Lost Lady*. Niel exemplifies a mythologizing impulse to replace his biological family, with its "air of failure and defeat" (30), with the glamorous, authoritative figures of Captain and Marian Forrester — surely paragons of "the noblest and strongest of men and the dearest and loveliest of women." He strives to portray Captain Forrester, a member of that old "railroad aristocracy" (9), and Mrs. Forrester, a member of a more "fortunate and privileged class" (19), as beings who are grander than their common companions. When the Captain gives his ritualistic "invocation" at the dinner table — "Happy days!" (50) — he lives up to Niel's ideal of him as a kind of King Arthur of "high courtesy" (51) and chivalric ideals. What his toast really invokes, to use Freud's words once again, is "the child's longing for the happy, vanished days" of an imaginary past, when his parents were the perfect lords and ladies of his dreams, and he himself was the majestic king at the center of their court.

Niel's search for an ideal foster home may well reflect an impulse in Willa Cather as well. Cather's own family in Red Cloud was, in many ways, as unsatisfactory to her as Niel's biological family is to him. As one of a family of eleven, she, too, grew up in a tiny, overcrowded, "frail, egg-shell house" (29). Moreover, Niel's real parents in the novel strikingly resemble Cather's own. Niel's mother was a "proud" Southern lady who "hated" the "commonplace" West to which they had been driven only by financial necessity — the need "to turn the crown into the pound" (30). She continually lamented the loss of a more gracious and aristocratic past epitomized in her Kentucky home; as Cather says, she "used haughtily to tell her neighbours that she would never think of living anywhere but in Fayette county, Kentucky" (30). Like Niel's mother, Cather's own mother, Mary Virginia Cather, was also a haughty, willful, and "domineering"[24] Southern belle. She was tyrannical in matters of family discipline, and exacting in matters of domestic proprieties. Just as Niel's mother pined for her old Kentucky home, so Cather's mother, similarly suited in temperament and background to live the genteel life of the Southern woman, greatly missed her old home in Virginia. She, too, had been uprooted to go west out of financial need, when the family lost its sheep and barn in a fire. She also failed to make the transition to life on the prairie. Homesick, and exhausted by her continuing pregnancies, Jenny Cather was ill for the year that the family lived on the homestead. She became increasingly cold and aloof and withdrew from the family. By all reports, Cather found her mother inaccessible, and they never developed a close relationship. Although Jenny Cather did not die, as Niel's mother did when he was five, Willa Cather may have felt that her mother "died" for her when the family traveled west.[25]

Cather's fictional account of Niel's father also seems largely modeled on her own. We are told that Niel's father "was a gentle, agreeable man, young, good-looking, with nice manners" (30); similarly, Charles Fectique Cather is described by Cather's biographers as gentle, easygoing, and mild mannered.[26] In the "air of failure and defeat" that characterizes Niel's father is also something of Charles Cather, the delicate man who, according to his biographers, was passive and ineffectual, lacking the strong will and indomitable drive of his wife. In the novel, Niel's father was defeated when he "lost his own property," and he began "invest[ing] other people's money for them" (30). He spent all of his time at the office, where "he kept the county abstract books and made farm loans" (30). In reality, Charles Cather suffered the same defeat, at least in his daughter's mind. He, too, lost the only property that was really his "own" when he sold the family farm at "Catherton" in 1884, held a public auction, and moved into Red Cloud. There, he, like his fictional counterpart, opened an office where he wrote title abstracts, made farm loans, and sold insurance.[27]

Niel's response to his parents and their failures may also be indicative of Cather's response to hers. Niel, described as being "proud, like his mother" (30), shares her contemptuous attitude to the modern world by emotionally withdrawing into the illusion of a more refined and glamorous past. Like his mother, he snobbishly blames his sense of loss and disorder on the common "people of no consequence" (29) who have failed to live up to his standards. Cather, too, was proud, like her mother.[28] Although in her actual relationships she was closer to her approachable father, in her imaginative life, and in her natural temperament, she modeled herself after her strong mother. Niel's refusal to follow his father to Denver, and his decision instead to return to Sweet Water, where "he clung to his maternal uncle, Judge Pommeroy ... [who was] a friend of all the great men who visited the Forresters" (30), reflects his allegiance to his mother's side of the family and her aristocratic pretensions. In Marian Forrester, the "high-and-mighty" (27) lady who dazzles Niel with her parasol and swirling petticoats as she daintily steps from a carriage, Niel finds a Southern belle who seems to reincarnate his first lost lady, his mother. Niel's defection from his father back to the town of his childhood and his mother's side of the family may mirror Cather's own imaginative return to the place of her childhood in search of the mother. As if to find substitutes for the real mother who had coldly detached herself from her, Willa Cather repeatedly sought, throughout her life, to attach herself to other mothers in other homes. As Leon Edel has noted, Cather found several such second mothers and second homes in her life: as a girl in Red Cloud, she found Mrs. Weiner; as a college student in Lincoln, she found Mrs. Westermann; and as a young journalist in Pittsburgh, she found the sisterly and motherly Isabelle McClung.[29] Cather found such mother substitutes not only in real women but in her characters. One such character is, clearly, Marian Forrester and her maternal prototype, Mrs. Silas Garber of Red Cloud. For Cather, as for Niel, the advantages of such a replacement of ideal characters for real parents are obvious but profound. In place of her weak and quiet father, who lacked the pioneer spirit and sold off the family property, Cather created in Captain Forrester the great conqueror who willfully claims a kingdom, just as he imperiously "commands" attention from others. In place of her elegant and aristocratic, but cold and withdrawn, mother, Cather created in Marian Forrester the lovely queen, who is both regal and yet at the same time, warmly affectionate and attentive to children. Cather's idealization of women, in her fiction as in her life, seems psychically motivated, in part, by her unfulfilled love for her own mother.

Critics have recognized that Niel wants Marian as a surrogate mother.[30] A Lost Lady enacts regressive Oedipal desires, not only aggrandizing the parents but also imagining a sexual relationship with the mother, expressed through Ivy Peters and Frank Ellinger. Niel's portrait of Marian Forrester uneasily vacillates between attraction to the erotic and the maternal. Although he voyeuristically imagines and participates in the lovers' seductions of the mother, he cannot recognize such impulses within himself at a conscious level, and so he recoils with excessive revulsion from his discoveries of her sexual relationships, seeing her in extreme terms as either angel or whore. Sharon O'Brien writes, "The 'lost lady' is ... the mother of earliest childhood whom we all must lose."[31] As readers, we acknowledge that the adolescent must lose his vision of the mother as pure goddess if he or she is to develop a mature awareness of her as a human being who is both sexual and fallible. For Niel Herbert, however, the mother of earliest childhood is an ideal that he refuses to give up. Although O'Brien and other feminist critics have argued that Cather means to undercut Niel's perceptions and judgments of Marian, I believe that the text as a whole works to confirm Niel's point of view and preserve his presexual impulses. Niel's imaginative constructions of Marian Forrester, although they are often conflicting and inaccurate interpretations of Marian as we might imagine her as a real person, nonetheless reveal and work out Cather's own ambivalent expectations, desires, and fears about "lost ladies" in her own life. Any criticism of Niel's point of view that the novel implies we might interpret as Cather's questioning of her own demands as a romantic artist. Generally, however, the novel presents Niel's point of view without ironic distance.

As caricatures of an aggressive and violent sexuality, Ivy Peters and Frank Ellinger also belong to the world of fairy tales where they enact the child's — and Willa Cather's own — distorting fears. Ivy Peters, with his swollen red face, his hard reptilian gaze, and his "unnatural erectness" (20), plays the part of the phallic "Peter," or snake. As his nickname, "Poison Ivy," confirms, he is the snake who poisons Marian with his sting; indeed, in a later scene, when Marian's sexual passions throw her into a fit of distraction, so that "her blue lips, the black shadows under her eyes, made her look as if some poison were at work in her body" (131), she suffers, at a symbolic level, from the deadly effects of Ivy's influence. Frank Ellinger, with "a restless, muscular energy that had something of the cruelty of wild animals in it" (46), plays the part of the big bad wolf; there is even "something wolfish" (65) in his ravenous eyes, "the look of a man who could bite an iron rod in two with a snap of his jaws" (46).

Ivy Peters's sexuality is characterized by a cold, vivisecting cruelty. In his first appearance on the fateful day that he intrudes on the boys' picnic in the Forresters' grove, he is armed with a daunting artillery: a gun, a slingshot, knife blades, hooks, curved needles, a saw, a blowpipe, and a pair of scissors. Ivy's instruments of torture, ordered through a taxidermy outfit ironically entitled the Youth's Companion, are more profoundly ordered by Willa Cather to manipulate our sympathies against Ivy's sexuality; a perverted boyscout if ever there was, Ivy takes his real aim not at helpless animals but at helpless females. His cruel blinding of the woodpecker is a displaced act of violence against women; making his real target explicit, he declares before he does the evil deed: "All right, Miss Female" (23). More specifically, Cather presents Ivy's project as an act of effrontery directed against the authority of Mrs. Forrester, whom he dares to come and stop him. Symbolically, the scenario contains an allegory of the plot of the novel as a whole, clearly forecasting Marian as the wounded bird, Ivy as her sadistic ravisher, and Niel as her heroic rescuer. In a subsequent scene where Niel catches Marian in the hammock, as if she were "a bird caught in a net," Cather makes the analogy explicit. Niel thinks, "If only he could rescue her and carry her off like this, — off the earth of sad, inevitable periods, away from age, weariness, adverse fortune!" (110). In the first scene, Niel would save the bird, and put it out of its misery, by killing it; with Marian, he reveals a similar strategy. Ironically, to capture Marian as an ideal in the net of his own consciousness, safely removed from time, suffering, and chance, Niel has to deny her existence in this world. In the first scene, the bird, after repeatedly "falling and recovering itself," returns to its familiar perch, and "as if it had learned something by its bruises, ... pecked and crept its way along the branch and disappeared into its own hole" (25). In Marian's subsequent story, Cather more broadly teaches the lesson of the bird's story: to recover from the wounding experiences of life, one must find a safe retreat. But, unlike the bird, who knows to crawl back in its hole and stay there, Marian is determined to climb out of her hole; as she tells Niel later in the novel, "[Ivy] honestly wants to help us out of the hole we're in" (124). Though we admire Marian's courage in trying to work her way out of debt and misery, Cather ensures that we see her efforts as deluded, since she is being aided by the untrustworthy schemer Ivy Peters. Moreover, as the novel bears out, Niel's disapproval of Marian's attempts to get out of her "hole" is meant to elicit our own.

Frank's sexual sadism, though less obvious than Ivy's, is no less dangerous. In an incident that recalls the painful hug that Uncle Joe gives Marie in *O Pioneers!*, but with more tension, Frank clasps Marian's hands so hard that she protests, "Be careful, Frank. My rings! You hurt me!" (65). At one level, Cather suggests that Marian will experience pain for breaking her wedding vows, signified by her rings; at a deeper level, she insists that all sexual encounters are bruising. Although we do not witness the actual union of the pair in the woods, Cather dramatizes its consequences in the scene that follows the couple's return to the carriage. Frank's power over the helpless Marian is analogous to Ivy Peters's power over the helpless bird in the earlier scene. Whereas Ivy had hidden the wounded bird under his "heavy black felt hat" (23), and had mercilessly crushed its panting body in his palm, so Frank "hold[s] her crushed up against his breast, her face hidden in his black overcoat" (66–67). Enshrouded by Frank's funereal coat, she herself has apparently given up on life, unable to rouse herself to say anything more than the indifferent refrain, "Nothing matters." Cather would have us believe that Marian has, in fact, been mortally wounded, like her counterpart, the bird. While Frank cuts some branches so as to cover up the spot where they have lain, little Adolph Blum watches Marian from his hiding place in the bushes. From his point of view, "When the strokes of the hatchet rang out from the ravine, he could see her eyelids flutter ... soft shivers went through her body" (67). As a veiled analog to Marian's seduction, this suggests that orgasmic shivers are induced by brutal and destructive attacks. Though Frank possesses no literal instruments of torture, as does Ivy, he seems biologically equipped with a more deadly weapon. Like the bird whose eyes Ivy had slit, Marian's "eyelids flutter" in response to the reverberation of Frank's cutting blows, and throughout the rest of the scene, she appears with "her eyes closed" (67), as if to suggest that she has, indeed, been cruelly blinded by her lover and needs to heal her wounds. As the rest of the novel confirms, Cather regards her heroine as irrevocably blinded by this sexual abuse — blinded both to her real identity and to the future direction her life should take.

As various readers have recognized, Niel's choice of erotic reading material, allowing him to lead "a double life, with all its guilty enjoyments" (81), suggests in his character a vigilantly repressed sexual energy. When he becomes a voyeur of the "sins" of living people, however, he is repulsed. The climactic turning point of part 1 of the novel is the scene of Niel's pilgrimage to Marian's bedroom window, a pilgrimage that ends not, as he hopes, at the scene of his childhood fantasy but at the scene of the disillusioning reality of adult sexuality that displaces it. This scene best organizes the issues at stake in the novel's competing claims for possession. The "impulse of affection and guardianship" (84) that compels Niel to pay homage to his lady reflects his possessive desire to guard his ideal of the pure mother of his presexual imagination. Above all, he wants to guard his childhood associations with the Forrester house, recalled that morning when he "awakened with that intense, blissful realization of summer which sometimes comes to children in their beds" (84). Niel's egoistic fantasy of being the child at the center of the universe is spoiled, however, by the thought of Frank Ellinger. Annoyed by "the intrusion of this third person" (78) in his imagination, Niel reveals that his biggest grudge against Frank is simply that he *is* a "third person," the one who divides him from his narcissistic union with the mother. Considering that Frank first intrudes his unwelcome presence as a repressed fear in Niel's consciousness, it is not surprising that he reappears in the flesh when Niel arrives at the bedroom window; symbolically, Frank must always reappear as an incarnation of the reality of sexuality that Niel cannot, for all his desire, repress or deny.

When Niel first gets to the Forresters' grove to find "an almost religious purity about the fresh morning air" (84), he seems to reenter the "dawn" before sexuality. This unfallen garden, with its "unstained atmosphere," recalls the garden in *O Pioneers!* before it was "stained" by the blood of the lovers. Symbolically, Niel's gift of roses outside the mother's bedroom window expresses his hope that she will forever incarnate the morning freshness and bloom of youth. Cather sympathetically portrays Niel as the innocent betrayed by a sordid and distasteful sensuality when, just as he bends to place the roses at the altar of his childhood, he hears the "fat and lazy" (86) yawn of Frank Ellinger. Niel, "his eyes blind with anger," is so outraged by the ugly intrusion of sexuality that he renounces Marian Forrester as his ideal. His disappointment stems from the same set of high standards that his author demanded from fiction when she wrote, in 1896, "We shall have poetry and beauty and gladness without end, bold deeds and fair women and all things that are worth while" (KA, 325). Having invested everything in a fair woman's grace, sparkle, and lovely voice, Niel now laments with an uncompromising absolutism, "All this was nothing" (87). Throwing the beautiful roses "over the wire fence into a mud-hole the cattle had trampled under the bank of the creek" (86), he most deeply resents Marian's sexuality as the vehicle that translates her, also, from the ideal, timeless realm of romance to the muddy ground of ordinary, physical experience.

In a letter to Zoë Akins, thanking her for some hyacinths, Cather wrote that such flowers always evoked an imaginative ideal she associated with the prototype of *A Lost Lady*.[32] Cather seems to share Niel's resentment against Marian on the grounds that "it was not a moral scruple she had outraged, but an aesthetic ideal" (87). The "something about [Marian]" that "could say so much without words" (35) resonates as "the inexplicable presence of the thing not named" that Cather valued as the indefinable power of the artist's personality. In terms that recall Cather's "overtone divined by the ear but not heard by it," Niel worships a quality in Marian's personality that distinguishes her above all others: "Compared with her, other women were heavy and dull; even the pretty ones seemed lifeless, — they had not that something in their glance that made one's blood tingle. And never elsewhere had he heard anything like her inviting, musical laugh, that was like the distant measures of dance music, heard through opening and shutting doors" (41–42). Though in earlier, confident novels like *The Song of the Lark*, Cather had celebrated her own possession of a light, effervescing vitality, now, as in *My Àntonia*, her surrogate must reclaim "that something" from another beautiful woman who serves as alter ego and muse. But Niel's disillusionment in his ruined aesthetic ideal seems to record the inevitable problem that Cather faced when she tried to create another person — possibly Isabelle McClung — as her soul mate and artistic inspiration. Contemplating "beautiful women, whose beauty meant more than it said," Cather, as much as Niel, wonders at the end of the episode whether "their brilliancy [was] always fed by something coarse and concealed? Was that their secret?" (87). Once Cather invested her ideal of a secret "something" in another person, it became corrupted, for others inevitably "fed" their spirits not with the divine currents of artistic genius but with other currents of life that Cather deemed polluted.

Although Cather's feeling of loss largely derived from the "corruption" of her muse, Isabelle McClung, certainly one corrupting agent had become time itself. All of Cather's dark novels of the 1920s are, at some level, about giving up that "something" that she had cherished as the creative source of her personality and art. Later in the novel, Marian's desperate assertion that she "had" something "left worth saving" (126) seems strained, as if Cather herself were coming to feel that such claims to self-possession were made in vain. Indeed, the fear that Niel feels for Marian — "When women began to talk about still feeling young, didn't it mean that something had broken?" (126) — seems to register Cather's fears as an aging, spent woman, "broken" in two. At the end of Cather's next novel, *The Professor's House*, the Professor must face the sobering fact that "he had let something go — and it was gone: something very precious" (PH, 282). Similarly, Myra Henshawe, the imperious heroine of *My Mortal Enemy*, expresses her defeat by life as the feeling that "something gives way in one" (MME, 89). Though Cather had worked so hard throughout her career to possess this precious vitality, these characters all seem to betray her anxiety about irrevocably losing it. As she despairingly wrote in a letter in 1941, she woke in the morning with a feeling of personal diminishment, as if something were lost out of herself and her world, leaving her no air to breathe.[33] Cather could no longer regain the joy of those early characters who wake up in the morning to an exultant sense of themselves. Now, it is Niel's inability to make the morning freshness last that records Cather's sense of loss.

As Cather had penalized the lovers in *O Pioneers!*, so she punishes Marian Forrester, though less dramatically, for heedlessly lavishing her passions on Frank. It is no coincidence that Marian's betrayal of Niel marks the turning point in her fortunes. The rest of her story is contrived to approve Niel's set of values and the superior kind of claim he would have made to her; when Marian goes her own way, disregarding his desires, she is shown to go astray, and to suffer for it. According to his childish fancy that puts Mrs. Forrester on a high pedestal, he perceives her as either the mythical lady or, as he later puts it, the "common woman" (170). The reversal in her fortunes is shown most dramatically in the scene towards the end of the novel where she gives her dinner party. By contrast to the first dinner party, in which Marian presided as the lively and gracious hostess, now she is portrayed as the frumpish "servant" (99), so dulled in her sensibilities and appearance that she must resort to artificial aids like "rouge" to give her the illusion of ardor. Whereas once she had commanded homage as the queen of a noble aristocracy, now she submits herself to the crude brats of the town. The proper hierarchy that Cather established in "Far Island" between the landlords and their "vassals" no longer holds: upstart "tenant[s]" (150) like Ivy Peters have become the landlords, and Marian Forrester must play the lady "going through her old part, — but [with] only the stage-hands ... left to listen to her" (167). Although on the surface Niel explains this degradation as a result of Captain Forrester's death, it follows more deeply as a result of his own disenchanted view of his lady. Whereas, in happier days, Niel and his uncle had been the only guests to come to the Forrester house for card games and dances in the moonlight, now he has to share her attention with all these others. In his jealousy, he perceives his lady as a trollop, stooping to the folly of entertaining vulgar boors. Niel's objections to his lady's role in this play within the novel anticipate Cather's objections to a version of Marian Forrester in an actual play that was written after the novel was published. As she complained in a letter to Zoë Akins in 1937, the language that the play-wright had put in Mrs. Forrester's mouth showed that he misunderstood her character; instead of conveying her grace as a fine lady, he had stamped her as the commonest slut.[34]

Though Niel's attitude towards Marian seems haughty and snobbish, Cather shares his contempt for the common, and even organizes the plot so as to punish Marian for violating Niel's ideal, according to his point of view. The most literal cause of Marian's plummeting fortunes is, of course, the closing of her husband's bank, a loss that leaves them bankrupt and vulnerable to shysters like Ivy Peters. Symbolically, how-ever, even this failure is owing to her "failure" in Niel's eyes. The losses occur simultaneously: as we later learn, it was while Marian was enter-taining Frank in her bedroom that her husband's bank collapsed in Denver. In its broadest implications, the decline in the Forresters' mone-tary fortunes is meant to illustrate their more general vulnerability to the hazardous world of fortune itself, to which Marian exposes them once she engages in the world of "men and their activities" (85). Like a fallen Eve, Marian is seen to be responsible for the loss of paradise and the subsequent necessity to struggle to survive in the real world.

Without warning or explanation, the bank forecloses because of a national "shrinking in values that no one could have foreseen" (90). At a psychological level, however, the bank failure is foreseeable as a symbol of the "shrinking in values" that results from Marian's affair with Frank. The failure of the bank serves as a metaphor for Marian's emotional bankruptcy in Niel's eyes, which makes him feel that he has unde-servedly suffered an irreparable loss. The juxtaposition of the scene of Niel's betrayal with the episode of the bank crisis contrasts the behaviors of Captain Forrester and his wife, so as to discredit Marian and justify Niel. The Captain, cast as the "man of honour" who "had either to lose his name or save it" (91), values the deposits that others have made in his name as "above price," and so makes sure that none of his depositors loses a dollar, even though, consequently, he and his wife will live in poverty for the rest of their lives. Just as the Captain's name had "meant safety" to all of his investors, so Marian Forrester's name had meant safety to Niel. On the morning of his pilgrimage, he had wanted to give her a valuable "gift" (85) from the heroic ages, yet Marian had defaulted on his imaginative investment in her. The Captain acts nobly to "save" his dignity, winning the praise of his investors that "his name meant a hundred cents on the dollar" (92); by contrast, Marian spiritually sells herself out to "lose" her reputation, forcing Niel to swear that her name means "nothing." The implication of Cather's analogies is that Marian has an obligation to live up to Niel's trust; like the Captain, she ought to put his interests before her own so as to help him gain compensation for all losses.

Indeed, Niel regards Marian as a kind of human savings bank in which he alone ought to be able to make imaginative deposits for his own profit. In his outrage that somebody else has, in a sense, drawn credit off his account, he cries,

> What did she do with all her exquisiteness when she was with a man like Ellinger? Where did she put it away? And having put it away, how could she recover herself, and give one — give even him — the sense of tempered steel, a blade that could fence with anyone and never break? (100)

As if human passion were a quantifiable asset like money in the bank, Niel seems to be asking Marian what kind of inner savings she has made. Above all, he wants to know if she has been able to store her essential personality in an inner vault, safe from the thefts of men like Frank Ellinger. As he phrases it, "Where did she put it away?" Clearly, he feels that no such savings account is possible in sexual relationships; Marian slept with Frank only to be robbed of herself. If Marian's vitality is a kind of "capital," then, in Niel's view, it is a limited amount that ought not to draw interest from her emotional investments in others; either she can save herself up for his imaginative use or she can spend herself in human relationships, only to become impoverished of her best self. Niel's theory of the economy of human relationships will permit no mergers among investors, no common stock, no common bonds. He and Frank cannot share Marian; she is a property whose value must accrue to one or the other.

We can further understand how the foreclosure of the bank symbolically reflects Marian's condition if we take a closer look at Cather's
attitude towards sexual relationships as a kind of material ownership. As
early as *Alexander's Bridge*, Cather had expressed her distrust of human
relationships for putting a "market value"[35] on the individual's original
ego. As we shall see in *The Professor's House*, Cather portrays social,
and especially sexual relationships, as intrinsically possessive and exacting. As the Professor complains, social bonds "are based on property"
(PH, 63). Marian herself implies the connection between sex and material
ownership when, in her jealousy over Frank's marriage to Constance
Ogden, she cries over the telephone, "How much stock did you get with
it?" (134) Cather implies what Marian herself fails to see: by letting
Frank physically possess her, she had also let herself be owned as a kind
of "stock," a material property degradingly held and controlled by
another, vulnerable to the fluctuations of the stockholder's interests. As
critics have noticed, the plot with Ivy Peters in part 2 of the novel largely
reenacts the plot with Frank Ellinger in part 1. That Ivy so readily substitutes himself for Frank suggests a correspondence between Frank's sexual claim to Marian and Ivy's financial ownership. By having Ivy exert
an "air of proprietorship" over both Marian's land and her body, Cather
suggests that these two kinds of claims are equivalent. Like Ivy's title
deed to Marian's land, his sexual claim to her is founded on a material
clause. Cather thus upholds Niel's original warning to Marian; if she fails
to "put herself away," she might as well put herself up for sale to the
highest bidder — be he the dashing ladies' man, Frank Ellinger, or the
shyster lawyer, Ivy Peters.

Niel takes narrative revenge on Marian by projecting his own sense of
loss onto her. As if she had spent too much of her exquisite self in sex, he
reflects that "he had the feeling, which he never used to have, that her
lightness cost her something" (99) — that unnamable allure of her flashing individuality. Later, at Marian's dinner party, Niel also conceives of
her efforts to entertain others as a wasteful giving away of self. He
regrets that "she was using up all her vitality to electrify these heavy lads
into speech" (162). Inconsistently, Marian is portrayed as squandering
her vitality before "heavy lads," but expressing a tantalizing charm when
she is with Niel; her energy seems valuably spent only as long as it is
spent exclusively on him. Like Jim Burden, Niel Herbert takes flight
from his beloved when her sexuality spoils his image of her. He also goes
away to school. In the guise of studying architecture at M.I.T., Niel really
hopes to reconstruct an aesthetic frame through which to gain a restorative view of his lost lady. He had been inspired to become an architect
through his reading, which gave him a "long perspective" (82) over

distance and time, a perspective that "made him know just what he wished his own relations with ... people to be" (82). Once he returns to Sweet Water two years later, however, he is dismayed to rediscover that in the close proximity of actual human relationships, ideal fictions are difficult to construct. Ivy Peters has replaced Frank Ellinger as the annoying third party in Niel's relationship with Marian, and so the story has to be told all over again.

In the second half of the novel, Niel once again tries to "save" Marian Forrester. He wins his greatest victory on the night that she comes to his office to call Frank Ellinger in her distress over his unexpected marriage. The scene takes place against the background of a stormy night and a flood that has washed away the bridge to the Forrester estate, hence destroying that protective moat against the outside world. As Marian recklessly crosses the creek in her impatience to contact Frank, she is in danger of drowning in the tides of her own violent emotions, which have similarly risen out of control. Arriving in Niel's office smelling "strong of spirits" (130), she is shown to be more drunkenly inebriated by her strong passions. In her rage at Frank, her beady eyes "shrunk to hard points," she is seen to be so utterly transfigured by her sexual jealousies that she resembles Ivy Peters. Marred by sensuality, Marian can apparently no longer be her true self. When she gets on the telephone with Frank, and her cheerful chatter turns into "quivering passion of hatred and wrong," Niel literally cuts the phone conversation short. In a dramatic gesture, he takes a pair of "big shears," conveniently left by the tinner, and cuts the wire behind the desk to the phone. Reflecting that "for once he had been quick enough; he had saved her" (134), Niel saves Marian's good reputation from any damaging scandal published by the gossips listening in on the line. More importantly, Niel saves his lost lady by severing her emotional and sexual connections to all other rivals. With his big scissors, bigger even than those that Ivy Peters possesses, Niel gains revenge in a gesture of symbolic castration against the cutting aggression of male sexuality.

On the surface, when the Forresters' misfortunes cause Niel to give up school so as to help nurse the Captain after his second stroke, Niel seems to assume adult responsibilities at a personal sacrifice that "cost him" (142) a lot.[36] In reality, however, Niel gets to live out a very selfish, regressive fantasy in the last section of the novel. We never see him doing any chores around the house or, indeed, ever caring for the invalid Captain at all. The one active thing he does is to rout out all of the gossips who have taken over the house. Far from being a selfless gesture, however, this housecleaning enables Niel to reconquer the territory as its sole ruler. Without having to worry about competing claims, Niel presides over the house, keeping nightly "vigils" (141) over the sleeping Captain and, more profoundly, over the secure and ordered world of his own childhood. Reflecting that "no other house could take the place of this one in his life" (142), Niel enjoys an infantile attachment to all the old familiar things "that had seemed so beautiful to him in his childhood" — his favorite chairs, his old books, and the card table that brings back happy memories of evening entertainments. Feeling "the satisfaction of those who keep faith," Niel feels that the scene has rewarded him, as in a wish fulfillment, for having religiously worshipped the myth of his childhood sovereignty. In the way that Marian had once ministered to him as a child in her bedroom, now she resumes "her place in the kitchen" (141), again busying herself to fulfill his needs.

The Captain knows of his wife's extramarital affair but, unlike Niel, does not reprove her for it. Niel realizes that "the Captain knew his wife better even than she knew herself; and that, knowing her, he — to use one of his own expressions, — valued her" (143). The Captain's tolerance of his wife has led critics to conclude that Willa Cather, likewise, does not pass judgment on Mrs. Forrester and hence is critical of Niel for harshly blaming her for what she has become. [37] Yet Captain Forrester "values" his wife for the same reasons that Niel does. The Captain also plays his part in Niel's fantasy. According to a clock-like schedule, the Captain gratefully submits to Marian's pampering care as she shaves him, feeds him, undresses him for bed, props him up on his pillows, and "tuck[s] him in" (122). With no hint of irony, she even tucks a dinner napkin under his chin like a bib when he eats. Though the double image of the Captain as the commanding mountain and the helpless baby is incongruous, it is explicable as a vicarious fulfillment of Niel's own juvenile desires. Whenever the Captain absentmindedly calls out, "Maidy, Maidy," and she, regardless of where she happens to be, or what she is doing, never-failingly replies, "Yes, Mr. Forrester," Niel feels a renewal of his own most deeply held childhood faith that the mother will always be on call to soothe his every anxiety. Although Niel objects to Marian's role as servant of the other town boys, her nickname "Maidy" ironically implies that his longing for her as a creator of comfort, order, and ease somehow erases the distinction between mother and maid. In Niel's childish needs, reflected in the Captain, we see how much Cather's own needs as a middle-aged writer have changed. The youthful fantasy characterizing the early novels of the child leaping out of his bed in the morning to conquer the world has diminished in scope to become the valetudinarian fantasy of the helpless child snuggled in his bed as a refuge against the world.

Of course, life once again takes away this fantasy of infantile dependence. In a betrayal scene that reenacts his earlier, parallel discovery at the bedroom window, Niel goes up to the dining room window one evening to admire the honeysuckle and sees Ivy Peters indifferently putting his arms around Mrs. Forrester, "his hands meeting over her breast" (169). Recoiling from the sight of Ivy's coarse familiarities, Niel swears to bring such repetitions in his experience to a final close: "'For the last time,' he said, as he crossed the bridge in the evening light, 'for the last time.' … It took two doses to cure him. Well, he had had them! Nothing she could ever do would in the least matter to him again" (170). As if true to his word, Niel leaves Sweet Water once again, this time never to return. Feeling nothing for Mrs. Forrester but a "weary contempt," he leaves without even saying good-bye.

Even more selfishly unforgiving than Jim Burden, Niel wishes that his lady were dead. As he looks back, he realizes that "what he most held against Mrs. Forrester" was "that she was not willing to immolate herself, like the widow of all these great men, and die with the pioneer period to which she belonged; that she preferred life on any terms" (169). Shockingly, Niel cannot understand why Marian desires to live rather than sacrifice herself on the grave of her husband as a memorial to his ideals. Understandably, the novel's feminist critics have seen this passage as grounds for Niel's unreliability. To be sure, Niel seems an unreliable guide to *our* views of Marian and what she represents. We see that, unlike Niel, who wants to take refuge in her timeless garden, "handed down from the heroic ages" (85), Marian is poignantly caught in time. She is forced to abide by the routines of daily living and the laws of the bodily, material world. As a human being who wants to form fulfilling personal relationships, she has no choice but to embrace "coarse worldlings" (85); moreover, her participation in the lives of others — a transgression against Niel's childish ideals — is what makes her human and adult. We certainly sympathize with the desire of a woman in the prime of her life to survive her husband. Finally, we recognize Marian Forrester's most compelling trait as an intense and passionate enthusiasm for life. Nevertheless, Niel's lack of sympathy for Marian does not discredit his narrative authority. By condemning Marian for "preferr[ing] life on any terms," Niel imposes on her the uncompromising terms of the choice that Cather herself had felt compelled to make throughout her career between life and art. Ever since she wrote *Alexander's Bridge*, Cather had refused "life on *any* terms" in order to affirm "art on her *own* terms." What Niel's disapproval of Marian most reveals is how life-denying Cather's own artistic aesthetic had become by 1922. In her selfish demands that life exist solely to feed her imaginative needs, she was forced, as she grew older, to reject a larger and larger amount of life itself.

Cather later recalled that she had gotten the idea for the novel while resting on her bed during a visit to the home of the Hambourgs in Toronto in 1921.[38] Though her reading in the Red Cloud paper of the death of Mrs. Silas Garber may have immediately reminded her of one "lost lady," surely her visit with Isabelle and Jan more deeply reminded her of another. As if time had given her a necessary emotional distance, Cather confronts her wounding loss of Isabelle McClung in *A Lost Lady* more directly than she had in *My Àntonia*; *A Lost Lady* enacts the sexual violation of the muse most painfully and irrevocably. In the guise of Niel, Cather herself seems to be imposing her expectations as an artist on the life of her soul mate, forcing her also to choose a life of imagination over the real world. Just as Marian plays the role of the supportive audience to the Captain's story, prompting him, cheering him on, approving him, so Isabelle had fully supported and inspired Cather's tale-telling. Like Niel, Cather had kept many a "vigil" in the McClung household, free to read and reflect within a secure and reassuring atmosphere, while Isabelle, like Marian, "took her place" in the kitchen or a nearby room, maternally taking care of Cather's physical needs and inspiring her with her beauty. But just as Niel bitterly regards Marian as guilty of a "defection" (156) when she withdraws her business from him and his uncle and gives it instead to Ivy Peters, so Cather resentfully regarded Isabelle when she withdrew from her to marry Jan Hambourg in 1916. Although, in reality, Isabelle's marriage to Jan was not a rejection of Willa Cather, Cather construed it that way; like Thea Kronborg singing to the Mexicans, Cather seems to have wished that her friends would "turn themselves and all they had over to her" (SL, 232) — and her alone. That Cather dedicated the first edition of the novel to Jan Hambourg, whose name she later removed, suggests that she initially connected some part of her story with Isabelle's husband.[39] Biographically, Cather's anger at Ivy Peters's "air of proprietorship" over Marian and her land has its roots in her resentment against Jan Hambourg's proprietorship over Isabelle and her estate. Like Niel, Cather felt that Jan's usurpation had deprived her of the scene and the company that had fostered her imagination. Ultimately, the novel expresses Cather's feelings of betrayal at being unjustly displaced from this ideal home. In Niel's bitterness that "ever since the Captain's death it was a house where old friends ... were betrayed and cast off" and "common fellows" (170) welcomed, Cather unconsciously expressed her own resentment that she had been cast off for the sake of an unwelcome intruder, one whom she preferred to think of as more "common" than

she. For Cather, too, the Captain's death may have held special biographical significance, for in the fatherly portrait of the Captain, we recognize,
in part, a portrait of Isabelle's father, the aristocratic Judge McClung. If
the death of the Captain marks for Niel a turning point in the life at
Sweet Water, so also, the death of Judge McClung marked a turning
point for Willa Cather, for a couple of months after his death, Isabelle
announced her engagement, and subsequently, the house was sold. [40]
Although, in reality, the death of Isabelle's father gave her liberation and
the financial means to marry, Cather implies through the fiction that the
"father's" death only left her more financially and sexually vulnerable, as
if without the insulating protection of his presence and the McClung
household, she could not afford to be her best, most well-bred self. At the
end of the novel, Niel gives his greatest loyalty to the Captain, reflecting
that "he had helped the Captain to die peacefully, he believed; and now it
was the Captain who seemed the reality. All those years he had thought it
was Mrs. Forrester who made that house so different from any other"
(170). In this we might read Cather's own last bit of consolation after
Isabelle's marriage: if Isabelle had transferred her loyalty to another, so
she, in turn, would transfer her loyalty from the daughter of the household to the father — the Judge whom she had watched over in his last
months, and who, she fancied, had been the truly noble presence that
dignified the estate.

Though Isabelle's marriage forced Cather to see that outside of her
own art, others exerted needs and demands as compelling as her own, she
protested bitterly against this fact, and, like Niel, punishes those who
have gone against her emotional and aesthetic demands. Yet, as if Cather
wanted, at some level, to reconcile herself to her lost lady, the novel ends
by attempting to restore Marian to Niel. Yet, it is only once Marian
becomes a "long-lost lady" (71), temporally inaccessible in the past, that
she becomes most imaginatively accessible to him. As he reflects years
later, "After she had drifted out of his ken, when he did not know if
Daniel Forrester's widow were living or dead, Daniel Forrester's wife
returned to him, a bright, impersonal memory" (171). Ironically, whether
the real Marian Forrester is alive or dead is irrelevant to Niel, for, as a
"bright impersonal" image, polished and safely erased of any tarnishing
passions, she transcends her temporal limitations as a "widow" and
becomes appropriable as the eternal and mythical "wife."

Finally, however, the novel is undecided whether to embrace Marian
as the mythical wife or as the temporal woman. In an unconvincing epilogue, Cather attempts to reconcile Niel to his lost lady, this time as a
real woman. In an unlikely meeting between Niel and Ed Elliott, a boy
Niel had always looked down on but whom he now greets as a long-lost

friend, Niel finds out the story of Marian Forrester since he had last seen her. His angry vow after his betrayal — "For the last time" — seems to give way to a desire to begin the acquaintance all over again, as, on the last page, he asks Ed, "Do you suppose ... that she could be living still? I'd almost make the trip to see her" (174). Although, on the surface, Niel seems full of goodwill and generosity, he betrays his hesitancy with an equivocal "almost," for the great stumbling block for Niel, as for all of Cather's characters, is the risky prospect that real life will disappoint his hopes. Indeed, the highly ambiguous account of Marian suggests that Niel has good reason to refrain from seeing her. Cather herself seems unable to decide how favorably to portray Marian — whether to forgive her or to continue to punish her. On one hand, Cather reinstates Marian as the loveliest of women according to the family romance; having married a distinguished "Mr. Collins" from England who, by report, "is the kindest of husbands" (174), she seems to have come up in the world. Yet Cather seems equally bent on keeping Marian in her place as the common woman who has sunk in her fortunes. It is unclear whether Marian's newfound wealth is a sign of her prestige or her crass materialism, for her husband is "quarrelsome and rather stingy" (173), they drive a flashy "French car," and move with a fast, bar-hopping crowd. We can hardly imagine the prudish Niel at ease in an atmosphere as exotic, wild, and sensual as this South America. Moreover, although Ed says that Marian's laugh hasn't changed a bit, her face certainly has. As a woman "a good deal made up ... like most of the women down there," wearing "plenty of powder" and rouge, her hair dyed black, Marian once again resembles the cheap and gaudy whore rather than the lovely lady. Cather spares Niel from having to decide whether he will *really* go to see Marian, and likewise spares herself from having to decide how to portray her, by removing her far away from the scene. As if the geographical distance to the southern tip of Argentina weren't enough, Cather removes Marian even farther away by killing her off. No sooner has Niel made his chivalrous offer than Ed relieves him of the burden of decision by telling him that Marian died three years ago — "I know that for certain" (174). In one sense, Niel gets his wish after all, for, just as he had wanted Marian to "immolate" herself on her husband's grave, so, symbolically, there she is laid to rest when her widowed husband perpetually sends flowers to Captain Forrester's grave "in memory of my late wife" (174). Niel's old claim upon Marian Forrester seems complete when, unbelievably enough, even her new husband vows to remember her as the widow of Captain Forrester. Equally ambiguous and unintentionally ironic are the novel's last lines:

"So we may feel sure that she was well cared for, to the very end," said Niel. "Thank God for that!"

"I knew you'd feel that way," said Ed Elliot, as a warm wave of feeling passed over his face. "I did!" (174)

It is hard to believe that boys as different as Ed and Niel would finally feel the same way about Marian Forrester — Ed, who had selflessly and humbly loved her in good times and bad, and Niel, who had selfishly and conditionally loved her only when she had gratified his needs. Beneath the surface benevolence and warmth that Niel expresses towards Mrs. Forrester, we must wonder just what he is thanking God for — that she was well cared for, or that, after all, she has met her "very end"? As the repeating and inconclusive patterns of the novel suggest, Niel is unable to bring closure to his own story until he can proclaim Marian Forrester dead. Surely some of this novel's inconsistencies and ambiguities reflect Cather's ambivalence about Isabelle McClung. More broadly, however, they reflect her increasing uncertainty about her choices and loyalties as an artist that the crisis with Isabelle had called into question. Cather would continue to try to write the rest of the story that she leaves unresolved at the end of *A Lost Lady*. In *The Professor's House*, she would more deliberately and honestly examine the conflict between the competing claims of art and life.

7
"Letting Something Go":
The Costs of Self-Possession
in *The Professor's House*

In her book *Willa Cather: Landscape and Exile,* Laura Winters asserts
that the "pervasive scheme of possession in the novels of Willa Cather is
most forcefully worked out in *The Professor's House*." In Winters's
view, Cather asks questions "concerning what can be possessed of
houses, of one's family happiness, of the artifacts of a bygone civilization, of control over one's time of death, of the patent on an invention, of
the vitality of a student who reminds one of lost youth, and of the landscape itself." [1] As this long list of themes suggests, the issue of possession
arises in nearly every episode in the novel. Most obviously, Cather
presents Professor St. Peter's family in a constant struggle for possessions and power. The family conflict stems from the fact that Louie
Marsellus, the Professor's son-in-law, has developed the scientific
research of his former student, Tom Outland, to amass an ostentatious
fortune. In addition to parading a show of expensive and gaudy luxuries
— jewelry, furs, motorcars, rugs, and furniture — the Marselluses are
building a decadent and pretentious "Norwegian manor house" on the
shores of Lake Michigan. Now that the Professor's daughter, Rosamond
Marsellus, can afford to indulge her expensive tastes, she has become
fastidious about money, disdaining to share her wealth with others. Her
absorption in her possessions has made her so callous that when she takes
her father on "an orgy of acquisition" (154) in Chicago, she not only
exhausts him but allows him to pay for his own room and expenses. As
the Professor's other daughter, Kathleen, and her husband, Scott Mac-
Gregor, vie to maintain a semblance of equality with the affluent Marsel-

luses, bitter quarrels and backbiting competition destroy family harmony. Material acquisitions — the best house, the best clothes, the best furs — consume the characters as if their self-worth were dependent on external marks of financial success. With the exception of Tom Outland and the sewing woman Augusta, greedy self-interest characterizes all of the novel's secondary characters. Langtry, the Professor's rival in the history department, uses his connection to an influential uncle in state politics to compete against him and win professional and social status in the university; Appelhoff, the Professor's landlord, is good-natured about everything except spending money; even Crane, the Professor's colleague who had always fought against commercial interests, selfishly tries to get a profit for himself out of Tom's research.

Hoping to elude "families and fortunes" (89), the Professor takes refuge in the study of his old house in order to escape the mercenary ambitions and petty rivalries of his family and colleagues. The mainstream of criticism has described the basic tension in the novel as a conflict between the materialism of industrial culture and artistic, spiritual ideals. The pattern of competition for possessions is only superficially an indictment of a commercialized society, however. Cather more deeply attacks human — and particularly familial — relationships themselves as grasping and possessive. More than the daily prose-poems that Scott writes for the local paper, his favorite expression, "Bang, bang!" (44), is the best editorial comment on the violent hostilities that Cather sees as inherent in family life. When Mrs. St. Peter announces to Louie, "It's Scott's dinner to-night. Your tastes are so different, I can't compromise. And this is his, from the cream soup to the frozen pudding" (109), the competition for possession extends even to meals. Cather's portrait of the family's acquisitiveness betrays her distrust of social relationships as intrinsically dispossessing of the self — that most precious and irreplaceable of possessions. In her essay "Katherine Mansfield," she describes the dynamics of family relations as a tug-of-war between the individual and the group in which "every individual in that household (even the children) is clinging passionately to his individual soul, is in terror of losing it in the general family flavour. As in most families, the mere struggle to have anything of one's own, to be one's self at all, creates an element of strain which keeps everybody almost at the breaking-point" (OW, 108–9). Similarly, as dramatized in the novel, what is really at stake beneath the familial rivalries is the Professor's possession of his own soul. Though Cather never married, she, like her Professor, experienced family life as a dispossessing strain throughout her life. As one of a family of eleven in a tiny, overcrowded house in Red Cloud, she had to struggle against "losing [her 'individual soul'] in the general family flavour." In a letter to her friend Irene Miner in 1943, she recounts that a recent visit from one of her nieces had been more draining than the toil of doing household chores.[2] In another letter a year later, she complains of being caught in the net of family obligations, graduations, marriages, babies, and illnesses, until she yearns to preserve a little of her life for herself.[3]

As in *A Lost Lady*, Cather depicts human relationships as grossly materialistic in order to warrant her repudiation of them for subjecting the individual to the will of others. To justify the Professor's uncompromising desire for autonomy, Cather portrays others' demands as excessively exacting, self-interested, and proprietary. The Professor proudly tells Rosamond that his relationship with Tom was different from hers because "your bond with him was social, and it follows the laws of society, and they are based on property. Mine wasn't, and there was no material clause in it" (63). The Professor is not just saying that the laws of society are based on property but that social bonds themselves have a "material clause" according to which one person can claim a kind of proprietary interest in another. He suggests that to be intimately involved with others is, at some uncomfortable level, to be "owned" by them; he feels that he cannot give up the claims of the self to accommodate others without mortgaging a part of himself. It seems no coincidence that the two verbs that the Professor wants to omit from his vocabulary are "to buy" (154) and "to love" (264), for, in his view, both are transactions that put a "market value" on things. Like Bartley Alexander, he imagines that his original soul "was [the] only ... thing that had an absolute value" beyond any form of exchange, and that all other relationships "were only functions of a mechanism useful to society; things that could be bought in the market" (AB, 39). He, too, imagines that to be "useful" to others is to be used by them for their profit. He thus regards the part of himself that has lived by conjugating the verb "to love" — getting married and having children — as his "secondary social" (265) self, as if this self were, indeed, inferior or incomplete for being connected socially and sexually to others.

By contrast, Cather maintains that the Professor's relationship with Tom, who "owed me no more than I owed him" (62), is free of burdensome obligations. Yet this friendship seems liberating only because it is not, strictly speaking, social at all, but purely imaginative: Tom Outland functions as St. Peter's own youthful alter ego. Ironically, though the Professor implies that his friendship with Outland is selfless, and hence superior to ordinary social ties, it is self-serving and narcissistic. As an imaginative relationship between two halves of one self, it seems unable to survive the realities of this world. The Professor envies Tom Outland, who, by dying young, preserved his autonomy and freedom. Leaving "the rewards, the meaningless conventional gestures" (261) to others, Tom escapes not only financial but social rewards, both of which would have devalued his original worth. Had his beautiful hand "had to 'manage' a great deal of money, to be the instrument of a woman who would grow always more exacting" (261), he would have had to succumb not simply to the materialism of society but to the equally material demands of others. The emblem of his hand holding money suggests that he himself would have become a kind of money, or property of exchange, in the hands of a grasping wife. Similarly, the Professor's desire to escape "materialism" betrays his deepest desire to escape all those "conventional gestures" and adult responsibilities that somehow lay a material, practical claim to his original sovereignty.

As in earlier novels, Cather presents self-possession and involvement with others as mutually exclusive. In defense of his decision not to join his family on its trip to France, for example, the Professor says that "one couldn't do one's own things in another person's way; selfish or not, that was the truth" (160). To enjoy an exclusive possession of his "own" way, he must withdraw into solitude. The Professor reveals the deepest cause of his depression as a feeling of self-devaluation and "diminution of ardour" (13) suffered through the costly "payments" he has made of himself to others. Explaining to his wife why he cannot join the family in France, he says, "I've lived pretty hard. I wasn't willing to slight anything — you, or my desk, or my students. And now I seem to be tremendously tired. One pays, coming or going. A man has got only just so much in him; when it's gone he slumps" (163). The Professor's problem is one that has preoccupied Cather throughout her career — the problem of spending and losing his youthful force. Since that possession is in limited supply, something that one "has got only just so much" of, it cannot be spent without loss. As the Professor increasingly tries to conserve his energies by retreating from others, his wife complains, "Now you save yourself in everything," so as to become "lonely and inhuman" (162). Lillian's criticism suggests that Cather herself sees some limitations to the Professor's self-absorption. She recognizes, it seems, that both the life devoted to the self and the life devoted to others exact a penalizing cost on the individual so that, as St. Peter says, "One pays, coming or going." Either one can give oneself to others, only to lose the original ego, or one can save oneself from others, only to lose one's more human, giving self — both choices result in emotional and spiritual diminishment.

To understand why the idea of "possession" is such a controlling metaphor in *The Professor's House*, we need to consider the personal investment that Cather had in her Professor. At fifty-two, Willa Cather, like her fifty-two-year-old surrogate, felt called upon to reevaluate the commitments she had made in her career, weighing the aesthetic life of the soul against the life of human relations. As in her first novel, *Alexander's Bridge*, she reveals an agonized awareness of the unsatisfactory, ambiguous nature of the choices involved. No longer so sure of herself as she had been earlier in her career, the choice was more painful, its dramatization more intense. At the end of the novel, after the Professor's brush with death, he suggests that the source of his alienation from his family lies in an injury or wound that he has received from them: "If his apathy hurt them," he reflects, "they could not possibly be so much hurt as he had been already" (283). Although the novel does not fully explain the cause of the Professor's wound, we can locate its source in his author. In a seminal article in 1957, Leon Edel suggests parallels between the Professor's situation and Willa Cather's.[4] The Professor has recently completed an ambitious history, *Spanish Adventurers in North America*, for which he has been awarded the prestigious Oxford Prize. Edel points out that Cather had also just won a prize — the Pulitzer Prize in 1923 for her novel, *One of Ours*. Moreover, he notes that the Professor's study is modeled on the little room at the McClung's house in Pittsburgh where Willa Cather lived from 1900 to 1906 and wrote her first volumes of poetry and short stories. Her room, like the Professor's study, was also in the attic at the rear of the house; it, too, was made snug "under the slope of the mansard roof" (16); with its little window overlooking a garden, it, too, was a room with a view. More tellingly, the room at the McClung's had also been the family's sewing room, containing dressmaker's dummies resembling the Professor's "forms." Just as for St. Peter "the notes and the records and the ideas always came back to this room" (25), so, for Cather, her ideas always came back to this favorite retreat, where she returned regularly to visit and to write for the next ten years after she had made her home in New York. Edel argues that the Professor's disillusionment has its origin in Cather's sense of betrayal when Isabelle married the violinist Jan Hambourg in 1917, forcing her to give up the cherished workspace that had afforded her such security and peace. This crisis was renewed in Cather's mind when she visited the Hambourgs at their French home at Ville-D'Avray in the spring of 1923. Isabelle had set aside a study for her that was meant to provide a replacement for the old room in Pittsburgh. Edel incorporates the testimony of Edith Lewis: "They had hoped she would make Ville-D'Avray her permanent home. But although the little study was charming, and all the surroundings were attractive, and the Hambourgs themselves devoted and solicitous, she found herself unable to work at Ville-D'Avray. She felt, indeed, that she would never be able to do any work there" (WCL, 131). Leaving Ville-D'Avray that September, Cather retreated to Aix-les-Bains, where she apparently conceived and began writing *The Professor's House*.[5] Edel suggests that the novel itself, focusing on the Professor's refusal to move from his old study to the family's new house, built with his prize money, suggests the reason why Cather could not accept her friend's invitation. As he writes, "The house at Ville-D'Avray becomes the new house built by the professor's family. It is no substitute for the old one, and the professor can no more share it with the newcomer to his family than Willa Cather could share the French home with both Isabelle and Jan. Isabelle was no longer a beloved figure exclusively possessed by her; she must be shared."[6] In the character of the rapacious Louie Marsellus, "a rather mackerel-tinted man" with a prominent "Semitic" (43) nose, Edel proposes that Cather creates an unsympathetic portrait of the Jew, Jan Hambourg. According to his reading, the novel enacts a drama of rejection and withdrawal, in which the Professor, hurt by his family, as Willa Cather had been hurt by hers, regressively clings to the womb-like security of his study.

That Cather used the money she made from *The Professor's House* to buy herself a new mink coat[7] — like the one she attacks Rosamond for wearing — suggests that her real quarrel was not with expensive luxuries. By broadening the target of her satire to the decadent commercialism of an age, Cather found an artistic means to express a deeper and more personal source of dissatisfaction. The struggle for possession against a society lacking aesthetic and spiritual values, while seemingly "typical and universal, not merely personal,"[8] nonetheless most deeply enacts Cather's own efforts to repossess the territory of her art and the sources of her artistic inspiration. Ultimately, the reason why the novel is so concerned with the vocabulary and implications of "possession" is that Willa Cather herself felt, due to alienating personal circumstances, more than ever in danger of being dispossessed of an inner power and autonomy. Doris Grumbach writes that *The Professor's House* "is the only novel by Cather ... which impresses the mature reader as dangerously threatening to his own self-possession."[9] The novel evokes this response, I believe, because we identify with the Professor's feeling of a self under siege, a portrait that projects Cather's own fears. Louie Marsellus is cast as the usurper who has robbed the Professor of his rightful imaginative property, as indeed, Cather felt that she had been robbed by Jan Hambourg. Most obviously, the Professor's retreat to his study dramatizes Cather's efforts to resist the demands of others so as to retain an imaginative hold on her attic room and all that it symbolized at the McClungs. At another level, the competing claims that the Professor and Louie make upon the women of the family has an analogy in Cather's attempt to keep a mental possession of Isabelle. Most intensely, the battle for possession is fought over the legacy and memory of Tom Outland. This conflict is a displaced version of the Professor's efforts to recover his own original soul and muse, embodied in Tom. The Professor's struggle to defend the "Outland patent" against the inferior claims of others enacts Cather's proprietary claims to her own genius and art.

The well-being of the Professor's mental life depends on his possession of his study. By letting her surrogate remain in his inner sanctum after his family has moved, Cather gave herself an option that she had, in reality, lacked. The Professor wants to stay in his old study above all because it is arranged the way he wants it; in his study, as in his garden, he alone has "the upper hand" (15).[10] As he explains to his landlord, he will continue to rent the old house in order "to have room to think" (52). The study is valuable as a space inhabited exclusively by his own thoughts. Glad that in his dismantled house there was "one room still furnished — that is, if it had ever been furnished" (16), the Professor most profoundly occupies the unfurnished room of consciousness that provided the paradigm for Cather's own art in her novel démeublé. Although he reflects that he has lived "two lives" (28) — the life of his work and the life with his family — these two lives have, in reality, been strictly separated and combined only in consciousness. Retreating to the study as the one place where he can "get isolation, insulation from the engaging drama of domestic life" (26), the Professor finds family life compelling only because he is safely shielded from it, having no more than a comfortably "vague sense" of the activities going on downstairs. As long as he appropriates others as part of a mental "drama," he can maintain a benevolent attitude towards them. If, however, he makes "that perilous journey" below to participate in ordinary life with its attendant distractions and confusions, he risks being dispossessed — "los[ing] his mood, his enthusiasm, even his temper" (27).

The Professor's values predate civilization, taking him back in time to reconstruct a myth of his own psychological origins.[11] As he looks out of his study window at Lake Michigan, "the inland sea of his childhood" (29), he sees embodied the interior reservoir of all his lost childhood power and vitality. Against its background, he seems to have no parents or family, nor indeed, any external constraints, for, as he fondly imagines, "You had only to look at the lake, and you knew you would soon be free" (30).[12] Just as St. Peter moves to Hamilton in order to have the "assistance" of the lake, a place where he can refresh himself when he is tired or not writing well, so Cather mentally returned to this scene in order to find new inspiration for her writing. The Professor's eastward view towards the dawn of his beginnings recreates the same imaginative scene that had sustained her, whether her windows had looked out upon cottonwood trees, a garden in Pittsburgh, Mount Monadnock, or the Bay of Fundy. Ultimately, though, the lake represents a subjective rather than an external reality, for it is "not a thing thought about, but a part of consciousness itself" (30), and, as such, we imagine, it embodies the mental purity and self-containment that Cather herself sought through her art. When Cather was charged with escapism and irrelevance in the 1930s, she defended herself on the grounds that art had always been a form of escape, a territory that, like the tantalizing Blue Lake, was exempt from the law courts and marketplace. [13]

As a writer, the Professor further resembles his author. His professional life, divided between "working so fiercely by night" while "he was earning his living during the day" (28), recreates Cather's years in Pittsburgh, during which she wrote fiction in her spare time while earning her living as a journalist and teacher. After fifteen years devoted to writing, he, like his author, "had got what he wanted" (29): financial success and recognition as well as creative fulfillment. His Oxford Prize for History, carrying with it 5,000 pounds, is the symbolic equivalent of Cather's Nobel Prize in 1922 and the financial equivalent of the royalties from Knopf that she had also received that year. [14] Moreover, we can see the critical reception of St. Peter's prize-winning, eight-volume history as analogous to that of Cather's own award-winning life-work of eight volumes. His first three volumes inspired no more interest than did Cather's first three works, *April Twilights*, *The Troll Garden*, and *Alexander's Bridge*. Yet, "with the fourth volume he began to be aware that a few young men, scattered about the United States and England, were intensely interested in his experiment" (33), just as Cather, with her fourth volume, *O Pioneers!*, began to win the admiration of a few critics such as William Heinemann in England (OW, 95). With his fifth and sixth volumes, corresponding to Cather's *The Song of the Lark* and *My Àntonia*, the Professor, like his author, became more widely reviewed and known, until, in his last two volumes, corresponding to Cather's *One of Ours* and *A Lost Lady*, he also secured "a certain international reputation" (33).

Moreover, the Professor's focus on *Spanish Adventurers in North America* bears resemblance to Cather's interests in her repeating story of adventurous conquerors. Like Cather, the Professor is a writer who takes a vicarious interest in his characters and, we suspect, creates them as self-projections. Although not of Spanish descent, he looks like a Spaniard, Cather says, because he has been writing about Spanish figures. Athletic and vigorous, with a look of imperial command like a "statue" (13) or a "warrior" on the Parthenon frieze, he incarnates all the heroic attributes of a conqueror. Though he criticizes Rosamond as a "Napoleon looting the Italian palaces" (154), he himself, originally christened Napoleon Godfrey St. Peter, embodies a spirit of selfish acquisition — not of material, but of imaginative spoils. The Professor, too, is an artist-conqueror who creates out of a grasping desire to appropriate the world in consciousness. On the day he takes the boat around the coast of Spain, he has his great epiphany of his future art: "Everything seemed to feed the plan of the work that was forming in [his] mind; the skipper, the old Catalan second mate, the sea itself" (106). As voracious as his prototype, Alexandra Bergson, who drinks in the Divide, the Professor visually devours the entire oceanic scene, including even his fellow sailors. Lying low in his boat, imagining that against the lofty mountains, rising "high beyond the flight of fancy ... the design of his book unfolded in the air above him," he sees art as the form that contains a world dissolved into the material of consciousness itself. For the Professor, the "design was sound" not just aesthetically but psychologically because of what it leaves out — namely, his wife and daughters, whom he has sent home from France so that he can voyage in search of inspiration alone. Years later, the Professor looks back on this day as the perfect scene for a picturesque shipwreck, and again, "his wife was not in it" (95). As Thomas Strychacz has observed, "St. Peter's mythic images of escape are in various ways attempts to fulfill an archetypal desire to remain young in a place without women."[15] The professor finds his artistic design sound for preserving a regressive and escapist fantasy of sovereign possession and authority.

In the golden past, the Professor had worked productively as if he had, in fact, been the ruler of his own private island. In those days, his daughter Kathleen had so dutifully honored his demand to work all morning in peace that even on the day she got stung by a bee, she refrained from knocking on his door; thereafter, she became his favorite daughter. But now the Professor is accosted by a continuous series of interruptions: "Am I interrupting?" (59); "May I interrupt?" (127); "Shall I disturb you?" (165)[16] As on his first visit from Rosamond, who comes while he is "resting his mind on the picture of intense autumn-blue water" (58), all visits force him to give up that psychic self-possession.

Yet, though life itself invades the Professor's repose, he holds Louie Marsellus most responsible for his disappointments. The deepest grudge that the novel bears Louie is not that he has materialistic values per se but that he presumptuously seizes what the Professor had imagined was exclusively his and then has the nerve to brag about it. Marsellus is blamed for corrupting with his Midas touch all that is dear to St. Peter —

Lillian, Rosamond, the life and achievements of Tom Outland. Cather says, "Since Rosamond's marriage to Marsellus, both she and her mother had changed bewilderingly in some respects — changed and hardened.... [It was] Louie who had done the damage" (161). But this change is not so bewildering if we consider Cather's repressed hostility towards Jan Hambourg. The change that comes over Lillian as she begins to dress well for Louie and Scott, "liv[ing] in their careers as she had once done in his" (79), seems to betray Cather's jealousy over the fact that Isabelle was now scheming in Jan's interests and no longer just in her own. Playing the part of one of those "beaux-fils, [who] were meant by Providence to take the husband's place when husbands had ceased to be lovers" (160), he is the newcomer who supplants Cather in Isabelle's affections by providing a sexual relationship that she could not. The Professor's dislike for Louie is most profoundly motivated by his own need for attention. Beneath his scorn for Louie as the one who can "pick up a dinner party and walk off with it" (47) lies Cather's painful feeling of neglect as the outsider while somebody else steals the show. Whispering to Lillian, "That's another secret we have to keep. We have such lots of them!" (76), Louie's smug conspiratorial airs seem to derive from Cather's feelings of being left out of her friend's private life, the friend with whom she had previously confided secrets. Louie's public displays of affection — kissing Mrs. St. Peter as his "dearest" (39), proudly showing Rosamond off to the world as his beautiful wife — are made to seem gloating and proprietary, as if he were lording his conquests over the Professor — a portrait that more deeply projects Cather's own jealousy over her thwarted possessive interests. Above all, what most grates on the Professor's nerves is having to hear Louie's constant use of the word "our" — "our place" (40), "our wonderful wrought-iron door fittings" (39), "our excursion" (157), and so on — a vocabulary which, again, has its derivation in Cather's own frustrated possessive desire to say "mine."

Like the Professor, who snidely poses his two sons-in-law in a pageant as the sumptuous and pompous Saladin of Jerusalem, and the haughty and thoughtless Richard Plantagenet, so Cather, at one level, uses her art for revenge; she poses Jan Hambourg as "this — this Marsellus" (87) — a kind of foppish Mohammedan emperor or Roman prince — and hopes, as does the Professor, that no one will see "[her] little joke" (74). As Leon Edel speculates, Cather dedicated the novel to Jan Hambourg "to overcome her guilt over the unflattering portrait she had painted, or to disguise what she had done."[17] Certainly the revenge she takes in *The Professor's House* is less savage than that she takes in *A Lost Lady*; we need only compare the caricature of the odious Ivy Peters with the mildly offensive character of Louis Marsellus to see that Cather was trying to school herself to be more tolerant. She preserves the semblance of the Professor's neutrality, and encourages her own, by attributing her most hostile criticisms of Louie to the Professor's allies, Scott and Kathleen. Moreover, she has Lillian defend Louie throughout the novel; even the Professor is forced to admit towards the end that Louie is "magnanimous and magnificent!" (170) Instead of simply making Louie the novel's scapegoat, Cather takes pains to try to be fair to Louie, even having the Professor make him a handsome apology for the behavior of his family.[18]

Although the novel blames others for being greedy and grasping, the Professor makes demands of his wife and daughters that are, in their own way, selfish and impossible. When, at the opera, he wishes that he and his wife could return to a time before they had raised a family and gotten middle-aged, he denies Lillian's sexuality and maternal responsibilities towards others in the family; in his efforts to imagine her as an extension of himself, he dreams not of being "picturesquely shipwrecked together" (94) but of being shipwrecked alone. Similarly, his daughters drop out of his deepest inner life. In a moment of bitterness, he asks, "When a man had lovely children in his house, fragrant and happy, full of pretty fancies and generous impulses, why couldn't he keep them? Was there no way but Medea's, he wondered?" (126). Hoping to "keep" his daughters forever as pretty children who dance in fresh dresses and bring him flowers, he loses them not because they become corrupted by the culture but because they grow up. In the Greek myth, Medea had killed her children to spare them from becoming slaves; St. Peter equally wishes to prevent his children from becoming "owned" by others. Although he doesn't resort to murder, he figuratively enacts Medea's solution by replacing his wife and daughters with the decapitated dressmaker's "forms" that occupy his study. The one, with its deceptively "ample and billowy" maternal bosom, in reality "the most unsympathetic surface imaginable" (18), serves as a surrogate for Lillian; the other, with its "sprightly, tricky air," as if it were "just on the point of tripping down-stairs, or on tiptoe, waiting for the waltz to begin" (18–19), serves as a surrogate for the lively young girls.[19] Whereas the Professor regrets that "cruel biological necessities" (21) and other people have taken away the actual women in his family, he vows to keep an exclusive imaginative possession of these substitutes, protesting to Augusta, who comes to claim them, "You shan't take away *my* ladies.... You can't have *my* women" (21–22, italics mine). Clearly, the Professor prefers the company of these headless and armless torsos to the real women in his family because they give him the illusion of company while being unable to hurt or disappoint him. Moreover, by dressing them up in gay frocks, Augusta can make those "terrible women entirely plausible" (101), again as beautiful and innocent little girls.

For Cather, the battle to possess the female muse had already been fought and lost in her previous novel, *A Lost Lady*. The central dramatic struggle for possession in *The Professor's House* is fought over Tom Outland, the Professor's youthful alter ego. Slipping on stairs, sweating profusely in his collar, eating potatoes off the back of his knife, Tom is a primitive, untaught in manners and the ways of civilization. As a boy whose hand "had never handled things that were not the symbols of ideas" (260), he is a transcendentalist, free of the encumbrances of traditions. From the day of his "fantastic" (257) entrance into the Professor's garden, as if by a strange destiny, his origins are mysterious. An orphan who has never known his parents and who "hasn't any birthday" (122), he is an ageless innocent, an unfallen Adam, without a past. His name suits him exactly because he is an Outlander[20] — with no more of a geographical than a historical connection to the world. If Tom comes from nowhere in time or space it is because he is not the semblance of a real person but a projected ideal of his author's. Maynard Fox has seen Tom Outland as a descendant of Huckleberry Finn,[21] and Richard Dillman has seen him as a descendant of Emerson's American Scholar,[22] but while both of these readings are illuminating, we can also understand Tom Outland in terms of Cather's own literary origins.

As Cather once wrote, the form of the book, with its inserted story, had been inspired by Dutch paintings in which a small square window opened out from the living room or kitchen:

> The feeling of the sea that one got through those square windows was remarkable.... In my book I tried to make Professor St. Peter's house rather overcrowded and stuffy with new things; American proprieties, clothes, furs, petty ambitions, quivering jealousies — until one got rather stifled. Then I wanted to open the square window and let in the fresh air that blew off the Blue Mesa, and the fine disregard of trivialities which was in Tom Outland's face and in his behaviour. (OW, 31–32)

Tom Outland comes out of the blue — out of the Blue Lake Michigan through the Professor's study window, and out of its recreation as the Blue Mesa, that other blue "ocean of clear air" (213). Most profoundly, he comes on the winds of inspiration from the free expanse of consciousness itself. Louie's comment to the Professor, as he walks into his study one day, "Your children were born here. Not your daughters — your sons, your splendid Spanish-adventurer sons!" (165), could as well refer to Tom Outland, the foundling who is most powerfully born as the offspring of the Professor's mind. A pioneer spirit who had grown up in that "great dazzling South-west country" (258), Tom is a character come to life. His arrival helped Cather, also, "to see old perspectives trans- formed by new effects of light" (258), for in his company, she could imaginatively revisit the country of her earlier literary pilgrimages to see with a restored vision. Like the Professor, Cather herself "had got as far as the third volume" — *Alexander's Bridge* — when she was visited by "a boy with imagination" — a second self. Now that she, too, has gotten to the eighth volume, Tom Outland returns to her as the primitive archetype of all her imaginative claimants. Like St. Peter, Cather "had had two romances: one of the heart, which had filled [her] life for many years, and a second of the mind — of the imagination" (258). When her romance of the heart with Isabelle lost its "morning brightness," she turned back to the life of the mind and its initial inspiration, incarnated in Tom Outland, who brings her "a kind of second youth" (258).

Like Cather's other protagonists, Tom is an exceptional personality. As the Professor reflects, he was "always very different from the other college boys, wasn't he? Always had something in his voice, in his eyes.... One seemed to catch glimpses of an unusual background behind his shoulders when he came into the room" (132). Tom's difference, like that of Alexandra Bergson or Thea Kronborg, lies in his possession of a unique "something" — a remarkable soul, or genius, that imbues the space around him with a personal aura. Ultimately, his "unusual back- ground" affords the Professor — and Cather — an entrance into the exemplary imaginative space of her own fiction. The only one allowed to share the Professor's private study and garden, Tom embodies that one passion in four walls. The conversations that the Professor holds with Tom in his study are resonant as the conversations that Cather must often have held with her companion self while writing her novels. Tom's diary, a "plain account" that strikes the Professor as "beautiful, because of the ... things it did not say" (262), is itself a version of Cather's spare style that strove to evoke beauty by indirect suggestion. Tom's diary, like Cather's "diaries" in the subtexts of her novels, is the private recording of his own emotions and imaginative desires, the more forceful for being held in reserve: "through this austerity one felt the kindling imagination, the ardour and excitement of the boy, like the vibration in a voice when the speaker strives to conceal his emotion" (262–63). Moreover, we might consider Tom's discovery of "the principle of the Outland vacuum" (40) as analogous to Cather's own invention as an artist of the novel démeublé — an empty space reserved for nothing but the pure life of consciousness — a vacuum of sorts. Although designed to fuel airplane engines, this vacuum more profoundly fueled the flights of

Cather's imagination. Like Tom, Cather had taken care to protect her art by "patent" (40), but she found that life, unlike art, refused to shelter her in the vacuum of her dreams.

Affirming Tom as an unworldly prince of virtue and integrity, Kitty laments to her father, "Yes, and now he's all turned out chemicals and dollars and cents, hasn't he? But not for you and me! *Our* Tom is much nicer than theirs" (132, italics mine). By juxtaposing the claims made by the Professor and Louie to Tom, Cather insists on the superiority of *her* Tom — an artistic ideal she wanted to keep untainted by the world and the claims of others. Louie Marsellus's commercial exploitation of the Outland vacuum to build "Outland," his overcrowded and over-furnished Norwegian manor house, more deeply signifies for Cather the invasion of her sovereign creative space. Tom Outland had "made a will in [Rosamond's] favour" (41) only to have her husband, Louie, exploit it. Similarly, Cather felt that she had willed the valuable inheritance of her art to Isabelle, only to have her husband, Jan, promote it. In a moment of reminiscence, Kathleen tells her father, "Now that Rosamond has Outland, I consider Tom's mesa entirely my own" (131). Similarly, Cather seems to acknowledge that now that Isabelle has Ville-D'Avray and Jan, she will turn back to the imaginative territory they had once shared and reclaim it for herself alone. Nobody, she seems to say, can take away from her that original estate.

Leon Edel has suggested that Ville-D'Avray is recreated as the house that the Professor's family is building, but more precisely, it is recreated as the Marsellus's Norwegian manor house, as "out of scale" (76) and foreign as a French villa. Rosamond, in fact, makes the Professor the same offer that Isabelle had recently made to Cather when, on a visit to her father's old study, she says, "Won't you let me build you a little study in the back yard of the new house? I have such good ideas for it, and you would have no bother about it at all" (59). Louie's efforts to convert their new house into "a sort of memorial" (42) to Tom Outland mirror the Hambourgs' efforts to set aside part of their new home as a tribute to Willa Cather and her art. Just as Louie eagerly promises, "We are going to transfer his laboratory there," so the Hambourgs had zealously promised Cather that in her new study at Ville-D'Avray, she would find all her "books and instruments, all the sources of [her] inspiration" (42). As Scott's comment, "Even Rosamond," reminds us, Cather would find "even Isabelle" — her greatest source of inspiration — at the new house, just as in the old days. However, though Cather had cherished Isabelle along with her other "instruments" at the old house, she could not, as Edel has suggested, bring herself to share all of these things with the interloper, Jan. She makes it clear that the new "Outland" is a vulgar sham that merely makes a travesty of all that Tom — the persona of her own original muse — had stood for. After Louie's boastful announcements at the dinner party, the Professor complains, "They've got everything he ought to have had, and the least they can do is to be quiet about it, and not convert his very bones into a personal asset" (47). In her resentment against Jan for taking away her most valued treasures, Cather was determined to cling all the more tenaciously to her own ego so as to prevent that, too, from being appropriated as his property. Cather thus claims that while Louie/Jan thinks he has played a role in Tom's discovery "until he almost thinks it's his own idea" (87), he really knows nothing about the true "genesis of the Outland engine" (41) at all. Speaking through Scott, she wants to let her antagonist know that he "had never so much as seen Tom Outland" (42), her original self, and that he never would. Outland is her affair, and hers alone.

Like the Professor, who insists to his wife, ""Hang it, Outland doesn't need their generosity!" (47), Cather wished to reject Jan's offers of patronage. St. Peter's remark to Rosamond, "Nothing hurts me so much as to have any member of my family talk as if we had done something fine for that young man, brought him out, produced him" (62), suggests that the enigmatic "hurt" that Cather felt she had suffered from her family has its source in wounded pride and compromised independence. As she portrayed herself as early as *Alexander's Bridge,* Cather had, in fact, been "brought out" and largely "produced" by her patroness, Isabelle McClung. She had been the raw Western youth, much like Tom Outland, whom Isabelle had helped to educate and refine into cultured society. Thanks to the financial support and background that Isabelle had provided, Cather had been able to write and publish her first works. But for Cather, there was a world of difference between Isabelle's welcome patronage and Jan Hambourg's. In fact, she had good reason to be sensitive about the degree of Jan's influence in her own career. In the way that Louie had helped Tom Outland "[get] the idea over from the laboratory to the trade" (41), Jan had helped Willa Cather make her art more marketable and profitable. As Alfred Knopf recounts, Jan Hambourg had been the biggest influence on Cather in one of the most major decisions of her career: on Jan's advice, she switched publishers from Houghton Mifflin to Knopf in 1920.[23] She had made the change for financial reasons. By the spring of 1920, *My Àntonia* had been out a year and a half, and as Edith Lewis remembers, it had made only $1300 in the first year, and a meager $400 in the second.[24] *One of Ours* was coming along slowly. When Cather herself recounted her decision to adopt a new publisher, she did not mention Hambourg but merely said, "It was a rather sudden decision."[25] For all her awareness of St. Peter's faults, Cather

seems to support him in his resentment of Louie for exploiting and com-
mercializing Tom Outland's pure idea for profit. It may be that in
Cather's largely negative portrait of Louie, she was working out her own
ambivalent feelings about Jan's involvement in her own career. Although
no doubt, at a conscious level, she recognized Jan's advice and assistance
as necessary and supportive, she did not like being indebted to others for
the welfare of her art. As much as she herself wanted to make her novels
a financial success, she liked to think of them as free and living messen-
gers of her soul. As she put it in a letter to Mary Austin, a book is like an
individual sustained by nothing but her own vitality.[26] Throughout her
career, Cather would feel a deep ambivalence towards sharing her art,
conceived in the most private of spheres, with all of the publishers and
critics who promoted it in the public marketplace. Increasingly, as Cather
grew older, she viewed the artistic enterprise as a matter of self-protec-
tion. After Cather received unfavorable reviews of her book of essays
Not Under Forty, in the late 1930s, she confessed to Zoë Akins that she
felt silly for having publicized her credo; she reflected that one ought to
keep and protect one's articles of faith as the most private of secrets.[27]
Possessing the articles of one's faith as the most protected of secrets is
what *The Professor's House* is largely about. In the guise of the Professor, who wonders, "Was it for this the light in Outland's laboratory
used to burn so far into the night!" (90), Cather seems to betray a fear
that the light of her own intellectual lamp that used to burn brightly
through years of solitary labor might be snuffed out by the distracting
claims of others encountered in the public limelight. As if to reclaim full
independence over the creation of her art, and deny commercial necessities, Cather portrays Louie Marsellus as the one who is "terribly indebted" (41) to her alter ego, Tom Outland, instead of the other way
around.[28]

The Professor feels that his prize money is not adequate compensation
for the "fun" he had writing his history, something "one couldn't get …
for twenty thousand dollars" (33). Cather had liked to think that for her,
as for the Professor and Tom, the value of art lay in the process of its
creation, not in its monetary results. In the process of selling her work
and gaining a public reputation, however, she found it increasingly difficult to preserve her imaginative engagement with her material. The inevitable cost of her "vulgar success" (150) was that her art got divided up
by profits and the worldly claims of others. In the novel, Cather defies
not only Jan Hambourg but all those with his "salesman's ability" (138)
— publishers, advertisers, and promoters who "[knew] the twists and
turns by which [her] patent could be commercialized" (137). In Dr.
Crane, Tom Outland's old laboratory partner, one who also wants to

claim his "rights in the Outland patent" (135), we see a representative of all those marketers who were demanding a commercial part in Cather's work. Although, ostensibly, the Professor wants to see Crane get his fair share, the novel's deeper impulse is to deny all other claims to the patent as selfish and fraudulent. In Cather's view, nobody can have a real share in Tom's profits, since those profits, like those she gained from her own art, were imaginative and not material. The Professor's hostile challenge to his colleague, "Just how much was it 'our' gas Crane?" (145), is simultaneously the challenge that Cather increasingly leveled at publishers and advertisers towards the end of her career. Her attitude towards her art, like the Professor's attitude towards Tom's patent and friendship, is emphatically proprietary; as her letters reveal, her books are "the one thing [she would] not have translated into the vulgar tongue" (62). Cather had wanted her books to sell well, but on her terms. Despising the crude industry of anthologies, Cather wrote to her old publisher, Ferris Greenslet, that Àntonia was a choice piece of property that they should keep to themselves.[29] When a scriptwriter named Totheroh dramatized *A Lost Lady* in 1936, Cather angrily wrote to Zoë Akins that he had no business squatting on her land when it was not up for sale.[30] For Cather, as for the Professor and Tom, art had a dubious reward when its completion translated it into a piece of property that could be possessed by others.

* * *

In "Tom Outland's Story" — the inset tale that Tom tells of his boyhood in the Southwest — Cather opens her narrative window to let the fresh air of the Blue Mesa into the stifling atmosphere of the Professor's house. The loving description of the stone village on the mesa, a sacred space of purity, beauty, simplicity, and uncluttered order, is largely a reproach to the messiness in which the Professor's family, and most families, live. But if, at one level, Tom's story of discovery provides a refreshing escape to a world transcending place and time, it is also a "story of youthful defeat" (176). Although Cather liked to emphasize how her story functioned in juxtaposition to the rest of the novel, it more deeply functions as a parallel reworking of the novel's central issue: the struggle for possession. Once again, Cather presents the crucial debate as a competition between material ownership and imaginative appropriation of nature. Like the Professor's art, Tom's art is converted into the only currency that his society understands, when his friend, Roddy Blake, sells the pottery and other Indian artifacts that they have excavated from the mesa to a German antiquarian. "Everything," Roddy explains in his defense, "come[s] to money in the end" (244). Overwhelmed by a feeling of irreparable loss and betrayal, Tom, in turn, tries to explain to Roddy "the kind of value those objects had had for me" (245). For him, the relics are important as stimuli to the imagination. Ostensibly, Cather roots this conflict in history and culture. She presents the legend of the Cliff Dwellers' extermination by the pillaging materialistic tribe, "without culture or domestic virtues" (221), as a desecration that she saw reenacted in her own time. When Tom makes his visit to Washington, D. C., to see if he can interest experts in his discovery, he encounters a twentieth-century version of these same philistines, now disguised in coat and tie: petty officials who are indifferent to all cultural and aesthetic values, interested only in acquiring material possessions and social status. But beneath this overlay of historical interest and cultural criticism, Cather dramatizes the conflict between Tom and Roddy out of a more personal need to defend her own artistic "patent" — this time conceived as the mesa and its relics. Moreover, she uses their dispute to reexamine the conflict, rooted in her own biography, between the artist's sovereign claim to an imaginative territory and her involvement with others.

On the surface, Tom chastises Roddy for selling a valuable national treasure; as he exclaims, "They weren't mine to sell — nor yours! They belonged to this country, to the State, and to all the people" (242). Beneath his patriotic Fourth of July rhetoric, however, Tom gives his real loyalty to the country of his own psychological creation. Wanting to see and touch everything "like home-sick children when they come home" (240), Tom emotionally returns to the territory of childhood that preserves his feelings of omnipotent power. Though we might see the mesa as a "monument" (190) commemorating a historic past, Cather presents it as a memorial to Tom's own creative spirit. In deliberate contrast to the pretentious "memorial" that Louie would erect in Tom's memory, the "naked blue rock" (186) of the mesa provides his proper background, as primitive and essential as the boy himself. It, too, is solitary, "set down alone in the plain." It is the place of escape where the wild things go. When their cattle run away to the mesa, Tom and Roddy follow, not to retrieve but to join them and lose the rest of the herd of common humanity. Indeed, the mesa seems "enchanted" and tantalizing primarily because of its mysterious inaccessibility; it has the charm of being uncharted ground that awaits the boys' sovereign claim. "Nobody had ever climbed" (186) the mesa, Tom fantasizes, until he first set foot upon it as its conqueror. When Tom returns to the mesa from Washington, he rejoices, "Once again I had that glorious feeling that I've never had anywhere else, the feeling of being *on the mesa,* in a world above the world" (240). Hardly a public space, the mesa offers the same psychological and aesthetic benefits as Cather's kingdom of art, that "clear firmament of creation where the world is not" (KA, 407). The boys inhabit the cliff city as Cather inhabited the sanctuary of her own art — as a "stronghold," safe against the threatening intrusions and bustling business of the nation. Suspended in air, the "cliff-hung villages" seem exempt from the laws of reality below. They have been "preserved in the dry air and almost perpetual sunlight like a fly in amber, guarded by the cliffs and the river and the desert" (202), as if they had been protected even from the elements and the wearing effects of time.

Such immortal repose could belong only to the static world of art — not the chaotic world of life — to uninhabited houses that are "as still as sculpture — and something like that" (201). Tom imagines that the Cliff Dwellers themselves were artists who "lived for something more than food and shelter" (219), dedicated to the life of the spirit. Indeed, if the mesa's air seems to "go to [Tom's] head ... produc[ing] a kind of exaltation ... very different from the air on the other side of the river, though that was pure and uncontaminated enough" (200), that is because it embodies the heady air of consciousness itself. As Cather wrote in her 1916 essay on Mesa Verde, the inspiration for her fictional mesa, "No sinister ideas lurk in the sun-drenched ruins hung among the crags"; rather, "human consciousness ... dwelt there."[31] Like the watchtower that "was the fine thing that held all the jumble of houses together and made them mean something" (201), Tom's is the contemplative Emersonian eye that integrates all the parts. When, after first beholding the mesa, Tom closes his eyes and imagines the scene as a picture "against the dark, like a magic-lantern slide" (204), we are reminded that, from the first, he most vividly sees a projection of his own desire. Cather herself had long imagined such a scene in the magical dimension of her mind, first projected in her story "The Enchanted Bluff." Illumined by the sunset to look like a giant inkwell — "like one great ink-black rock against a sky on fire" (193) — the mesa looms most impressively as a symbol of Cather's vocation as a writer.

By selling the artifacts, Roddy assigns a worldly value to the sanctuary that Tom wanted to reserve for art. While Tom was cherishing the mesa as "a world above the world," Roddy was remembering that Tom "had [his] way to make in the world" (243). Roddy's transgression focuses the conflict between the necessities of art, as Cather saw them, and the demands of life. Though Tom has a strong allegiance to his best friend, he has an even stronger allegiance to his own ego and artistic genius — that "something else that made [him] absolutely powerless" (247) to compromise and detain him. Tom can't get around the fact that Roddy's selling of the Indian pottery, in which he had invested something of himself, cheapens his own nature. Like Cather's previous imaginative claimants, Tom "idealized the people he loved and paid his devoir to the ideal rather than to the individual" (172). As long as Roddy behaved as the "sort of fellow who [could] do anything for somebody else, and nothing for himself" (185), he lived up to Tom's self-gratifying ideal. However, just as Jim had rejected Àntonia, and Niel rejected Marian, so Tom drives Roddy off the mesa when he discovers to his dismay that his companion no longer shares his consciousness.

Though Tom denies that he regards the artifacts as his "private property" (245), his spiritual investment in them does, as Roddy implies, make them exclusively his. After Roddy leaves the mesa, it becomes even more clear that only one can inhabit Tom's imaginative world. Secure on a "solitary rock ... like an island" (250), Tom lives out the Professor's fantasy of total escape from all others. Only now that he is "up there alone, a close neighbour to the sun" (251), but to no other human beings, is he fully free to inhabit the mesa as a high plateau of consciousness. Like St. Peter lying low in his boat in the purple water, Tom, lying at the bottom of his purple canyon, watches his thoughts unfold in the air above him. He finds that "the climb of the walls helps out the eye, somehow" because it blots out the rest of the world and lets him focus his vision on the halo of his own divine nature, suggested by a silvery blue "arc of sky" (250). The sunset also helps out his eye, dissolving the physical reality of the canyon walls until "only the rim rock at the top held the light." Himself "full to the brim" with "that consuming light" (252), Tom may have lost the vessels of pottery but he imaginatively transforms the entire rock canyon into a vessel filled with his vitality.

Like Thea Kronborg, who enjoys a feeling of being "all there" as a fully reconstituted self in Panther Canyon, Tom reflects that "that was the first night I was ever really on the mesa at all — the first night that all of me was there" (250). In his great epiphany, he recognizes that "something had happened in me that made it possible for me to co-ordinate and simplify, and that process, going on in my mind, brought with it great happiness. It was possession" (250–51). By merely recovering an inner unity, Tom Outland, like Emerson's poet, is able to take imaginative "possession" of the landscape as an extension of his soul. Reorganizing the unpeopled landscape around the coordinating axis of the self, he sees his world "as a whole" (250) that mirrors his own undivided nature.

We can appreciate the intensity with which Cather identified with Tom Outland's "possession" of the mesa if we consider her own motives for traveling to such inviting scenes. Between Cather's return from

France to write the novel in 1923 and the date of its publication in 1925, she traveled extensively for visits and vacations to the Poconos, Nebraska, Michigan, Grand Manan, Arizona, New Mexico, Colorado, and Maine. In her many personal journeys, Cather sought a spiritual self-restoration. Of a trip to Italy in 1935 after an illness, she wrote to Carrie Miner that the solitude near the lakes had allowed her to recover her lost soul.[32] Perhaps the first time that Cather recovered her soul from the contemplation of a beautiful landscape was in France, where she and Isabelle visited in 1902. She reported to *McClure's* of the seaside village, Lavandou, that "nothing else in England or France has given me anything like this sense of immeasurable possession and immeasurable content"(WP, 944). As "possessors of a villa on the Mediterranean and the potentates of a principality of pines," she and Isabelle gained a sense of power over their own private kingdom that was "good for one's soul" (WP, 944). Jaffrey, New Hampshire, and the island of Grand Manan, New Brunswick, where Cather and Edith Lewis had a cottage, yielded the same emotional return in her later years. Feeling bereaved of herself in the chaotic city of New York, Cather habitually escaped to Jaffrey, where she could recoup her losses. As she recalls in a letter written at the Shattuck Inn just one year after *The Professor's House* was published, the only way she could live freely so as to possess her soul was to escape New York City for at least eight months of the year.[33] As her novels suggest, the American Southwest offered Cather the fullest sense of possessing her soul. A symbolic composite of all the places Cather chose to visit for her own self-restoration, Tom's mesa embodies a mental space that cannot be located on any map. It seems that the more Cather felt dispossessed of herself by others, the more she, like Tom, turned for compensation to nurturing landscapes.

Nevertheless, "Tom Outland's Story" does reveal Cather's shaken faith in both the efficacy and the moral validity of such imaginative conquests. As Tom wakens, after his falling out with Roddy, to "the feeling that I had found everything, instead of having lost everything" (251), Cather seems to admit that her myth of possession is a strategy conceived out of loss. As if the language in the scene were claiming too much for itself, we are aware that the compensation it provides is ultimately an illusion, concealing an underlying dissatisfaction. For all that clear air, Tom's self-possession on the mesa is clouded by his tragic loss of Roddy. His story ends by registering a note of guilt and regret: "But the older I grow, the more I understand what it was I did that night on the mesa. Anyone who requites faith and friendship as I did, will have to pay for it. I'm not very sanguine about good fortune for myself. I'll be called to account when I least expect it" (253). Reevaluating the balance of payments in human relationships, this passage signifies a major change in Cather's fiction. Whereas, ever since *Alexander's Bridge*, she had put a premium on the individual's precious possession of self, now she weighs the scales in favor of a greater "fortune" to be found in friendships. Although she had feared that human relationships would diminish the self, here she admits that self-absorption exacts an equal cost on human relationships: to save his soul, Tom has had to pay the price of giving up his dearest friendship; the exchange seems an unfair trade, as if his possession of selfhood were only the second best thing to having companionship. As Tom imagines being "called to account" to pay his dues in the future, he secretly admits that he has committed a kind of crime for which he must seek exculpation. Cather thus implies that we do "owe" a debt of sympathy to our friends, even if they do not fully meet our needs. She concedes that Tom's solitary epiphany on the mesa is not enough to sustain him; he must also involve himself in mean-ingful social relationships if he is to reap the most valuable rewards of experience.

Throughout the argument between Tom and Roddy, Cather betrays her qualms about the rightness of Tom's position. For one of the first times in her fiction, she shines a sympathetic light on a character who disagrees with her protagonist-surrogate. Roddy's reproach to Tom, "Motives don't count, eh?" (246), seems just, reminding us that he had deposited all of the money in the bank in Tom's name to put him through school. By contrast, Tom's disdain for the money, which he'd no more touch than if Roddy had "stolen it," seems self-righteous and heartless. When, during his farewell, Roddy wishes Tom good luck, adding, "I'm glad it's you that's doing this to me, Tom; not me that's doing it to you" (247–48), he leaves us with the impression that he is the most generous and least to blame of the two. Indeed, Cather takes some pains to exonerate Roddy, as suggested by Tom's ambivalent attitude towards him throughout the scene. Feeling simultaneous antipathy and sympathy for his friend, Tom curses Roddy's "stupidity and presumption" (239) but concedes that he didn't mean to sell him out. Although he insists that Blake must have known how he felt about the mesa, he admits that he had never talked with him about it directly. In reality, Roddy had good reason to assume that Tom had hoped to sell the artifacts to the government. Furthermore, Tom realizes that he himself did not know how much he cared for these things until after he had lost them. In the course of their argument, he has the candor to confess that he is not completely honest with Roddy about his own motives; he "lie[s]" (243) that he had made plans that would have enabled them to continue their excavation. Finally, when Roddy prepares to leave, Tom's emotions are divided; even though he is constitutionally unable to stop him, he nonetheless felt "an ache in my arms to reach out and detain him" (247). Thereafter, Tom's efforts to find Roddy attest to his nagging misgivings about his decision.

Finally, Cather regretfully admits, for the first time in her career, that her own story has been one of defeat as well as victory, irrevocable loss as well as gain. The most important reason that Roddy is on the Professor's "conscience" (131) is that he — or she — is on Willa Cather's, too. Leon Edel has suggested that Cather identified the mesa and tower with the McClung's house in Pittsburgh, a retreat similarly situated on high ground. He cites her dedication to Isabelle McClung in *The Song of the Lark*, the first novel to draw upon the Southwest:

> On uplands,
> At morning,
> The world was young, the winds were free;
> A garden fair
> In that blue desert air,
> Its guest invited me to be.

As Edel makes the analogy, "Uplands has become Outland. The world in the 'blue desert air' of the mesa is a re-creation of the feeling of freedom Willa Cather had experienced in her life with Isabelle, patron of the arts, and in the sewing-room sanctuary of the Pittsburgh mansion."[34] Edel then suggests that Cather incorporates her "fantasy of rejection and loss" into the story of Tom's betrayal by "his 'loyal' buddy [who] has denuded his cliff sanctuary of all that was precious to him." By projecting her sufferings through Outland, she could say, "I was robbed, robbed, robbed!"[35] Tom "reads" evidences of human labor in the mesa "as a sort of message" (194); similarly, Cather seems to engage in an imaginative act of archeology, excavating and interpreting the "secrets" of her own personal past.[36] The fictional exploration of the mesa recreates the time when Cather shared with Isabelle that "garden fair" in the McClung mansion, making discoveries about herself and her art. Like Tom, she had assumed that she and her companion were valuing the relics of her art in the same way, as containers of the artist's desire. By getting married, Isabelle had, in Cather's view, betrayed these sacred tokens of her creativity, exchanging them for the things of the material, social world — houses and jewels, marriage and family. The selling of the relics becomes Cather's metaphor for her friend's "selling out" — letting others in on the private world of art and its treasures that Cather had so zealously tried to dig up and possess for herself and a select few ever since she wrote "The Treasure of Far Island." We recall that when Tom

first finds the mesa, "hidden away" for centuries, he wonders if he ought
to tell even Roddy about it. Very probably, Cather felt that she, too, had
done Isabelle a favor by initiating her into the sacred kingdom of her art.
According to the rules of the play, it was not Isabelle's prerogative to
admit somebody else into the camaraderie without Cather's permission.
Rather than just repudiate Isabelle for her defection from the partnership,
however, as she had done through her fictional disguises in *My Àntonia*
and *A Lost Lady*, she now acknowledges the absence of her friend in her
life as a real loss. She even is willing to admit that her own selfish devotion to her art, and her own blindness to human needs, may have driven
her companion away. She confronts the disillusioning reality that she and
Isabelle, like Tom and Roddy, may have been living in different worlds
all along, and that it was only when she, like Tom, was "betrayed" that
she fully appreciated the differences in those values.

Though "Tom Outland's Story" was in part inspired by Cather's trip
to the Southwest with Edith Lewis in 1915, its compositional history
suggests that its more profound psychological genesis lay in Cather's
rupture with Isabelle McClung in 1916. Cather began "Tom Outland's
Story" as a piece called "The Blue Mesa" during the late summer and fall
of 1916; she had put *My Àntonia* aside in her disappointment over
Isabelle's impending marriage.[37] On 22 August 1916, she wrote to Ferris
Greenslet that she was planning a book called *The Blue Mesa* that would
be impelled by love and hate.[38] Presumably, the book never became a
book but was later incorporated into *The Professor's House* as "Tom
Outland's Story." In a sense, "The Blue Mesa" serves as the missing link
between the introduction to *My Àntonia* and the body of that novel, as it
deals more directly with the painful biographical material that Cather was
trying to evade. In the diary that Tom Outland leaves behind him on the
mesa, we can see an analogy to Cather's story "The Blue Mesa" — for
her, also, a personal record of a past imaginative experience put away
and preserved over the years. Like the stories about the noble and heroic
Roddy that he loved to tell the little girls, Tom's diary had no "shadows"
(123); written before his "fruitless errand" in Washington and his break
with Roddy, it is a sunny story of perfect joy. When Tom returns to live
on the mesa alone, he doesn't resume his diary, reflecting, "I didn't want
to go back and unravel things step by step. Perhaps I was afraid that I
would lose the whole in the parts" (252). Tom can preserve his feeling of
wholeness on the mesa only at the expense of the parts — like Roddy,
whose part in his drama Tom chooses to repress from his memory that
summer. By keeping his diary safely "sealed ... up" in its "stone cupboard" (259), Tom symbolically preserves his happy memories in an air-
tight, vacuum-sealed container. If we take Tom's diary as the emblem of

the "vacuum" that he later discovers, we can see him as an artist who, like his author, seeks to create in art an unfurnished sanctuary occupied only by the spirit. By setting aside "The Blue Mesa" for nine years, Cather, too, was trying to seal her story off in a vacuum of its own, impervious to the disturbing parts of human experience. The fact that Tom puts his diary in the Eagle's Nest, where he had found "Mother Eve," the corpse of the woman murdered for adultery, suggests Cather's own neat substitution of eternal art for agonizing social and sexual relationships and betrayals. In the narrative form of the novel that sets Tom's story apart from the main plot, like a "turquoise set in dull silver,"[39] Cather similarly attempts to isolate and protect his joy on the mesa in an imaginative world of its own.

Like Tom, Cather may have originally composed her "diary" as a way of gaining a compensatory feeling of wholeness against loss; as Edel has suggested, "Tom Outland's Story" fulfilled Cather's needs as a cathartic "self-rescue."[40] At the same time, it provided her with painful self-criticism. The story that Cather tells in "Tom Outland's Story" is a more complicated and honest version of Tom Outland's diary. In spite of its attempt to be a fantasy, it is a realistic tale that includes the sorrowful story of Tom's loss and ends by foreboding a day of reckoning for its author. Ultimately, Cather is the author who is "called to account" when she reexamines the story of her past history. Through the Professor, whose primary occupation in the last section of the novel is to edit Tom's diary, Cather, in effect, engages in a mature process of editing, or annotating, her own career and artistic achievement. In the guise of the Professor, who returns to the mesa to retrieve the journal from its stone cupboard, where it has been packed away for many years, Cather returns after many years to her abandoned story, "The Blue Mesa." She removes her art from its insulation within the empty and self-enclosed space of dreams, and examines it and its values in the light of real life, with its hardships, compromises, and multiple experiences and points of view. As the editor and annotator of Tom's diary, the Professor faces a "bother[some]" (171) task. He must write both an introduction and a conclusion in order to make sense of the boy's experience on the mesa. It would not be enough to write merely about Tom's subsequent scientific work; "that was not all the story" (172). More importantly, he must relate the diary to Tom himself, "a many-sided mind" (172) and to "his later life and achievements" (171). Certainly for Cather, too, such a task was not as much "fun" as her earlier writing. She seems to accept that the story of artistic discovery is "not all the story," after all; the complete story is more problematic and must go beyond that joyful beginning. Though we never find out whether the Professor finishes editing Tom's diary, we might say that he completes the task by undergoing a change in his own life. Though his initial excavation of the diary helps him to recover his own first youth, and thus figuratively to write an "introduction," his subsequent annotation of the diary helps him to bring Tom's life, and his own, to a new conclusion. Whereas Tom had discarded "the parts" of his life to preserve the spirit of the whole, the Professor must reintegrate such particulars into Tom's account — and his own life — if they are to be accurate and true. By writing the Professor's story in part 3 as the appended conclusion to Tom Outland's story, Cather concedes that life goes beyond the ending of the tales she had told in the past. In his reincarnation as the Professor, Tom Outland grows up.

* * *

While reading Tom Outland's stirring account of his imaginative possession of the mesa, the Professor takes stock of his own "estate" (266) — his innate inheritance as "the original, unmodified Godfrey St. Peter" (263). Recalling how his grandfather, the old Napoleon Godfrey, had recovered his "first nature" (267) in his last days, the Professor read-opts the "Napoleon" within himself — that youthful conqueror who had claimed the world as his own. He had "abbreviated" (163) his name when he got married, just as he had abbreviated his essential self through social and sexual roles; "even his daughters didn't know what [his name] had been originally" (163), for the original self had to be an outcast from his socially constructed self. His "secondary" (265) life as a husband and father, based upon a sexual identity that "grafted a new creature into the original one" (267), divided the being he was back in the beginning. His wife, children, friends, colleagues — all were accumulated by the social and sexual self as secondary possessions, and like Thea Kronborg in her cave, he casts them all away in a consummate gesture of egotism. Reflecting that he went astray when he became a "lover," he decides that he no longer needs to negotiate the distance between himself and other people and things; hereafter, he will narcissistically conjugate "to love" with only one object: himself. Discounting his adult life as the life of another person, he returns to his point of origin as an amoral and solipsistic primitive, at one with himself and the earth he came from. Like Tom on the mesa, absorbing the solar energy in a direct way, he basks peacefully in the sunshine, content simply to exist. It infuriates the Professor that ever since early childhood, his life had "been accidental and ordered from the outside" (264). Yet, by imagining that events have just happened to him, he escapes accountability for his life. As many critics have remarked, the Professor's identification with a presexual self is a way of denying his human, adult responsibilities.[41] The true, unfettered "God-free" need feel no obligations towards a wife and daughters.[42] Moreover, his retreat to childhood allows him to heal the wounds of his adult life: his sense of betrayal by Lillian, his disappointments in his daughters' lives, his grief over the loss of Tom Outland, even his dissatisfaction with his histories.

Tom's death seems to be an admission that the only way that the self can live exclusively on its own terms, as its "own master" (121), is by escaping life's obligations altogether. In the Professor's view, death comes as a blessing to Tom by immortalizing his innocence and wholeness that his duties towards others would have corrupted. Tom thus remains the romantic hero who discovers and conquers a world. When the Professor yields himself to the chance of accidental extinction from the gas stove in his study, he is motivated by a subconscious wish to recover his essential self through death also. As he lies down on his "box-couch" (277), looking up at the ceiling, he assumes simultaneously the position of Tom Outland, lying down in his "box canyon" (200), and a dead man lying in his box-coffin; Cather implies by analogy that in death, one can achieve complete possession of the self and the world as a lasting elation.

Finally, the Professor's instincts to survive prove stronger than his wish to die. Falling on his way to get to the door, he alerts the dutiful sewing woman, Augusta, who comes to his rescue. By having St. Peter live, Cather admits that the life of the original ego, able to thrive only at the sacrifice of the Professor's life, demands too great a cost. As in *Alexander's Bridge*, Cather conceives of a choice for her hero between two mutually exclusive and unsatisfactory alternatives: he can experience either a life-in-death or a death-in-life, and she chooses the latter. The life of the soul, though compelling and beautiful, is less important than life itself, even if that life is now reduced to its lowest terms as a matter of mere survival. The Professor is resurrected not into a new life of hopeful promise but into a life of stoic resignation.[43] Augusta models the new life that is possible for the Professor in his older years. As counsel for the future, she embodies the "bloomless side of life" (280) that he had always found unendurable. But, whereas his forbear, Niel, had been outraged at losing the early morning "bloom" of his existence, the Professor steels himself to live without delight and passionate joy in the future. Adjusting to a different reality, he reflects that, "he had let something go — and it was gone: something very precious" (282). Most critics have been puzzled by this cryptic reference. Doris Grumbach, for example, says that the Professor "has surrendered 'something,' ... but all we know of the something is that it was 'very precious.'"[44] Precious indeed, for we recognize what the Professor lets go as his own primary, original soul.

Bartley Alexander had been divided between awe and fear of that "something" in his own breast; Alexandra Bergson had held on to that "something" embodied in the land; Thea Kronborg had vowed to express and preserve that "something" in her music; Jim Burden had vicariously recovered that "something" in his childhood friend, Àntonia. Those, like Niel Herbert, who had failed to recover that ideal had bitterly protested against the loss. However, unlike each of his prototypes, who, in one way or another, tenaciously clings to this impulse of vitality at all costs, the Professor willingly releases it. Although his gesture of self-abnegation concedes that the ego is no longer sovereign, it finally empowers us because it suggests that if we relinquish that first identity we can take our places in the human family and go on living.

Writing in a gift copy of the novel to Robert Frost, "This is really a story of 'letting go with the heart'" (WC: AM, 215), Cather herself seems to let go her faith in an original ego, as if to acknowledge it as a fictitious construct. Wondering if Tom Outland had been only "some fugitive idea" (132) after all, she seems to doubt her myth of the romantic self as no more than a glittering illusion, an "idea" of the original, but not the original itself.[45] As an aging writer, she lets "something go" that has, in a sense, already departed. She lets go not only the physical vitality of her youth but the imaginative power to believe in that illusion as a reality. When, during the storm, the Professor's window shuts and the fire in his stove goes out, Cather acknowledges the loss of her own sources of inspiration — the loss of access to the imaginative region of the mesa and its pure air, the loss of vitality from the fires of her own ebbing genius. The attic that was once a garden fair threatens to become a suffocating tomb, commemorating an imaginative life that is no more. From now on, life will be, in the words of Frost's poem, a diminished thing.[46]

In its place, Cather gains a new territory that she has never before been willing to claim: reality. With the aid of Augusta, a being who is not in a world above the world but "on the solid earth" (281), Cather, like the Professor, can "[feel] the ground under [her] feet" (283). She descends to the plane of ordinary experience where facts and circumstances prevent the individual from having her own way. In the beginning, Cather, like the youthful Professor, had worshipped a theology of the will, believing that "a man can do anything if he wishes to enough" (29). But she progresses to believe that will, or desire, is not enough to control one's fate. Behind the Professor's realization that his family won't even notice his apathy lies Cather's acceptance of the fact that she is not the center of the world. As John Randall has observed, Cather reaches a new stage in her career where "she sees that the world is fundamentally indifferent to her; that it includes countless other people besides herself who have desires and wishes that they will try to follow despite her own desires and wishes."[47] Yet, for all the stoicism and pessimism of the novel's ending, it sounds a subdued note of optimism and recommitment. Instead of rejecting the world and retreating into the past, as she did in *A Lost Lady*, Cather forces herself, with her Professor, to move on to "face with forti-tude the *Berengaria* and the future" (283). For the Professor, the prospect of new life is vividly symbolized by the baby that Rosamond and Louie are expecting. Cather, too, seems to anticipate a new life when her family, like the Professor's, will return on that boat from France.[48] Having let go some of her own ego and pride, she will be able to accept future invitations from them. She, too, will be "outward bound" (281), even to onerous social conventions and responsibilities. Following the example of the good Catholic Augusta, who represents the commitment to community, she seems to see some salvation in the ideal of service to others. As if accepting that art in a "vacuum" is, after all, empty and sterile, she expresses a willingness to let others — even Jan Hambourg — inhabit her novel démeublé. Like the Professor who, in an early scene, separates his manuscripts from Augusta's patterns in the box-couch (22), Cather had tried in the course of the novel to separate her life work from the patterns of others' lives in hopes of preserving its integrity. As the symbolic repository of art, however, the box-couch suggests Cather's ambivalence towards her artistic priorities. As a container of manuscripts alone, designed to preserve the Professor's eternal solitude and auton-omy, the box-couch becomes a box-like coffin. Rejecting this paradigm of art, Cather seems willing to let the box-couch regain its intended function. By the end of the novel, she allows manuscripts and patterns to interpenetrate her imaginative space once again. Future visitors to the Professor's study will have a place to sit.

8

"How to Recover a Bishopric":
Cather's Recovery
of the Imaginative Territory
in *Death Comes for the Archbishop*

In a letter to Ida Tarbell, Cather wrote that her composition of *Death Comes for the Archbishop* (1927) was the most untarnished enjoyment of her life. She had shared the Archbishop's happy and serene mood, and when she finished writing the novel, she missed his companionship terribly. [1] What made writing *Death Comes for the Archbishop* such an enjoyable experience for Cather was that, once again, she managed to work with her protagonist as an alter ego who could successfully enact her own desires. In the prologue, Cather establishes the exalted "mission" of her missionary priest in terms that are analogous to her own mission as an author. In the Sabine hills above Rome in 1848, an American Bishop meets with three Cardinals over the appointment of a new Vicar who can impose "order" (8) on the undisciplined territory of New Mexico. According to the report of the American Bishop, the dissolute priests are breaking all the rules of ecclesiastical decorum, indulging in worldly pleasures and openly living in concubinage. As he states the challenge for his proposed new Vicar, Jean Latour: "If this Augean stable is not cleansed, now that the territory has been taken over by a progressive government, it will prejudice the interests of the Church in the whole of North America" (7). On the surface, Latour's religious and moral mission has little in common with Cather's commitments as an artist, which were more deeply aesthetic. In an 1894 essay, she wrote, "An artist should have no moral purpose in mind other than just his art. His mission is not to clean the Augean stables; he had better join the Salvation Army if he wants to do that" (KA, 406). But, though Cather did not want to engage in social causes, she wished, as an artist whose moral purpose was her art, to purge its domain of polluting elements. Spending most of the novel dutifully banishing the priests who threaten to usurp his authority, the Archbishop carries out a more profound appointment by Willa Cather to clean "the Augean stable" so as to restore it as the province ruled solely by the artist.

Death Comes for the Archbishop is an episodic novel (or, as Cather preferred to call it, "a narrative" [OW, 12]) loosely organized around the adventures of two priests and embedded with various anecdotes about the religious history of the Southwest. For many readers, the novel is so lacking in dramatic climax or emphasis that it becomes uninteresting; John Randall, for instance, has described it as a "hodgepodge leading nowhere."[2] Yet the novel is constructed to achieve a definite narrative goal. As James Woodress has noted, "What plot there is concerns itself with the gradual organization of the vast diocese and the bringing under a central authority, after decades of neglect, all the parishes scattered over hundreds of miles of mountains and deserts."[3] Interestingly, the plot's movement to bring all the people and places in the novel under the central authority of Bishop Latour merely literalizes the subtexts of Cather's earlier novels, which also seek to reorganize the world around the authority of her protagonists. We can best understand the Archbishop's spiritual conversion of others in the name of the Church as a disguised expression of an imaginative assimilation of others in the name of the self. In the guise of redeeming the landscape, the Archbishop appropriates it; while "claiming it for the glory of God" (22), he more deeply claims it for the glory of his own ego. The contest for "jurisdiction" (6) between the worldly, sensual priests and the intelligent, refined Archbishop is another version of the competition between the materialistic claims of the philistines and the imaginative claim of the artist that had preoccupied Cather in *A Lost Lady* and *The Professor's House*. Latour's displacement of his rivals allowed Cather to win the struggle for control of the kingdom of art that she had fought and lost in these earlier tormented works. According to Cather, the writing of the novel took only a few months "because the book had all been lived many times before it was written" (OW, 10). Inspired by a faith in the power of the individual to take imaginative possession of the world, the Archbishop reveals that Cather had kept faith with a story that she had told many times before in her career.

The American Bishop knows that of all the leaders in Christendom, only the parish priest from Canada, Jean Latour, will fulfill his requirements for the prestigious position in the New World. As he convinces the

Cardinals, "The new Vicar must be a young man, of strong constitution, full of zeal, and above all, intelligent" (8). As the outstanding individual chosen to fulfill a great destiny, Jean Latour conforms to the blueprint of Cather's earlier characters such as Alexandra Bergson and Thea Kronborg. Like them, he possesses that peculiar mark of genius — as Cather described it, "something fearless and fine and very, very well-bred — something that spoke of race" (OW, 7). Granted power over "a country larger than Central and Western Europe" (6), he asserts the most extensive claim of any of Cather's characters, getting to determine the fate not only of a farm or a town but of a virtual continent and its people. Yet, Latour's claim to his great diocese is not, finally, as bold as the imaginative claims of his predecessors. Edith Lewis once praised Cather's "magical gift" for writing history: "She could make the modern age almost disappear, fade away and become ghostlike, so completely was she able to invoke her vision of the past and recreate its reality" (WCL, 120). Lewis's wide-eyed praise for Cather as a writer of history unwittingly reveals another truth: that Cather's gift for historical reconstruction was more deeply inspired by a need to imaginatively erase the current age and refuse to come back to it. As if Cather realized that she could not win her struggle against modern-day materialists, she retreats from an uncongenial present into history, resetting the scene of the conflict in the mid-nineteenth century. Since Archbishop Latour's domination over the Southwest had a precedent in the success of his prototype, Archbishop Lamy of Santa Fé, [4] Cather could rest secure that history had already won her battle for her. Further escaping the limitations of the real world, Cather makes her hero a priest who, like the Acoma Indians, takes a "leap away from the earth" (97) to found a purely spiritual territory. His religious office grants him not only a safe insulation from the things of life but an automatic authority to fulfill his desires. Paradoxically, Latour's very power as a figure in the Church suggests the diminished confidence of his author. Whereas, in earlier novels, she had celebrated imaginative claimants who drew their strength from an innate genius, Jean Latour must depend on the incontrovertible institutional power of the entire church of Rome.

When Cather first published *Death Comes for the Archbishop*, she fooled many readers into thinking that she had converted to Catholicism. [5] Even Catholic commentators themselves have praised *Death Comes for the Archbishop* for its sympathetic and understanding treatment of Catholicism. [6] In an important article examining the Christian implications of the novel, John Murphy discusses the ways in which Father Latour's spiritual pilgrimage is patterned on Dante's journey from Hell to Paradise in *The Divine Comedy*. [7] I agree with Murphy's insight that

"Cather's attraction to a Dantean system was not a matter of orthodoxy so much as a desire for an integrating spiritual context."[8] In my view, Cather appropriates the vocabulary and structure of Christian pilgrimage and mythology not to affirm Christian values per se but to affirm "an integrating spiritual context." I believe that this "integrating spiritual context" is unorthodox indeed.[9] In Cather's next novel, *Shadows on the Rock*, she describes the faith that the dying Count Frontenac has in God as the destination of his spirit: "His spirit would go before God to be judged. He believed this, because he had been taught it in childhood, and because he knew there was something in himself and in other men that this world did not explain" (SR, 247). For Count Frontenac, as for his predecessor, Father Latour, faith in God is indistinguishable from a faith in "something in himself and in other men." It is not God's presence as a higher power, but an inner "something" possessed most strongly "in childhood" that sustains Cather's faith in the inexplicable mystery of life. Jean Latour dedicates his life to finding this "something in himself," which he, like Count Frontenac, ultimately finds in death, when he comes back to New Mexico to die in exile for the sake of it. Through her surro-gate, Cather accepted the authority of the Church as a medium through which she could liberate her own sacred spirit from worldly concerns and integrate it in its original wholeness. Cather appropriated religion in *Death Comes for the Archbishop* in order to sanction both the aesthetic creed and the primal fantasy that had underlain her work all along.

In her letter to *The Commonweal* in 1927, Cather justified the episodic form of her narrative as an attempt to capture in prose the effect of the hagiographic frescoes of the nineteenth-century French artist Puvis de Chavannes:

> Something in the style of legend, which is absolutely the reverse of dramatic treatment ... something without accent, with none of the artificial elements of composition. In the Golden Legend the martyrdoms of the saints are no more dwelt upon than are the trivial incidents of their lives; it is as though all human experiences, measured against one supreme spiritual experience, were of about the same importance. The essence of such writing is not to hold the note, not to use an incident for all there is in it — but to touch and pass on.... In this kind of writing the mood is the thing — all the little figures and stories are mere improvisations that come out of it. (OW, 9–10)

Cather's references to the frescoes and the medieval manual of ecclesias-tical lore imply that in her novel, great and little events are treated as equally important when measured against the supreme vision of heaven.[10] But there is a more covert organizational principle at work:

Cather makes all events and characters in the novel seem incidental next to the "one supreme spiritual experience" of the self. Like St. Geneviève in the Puvis de Chavannes frescoes, the saintly Archbishop stands out as the central figure in relief against peripheral, minor figures and objects. By simplifying and stylizing secondary characters as if they were two-dimensional figures allegorizing Christian virtues and vices, Cather minimizes their importance and confirms the centrality of her hero. Her narrative "without accent" gives her a formal pretext to "touch and pass" over disagreeable characters and facts of experience so as to subordinate all fictional elements to her central "mood." Omitting any discussion of her saint's "martyrdom" or sacrifices, and refusing to dwell on the "trivial incidents" of his conflicts with the other priests, Cather white-washes the plot in an atmosphere as calm and still as that of the static, flat-toned frescoes, an atmosphere that reflects the Bishop's own consciousness. Although, as a Frenchman, Latour is presented as one of "the great organizers," it is in his capacity as an artist that he is equipped to "arrange" life according to a proper "sense of proportion" (9), for he, too, knows how to subordinate the disparate parts of experience to his own ego.

From the beginning of her career, Cather had appropriated the rhetoric of religious incantation to exalt her quest as an artist. She saw the artist as the pilgrim-knight who was called to leave his home and renounce the things of this world to journey through the desert sands in search of "the holy sepulchre" (KA, 417). The artist had to be as exclusively devoted to his art as a religious convert to his religion, for, as she put it, "In the kingdom of art there is no God, but one God, and his service is so exacting that there are few men born of woman who are strong enough to take the vows" (KA, 417). Rosowski puts it well when she writes, "Cather replaced the kingdom of heaven with a kingdom of art, and she gave godhead to the Artist.... Cather did not make the artist a priestly representative of God so much as she made God a highly effective Artist."[11] I would reverse Rosowski's emphasis, however, to say that Cather imagined God as an artist in order to sanction her own aspirations towards godhead. In her 1894 description of God, Cather describes her image of the divine artist as an imaginative claimant who can appropriate all time and space: "The world was made by an Artist, by the divinity and godhead of art, an Artist of such insatiate love of beauty that He takes all forces, all space, all time to fill them with His universes of beauty ... [and] dreams" (KA, 178). Cather claimed the powers of a God to "take" and reorganize the universe as an ideal fictional kingdom that sanctioned the great forces of human passions. We can best understand Cather's religion of art by recalling Professor St. Peter's lecture on the superiority of art to science. As Cather herself lectures us,

As long as every man and woman who crowded into the cathedrals on Easter Sunday was a principal in a gorgeous drama with God, glittering angels on one side and the shadows of evil coming and going on the other, life was a rich thing. The king and the beggar had the same chance at miracles and great temptations and revelations. And that's what makes men happy, believing in the mystery and importance of their own little individual lives. It makes us happy to surround our creature needs and bodily instincts with as much pomp and circumstance as possible. Art and religion (they are the same thing, in the end, of course) have given man the only happiness he has ever had. (PH, 68–69)

David Stouck has argued that, for Cather, "art and religion ... are a lasting source of happiness because they transcend personal desire."[12] Cather's view of religion is not so orthodox, however. Far from depending on the individual's renunciation of power, Cather maintains that religion, like art, provides happiness precisely because it sanctions personal desire: it reassures human beings of the importance of their existence in the great scheme of things. By surrounding the self with "pomp and circumstance," Cather hoped to exclude those unpleasant aspects of physical experience — especially bodily appetites and biological functions — that she imagines to weaken the power of the self. Even though the Archbishop has a clerical role, he is as unbound by notions of a conventional God as is his skeptical prototype, "God-free" St. Peter. The Professor says that "cathedral-builders" as well as "theologians" might "without sacrilege, have changed the prayer a little and said, *Thy will be done in art, as it is in heaven*" (PH, 69). To Cather's mind, God didn't work his will very well on earth, but he could in art, because on that "stage" (PH, 69) the self could play His part. The real "miracle" of religion is that it enables the individual to cast himself as a "principal" in a wondrous, beautiful "drama." Wishing "to leave nothing to chance" (242), the cathedral-builder Jean Latour builds his church as a stage where he, as leading actor, can rule according to his own "will."

The first scene establishes both the Bishop's central problem and its resolution in the novel as a whole. Having "lost his way" (17) somewhere in the middle of the desert of New Mexico, the solitary horseman finds himself "wandering in some geometrical nightmare" of endless "flattened cones ... the shape of Mexican ovens" (18). Though on the surface he is oppressed by the heat and the interminable monotony of the landscape, his "geometrical nightmare" is more profoundly the projection of a psychological nightmare. His losing the trail becomes a metaphor for a more disturbing sense of displacement. He gets lost because he has been absentmindedly pondering a problem: "how to recover a Bishopric" (20). Although he had ridden into Santa Fé, "claiming it" (22) as "his seat" (23) of power, he had been devastated to find that other rival priests had "refused to recognize this authority." He had been "thrust out; his flock would have none of him" (20). The Bishop's exile in the desert is not only archetypal in a religious context but paradigmatic in the context of Cather's own art. It reflects the deepest fear at the heart of her fiction: he has been dispossessed of his rightful territory by the competing claims of others.

We might read this scene of dispossession, occurring off-stage before the novel opens, as an analogy to Cather's own experience as an author whose control of her imaginative kingdom in novels like *A Lost Lady* and *The Professor's House* had been challenged. She would try to solve the problem of "how to recover" her own authorial domain in the course of writing the novel. In her pose as the Archbishop, she once again casts herself as an "exile" (36) in search of a home — one that she located psychologically in her art. This home is suggested by the Bishop's first view of Santa Fé as a welcoming and nurturing idyll. Nestled within an "amphitheatre of red hills" that "curved like two arms about a depression in the plain" (22), the scene offers the security of a maternal embrace that Cather had associated with the Sweet Water estate in *A Lost Lady*. The church from which the streets "seemed to flow … like a stream from a spring" (22) invites the soul to replenish itself at the font of life and inspiration. The gracious poplars, "inclining and recovering themselves in the wind" (22), assure the onlooker of her own perpetual and effortless self-recovery.

To be dispossessed of this primal scene is to be cast out of paradise — lost and alone, abandoned to an indifferent and hostile waste. Echoing the Lord's passion with his cry, "J'ai soif!" (20), the Bishop reveals himself as the Lord who has been scorned and rejected by others; he thirsts more profoundly for a vanished vitality and power. Most revealing of the source of the Bishop's anxiety are the conical hills. No mere geological outcroppings, these hills are suggestively anthropomorphized: "The hills thrust out of the ground so thickly that they seemed to be pushing each other, elbowing each other aside, tipping each other over" (18). These shapes horrify the Bishop, for they incarnate the pushy authorities that have "elbow[ed] [him] aside" (18), and "thrust [him] out" (20) of his bishopric. "Crowding down upon him in the heat" (18) so as to fill him with dizzying "seizures of vertigo" (20), the hills inspire terror at having been overwhelmed and unbalanced by the claustrophobic assaults of others. The country that "was so featureless — or rather, … crowded with features, all exactly alike" (17), projects his dread of confronting the stupid faces of his enemies — faces that have no distinctive features by comparison with his own and that all look alike by virtue of their opposition to him. "Repeated so many hundred times upon his retina" (18), these shapes suggest Latour's alarmed paranoia that multiplies a few antagonists into an army. A man who is "sensitive to the shape of things," he is glad to escape the threat of "the intrusive omnipresence of the triangle" (18). As a Catholic priest, he might be expected to recognize a three-sided figure as an emblem of the trinity. But three-sided configurations are to the Archbishop a repugnant reminder of the unwelcome intrusion of others — third parties — that divide his sacred union with the self. By contrast, he kneels with a sense of relief before the cross, for in that shape he recognizes a point of unity within himself that is the intersection between the human and the divine.

The Bishop's recovery from his vertigo foreshadows the way in which he gains a subsequent victory over the mutinous priests of his diocese. Instead of exerting himself against the wilderness, he withdraws from the physical world, and, as Rosowski has pointed out, charts his way by neither sun nor compass, but "orients himself spiritually by a symbol."[13] After closing his eyes in meditation, he opens them to see a miraculous sight: the form of a cross in the parted green branches of a juniper tree. As he dismounts and kneels at the foot of the tree, he seems, as Rosowski and others assume, to be praying to a higher providence. In that "one juniper which differed in shape from the others" (18), however, he most deeply recognizes not a symbol of God but a mirror of the self. As Cather reminds us, he kneels before the cross as if he himself were "a priest in a thousand, one knew at a glance" (19). Cather emphasizes that Latour, like the juniper cross, differs "in shape" from the others; from "his bowed head [that] was not that of an ordinary man ... [but] built for the seat of a fine intelligence" (19), to his hands, molded with "a singular elegance" (19), he stands out as an extraordinary being. As if in answer to the skeptical priests who had demanded to know, "Where were his credentials?" (23), Cather affirms her hero's qualifications not on the basis of his piety but on the basis of his gentility; a "man of gentle birth — brave, sensitive, courteous" (19), he has the courtly demeanor of a natural aristocrat or chivalric prince. Worshipping the juniper cross for being the only one of its kind, Latour "discover[s] the logical relation of things" (9) in a connection between the cross-shaped tree and himself, and so, symbolically confirms his own exceptional nature.

As he goes to sleep that night, the Bishop looks back on the day as "a miracle" (29). He might just as well call the day a wish fulfillment. In a later conversation with Joseph, Latour argues that "miracles" are not divine interventions in human life but a consequence of "our perceptions being made finer" (50). Above all, the settlement named "Hidden Water" stands as proof that there will always be "a miracle" near us, merely hidden from view, if only we have enough faith in our creative perceptions to conjure it.[14] "Refreshed" (19) by his vision of the juniper tree, the Archbishop has his faith in his wonderful perceptions rewarded when he immediately encounters the inviting prospect of a running stream and brilliant, verdant gardens — a new Eden, "greener than anything [he] had even seen, even in his own greenest corner of the Old World" (24). He comes upon the scene as a mirage, a mere "delusion of thirst" (24), as if, once again, the landscape becomes transfigured as a projection of his desire. The spring in the desert quenches all his thirsts — most importantly, his thirst for admiration. When he arrives at the family of the Mexicans, he is greeted by the daughter with incredulous wonder and joy, as if he himself were the son of God, appearing in a second coming: "'A priest?' she cried, 'that is not possible! Yet I look at you, and it is true. Such a thing has never happened to us before; it must be in answer to my father's prayers'" (25). This first scene is paradigmatic of the course of Latour's travels in the novel as a whole; for him, as for the early Franciscan missionaries, his "way through the wilderness blossomed with little miracles" (279). Although the Bishop leaves his boyhood home in France, he never has to experience alienation or separation, for in his role as priest, he is provided with a "friendly ... welcome" (277) into a series of well-tended, hospitable homes, sanctuaries, and gardens. Ultimately, by beautifying the desert as his own garden at the end of the novel, Latour outwits the fate of his typological predecessor in the Genesis narrative. Believing that "man was lost and saved in a garden" (267), he satisfies his deepest longing to see all that is lost restored.

In one of the most unlikely of all fictional friendships, Jean Latour is good friends with the trapper and scout Kit Carson. As Cather describes them, "The two men were about the same age, both a little over forty, and both had been sobered and sharpened by wide experience" (76). But, though dressed as a rugged man of the trail who undergoes periodic physical hardships, Latour is never seasoned by harsh experience. Unlike Kit Carson, the Archbishop is accompanied by the guardian angels of Providence. He can be certain of overcoming all dangers, and even murderers like Buck Scales, because he is always given "evidence that some protecting power was mindful" (70) of him. Just as Thea Kronborg had fairy godfathers, now Latour has both a fairy God the Father and a Mother Mary to watch over him in his times of need.

In fact, the Bishop came to the New World in the first place to escape to a fundamentally different reality. He recalls how he had to convince his boyhood friend, Joseph Vaillant, to leave their home in France to join him as a missionary in America. Torn between "the desire to go and the necessity to stay" (299), Vaillant had conscientiously felt guilty about turning his back on his familial responsibilities, especially his obligation to care for his sick father. But Latour had felt no such conflict between the call of "desire" and the demands of "necessity." As he later reflects, "That parting was not a parting, but an escape — a running away, a betrayal of family trust for the sake of a higher trust" (204). Though disguised as a self-sacrificing response to a "higher" call from God, Latour's departure from France is more deeply a self-indulgent "escape" from the facts of adult experience — the responsibilities of caring for a real family and aging parents, the burden of assuming a sexual role, the obligations of fitting into the social structure of community, the drudgery of having to earn a professional living. He leaves all this behind him for a land where "desire" can make miracles come true.

Cather rarely dramatizes any of the conflicts between Latour and the other priests, instead resolving crucial action off-stage.[15] Far from being an aesthetic choice alone, the static plot was for Cather a psychological necessity that enabled her to empower her Archbishop. Only because all dramatic conflict is scrupulously avoided is the Bishop able to win his struggle for power at all. Just as Cather had used Thea Kronborg's faith in her art as a way of reorganizing the cast into two camps, so now she uses Latour's faith in his religion — which is really the same thing — as a way of justifying his adolescent desire to divide the world into the good who are "for me" and the bad who are "against me." By taking up the cross, Latour enjoys the automatic right to banish all who reject his authority as unreclaimed heathen, and to surround himself with a faithful flock.

Typically, while Latour has to do no more than exert his authority, he sends his Vicar Joseph Vaillant to the parishes to institute reforms. For example, when Latour returns from Hidden Water to Santa Fé, he miraculously finds "amity instead of enmity awaiting him" because Father Vaillant has "taken possession of the priest's house" (33) and put it in order. Joseph's "destiny" is "to serve ... in action" (41), but for the first half of the novel this calls him to serve not God but his "superior," Jean Latour. Just as Alexandra Bergson had her brothers, Lou and Oscar, cultivate her fields, so Latour has his spiritual "brother" Joseph do the dirty work of cleaning the actual Augean Stable — disciplining the bad priests, making converts, raising money, getting provisions, hearing confessions. It seems proof of Latour's inability to deal with real people who are immersed in the difficulties of living that he never once hears a confession. Although Latour performs plenty of baptisms and sanctifies many unblessed marriages in an effort to purge the world of sin and the scourge of sex, he avoids ministering confessions because in that role he would have to become the repository of the world's carnal sins. Vaillant, however, made to seem naturally preoccupied with "material cares" (54) and unmindful of the "ugly conditions of life" (228), is the realist in the novel who conveniently liberates the romantic Latour from all such unsavory obligations to lead a contemplative life in his study or garden. Reminiscent of Ray Kennedy's crushed bones laid at the monument of Thea Kronborg, Vaillant's calloused feet and broken bones seem to be the necessary sacrifice for Jean Latour to reconstitute his spiritual wholeness.

Padre Gallegos of Albuquerque, who drinks, hunts, plays poker, and dances the fandango, is one of the most colorful characters but clearly an unbecoming model of ecclesiastical proprieties. Without confronting Gallegos in conversation or argument, the Bishop rides away from him, deciding that "there was but one course: to suspend the man from the exercise of all priestly functions, and bid the smaller native priests take warning" (84). The Bishop's most threatening rival is, of course, Padre Martinez, the profligate who has become the dictator to all the parishes in northern New Mexico. Martinez is the most brazenly contemptuous of Latour's authority, boasting, "We pay a filial respect to the person of the Holy Father, but Rome has no authority here" (147). He terrifies Latour with his "big head, violent Spanish face, and shoulders like a buffalo" (32), but despite his animal physical force and imperious will, he is defeated as easily by Latour as is Padre Gallegos. As if Latour had the benefit of Cather's own historical hindsight, he is not troubled by Martinez's revolt in Santa Fe; reflecting that "the day of his tyranny was almost over" (32), Latour effortlessly disenfranchises Martinez because history has already made him a relic of the past. Though, at one point, the two clash in a disagreement over the issue of priestly chastity, all tension is dissipated when the Bishop chooses to ignore the issues that are raised. When Vaillant asks Latour what he plans to do about Martinez, he says, "Oh, there is no question of discipline! He has been a little potentate too long.... For the present I shall be blind to what I do not like there" (156). In order to avoid risking a showdown with his enemy, the Bishop ratio-nalizes that he cannot take action against the rebellion; like many of Cather's other protagonists, he blinds himself to what he chooses not to see. Though his willful ignorance seems naive and self-deluded, Cather upholds his vision as the dictator of experience: what he wishes not to see simply goes away. Latour does not have to do anything to attain his goals; he need merely will them into existence.

Safe at his desk from the embroiling perils of human conflicts, the Bishop wages his war on paper — as Cather was waging hers. He, too, has omnipotent power as an author over his experience, rearranging and eliminating the figures in his diocese as if they were characters on a blank page. At first, he issues a mild "suggestion" (159) that Martinez formally resign his parish with the condition that he can still celebrate mass on perfunctory occasions. Although potential conflict arises once again when Martinez "flatly refused to submit" (159) and forms a schism church of his own, that drama is also quickly quelled when Latour writes a letter that "stripped Father Martinez of the rights and privileges of the priesthood" (162). Similarly, he writes a "letter of excommunication" (162) against Father Lucero, the priest who greedily hoards $20,000 under his bedroom floor. Latour has merely to pronounce his word to gain the gratification of having it instantly accepted as a divine fiat. He even seems to have a fatal power over others' lives, for almost immediately after his edicts, both Martinez and Lucero drop dead. Similarly, in her guise as the Archbishop, Cather gets to resolve all conflicts in her favor as if hers were the word of God.

Padre Martinez is the greatest threat in the diocese because he is the personification of lust. With his "full lips thrust out and taut, like the flesh of animals distended by fear or desire" (141), he is, like Frank Ellinger or Ivy Peters, a cartoonish depiction of violent, unbridled passions. As in a Gothic novel, he has debauched virgins and nuns and then sold them into slavery as tenants on his farms. He further makes a mockery of the priesthood by living with his son, Trinidad, whom he is training to take orders. Always "stupefied by one form of sensual disturbance or another" (145), Trinidad is portrayed as a subhuman creature of appetites who hungers for women "in the same greedy way" that he devours his mutton stew. As if his physicality were dissolving his humanity, Cather notes that "his fat face was irritatingly stupid, and had the grey, oily look of soft cheeses" (145). Cringing at a woman's hairpiece strewn on the floor, Latour in his "fastidious taste" cannot bear "the disorder" (144) of the unchaste household; if he is to clean the Augean stable, he must rid it above all of sexuality. His excommunication of Martinez to make sure that he is "really impotent" (141) enacts a kind of castration. When he tells the old reprobate that he will impose reforms "until there is not a priest left who does not keep all the vows he took when he bound himself to the service of the altar" (146), he more deeply promises to keep Cather's "vows" to the "altar" of her art. Having failed to make others keep these vows in *A Lost Lady* or *The Professor's House*, Cather ensures her success in *Death Comes for the Archbishop* by donning a cassock.

Finally, the Bishop only imagines that he can win his war against the flesh. The scene in which he and his guide, Jacinto, take refuge from a snowstorm for the night in a cave reminds us that he cannot rout sexuality itself out of existence. If Latour "did not like the air of [Martinez's] house" (149), he cares even less for the "fetid odour" (127) of this cave. He long remembers the place "with a shudder of repugnance quite unjustified by anything he had experienced there" (133), for, ultimately, his distaste is conditioned by Cather's own horror of the cave's associations with sexuality. Having been used for ancient Indian fertility rites, the cave is said to contain in its dark depths a great serpent. This phallic serpent lurks hidden in a cave whose configuration anatomizes the female body. The cave is called "stone lips," named for the two ledges that thrust outward from its opening "orifice" (127). At the rear wall of the cavern inside is "a hole" of "an irregular oval shape" that is "solitary, dark," and seems "to lead into another cavern" (128–29). From within that inner tunnel is heard "the sound of a great underground river ... a flood moving in utter blackness under ribs of antediluvian rock" (130). Just as Jim Burden had confronted the snake as "the ancient, Eldest evil," so the Bishop lays his ear to a "crack" to hear "one of the oldest voices of the earth" — some primordial current of force — and he pronounces, "It is terrible." Overwhelmed by a sense of "vertigo" (129) in the face of unconscious energies and powers he cannot control, the Archbishop is relieved when Jacinto plasters up the seam in the rock with clay as if in response to his repressive wish. Although the Bishop tries to suppress thoughts of sexuality by reading his breviary, his mind unaccountably wanders to "other than spiritual things" (131). He even indulges in a sneaky fantasy that he might waken later that night while his companion is asleep and "study a little the curious hole his guide had so carefully closed." When he does waken, however, he finds that Jacinto has beat him to it. Saved from temptation, he emerges from the cave the next morning into a "gleaming white world" of "virgin snow" (132). Though, on the surface, the problem of sexuality seems resolved, it is only temporarily evaded. As a repressed urge or fear, sexuality returns to haunt the Bishop, who "did not cease from wondering about it" (133). Indeed, somewhere in that diocese, there will always be a "great serpent in concealment" (134), ready to raise its ominous head. Cather herself had tried to plaster over the "crack" of sexuality in her fiction but had been unable to silence or answer its irrepressible voice.[16]

Cather writes that the plains had an appearance "of incompleteness; as if, with all the materials for world-making assembled, the Creator had desisted, gone away and left everything on the point of being brought together, on the eve of being arranged into mountain, plain, plateau. The country was still waiting to be made into a landscape" (95). God has vacated the premises, leaving the "stage" clear for Latour, the real Creator, to bring order and meaning out of raw materials. The Archbishop most powerfully fulfills his mission when, after rejecting the sexual cave, he finds the rock with which to build his spiritual cathedral, his greatest ambition in the novel. In an early review, Cather made an analogy between writing a novel and building a cathedral, both of which required "a continuous flow of feeling and thought and a vast knowledge of technique and of the artistic construction of the whole" (KA 339). Though critics have accepted the cathedral on religious grounds, according to the terms of Cather's masquerade, Cather uses it as a metaphor for her own art and the romantic principles that shaped it.[17] While it is Father Vaillant's charitable mission to save the souls of others, it is Father Latour's mission to "save" his own soul. Although ostensibly built and dedicated to the greater glory of God, the cathedral is significant as a vessel that enshrines the Archbishop's own ego. Latour wishes to build his cathedral not as the house of the Lord but as "a continuation of himself and his purpose, a physical body full of his aspirations after he had passed from the scene" (175). His motives are not religious or communal in nature, but aesthetic and personal. Though the communion is supposed to celebrate the "physical body" of Christ, the Archbishop would resurrect himself as the living Host through the transubstantiation of art. Wondering what legacy his Bishop will leave behind him, Vaillant speculates, "Perhaps it pleased Him to grace the beginning of a new era and a vast new diocese by a fine personality. And perhaps, after all, something would remain through the years to come; some ideal, or memory, or legend" (254). Although the biblical story says that it pleased God to send his only begotten son, Jesus Christ, to redeem man with the gift of "grace," Cather's appropriation of the story reads that it pleased God to send Jean Latour to redeem man with the "grace" of his own "fine personality." "The beginning of a new era" founds not the kingdom of heaven but the legend of Jean Latour.

Although the Archbishop tells his Vicar, "Our own Midi Romanesque is the right style for this country" (243), he decides to build his cathedral in the French style out of a need to set himself apart from the indigenous landscape; he would be seen as an individual with a style all his own. Christ had called his disciple St. Peter the "rock" of his church, and for Christians, the "Church" refers to the body of its people. With an exaggerated literalness, however, the Archbishop builds his church out of a physical rock that incarnates not the many but the one; he values the rock for being "the only one of its kind" (241). One afternoon, while riding through the landscape, the Archbishop comes across a particular hill that shines with the stone he has "always wanted" and, in a moment of epiphany, he "knew instantly that it was *my* Cathedral" (242, italics mine). His joyful recognition of the rock reenacts his discovery of the juniper cross in the first scene; it, too, is remarkable for its unique color. As he recounts to Joseph, "It is curious, is it not, to find one yellow hill among all these green ones?" (241). We recall that Cather had imagined Thea Kronborg as "a goldfish darting among creek minnows," or "a yellow butterfly soaring above a swarm of dark ones" (SL, 235); similarly, she identifies the Bishop's vitality with the only yellow rock among miles of ordinary green ones. The hill marked out for Latour "stood up high and quite alone" (241), as if it were a natural tower declaring the noble derivation of his name. Exposed where "the western face [of] the earth had been scooped away," the rock hill, like Tom Outland's mesa, provides the material of art that exists in a world above the world. It reminds Latour of "something nearer home" (242) — of his childhood home in Clermont, but at a deeper level, of "something" nearer his own heart. Like Alexandra Bergson or Jim Burden, Latour significantly has his revelation of the landscape while he is taking the "way home" (242), for, symbolically, his journey by a different path is also a homecoming to the self. The picks and crowbars that lie about the "gold" rock suggest a comparison between the "gold" that Latour digs for and the gold that the prospectors are digging for in the Colorado camps, where Vaillant is headed. Latour's gold signifies an imaginative treasure. Latour tells Vaillant, "I would rather have found that hill of yellow rock than have come into a fortune" (245), for he knows that his "gold" incarnates the priceless value of his own consciousness.

Cather had long been fascinated with the preacher as a man who could command power over his audience. In an 1893 sketch, she describes an eloquent minister whose "voice had in it a sympathetic quiver born of excitement and the grandeur of his subject" (WP, 5). His voice sounds a sympathetic note in his consciousness that he is inspiring others with sympathy for him. Like Emerson's orator in "The American Scholar," the minister believes himself to be spiritually united with his audience as "the complement of his hearers."[18] As he looks over the crowd, "his interest quickened under the pleasant knowledge that he was being appreciated" (WP, 5). His voice "trembled with enthusiasm … over his own eloquence and conscious power." While preaching a sermon on "the brotherhood of man," the minister really ministers to the selfish needs of his own ego. Though, as readers, we may see this as ironic, Cather upholds the minister's power over his audience for the same reasons that she upholds the power of the artist over her audience. Identifying with the minister as a kind of artist who can evoke powerful feelings through language, Cather celebrates true brotherhood as the community that sympathetically lives through the thoughts and feelings of the gifted artist or orator. Cather does not see the minister's narcissism as inconsistent with the role of Jesus Christ; rather, she casts him as a true follower of Jesus Christ, whom, as she says, "any of us" could resemble "if we only had egotism enough" (WP, 6). Instead of seeing Christ as a model of humility and self-sacrifice, Cather, like Emerson, appreciates him as the greatest egotist of all, since he showed man his inner divinity. Collecting generations of souls who would live through him as "His property," Christ inspired Cather as the archetypal imaginative claimant of people. Latour is an equally great egotist when he claims the souls of the Mexicans as "his people" (81).

The self-important relationship that Latour establishes with the native population is best illustrated by his friendship with his Indian guide, Jacinto. Unlike the powerful priests, who present an "intrusive omnipresence" (18), the Indians possess an "unobtrusive demeanour" (235) that allows Latour to assert his omnipresence over them. Jacinto so fades into the background that he is unrecognizable as a personality. In fact, Cather most often describes him indirectly by analogy to the landscape. On the evening that Latour and Jacinto camp out, they look up to see "high above the horizon the evening-star ... , and close beside it ... another star of constant light, much smaller" (92). Making the symbolism explicit, Jacinto points out that the Indians call the little star "the guide." Like his predecessors in Cather's fiction, Latour collects loyal disciples as his satellites. Cather again uses the landscape to provide an analogy to the relationship between Latour and Jacinto when she describes how every mesa is "duplicated by a cloud mesa, like a reflection.... The great tables of granite set down in an empty plain were inconceivable without their attendant clouds, which were a part of them, as the smoke is part of the censer, or the foam of the wave" (95). Jacinto, the "attendant" cloud who hovers vaguely in the background of Latour's great and imposing facade, is seen not as a separate individual but as an auxiliary imaginative property, or "part," of his master's appropriating consciousness. That Latour's psychic configuration seems "inconceivable" without his supplementary "reflection" suggests that he, like Thea Kronborg, has a narcissistic need to see himself mirrored in others, and that without them, he is incomplete. Whereas Thea had readily appropriated the Mexicans, however, Latour can appropriate Jacinto only by reimagining him as part of the landscape. Though Cather continued to need to confirm herself through others, she had realized by this late point in her career that it was safer and easier, if not more rewarding, to claim a landscape than another person for her imaginative property.

Cather portrays the Mexicans, who "vie with each other in acts of loyalty" to the proper "master" (117–18), as children who wish to be controlled by a strong paternal authority. Although, as in a wish fulfillment, Latour appropriates the Mexicans and the native population as effortlessly as he appropriates the landscape, he has more difficulty retaining his hold on his best friend, Joseph Vaillant. His loss of Vaillant's companionship is the major, and indeed, the only "bitter personal disappointment" (208) that he suffers in the novel. Twice Latour appeals to his friend to give up his missionary work so as to keep him company in Santa Fe, and twice Joseph breaks ties and leaves, first for Mexico, then for Colorado. Joseph's departures "spoiled a cherished plan" (208). Latour would have liked to recreate the days when they had lived together, almost like a happily married couple, Joseph dutifully cooking dinners and keeping pinon logs on the fire, he writing his letters.[19] "Countrymen ... bound by early memories" (253), Jean and Joseph resemble other pairs of childhood friends — Alexandra and Carl, Jim and Àntonia, Tom and Roddy. At one point, Latour expresses his love for Vaillant by saying, "I do not see you as you really are, Joseph; I see you through my affection for you" (50). In the guise of blessing Joseph with a "divine love," Latour, like his fellow idealists Jim and Niel, appropriates him according to his own perceptions. Much like Jim's Àntonia, the Bishop's Vicar had played the gratifying role of the subordinate admirer.[20] In personal relationships, however, Latour's automatic authority as Bishop breaks down. Despite his formal letter of recall to "his Vicar" (231) in Tucson, Joseph refuses to be just Latour's imaginative property; as he passionately cries just before he leaves to aid the Mexicans, "But you do not need me so much as they do! ... I am *their man!*" (208).

In *The Professor's House*, her most mature novel, Cather had honestly assessed the painful and costly choices that people must make. Tom Outland suffers an irrevocable loss when he requites Roddy's friendship, and as if to do penance for that transgression, the Professor suffers an equally painful loss when he lets go a part of himself to rejoin his family. Through these conflicts, Cather had squarely confronted the consequences of the choices that she had imposed on herself as an artist; for once, she had admitted that she had had to give up valuable human ties by devoting herself so exclusively to her art. Once again, the Bishop's loneliness in his study after Vaillant's departure potentially raises the conflict between an involvement in community and a devotion to the self in art. After bidding Joseph a final farewell on his way to Colorado, the Bishop rides home to his solitude. He, like his author, has always been more at home in the world of "scholarship" (253) and "delicate perceptions" (254) than with people. But without Joseph's kindling energy and warmth, his life seems empty and "a little cold" (261–62), and he yearns for the companionship of nephews or nieces who could enliven his household. His thoughts, "such ... as any bachelor nearing fifty might have" (255), reflect the self-doubts and anxieties of his fifty-four-year-old unmarried author. As John Randall has astutely noted, "It is easy to see the Bishop in his solitude as a type of the author herself who has given up everything for art, and wondering whether after all the choice really was worth while."[21] As Cather grew older, it began to seem that companionship with ideas could not substitute for connectedness to human society. Having herself, like Latour, lost valuable friends, she makes her confession that "the loneliness of his position had begun to weigh upon him" (253). Yet she "could not form new ties" any more readily than her surrogate.

Cather uneasily confesses that Latour "missed Father Vaillant's companionship — why not admit it?" (223) Yet, ironically, Cather herself refuses to admit this loss. She evades the crisis in Latour's personal relationships as calmly as she had glossed over his conflicts with the insubordinate priests. No sooner does she describe Latour's loneliness than she matter-of-factly denies it. Entering his study, he finds, as if by a miracle, that "the curtain of the arched doorway had scarcely fallen behind him when that feeling of personal loneliness was gone, and a sense of loss was replaced by a sense of restoration" (256). As the falling curtain over the door signals, Latour returns not to "reality," as the text states, but to a world staged as a drama in his imagination. Cather provides "the sense of a Presence awaiting" the Bishop to reassure him that he need never suffer the pangs of self-sacrifice. As a religious man, Father Latour might be expected to undergo some sort of soul-searching, trial of faith, or personal renunciation.[22] As Randall has argued, however, Cather tries "to convince herself that rejection of human ties involves no real loss, that what the Bishop has given up, he has not given up.... [R]eligion is made easy, and renunciation is robbed of its sting."[23] In *Death Comes for the Archbishop*, the anguished tension that had made *The Professor's House* so relevant to our own lives is gone, and human conflicts, instead of being confronted, are wished away by the panacea of religion.

The compensatory "Presence" who visits the Bishop is not Jesus Christ, who is virtually absent from the novel, but the Holy Mother. Comforting the Bishop that his life "need not be cold, or devoid of grace in the worldly sense" (256), the "Virgin-mother" — the supreme dream of the flesh — offers the very "worldly" salvation of a warm maternal embrace. In the guise of worshipping the Virgin Mary of the Church, the Bishop worships the perfect virginal Mother of his dreams — an asexual woman who herself had an immaculate conception — and so fulfills the unsuccessful quests of Niel Herbert, Professor St. Peter, and Willa Cather herself. In his dark night of the soul after losing Vaillant, the Bishop finds consolation in the fact that "there was a Kind Woman in Heaven, though there were such cruel ones on earth. Old people, who have felt blows and toil and known the world's hard hand, need, even more than children do, a woman's tenderness" (217). This revelation reminds us that one reason why the novel is so serene in mood, unlike *The Professor's House*, is that, to use Cather's own words, it has "no woman in it but the Virgin Mary."[24] Unlike any real woman, the Virgin Mother can be possessed exclusively in imagination. Although Vaillant's departure in an earlier scene leaves Latour feeling as if he had "nothing within himself" (211), the devoted attention of the Mother reassures him that *"whosoever is least among you, the same shall be first"* (218) in the heaven of her nurturing kindness. Far from encouraging him to renounce power, the beautiful concept of Mary disguises an infantile yearning for the Mother who, through her nurturing and healing love, can reassure the baby that he is "first" as Lord. Revisiting his own childhood, Latour imagines the Virgin Mary most vividly as "one of these nursery Virgins" (256), a wooden figure that the women of the parish love to dress up in handmade clothes: "She was their doll and their queen, something to fondle and something to adore, as Mary's Son must have been to Her" (257). John Randall has observed that in this passage, "the whole cult of the Virgin Mary is reduced to the image of a little girl playing with her doll."[25] Indeed, Cather transforms Christianity into toyland. Religion — as well as Cather's own earlier aesthetic — is founded on a faith in the unseen. But now, as Cather idealizes the physical "things of the altar" as the most precious "possessions" (217), she holds on to the security of the seen. With its emphasis on ritual and art, Catholicism gave her a way to surround herself with lovely artifacts that she could treasure for consolation and security.

Despite Cather's affirmation that the Bishop's life in his study "was not a solitude of atrophy, of negation, but of perpetual flowering" (256), he resists growth and affirmation of life in a series of regressive fantasies. After Vaillant leaves him, Latour, like other protagonists in Cather's fiction, finds compensation for personal loss in his art: "The Cathedral ... had taken Father Vaillant's place in his life after that remarkable man went away" (271). In the winter, just before his death, Latour listens to the ringing of the bell and reflects, "How it was of the South, that church, how it sounded the note of the South!" (271). Although the bell overcomes him with a nostalgic "feeling of place" (43) that takes him back to a special "garden in the south of France" (43), it more powerfully recalls him to another time — the perpetual springtime of his own youth. The garden where he was sent "in his childhood to recover from an illness" (43) lures him back as an old man to recover himself again, this time from the debilitating experiences of life.

The Bishop tries to enter the kingdom of heaven by giving a literal interpretation to Cather's favorite biblical injunction: "Unless ye become as little children" (206). Cather herself had fondly recalled, "Writing this book ... was like a happy vacation from life, a return to childhood, to early memories" (OW, 11). In order to preserve the Bishop's integrity and the carefree mood in which she was writing, however, Cather had to take more than a "vacation from life"; taking the Bishop back to childhood, and even farther back to death, she had to take permanent leave of life itself. In *The Professor's House*, Cather had brought the Professor back from the grave in an ultimate allegiance to life. She had forced him to recognize limitations to his will so that he could accommodate other people and embrace the future. But she undoes that process of growth towards maturity at the end of *Death Comes for the Archbishop*. As if Cather were still haunted by a fear of life's dispossessions, she imagines that the cathedral walls can shut out the world and give repose to the spirit only if they are made as thick as the walls of the grave. In the end, the Bishop comes to feel "a grateful sense of nearness to his Cathedral" in the knowledge that it "would also be his tomb. He felt safe under its shadow; like a boat come back to harbour" (273). With its imposing "sea-wall," the cathedral suggests that Cather had increasingly come to view the kingdom of art not simply as a place of self-worship but as a fortress, armed against the marauding invasions of life.

Although he might have lived in France after he retired from his duties as Archbishop, Latour decides to spend his last days in New Mexico in order to recapture the "peculiar quality" of the morning air. As he reflects,

> He did not know just when it had become so necessary to him, but he had come back to die in exile for the sake of it. Something soft and wild and free, something that whispered to the ear on the pillow, lightened the heart, softly, softly picked the lock, slid the bolts, and released the prisoned spirit of man into the wind, into the blue and gold, into the morning, into the morning! (275–76)

Cather once again argues that nothing can compensate for the loss of that special "something" which releases the heart and soul into the unvanquished freedom of youth. She had let go that "something" at the end of *The Professor's House*, but now, as age and disappointments weigh more heavily on her, she celebrates the soul as the only thing worth living, or dying for, after all. Whereas Christ had died in exile for the sake of mankind, Latour is no martyr; he dies "in exile" for the sake of his own romantic ego.

Just before his death, as the Archbishop "sat in the middle of his own consciousness" (290), he blots out the world so as to find his greatest sense of centeredness in his own self-possession. Inhabiting the exemplary space in Cather's fiction as the one passion in four walls, he has fulfilled his mission to weld her world whole again. He has transcended not only physical space but calendared time to gain the illusion that "none of his former states of mind were lost or outgrown. They were all within reach of his hand, and all comprehensible" (290). Reaching back to recover his own beginning as his end, Latour himself becomes the alpha and omega who unites all experience into an eternal present. His appropriation of history is a way of denying time and the errors of adulthood so as to grasp his elusive origins as a tactile reality. Just as the Professor had dismissed his life after adolescence as a random chain of events that had nothing to do with his essential self, so Latour reflects, "More and more life seemed to him an experience of the Ego, in no sense the Ego itself.... The mistakes of his life seemed unimportant; accidents that had occurred *en route*, like the shipwreck in the Galveston harbour" (289–90). Once again exploiting his powers as priest, Latour readily absolves himself for his past. Far from doing any penance for his sins, as would a real Catholic at confession, the Bishop puts his faith in the omnipotence and indestructibility of an unfallen Adamic "Ego" that grants him an immunity to the accidents of fortune and an exemption from the consequences and penalties of his actions. As Cather got older, she, like her Archbishop, wanted to believe that ill health and the perpetual inconveniences of the present could be escaped by reaching back to her first identity. As if she wanted to experience the Archbishop's self-possession, she wrote to Carrie Miner in 1941 that her foreshortened perspective at the end of the road had allowed her to possess simultaneously all the phases of her life.[26]

The closing scene of Latour's death is an odd death scene for a priest. Whereas all the other dying priests in the novel receive the last sacrament and make their confessions according to Catholic tradition, the Bishop is attended by no priests, nor even a Bible. The self at the center of his faith has already redeemed him. Yet his mission to appropriate the world in his consciousness is not complete until he reabsorbs others into himself as well. That he is surrounded by faithful attendants, including his surrogate son Bernard, fosters his fantasy that all others devotedly minister to his needs as the supreme "Father" (299). Then, withdrawing to "some other part of the great picture of his life" (290), Latour has a private deathbed revelation. Far from being illumined by a vision of God, however, he egoistically imagines himself in the role of God. His last thoughts take him back to the day in France when "he was trying to forge a new Will in that devout and exhausted priest" (299). When Joseph had taken up the cross and followed him as his disciple to the New Jerusalem, he obeyed Latour's wish, as if to say, Thy will be done. Though, in the intervening years, Joseph had diverged to pursue a path of his own, abandoning him to an empty wilderness, Latour imagines by way of compensation that he can lead his companion after his example once again.[27] Finally, when "the old Archbishop lay before the high altar," so that the whole "Mexican population of Santa Fé fell upon their knees" (299), he seems to have reasserted the proper "sense of proportion" (9) and hierarchy to the bishopric. As the cathedral bell tolls, it welcomes him back home with a joyful tune to the garden of his childhood, where his Will reigns above all others'. It announces Death comes *for* the archbishop as a reward — a gift of grace for putting his faith in the momentous beginning of things.[28]

9

"The Ownership that was Right": Imaginative Bonds of Slavery in *Sapphira and the Slave Girl*

Edith Lewis notes that "publication of the *Archbishop* marked, in a way, the close of an era in Willa Cather's life" (WCL, 148). According to Lewis, this era ended in fall 1927, when she and Cather had to leave their apartment at 5 Bank Street because the building was to be torn down. Lewis reflects, "I think Willa Cather did her happiest writing in the fifteen years she lived there" (WCL, 148). Certainly, the years from 1912 to 1927, when Cather completed *O Pioneers!* and worked on all her books through *Death Comes for the Archbishop*, witnessed her most significant artistic achievement. The hard years that followed, however, "took something permanently from her vital force" (WCL, 163). Cather lost not only her secure residence at 5 Bank Street but her father, who died of a heart attack in 1929, and her mother, who died in 1931. In close succession in 1938, the deaths of her favorite brother, Douglass, and her cherished friend, Isabelle McClung, left her even more bereft. The outbreak of the Second World War in 1939 seemed to give her personal losses a worldwide resonance. In the meantime, her own health had rapidly deteriorated. She suffered her most disabling setback in 1933 when her right hand had to be immobilized due to a serious inflammation of the sheath of the tendon; from this time on, she had to endure long periods when she could not write. All of these losses took their toll on Cather's art. Even the devoted Edith Lewis, who tries hard to conceal in her memoir all of Cather's shortcomings, admits: "It seems to me that it is in this quality of vitality that Willa Cather's last three novels — *Shadows on the Rock, Lucy Gayheart, Sapphira and the Slave Girl* — differ from those that go before" (WCL, 167). Unable to "get back that power to work which comes from the sense of limitless reserves of strength, to use or throw away" (WCL, 177), Cather's last novels betray the diminished energies of their author.

Less often read and discussed, these novels are nonetheless worth examining. I wish to focus on Cather's last completed novel, *Sapphira and the Slave Girl* (1940), because its heroine — the domineering and willful matriarch of the Southern plantation, Sapphira Dodderidge Colbert — is most clearly a descendant of earlier artist-claimants like Alexandra Bergson. In fact, the reason why Sapphira Colbert seems a stronger, more vividly realized, and memorable character than the heroines of *Shadows on the Rock* and *Lucy Gayheart* is because she, as Cather's last imaginative claimant, selfishly strives to possess her own soul. Though not as aesthetically achieved as her earlier novels, this last novel recapitulates Cather's central narrative in interesting ways, throwing earlier patterns into starker relief. The childhood fantasy of power gets played out once again, but this time it assumes stunted and distorted, even grotesque, expression. Like the reflection of a child in a twisted amusement park mirror, these distortions exaggerate the features that the subject has possessed all along. By enlarging our perception of these features, *Sapphira and the Slave Girl* shows us the final disproportions of Cather's vision of the self. Moreover, it suggests how Cather herself, in these last years, may have been using her fiction to examine the reflection of an older and less resilient self with a growing sense of desperation.

Cather wrote *Sapphira and the Slave Girl* in a period of personal duress, beginning the novel in the spring of 1937 and not completing it until three and a half years later, in 1940. As if to capture the memory of her pleasant visit to the Virginia countryside with her brother Douglass in the spring of 1938, she returned in this novel to the pastoral scenes of her childhood. *Sapphira and the Slave Girl* takes place in Back Creek Valley, Virginia, in 1856, during the last years of slavery. In the outlines of its plot, the novel resembles a melodramatic Gothic tale of seduction and intrigue.[1] In brief, Sapphira Colbert, the proud mistress of the estate, suspects that her husband is having an affair with her young slave, Nancy Till. In order to get rid of Nancy, she sets the scene for her rape; she invites Martin Colbert, her husband's lecherous nephew, to stay for an extended visit at the plantation, and then schemes in various ways to facilitate his sexual advances. Sapphira's daughter, Rachel Blake, an abolitionist, interferes with Sapphira's schemes by helping Nancy to escape to freedom in Canada. As the novel progresses, however, the white and black characters are all reconciled to each other. In an epilogue written many years later, told from the point of view of the young Willa Cather herself, as witness, Nancy returns to see her aged mother.

Sapphira's racist and sexist exploitation of a young black woman has understandably disturbed the novel's readers. Critics have agreed that Sapphira is the novel's villain, yet they have puzzled over why Cather would make her heroine such a sinister character with whom the reader cannot empathize. As James Woodress raises the question, "How does one reconcile Cather's own statement to Carrie Sherwood written as she put the finishing touches on this novel: that she could only write success-fully when she wrote about people or places which she greatly admired or actually loved? Sapphira is ... a person without a moral sense, a figure of ambiguity, someone no reader could love."[2] Merrill Skaggs helps to resolve these tensions in the novel by arguing that Cather was aware of her heroine's shortcomings but nonetheless "acknowledges the nature of her own blood, judges it coldly, and then accepts it."[3] Skaggs recognizes that Cather regards Sapphira as her own progenitress with whom she shares a common nature. I would like to extend Skaggs's argument to suggest that as Cather looked back to identify with her biological fore-mother, she used her as her own surrogate to explore the complexities of a self-centered disposition. Skaggs eloquently writes that Cather "forces us to realize that Sapphira's sins and her virtues spring from the same self-confident dependence on herself, from her arrogant willfulness, and from her unfaltering courage and self-love.... Cather insists that we see Sapphira as a woman whose selfishness most enviably preserves and sustains her."[4] Willa Cather accepted Sapphira, despite her unlikeable qualities — even portraying her as a character with nobility — because she imagined in her the unwavering self-love that had empowered Cather herself throughout her career.

Elizabeth Ammons has persuasively argued that the racism in the novel "makes totally untenable the usual comfortable view of Cather as a writer of broad and inclusive sympathies and imagination."[5] As she points out, Cather fills the novel with stereotypes of blacks ranging from fat cooks to shuffling, docile servants, referring casually to the "emotional darkies," and the "foolish, dreamy, nigger side" (70, 178) of a character's nature. Ammons shows that Cather, in her racism, was a product of her times, and that we need, therefore, to read her critically. What is important to recognize, in addition, is not simply that Cather in-cluded racist stereotypes but that she used them as part of a larger fic-tional strategy. I would like to explore how the novel's manipulation of race affirms Cather's deeper aims as an artist. In her book *Playing in the Dark: Whiteness and the Literary Imagination*, Toni Morrison discusses the various strategies by which white American authors have used stereotypes of black characters to confirm and enpower the qualities of white characters. She recognizes that in *Sapphira and the Slave Girl*, "Sapphira's plotting, like Cather's plot, is without reference to the characters and exists solely for the ego-gratification of the slave mistress."[6] Playing off the novel's title, Morrison shows that the story transforms Nancy from an individual into "the Slave Girl" — a mere stereotype and cipher, as voiceless as she is invisible — in order to accommodate Sapphira's self-interests. She points out that the status of Nancy and her mother as "the unconsulted, appropriated ground" of Sapphira's scheming is a dynamic made thinkable only because the characters involved are black and therefore "wholly available and serviceable" to the needs of the white characters.[7] As Morrison suggests, their stereotypic subjugation and homage to the white mistress is the necessary foundation that supports the illusion of Sapphira's supremacy. As Sapphira sets a drama in motion and then sits back to watch it unfold as if it were "as good as a play" (199), she, like her author, assumes the role of the stage director, or artist, of her own experience. She manipulates the slave Nancy Till for the same reasons that Cather manipulates her black characters: to make them take part in her own childhood fantasy of power.[8] In Sapphira, Cather recognizes the autocracy of the artist who, rather than being simply the agent of vision, is the despot, a diminutive god.

On the surface, Cather seems to raise moral objections to the system of slavery. After all, Rachel Blake steals Nancy away from the perils of an evil institution that threatens her with sexual violation. In what seems the novel's most serious indictment of slavery, Rachel reflects that "it was the *owning* that was wrong, the relation itself, no matter how convenient or agreeable it might be for master or servant" (137). If Cather agrees that slavery is "wrong," however, it is only in an abstract sense, for she portrays the relation as convenient and agreeable for both master and servant. She objects to slavery not on strong moral or ethical grounds, but on the grounds of a legal technicality — it was the literal "owning" that was wrong. Though she deplores Sapphira's legal ownership of her slaves, she condones the paternalistic spirit behind it. In fact, Sapphira's ownership of slaves merely literalizes the kind of imaginative possession that Cather's protagonists take over others whom they appropriate as parts of consciousness. Throughout the novel, Cather refers to the slaves as "servants"; her euphemism suggests that she wishes to deny the harsh injustice of slavery while participating in its psychological rewards. The relationship between the "Mistress" Sapphira and her black slaves recreates the paradigmatic relationship of power which Cather idealizes throughout her fiction between the artist and the "vassals" who are servants to his or her imagination and, hence, can be claimed as mental property. We recall that in "The Treasure of Far Island," the fantasy of the two children who rule the territory is bolstered by the willing participation of the other children, who play the role of "vassals ... who claimed no part in the craft" but gladly toiled and sweated according to their assigned roles because "this fascinating play world ... was so much more exhilarating than any they could make for themselves" (CSF, 277). The attack on Cather's racism in the novel would be better directed towards Cather's egoism as an artist. While it is true, as Morrison suggests, that the minority status of the slaves facilitates Sapphira's appropriation of them, race is not an essential ingredient to such appropriation. Cather's artist-claimants regard all those who intensify their inner lives as "vassals" or servants completely available for their imaginative use. Cather's artist-claimants, like the two children of Far Island, appropriate other people — men, women, Mexicans, Indians, and now Blacks — not, primarily, out of racism or sexism, but out of an unabashed egoism. Like the poet in Whitman's "Song of Myself," Cather's artist-claimant indiscriminately embraces all, regardless of color or creed, who seem to embody or confirm a part of the poet's own nature. The black woman, Nancy Till, is denied her selfhood through Sapphira's appropriation of her and her story in the same way that the white woman, Antonia, is denied her selfhood through Jim Burden's assimilation of her.

When Cather casts her fantasy of imaginative possession in terms of the system of slavery, the racist implications inhibit our emotional participation as readers; we see her heroine transformed from a courtly lady into an evil schemer. The dark and sinister aspects of the romance suggest that Cather may have been deconstructing her own ideology with some ironic distance. As if she were being critical of herself and her earlier surrogates, Cather acknowledges that Sapphira "was entirely self-centered and thought of other people only in their relation to herself" (220). The story of Sapphira shows how such an egotistical view of human relationships can lead to a self-destructive paranoia and an inhumane exploitation of others. Yet, if the novel is partly confessional and self-vilifying, it is more deeply self-vindicating. Cather recognizes Sapphira's selfish egoism but nonetheless accepts it as the source of her strength, and takes pains to exonerate her. She makes allowances for her heroine as if to suggest that the artist prevails through a tyrannizing imagination. Though Cather's decision to dramatize an imaginative possession of others as a literal ownership may suggest that she was undermining her past vision, it also is symptomatic of her increasing need, in her later years, to embrace realities that were fixed and firm, when the world around her seemed to be ending in catastrophe.[9] Now that her personal sense of power was especially fragile at the end of her life, when she was ill and had lost many loved ones, she tried to augment it by imagining that the bonds she idealized between herself and loyal friends could be solidified and made permanent through an institutionalized and socialized structure, even though, of course, slavery had been historically abolished. Her casting of the relationship between the artist-claimant and her devoted retainers in terms of race suggests that she needed to depend on a hierarchy of power that was, so to speak, unambiguously black and white. Above all, Cather's collapsing the distinction between imaginative and literal ownership of people in *Sapphira and the Slave Girl* confirms that human relationships appealed to her imagination primarily as a means to power. Ironically, what Cather unwittingly proves in this dynamic is that she is the one who is enslaved to the primal patterns of her fiction. *Sapphira and the Slave Girl* has been Cather's least popular novel. As Morrison has observed, the source of the novel's flaws is not just the failure or exhaustion of Cather's gifts but its problematic portrait of race. [10] The novel makes its readers uncomfortable because it asks us to participate in a childhood fantasy of power that conflicts with our ethical and moral codes as readers who have the advantage of a heightened sensitivity in the second half of the twentieth century to issues of race and power.

Like Myra Henshawe and Marian Forrester before her, Sapphira Colbert is portrayed as a queen in "exile" (25) who must maintain her authority over her "stage-hands" (LL, 167) and slaves. Yet Sapphira's exile is a voluntary one that she seems to enjoy. Although other characters wonder why she chooses to marry beneath her and move from a much richer county east of the Blue Ridge to the poorer Back Creek, the reason seems to be that she wishes to play the role of the one superior being amidst commoners. Riding in her coach as a "mysterious stamp of superiority" (35), she is the only one in the area to have slaves, the implication being that she is the only one with the personality and breeding commanding enough to deserve them. Far from being resented for her haughtiness, Sapphira is surrounded by an admiring audience that confirms her right to act as dictatorially as she pleases; as everyone, black and white, admits, "A woman and an heiress had a right to" (5).

We might imagine that Cather dramatizes the dynamics of slavery to explore its psychological handicaps, vividly illustrated by her literally crippled heroine. Like Sapphira's self-serving exile, however, her physical illness only seems a disability while it really confers power. It is telling that on so many occasions she calls for her servants while only pretending to be sick, for her affliction from dropsy grants her all the privileges of childhood but with all the authority of adulthood. As an invalid, she enjoys the luxury of being pampered by her slaves at all hours of the day or night. Of course, as the mistress of slaves, Sapphira would automatically enjoy the power to command such attentions; I suspect that Cather made her heroine an invalid because she herself, suffering from a paralyzed hand and numerous other illnesses, had come to know the meaning of being "crippled and incapacitated, not to come and go at will, to be left out of things as if one were in one's dotage" (105). In Cather's valetudinarian state, the thought of Till and her mother Nancy rushing to the bedside to offer warm compresses and prompt sympathy would have been consoling. Cather further creates a bitterly ironic sense of sovereignty by imagining her heroine sitting "in her crude invalid's chair as if it were a seat of privilege" (15). Even from her invalid's chair, Sapphira is "still able to keep her servants well in hand" (54); like Alexandra Bergson, who conquers just by sitting still, Sapphira conquers by being, not doing; her confinement in her chair is a test of the sheer power of her will to overcome circumstances and make the world obey her desire. On each side of her chair are two iron rings into which her "bearers" (86) thrust hickory saplings; as Sapphira is actually carried around the estate in this chair as if it were a throne, her role as her majesty the queen becomes transparent. Though Cather presents her heroine's deportment in her chair as a sign of stoic fortitude, it is really a sign of infantile narcissism. Sapphira is most deeply living out the fantasy that Willa Cather herself loved indulging in as a child when she would often sit in an "imaginary chariot" made of one chair upside down on another; as her parents recalled, "Here she would sit in complete silence, driving the chariot, while an invisible slave ran beside her, repeating at intervals, 'Cato, thou art but man!'" (WCL, 10). Although now Cather surrounds her surrogate with actual slaves, they are no more visible as real people than they were in her childhood fantasy, for they still exist as solipsistic projections of her imagination. Finally, the childhood fantasy is made explicit in Cather's description of Sapphira's bedroom, where she sits for several hours after supper, watching the sun set over the creek: "The room had an air of settled comfort and stability.... The deep-set windows made one feel the thickness of the walls. A child could climb up into one of those windows and make a playhouse" (41). As thick and protective as the walls in *Shadows on the Rock*, these walls ensure that Sapphira can sustain the make-believe world found only in children's fairy tales, where kings and queens can rule over golden empires and never grow feeble or old.

Although on the surface Sapphira seems to be the malicious villain in the romance, the novel lays blame for Nancy's fate not on Sapphira but on her husband, Henry. Sapphira's childhood fantasy of power depends on a rigid caste system in which "whoever came, friend or stranger, was made welcome and cared for according to his place in the world" (159). This ruling principle of social order extends even to the grave. The family burying ground is emblematic of the proper relationship that must be kept between the rulers and the slaves: though the graves of the slaves are included with those of the rest of the family within the wall, their headstones — slate, rather than marble, and bearing single names — are divided from the rest by a wide gravel path; the spatial arrangement suggests the proper distance between slaves and their masters: related but subordinate, close, but unprotestingly in "their places" (203). Correspondingly, Sapphira's manner with inferiors, we are told, is always "irreproachable" (81); she is courteous but not too familiar. When the cobbler, the butcher, or the weaver come to visit, "she knew just how to talk to them" (81).

By contrast, the lesser-bred Henry Colbert does not know how to observe proper social decorums and distinctions. By insisting that only Nancy clean his room at the mill, he betrays a special fondness for her that arouses suspicions among the blacks that do no credit to either Nancy or himself and the Mistress. At the funeral of the old black woman Jezebel, Sapphira witnesses Henry disobeying the code of acceptable conduct between white masters and black slaves. He and Nancy stand apart from the others just outside the graveyard's stone wall — and thus symbolically in a kind of no man's land beyond the boundaries that define social harmony between the races. He speaks "very earnestly, with affectionate solicitude" (103) while she stands in an attitude of dejection, as if offended by his attentions. Sapphira is indignant: "Never before had she seen him expose himself like that. Whatever he was pressing upon that girl, he was not speaking as master to servant; there was nothing to suggest that special sort of kindliness permissible under such circumstances. He was not uttering condolences. It was personal. He had forgotten himself" (103–4). Henry's fault is that he forgets his superiority and treats Nancy as an equal. He has "exposed" himself to public scrutiny and thus threatens to break down the whole fragile structure of power on the estate. That night, as Sapphira lies in bed, worrying about the meaning of what she has seen, she is concerned that she will "be deceived and mocked by her own servants in her own house" (105); regardless of the truth of the rumors, she cannot tolerate such gossip and still retain her authority. We see that the problem here lies in the system of slavery itself that puts those in power in the vulnerable position of defending their authority before so many curious, probing eyes; it is the system of slavery that really enslaves Sapphira to the perceptions and opinions of her servants. Cather, however, does not indict the system itself, only those breeches of propriety that threaten it.

Moreover, Sapphira's suspicions about Henry's "intimate conversation" (105) with Nancy in the graveyard are confirmed by the sexually charged language of the passage: he had "forgotten himself" as if he had become carried away with passion, "expose[d] himself" as if he had figuratively stripped himself naked of his clothing. "Whatever he was pressing upon that girl" implies an urgent sexual need. In fact, as the novel unfolds, it becomes apparent that Henry has a latent sexual attraction to Nancy, made conscious to himself by the arrival of his notorious nephew, Martin Colbert. Cather chooses to make Nancy's pursuer a close relative of Henry in order to dramatize the dangerous sexual potential within Henry himself. As if sexuality were an aberrant genetic trait, rather than a universal fact of life, Cather links Martin and Henry as twins infected by the same bad blood. As Henry lies awake at night, thinking about Martin's nefarious designs, "the poison in the young scamp's blood seemed to stir something in his own. The Colbert in him threatened to raise its head after long hibernation" (209). With an almost comic literalness, the sexual aggressiveness in Henry wakes up under Martin's influence, like a phallic snake that has been too long asleep. Though Henry watches Martin making free with Nancy while she does the laundry in the barn, he ignores it, as he does all of Martin's advances, because he is torn between a desire to get rid of him and a desire to participate, vicariously, in the seduction. When, in his dreams, "the sense of almost being Martin, came over him like a black spell" (209), he is able to act out through an alter ego his own guilty sexual fantasies.

In a seemingly digressive episode, when Rachel Blake goes to visit Mrs. Ringer, we find out that both of Mrs. Ringer's daughters have been seduced by country rakes; the relevance of the story is made clear when Mrs. Ringer pronounces with folksy wisdom, "Fellers is skeered to make free with a gal that's got able men folks to see she gits her rights" (122). Although Sapphira sets the wheels for a sexual seduction in motion by inviting Martin Colbert to visit, it is up to Henry to prevent it. His incapacity to intervene on Nancy's behalf proves that Sapphira's doubts about him are well founded and that her precautions are prudent. Of course, Sapphira's fears about Henry's untrustworthiness reveal much about her own preoccupations with sexuality. Psychologically, her repressed sexuality (expressing Cather's own) emerges as the fantasy of Henry seducing Nancy, but the self-fulfilling nature of the repressed fear is not apparent to Sapphira or Cather.

In the battle between two competing notions of "inheritance" — Henry's "family inheritance" (192) of blood tainted by sexuality, and

Sapphira's "inheritance" of breeding according to a genteel Southern tradition — Sapphira wins in the only way she can. Although her setting the scene for a rape seems, from one point of view, to introduce sexuality into the pastoral idyll, it is really aimed at removing that threat. It is surely one of the novel's greatest ironies that Sapphira must resort to a devious plot of seduction in order to evade the consequences of sexuality. This inconsistency implies that Cather considered the integrity of a black woman expendable if that meant preserving the honor of a white woman. When old Jezebel, Nancy's grandmother, dies, Sapphira arranges to have her buried in one of her own embroidered nightgowns that she used to wear as a girl. Her redressing of the black woman is emblematic of the way she wishes to clothe all of her slaves in the garb of her own childhood innocence. Sapphira wishes to keep Nancy as an incarnation of preadolescent youth off of which she, bitterly aging, can feed. When Nancy becomes no longer a girl but a woman of sexual maturity, she must go. Sapphira must cast Nancy out in order to preserve her dominion over a kingdom of childhood. Interestingly, it doesn't matter to Sapphira whether Nancy has actually had any sexual experience. The mere fact that she has allowed herself to be perceived as a sexually attractive woman is what Sapphira cannot forgive. The point is reinforced by Henry's response to Nancy, which is equally narcissistic. He had valued her as a child, "more like an influence than a person" (192), who came to fill his room with the soft spring breezes of youth. But, Cather says, "Now that he must see her as a woman, enticing to men, he shrank from seeing her at all" (193). Despite Nancy's innocence, Henry rejects her for the same reason that Jim Burden rejected Àntonia after the Wick Cutter episode. The analogy suggests that, as racist as the novel is, its main quarrel is not with race per se but with sex, though projecting sexuality onto blacks is a very traditional racist gesture.

As an imaginative claimant plagued by old age and its infirmities, Sapphira Colbert is in a double bind. Like her prototypes in earlier novels, she needs others to confirm her identity and give her a vicarious sense of youth. Unlike them, however, she is also threatened by that youth. Like Snow White's stepmother, Sapphira looks into the mirror of others to see that she is no longer the fairest of them all; the golden girl, Nancy,[11] is more attractive and youthful than she. Paradoxically, she finds that the young, instead of replenishing her vitality, merely arouse her jealousy, reminding her of her own age and decrepitude. Ironically, the most fundamental reason why Nancy no longer suits her mistress is that she reminds her of all that she has lost. As if Cather's old dream of maginative self-recovery through an alter ego were breaking down, Sapphira has to concoct the whole plot of sexual intrigue as an excuse to get rid of the servant who can no longer fulfill her insatiable needs.

Nancy's departure is necessary for the restoration of Sapphira's supremacy. Moreover, everything beginning with Nancy's escape is contrived to reinstate Sapphira in the reader's favor. As soon as Rachel helps Nancy to escape, she regrets what she has done. For her, the freeing of another human being is not worth the cost of hurting her mother's pride. In the next chapter, the death of one of Rachel's daughters from diphtheria provides the pretext for Rachel's grateful reunion with her mother; though we would think that Sapphira would be in need of forgiveness herself, she is the one who forgives Rachel for stealing her property. Sapphira gets to play the role of the "kind woman" who is "good to a great many folks" (268) when she rallies around the sick girls, gets the doctor for them, and then condescends to invite Rachel and her granddaughter Mary to live with her. Sapphira also wins the adoration of Henry. Through his admiration for her resolute courage in the face of her worsening illness, Cather is able instantaneously to transform her heroine's "heartlessness" into a perceived "strength," for "as long as she was conscious," he reflects, "she would be the mistress of the situation and of herself" (268). The lesson that Henry draws from the episode with Nancy provides the novel's moral: "There are different ways of being good to folks," he tells his wife. "Sometimes keeping people in their place is being good to them" (268). Seen as a noble effort to keep people like Henry and Nancy in their place, Sapphira's cruel designs in the novel are sanctioned.

The chapter entitled "Nancy's Flight" could more accurately be called "Nancy's Exile," for it portrays how even the black slave escaping to freedom mourns having to leave her happy home. We learn that it is not slavery that is a hard pill to swallow but freedom, which makes the slave feel "drugged ... by the bitterest of all drugs" (239). As Ammons has noted, the fact that no slaves in the novel hate slavery reveals that "a lifetime of observation and experience had done nothing to deconstruct the sentimental racist myths of [Cather's] Virginia girlhood."[12] So, too, we could say that Cather uses the black characters to participate in and confirm her own more personal myth of childhood sovereignty. Nancy's desire to stay on the plantation as the white people's dependent is meant to pay tribute to Cather's surrogate. Her last words before she crosses the river express a desire to go home out of loyalty not to her own mother but to her white mistress: "Why, she brought me up, an' now she's sick an' sufferin'. Look at her pore feet. I ought-a borne it better" (237). Per haps out of an unconscious need to win sympathy for her own ailing condition, Cather confirms the stereotype of the black "mammy" who feels more pity for her white mistress's sore feet than for her own aching and enslaved body.

Cather envisions blacks as children out of her own childish needs, and she herself appears as the real child in the epilogue, reminding us, as Cather's biographers have noted, that the story in the novel was based on an actual episode in the Cather family history. Rachel Blake is a fictional portrait of Cather's own maternal grandmother, Rachel Seibert Boak, and Rachel's daughter Mary is directly drawn from Cather's mother, Mary Virginia Cather. Sapphira Dodderidge Colbert may have been suggested in part by Cather's maternal great-grandmother, Ruhamah Seibert, though, as James Woodress points out, the family history records little about her, and she died before Cather was born.[13] Sapphira is most likely a fictional invention of the kind of woman Willa Cather imagined as her ancestor. Nancy and Till were based on real blacks of those names. In the epilogue, Cather recreates the scene that she vividly remembered from her childhood in Virginia, of the return of Nancy Till. As she recalled in a letter, her opportunity to witness the reunion of Nancy and her mother was the most thrilling event of her life up to that time.[14] After their long separation, Nancy is coming home to see her aging mother at Back Creek. However, because the five-year-old Willa has a cold and cannot leave her mother's bed at Willowshade to witness the reunion, her mother persuades the two black women to postpone and relocate their meeting so that it can transpire in front of Willa. The reunion thus assumes a staged quality, as if it were performed more for the imaginative benefit of little Willa than for the satisfaction of the two black women involved. For the girl Willa, as for her great-grandmother Sapphira, human relationships are most interesting as a "play" staged for her own imaginative stimulation. Other people have little autonomy or agency in creating their own stories but are appropriated as part of her child's lively fantasy. Till readily plays her part in Cather's script, putting aside her own desire to see her daughter in order to accommodate the child's wish. Cather's recreation of herself as a child in this scene suggests the psychological vantage point from which she has regarded Sapphira's story all along. Indeed, though Sapphira Colbert is now dead, she is reincarnated in the presence of Willa Cather herself. Sick with a cold in her mother's bed, the five-year-old Cather occupies the same psychological space at center stage that Sapphira had enjoyed in her invalid's chair. Once again, the bed of illness has become the throne of privilege, where the child can be waited on, nursed, and entertained. The scene reminds us that as

Cather was writing the novel in her invalid's chair, she sustained herself in spite of her ebbing vitality by recalling the days of her own childhood at Willowshade when she had enjoyed a secure place of importance. As Cather fondly describes in a letter how her mother used to sing her to sleep in her bed with the old song about the black girl Nancy Till, we can see why Cather felt that the old times were beautiful. [15]

As a novel in which Willa Cather explores how her own female lineage shaped her artistic vision, *Sapphira and the Slave Girl* is a biographically significant work that has interested feminist critics. Sharon O'Brien, the first to consider the novel in terms of Cather's search for her artistic origins, argues that the epilogue reveals the "harmonious bond between mothers and daughters" that played a "central role in nourishing [Willa Cather's] creativity." [16] The mother-daughter bond does seem to have provided Cather with an important nurturing source of creativity. But, whereas O'Brien sees the maternal bonds portrayed in the text as paradigms of fostering "compassion" [17] for others, I see them as relationships imagined to confirm the child's own self-love. The "compassion" that Willa's mother shows her when she agrees to arrange the meeting of Nancy and Till in her bedroom might more accurately be seen as indulgence of the child's egocentric needs. In fact, what little we discover about Cather's "mother" Mary in the novel confirms that selfishness, rather than selflessness, is the legacy that Cather inherits from her female ancestors. Cather includes the seemingly digressive episode of the illness of Rachel Blake's two young daughters, Betty and Mary, as a kind of parable. It seems no accident that the two girls meet with very different fates when they contract diphtheria. Betty, a self-abnegating and "gentle spirit" (266) who embodies the female quality of selflessness according to the nineteenth-century genteel tradition, dies of the disease. Mary, on the other hand, a strong-willed and self-centered girl who takes what she needs from life, greedily drinks the doctor's soup, despite his orders, and lives. Mary, not Betty, is the one who wins Sapphira's approval as she pronounces, "Mary will get *so much more* out of life!" (266) By privileging Mary over Betty, Willa Cather breaks from her literary inheritance of female sentimental writers who cared more about otherworldly salvation than survival. By contrast, she seems to trace her maternal lineage from her own mother back to Sapphira, the most selfish woman in all of her fiction, as a model of the acquisitive egotism that is necessary to thrive.

The experience of the young girl Willa in the epilogue is aimed at reconnecting her to her origins in her regal ancestor, Sapphira. Sitting as the audience to the stories told by Nancy and Till, Cather bears witness to her own aristocratic past. A lot has happened to Nancy in twenty-five years — she has escaped to Canada, married, and had three children —

but she wants only to talk nostalgically with her mother about the "old times" when they had the pleasure of serving the gracious Sapphira. More than anything, Nancy wants to hear stories about Mrs. Colbert. Till obliges her (and more deeply, Willa Cather), by indefatigably praising Sapphira as a "lady" in a place "where nobody was anybody much" (295) — presumably, including herself. Till takes little Willa to the graveyard to put flowers on her great-grandmother's grave, but Till's own cabin serves as a kind of memorial to her. Holding no secrets about Till's own past, her cabin is a museum housing momentoes of the Colberts — the miller's books, Sapphira's lace caps and velvet slippers, and even locks of her hair — which Willa gladly appropriates as evidence of her fictional great-grandmother's illustriousness. Like Nancy's experience of freedom in Canada, where she worked respectfully for a "mistress" and "master" (285), her return to the Virginia plantation after the slaves have been set free merely replicates her earlier situation in slavery. Nancy and Till now voluntarily adopt the servile position that worships their mistress's memory. Cather fully restores that imaginative hierarchy between mistress and servant; purged of the stigma of "ownership," but remaining essentially unchanged, that relationship is now presented as exemplary, and Willa Cather's ancestor is honorably redeemed.

Till is especially impressed by her memory of Sapphira's death when, dignified till the end, she died "upright in her chair" (294), with her head held high. But though Till imagines her old mistress dying like a lady, Sapphira really dies like a child in a scene that is once again staged to foster the world of beautiful illusions. As she sits in her throne, looking out her bedroom window, she contemplates not the world but a reflection of her own selfish desires. Till has arranged the candles on the tea table in such a way that they replicate themselves in their reflections in the window; as Till describes the effect, "It looked like candles shining in a little playhouse ... and there was the tea-table out there too, all set like for company" (294). Sapphira presides over this scene smilingly, like a little girl playing house, or having tea, with imaginary guests — spirits of the "fine folks" (294) who used to come to her old home on Chestnut Hill to pay homage to her as the patrician lady. Sapphira's death is not a reunion with God but a return to her proper place at the top of the social scale, and thus, a spiritual homecoming to herself only. In this final scene, Cather, too, imaginatively recreates the bright occasions of the past, summoning back from the dead the supportive presence of others as flames of youth that reflect the glow cast by her own central aura. Death allows Sapphira to die happy in her memory of a bygone childhood power, and this, we suspect, is where we also leave Willa Cather at the end of her career, looking forward, through her fictional surrogate, to her own death. Still her unvanquished self, she goes through her old part to the last. Upright in her chair, she looks out at the world as a mirror that reflects back to her a sense of her own indomitable sovereignty.

10

"Making it Over Until it Becomes
a Personal Possession":
Willa Cather and the Reader

If one measure of an artist's merit is her staying power, then Willa Cather must be deemed an important writer. In 1938, Sinclair Lewis declared that he would vote for Willa Cather as the "greatest American novelist."[1] Despite the critical disfavor in which she was held by a minority of critics in the 1930s, George White could still declare in 1942, "There is in her novels the genius of permanence.... [H]er own world broke in two about 1922. Not so the world of her novels. It is as strong as ever."[2] White's words were prophetic. Certainly, the sales record of Cather's novels bears testimony to her enduring popularity with her readers. Early in 1913, Ferris Greenslet, Cather's publisher at Houghton Mifflin, was confident that *O Pioneers!* "ought to ... definitely establish the author as a novelist of the first rank,"[3] and the following year, he could gladly report that the novel was "selling more steadily than the popular successes of last fall."[4] Of Cather's next novel, *The Song of the Lark*, Greenslet was similarly happy to inform her that "it is the steadiest and most persistent seller of all of our 1915 novels."[5] Faring better than *O Pioneers!*, *The Song of the Lark* sold 8,000 copies in its first six months,[6] which Greenslet deemed "after all pretty exceptional" for a "book of so high a quality."[7] No bookstore was overstocked with it, and he was continually receiving reorders. In 1918, he wrote to Cather that he had spent a day in Glens Falls, New York, and was impressed to see that the circulating copy of the novel in the public library had been taken out 167 times.[8] *My Àntonia*, appearing in September 1918, has proven the most popular of all of Cather's novels. It immediately sold well, profitably passing the

5,000 mark in just three months so as to earn, according to Greenslet, "a definite place as an 'American classic.'"[9] Pleased with the increasing ascendancy in sales of *My Àntonia* over Cather's other novels, Greenslet wrote to Cather in 1921 that he was printing a new edition of 2,000 copies, which he thought "unusually large ... for a work of fiction after its first year."[10] Cather's substantial sales have been especially impressive, given that she strenuously objected to the constant pressure to dramatize, anthologize, and reprint her books in inexpensive editions. Today, now that Houghton Mifflin has brought Cather's novels out in paperback, *My Àntonia* is selling more copies than ever, reaching approximately fifty thousand a year in the early 1980s and seventy thousand a year in 1992. According to Alan Andrés of Houghton Mifflin, "*My Àntonia* has been for many years one of Houghton Mifflin's best-selling backlist titles."[11]

Cather's subsequent novels, published by Knopf, have also done remarkably well. Although Cather received her first large-scale negative criticism for *One of Ours*, the book became an immediate best-seller, selling 16,000 copies in its first month, and 54,000 copies within the year, after seven reprintings. With its large royalties, Cather was financially secure for the rest of her life from this one book alone.[12] The publication of *A Lost Lady* in 1922 turned Cather into a huge critical and popular success. Paying her their first official homage, the people back home in Nebraska commissioned Leon Bakst to paint Cather's portrait to be hung in the big public library in Omaha. In 1923, Warner Brothers in Hollywood purchased the movie rights to *A Lost Lady* for $10,000, and then remade the film in 1934 with Barbara Stanwyck.[13] According to Edith Lewis, *Death Comes for the Archbishop* so surprised the publishers as an "instant and overwhelming success" that it ran out of stock and booksellers could not supply the demand for it (WCL, 146). Still considered one of her most popular novels, *Death Comes for the Archbishop* has sold over 250,000 copies in hard cover alone.[14] After the favorable reception of *Death Comes for the Archbishop*, *Shadows on the Rock*, published in 1931, enjoyed the largest immediate sales of Cather's career. Promoted in part by its selection by the Book of the Month Club, the novel sold 167,679 copies from ten printings before the end of 1931, and in future years was reprinted ten more times.[15] *The New Yorker* honored the book's publication by running a profile of Cather by Louise Bogan, and in February 1933, *Time*, hailing Cather as "our finest novelist,"[16] put her on its cover. In 1933, *Shadows on the Rock* won the Prix Femina Americain, adding to the long list of Cather's other honors and awards.[17] At the end of Cather's life, her reputation as one of the most important and influential American novelists was secure; her books were continuing to sell well and be widely read, her admiring public continued to grow, and her novels were being translated into at least ten different languages: Swedish, Spanish, Hungarian, Danish, Dutch, German, Swiss, French, Italian, and Argentinian.[18]

All of Willa Cather's twelve novels, three collections of short stories, and a volume of poetry that she approved for publication in her lifetime are still in print. This surprising fact reflects not only our commitment to an expanding canon of American literature but the incredible popularity that Willa Cather has won with an American and international audience. Deserving as Cather is of critical recognition, her popularity is owing not simply to her literary merit as to the deeper emotional need that her books fulfill. Cather herself cared more that her fiction stir the average reader than the professional critic. When, for example, a former president of the Missouri Pacific praised *The Song of the Lark*, Cather "felt a contentment more instinctive and complete than any purely literary critic could give her."[19] Despite her usual objection to cheaper editions, she agreed to a special edition of *My Àntonia* for a worker's union because she liked to think that "Àntonia" had always been beloved among working people.[20] Clearly, Cather has succeeded in reaching her intended audience. Today, conferences on Willa Cather — unlike typical academic conferences — are attended not only by professional scholars but by many of her faithful everyday readers — housewives, lawyers, business managers. Cather's broad appeal confirms that one does not have to be trained in explicating complex literary allusions to be able to experience the pleasures afforded by Cather's uninvolved narration; instead, one has only to respond to the kindling of emotion aroused by the drama of an ardent living soul. Cather's novels inspire passionate sentiments in her audience. As one of Cather's first reviewers felt, the power of Cather's "unforced emotion ... lift[s] [her novels] far above the ordinary product of contemporary novelists."[21] So strong is this emotional power that it compelled even a professional critic like Robert Morss Lovett, writing in 1927 of *Death Comes for the Archbishop*, to admit ingenuously that it "moves one to tears."[22] One has only to attend a Cather conference or teach a class on *My Àntonia* to witness the heartfelt and often teary-eyed testimonials of personal attachment offered by her loyal readers.

If one asks people if they have read Willa Cather, the typical response is something like, "Oh, I just LOVE Willa Cather!" Cather's readers feel a strong personal investment in her fiction. Reviewers and ordinary readers often express this devotion by talking about Cather in superlative terms — she is their "favorite" writer, and there is no writer like her. In an article that appeared in the *Bookman* in 1926, for example, Zona Gale describes Tom Outland as "my favorite character in fiction" because "the passion and the hope and the understanding which he puts into [his] quest" is "so emotionally thrilling."[23] Tom Outland's story similarly impressed one James Ford, who exclaims in his 1925 review, "Never have I read such a thrilling account of a dead-and-gone civilization as I find in her pages."[24] Recalling how, "when I read that story I felt as a prospector might feel on coming upon a very rich vein of the precious metal," he identifies with Tom's discovery on the mesa so as to treasure in Cather's novel a valuable possession. In fact, the passionate response of many of Cather's readers seems inspired by their empathy with her characters as if they were real people.

In particular, male readers of *The Song of the Lark* sound very much like Thea Kronborg's admirers within the novel itself. In a 1915 review for *The Nation*, H. W. Boyton avows that whereas other prima donnas in fiction have been alleged in vain, "Thea Kronborg we believe in. She triumphantly refutes the legend of the invertebrate artist."[25] Also seduced by Thea's victorious power, René Rapin, in his 1930 book on Cather, implicitly puts himself in company with Thea's worshippers in the novel, explaining that

> egotism carried so far compels admiration, it is not usually provocative of any tender emotions. Yet, as witness Ray Kennedy's, Dr. Archie's, Harsanyi's, or Fred Ottenberg's experience in the book, men not only admire Thea (their weaker natures bowing to her strength), they actually love her. For Thea *is* lovable. She is lovable because she is so intensely alive, so constantly 'pulsing with ardor and anticipation' (140); ... lovable also because, however ruthless her devotion to her aims, her ideal is a high one, and there is no littleness in her, only an unqualified giving of herself to the realization of the best in her; lovable because of her quick instinctive appreciation of passion and of beauty, her utter disregard of prejudice and conventions, her powerful and delicate imagination."[26]

Fully recognizing Thea's "egotism," Rapin nonetheless gets carried away in professing his love for her, precisely because her indomitable sense of self invites his vicarious identification. In surely one of the most ecstatic "love" letters that Cather ever received from a reader, John Curran describes a living and breathing Thea Kronborg as if she were his best friend: "Thea is very precious to me. She is much more important than the friends I have about me every day. I have no real friends like her. Our everyday people, you know, hide themselves from us, just as we hide from others. But I know Thea better than I know my own sister, and I love her just as much."[27] In the way that Jim Burden possesses Àntonia, not as a real friend or lover but as an imaginative companion, so this reader recognizes that his bond with Cather's characters is in some ways more complete and satisfying than even his close familial relationships. As readers, we share the same pleasure that Willa Cather herself got from her characters as fellowship with another soul.[28]

Readers have shared the sense that Cather's novels often cling tenaciously in the mind, and yet they have found it difficult to determine the source of the novels' haunting resonance. In discussing *The Song of the Lark*, E. K. Brown observes that "without quite knowing why a sympathetic reader is suffused with warmth as he moves through the story, and long afterward when most of the events have been forgotten and most of the characters have grown dim, a mention of *The Song of the Lark*, a sight of the faded blue cover on the bookshelf of a friend, is enough to bring back a radiant feeling that no other writing by Willa Cather can evoke."[29] Floyd Dell, writing about *O Pioneers!* in 1913, says that the novel is "invested with dignity" but "despair[s] of being able to show why."[30] Francis Connolly, testifying to Cather's popularity in 1952, acknowledges that, "like all popular admirations, its source is not altogether clear. The springs of devotion are deep in instinct, disguised in latent assumptions, and they often bubble up in generous but imprecise enthusiasms at very great distances from the true source of the pleasure they inspire."[31] One reason why critics are unable to identify the mysterious source of Cather's emotional power is that they are responding to the power of Cather's own projected romantic ego — the inexplicable thing not named. To use Connolly's metaphor, the springs of devotion have, indeed, bubbled up at great distances from the original source of the pleasure that feeds them; although many readers have unconsciously responded to the childhood fantasy of power that operates in the novels, few, in their intellectual attempts to analyze different aspects of Cather's fiction, have recognized this as the emotional source of Cather's inspiration.

Cather's fiction has served as a mirror for a broad spectrum of critical interests; only because critics have put a variety of faces on Willa Cather's art has she been taken as a writer of breadth. The transparent fantasy of childhood has been taken to look like whatever the critic most values — real life, art, civilization, religion, history, local color, family values and community, environmentalism and the land, women's issues, or lesbianism. The "inexplicable presence of the thing not named" has been repeatedly called by different names. For example, critics such as H. L. Mencken, Carl Van Doren, and Maxwell Geismar, who value literary realism, see the essence of Cather's art as "the sweetness and splendor of life" in the world.[32] A lover of art, Edward Everett Hale imagines that Thea Kronborg is dedicated to a sense of "something less common than life: namely, art as it exists in life."[33] Not surprisingly, the opera buff Don Beckman, writing for *Opera News*, thinks that *The Song of the Lark* is primarily about the career and technique of the Swedish-born singer Olive Fremstad.[34] E. K. Brown, himself devoted to preserving "the essences which are central to all civilization," imagines that Cather's art is dedicated to the high aesthetic and moral ideals of "civilization"; as he appraises her work, "what she cares for in humanity and in nature many sensitive and cultivated people have cared for in every time."[35] Catholic critics are convinced that Cather writes about Catholicism. The Catholic commentator for *Commonweal*, Michael Williams, for example, admits his agenda when he writes: "Let us hope that among [future American writers] may be a few Catholics. American Catholics sorely lack, and even more sorely need, authentic artists." He finds what he seeks in Cather's *Death Comes for the Archbishop*, professing, "I consider it the duty of Catholics to buy and read and spread Willa Cather's masterpiece."[36] Like a priest on an evangelical mission, Williams wants to pass on Cather's novel as if it were a new Bible.[37] The Western literary historian David Harrell joins company with Louis Auchincloss and others when he argues that Cather is adapting history to fiction in novels like *The Professor's House*.[38] Those who wish to endorse traditional family values, like J. W. Donohue, writing for the family magazine *America* in honor of Cather's centennial, portray Cather as a writer whose own family feeling gave her "wider human sympathies and ... a moral sense of the ideal human community."[39] Nebraska critics, like Mildred Bennett, Bernice Slote, and Bruce Baker, seeking to inspire public appreciation for their home state, argue that Cather focuses on transforming regional material into universal situations and timeless folk literature.[40] James Keough, writing for *Sierra,* reads Cather through the lens of his own environmentalist concerns, imagining that she "was at heart a preservationist"[41] who loved, above all, the land, and deplore[d] people who merely take from the land with no moral commitment or attachment to it."[42] Feminist critics wish to use Cather to advance their theories of women as selfless, nurturing, and giving. Lesbian feminist critics like Judith Fetterly argue that Cather is writing lesbian subtexts.[43] In response to the treatments of Cather's sexuality, some traditional male critics, in their turn, take a proprietary interest in preserving their ideal vision of Cather as wholesome and mainstream. John Murphy, for example, regrets the "unfortunate trend in Cather criticism in which the novelist's fiction is confused with her life in order to destroy her traditional, healthy image."[44] James Woodress and his followers have been especially distressed by the emphasis on Cather's lesbianism. At the 1987 National Willa Cather Seminar in Hastings, Nebraska, Woodress expressed in his closing remarks his satisfaction that Cather criticism had taken a more sensible and profitable direction since people had stopped focusing on Cather's supposed lesbianism, as they had in the previous conference.

The new historicist Jane Tompkins helps us to understand that "great literature does not exert its force over and against time, but changes with the changing currents of social and political life."[45] To a degree, we can understand the response to Willa Cather as a reflection of the preoccupations and values of the historical period in which she has been read. In determining the historical response of the average reader to Cather, I have consulted not only scholarly articles but ordinary newspaper and magazine reviews as well as older anthologies. During the 1920s, when American literature was just beginning to be studied in the universities, its commentators tried to make a case for a strong indigenous literature, as worthy as Britain's, by emphasizing peculiarly "American" national themes.[46] Clearly conscious of his mission to distinguish American literature, T. K. Whipple writes in 1923, "To the query whether it is possible for an artist to exist in the United States, the best answer would be: Go read Miss Cather."[47] Her books are "richer and more varied than those of any other living American novelist."[48] Eager to defend against the view of American literature as provincial, critics of the 1920s were sympathetic to Cather's efforts to transform the Western landscape into the scene for heroic pioneer endeavor. Carl Van Doren, regarding Cather's idealized epic narratives as actual history, exults in the fact that "in [her] quarter of the country there were still heroes during the days she has written about."[49] Similarly, Edmund Wilson embraces Cather because he sees her as "one of the only writers who has been able to bring any real distinction to the life of the Middle West" insofar as she stirs us with the "pathos of the human spirit making the effort to send down its roots and to flower in that barren soil."[50] Themselves pioneers in literary criticism, hoping to foster the growth of a native American culture, Whipple, Van Doren, Wilson, and others saw Cather's pioneers as consecrated to an analogous mission: the fulfillment of a national destiny. Reflecting this time-bound agenda that great literature must "dedicate the complicated organization of our contemporary life to some great ends ... some significant purpose,"[51] Lloyd Morris believes that in Cather's novels, "the frontier was to be conquered that a national destiny might be inaugurated."[52] One of the first reviewers of *O Pioneers!* strikes the same patriotic chord when he sees Alexandra Bergson's story as a winning of glory not only for herself but for her "beloved country."[53] The "big spaces and big emotions of Western life" in Cather's fiction that engage his imagination reflect the national sense of America's grand mission. Inspired by "the suffering and the glory of those who have taught a desert to feed the world," he takes the story as confirmation of the myth of the supremacy of America in its role as breadbasket of the earth.

Cather came under attack in the 1930s as an escapist writer when the depressed economic and social conditions of the country reinforced the belief of a small group of Marxist critics that art should come to grips with the harsh political, economic, and social facts of the day. Leftist critics believed that American artists should comprehend the growth of capitalism and its negative side effects, such as war, depressions, and the exploitation and alienation of the working class. Judged not according to aesthetic standards but solely according to the ideological interpretation of the class conflict, Cather appeared to lack vision. Louis Kronenberger, for example, objects to the way that the distancing aesthetic effects of light and color in Cather's historical novels make "it impossible for her to give any sort of valid interpretation to life."[54] Similarly, Clifton Fadiman faults Cather for ignoring and evading pressing social and political crises: "Of all conceivable temperaments the Vergilian is perhaps the least suited to portray an epoch like ours, darkly colored with brutal struggle and mass disaster."[55] In his view, Cather's novels are limited because they trivialize and sentimentalize the problems of war, do not portray sexual relationships convincingly, and do not serve as guides for conduct in the America of her time. Lionel Trilling also berates Cather for having "gone down to defeat before the actualities of American life," and retreating into the past.[56] In perhaps the most influential critique in subsequent years, Granville Hicks sounds the keynote of this polemical brand of criticism when he charges that Cather "has never once tried to see contemporary life as it is."[57]

After Cather's own career came to an end in the 1940s, it became possible for the critics of the 1940s and 1950s to try to understand her work as a whole and to place her more objectively within historical traditions. Maxwell Geismar, in *The Last of the Provincials*, for example, sees Cather as part of a generation of writers in a unique era that included Anderson, Lewis, Mencken, and Fitzgerald.[58] Less partisan and censorious than the criticism of the 1930s, the criticism of the 1940s and 1950s was characterized by a new detached tone and an impulse to judge the significance of the art as art. Alfred Kazin's *On Native Grounds*, published in 1942, marked the beginning of a New Critical approach to Cather that subordinated social and historical issues to "a full devotion to what literature is in itself."[59] He is interested to find in Cather "the uniqueness of the gift, of the essential vision, through which I hope to penetrate into the mystery and sacredness of the individual soul."[60] Critics such as Kazin, E. K. Brown, David Daiches, and Van Wyck Brooks, among others, pay attention to the beauty of craftsmanship, sensuous style, sense of economy, command of rhythms, and richness of texture, atmosphere, and surface in the novels.[61] The main thematic emphasis during these decades is on the "values" in Cather's fiction.[62] Whereas critics of the 1930s had condemned Cather for her inability to deal with contemporary realities, the critics of the 1940s and 1950s see her art as exemplifying a necessary retreat from a degraded present in order to preserve the "exquisitely futile values"[63] of the past, embodied in a pioneer tradition of order and humanism. Kazin, for example, views Cather's escapism as the sign of an elevated cultivation and sensibility; whereas her contemporaries "were lost in the new materialism, satirized or bewailed it; she seceded, as only a very rare integrity could secede with dignity."[64] Just as Cather viewed her own characters as noble beings defeated by life, so Kazin sympathetically portrays Cather as too good for this world. She, like her characters, "withdrew ... because she had fought a losing battle that no one of her spirit could hope to win."[65] Kazin seems to reveal a kind of superior contempt of his own for the emptiness of modern industrial culture in which primary, spiritual values seem to have been lost. Other critics of the period seem to share this incommunicable sense of loss and, hence, appreciate Cather's vision, calling her escapism instead a high-minded allegiance to lasting values. Maxwell Geismar excuses Cather's evasion of the social environment on the grounds of her commendable values: "As early as her first novel you will realize how sure and sensitive her values are in the human area at least.... She is the defender of the spiritual graces in the midst of an increasingly materialistic culture."[66] Similarly, Henry Steele Commager and Van Wyck Brooks regard Cather as the guardian of the faith in spiritual and moral over material values.[67] Frederick Hoffman suggests that Cather's two central symbols of the softly lighted drawing room and the garage stress how "the values of traditional religion" succeed "in vanquishing ... the unholy modern trinity of science, invention, and war."[68] Hoffman's words remind us that the critics of this period identify with Cather's indictment of modernity not only out of an aversion for the corrupt values of an industrialized present but out of a historically conditioned disillusionment with the war. Having themselves suffered through a period of violent disruption and social change during World War II and its aftermath, the critics of the 1940s and 1950s sympathize with Cather's desire to maintain values in difficult and threatening times. They share what they view as her nostalgia for the indestructible things — humanistic values that are central to civilization and anchored in the West or in European or immigrant traditions. They also appreciate her absolute investment in art for art's sake. Interestingly, Cather's recovered popularity during the war decade that also saw the rise of New Criticism suggests

that she and her critics of this period together looked towards the sanctuary of art as a way to escape the annihilations of a chaotic and petty
present.

James Schroeter, in his book *Willa Cather and her Critics*, presents
the 1960s as a period in Cather scholarship when thematic and mythic
criticism was in vogue.[69] He discusses how, for instance, John Randall's
emphasis on the dialectical opposition between "civilized" and "frontier"
values in his book *The Landscape and the Looking Glass* (1960) is influenced by Henry Nash Smith's notion of the "garden of the world" as the
controlling American myth. He categorizes the Blooms' book, *Willa
Cather's Gift of Sympathy* (1962), as another example of one of the first
"thematic-symbolic" treatments of Cather in its similar concern with the
conflict between the values of the frontier and civilization. Schroeter's
idea of the mythic helps us to see a common interest during this decade;
for example, Robert Scholes, in his 1962 essay "Hope and Memory in
My Àntonia," examines the implications of the Adamic myth in that
novel.[70] Perhaps we can understand the emphasis on the pastoral idyll in
Cather as symptomatic of the social and political consciousness of the
1960s that was characterized by a heightened idealism, skepticism of
technological progress, and desire to return to a simplified life in nature,
uncluttered by material possessions. Talking about Cather on the brink of
the 1960s, Leon Edel relates his audience's love of Cather to the contemporary resistance to a new age of mechanization, standardization, and
consumerism. Stressing how far we have moved away from Cather's
world, he says, "We wonder, sometimes, whether we have awakened
from the realities of our childhood into the fantastic world of science fiction" with our huge "big-finned automobiles ... the sonorities of the jet in
the sky, or the cacophony of the dishwashing machine in the kitchen, or
the vibrations of Hi-Fi and television within the walls of our
dwellings."[71] Certainly, Edward and Lillian Bloom respond in Cather to
"the threat to [the spirit of the frontier] in the encroachments of materialism and selfish acquisitiveness,"[72] in part because they see that their own
times have become spiritually devitalized as a wasteland of conformity
and aimless enterprise; in looking back longingly to Cather's frontier,
they express the general desire of the decade to get back to a more spiritually sustaining life in nature, away from a machine-made materialism.
Revealing the unorthodox spirit of the 1960s that celebrated a youthful
and rugged individualism, they are attracted by Cather's unconventional
artists and creative souls; in what could be taken as a 1960s' manifesto,
they write, "She understands well enough that the artist is by necessity a
nonconformist who cannot yield to arbitrary social pressures and conventions."[73] For the Blooms, the nonconformist must be driven by a

moral purpose: "For most serious writers of modern times, moral or social responsibility must coincide with esthetic awareness."[74] Viewing
Cather through their contemporary lens of social commitment and idealism, the Blooms imagine that the quest for personal salvation in Cather
lies in high-minded moral action.

How should we analyze the historical response to Willa Cather?
Examining the politics of canon formation, Sharon O'Brien has recently
argued that Cather possessed canonical status in the 1920s only to lose it
in the 1930s because of the efforts of male reviewers, critics, and
academies to create a respectable American literary canon that excluded
women.[75] O'Brien looks at a subtext of sexist language in the attacks on
Cather by the leftist critics who came of age in the 1930s — Geismar,
Hicks, Trilling, and Kazin — to show that "gender may have been the
dominant, if unacknowledged, variable in shaping the case against Willa
Cather."[76] Surely, as O'Brien contends, some male critics of the 1930s
and 1940s did have sexist reasons for demoting Cather in the canon; they
applied standards to her art that they would not have applied to male
writers. Certainly, Cather did not assume a prominent place in college
curriculums until a revival of interest in women's literature within the
last couple of decades. In spite of this gender bias, however, even
Cather's harshest critics of the 1930s reserve praise for her earlier novels.
That they criticize primarily her later works, written after *Death Comes
for the Archbishop*, suggests that their criticism was motivated, at least in
part, by political and aesthetic concerns. Louis Kronenberger, for example, though he attacks Cather's last two historical novels on familiar
grounds, passionately admires her early novels with strong heroines.
According to Kronenberger, the most "human and solid"[77] novels of the
past twenty years are *My Àntonia* and *The Song of the Lark*. Although the
vocabulary that he uses to describe *Shadows on the Rock* and *Death
Comes for the Archbishop* — "minor," "pale," and "thin" — seems to
diminish Cather's art as too feminine, he most obviously criticizes Cather
not for violating a "male" standard but for failing to come up to her *own*
standard. As he says, "All her later work is distinctly minor, pale beside
the rich earthiness of the earlier novels, thin beside their vibrant sturdi-
ness, sterile where they were fecund. This sterility cannot, of course, do
damage to her past achievements: she remains, by past performance, the
best American woman novelist of her time. *The Song of the Lark* and *My
Àntonia* are books that one will want to read tomorrow."[78] Kronenberger's contrasts between "pale" and "thin" and "rich" and "vibrant" suggest
that what he is really responding to is a difference in emotional intensity
and texture between the early and late novels; in the early novels, the
female characters are stirred by youthful ardor, and the style is similarly

charged with more intense passion. The early novels, "set in a fresh and open world," about "women en route to their proper destinies," win him over with their strong "affirmation of life."[79] As long as this feeling of affirmation permeates the novels, Kronenberger finds them "emotionally satisfying";[80] he notes that, with the exception of *A Lost Lady*, Cather "is a success with success, a failure with failure."[81] Although we would think that a Marxist critic would find more to like in the novels of Cather's middle and late phases, where the intrusions of the world are acknowledged to prevent her characters from magically fulfilling their desires, he, like many of her other critics in the 1930s, clearly prefers the earlier happy novels in which the burdens of life are simply more successfully and transparently escaped. Interestingly, despite his own Marxist allegiances, Kronenberger is fully taken in by the wish fulfillment qualities of the early fiction. Similarly, Clifton Fadiman, who, initially seems to be another hostile male critic, also writes a balanced review. Although he thinks that Cather's "hypertrophied sense of the past" in *Shadows on the Rock* and *Death Comes for the Archbishop* "may permanently transport her to regions where minor works of art may be created, but major ones never,"[82] he regrets that this might be so. "This is a sad thing to contemplate," he writes, "for the author of *My Àntonia* and *The Song of the Lark* was not a minor writer, but a major one." What is surprising and noteworthy is not that Fadiman faults Cather's late works as "minor," but that he unreservedly recognizes the early works as "major." Those first novels he praises for their "fresh morning vigor and warmth"; by contrast, the late novels he disparages for a "continuous diminution of vitality." Even Granville Hicks has praise for the early novels that still possess richness of feeling.[83] What this evidence suggests is that Cather was not simply the victim of a male conspiracy in canon formation but a victim of her own ebbing powers as a writer. It is significant that it was with the publication of *Shadows on the Rock* in 1931 that Cather first felt the real bite of critical disapproval; as the critics of the 1930s suggest, one reason for its unpopularity was its lack of a compellingly vibrant heroine who had a transfiguring sense of imagination and vitality. Cather's reception suggests that if older writers would quit writing earlier, their reputations would often be more secure.

Despite Cather's growing reputation as a writer of peculiarly female sensibilities who appeals primarily to a female audience,[84] I have found no significant pattern of difference between the emotional response of male and female readers of Cather over the years. Beneath slight historical variations, the response of male and female readers alike to Willa Cather's fiction has remained remarkably consistent. The power that Cather has exerted over her readers is profoundly ahistorical and undictated by gender. A close reading of Cather's reviews shows how a variety of her readers, despite their varying assumptions about her art, betray their deep attraction to the wish fulfillment qualities of her childhood fantasy. One reason why Cather has held her own is because her readers have responded to her fairy tale of imaginative possession as a means to power. Approaching Cather's work through a kind of cultural psychology, we can see how generations of readers have found in her books a sense of personal hope and restoration.

Cather's work has been held in awe as a "miracle" by both female and male readers. In 1931, Louise Bogan writes that Cather had "accomplished ... a miracle which should cause any university ... to forget and forgive her sex."[85] In 1923, T. K. Whipple also praises Cather's achievement as so rare as "to verge on the miraculous."[86] Remembering Cather's novels for their sense of "transfiguration,"[87] Louis Kronenberger and Justice Oliver Wendell Holmes respond to the same magical quality in Cather's fiction: her ability to transform the common and everyday into the miraculous. Clearly, readers have participated in Cather's celebration of the exceptional being with an appointed destiny to conquer. Although Alfred Kazin focuses on Cather's "values," he identifies the "secret" of her power in "the individual discovery, the joy of fulfilling oneself in the satisfaction of an appointed destiny."[88] When *O Pioneers!* was first reviewed in *The Nation* in 1913, it was Alexandra's ability to make the world conform to her desire that captivated the imagination of the reviewer, who, appropriating Cather's language as his own, comments that "only here and there a strong heart, like that of the heroine of the story, refuses to be discouraged, persists in believing that the country has a future ... [until] the years justify her, bringing wealth to her and to her beloved country."[89] For Carl Van Doren, it is Cather's ability to fill her scenes with "a spaciousness and candor of personality"[90] that makes her art superior to that of the local colorists. He eulogizes her heroic pioneers, who "ride powerfully forward on a wave of confident energy, as if human life had more dawns than sunsets in it."[91] Henry Seidel Canby also prefers Cather's characters to their naturalistic counterparts in Dreiser or Garland because, in their "rich, subtle natures," they are "not types of social classes or particular environments," and therefore they are somehow immune to fortune and circumstances, having "no relation to success or failure as our world sees it."[92] Finding in Cather's novels more "opulence" than in those of her realistic contemporary Sherwood Anderson, T. K. Whipple is won over by the optimistic myth of the superior individual who can bring about "the triumph of mind over Nebraska."[93] Of Cather's characters, he writes, "Theirs is not a tragedy of frustration," for Cather "champions the poetic temper and the life of

realization [of dreams] against practicality."[94] No doubt one reason why
Cather's earlier novels have always been more popular is that her early
pioneers and artists have the strength to dominate over experience. The
reaction of Percy Boynton in 1924 is typical. He thinks that Cather has
lost her bearings in writing *A Lost Lady*, and hopes that she will "find her
way back to the elemental people whom she really knows" — the
Alexandras and the Àntonias; whereas "the lost lady is a weakling,"
"their victories are worth winning."[95]

Most readers are so swept up by the aura of the great personalities in
the novels that they accept with wide-eyed admiration the sacrifices of
life and people made on their behalf. Randolph Bourne, reviewing *The
Song of the Lark* soon after its publication in 1915, likes best the beginning of the novel "where Thea's artistic soul rises against the disapprov-
ing conventionality of the little town." Far from questioning Thea for her
selfish rejection of all those who do not worship her, Bourne privileges
her as much as her author does, concluding that "in this fair and self-
centred girl with her passion for her music, with that clutch at her soul
which held her aloof from every environment, that urge which impelled
her to realize her very self though it meant shutting out the whole world,
Miss Cather had a great story."[96] Similarly, George White, defending
Cather in 1942 against the 1930s charge of escapism, is so enthralled by
her romance of self-creation that he, along with Cather, dismisses all
externals as no more than superficial illusions next to man's sole spiritual
responsibility to himself. Preaching Cather's fictions as his own faith, he
writes,

> Man must know himself. He must weigh his gifts against the gifts of his
> world. If Americans are really 'self-reliant,' in the Emerson and Cather sense,
> they will soon discover that most of their world is made up of illusions —
> self-formed images that take the sting out of time and place. These illusions
> may be love, fame, ambition, money, family, war, art, or life itself. If the
> individual is to achieve that best for his life, and here Willa Cather repeats
> herself in every novel, the illusion must be destroyed."[97]

Believing that Godfrey St. Peter "had to destroy the illusion of family life
before he could become the uninhibited scholar,"[98] White adopts
Cather's faith in the preeminence of the self against which even the reality of one's own family is negligible and earnestly denied. In a review
that Cather praised for expressing her own articles of faith,[99] Margaret
Lawrence describes as her central theme the "magnetic inspirational
people" whose "shine of the spirit ... binds other people to [them] either
in love or in curiosity."[100] Certainly Cather's readers have been drawn to
her characters with just such faithful loyalty.

The early, relatively unsophisticated criticism of Cather during the 1920s, 1930s, and 1940s most transparently responds to Cather's fictional myth of conquest and individual power, yet puts the emphasis on such issues as national destiny, realism, social history, or moral values. More recent criticism of Cather in the 1960s, 1970s, and 1980s has been less willing to acknowledge the primal fantasy of power. Critics of this period, eager to secure Cather's reputation as a serious and important writer, have worked hard to deny her simplicity, emotionalism, and optimism, as if those qualities would diminish her literary status. One reason for their discomfort is that they have inherited the assumptions of New Criticism, with its modernist demands for psychological complexity, conflicting thematic threads, moral ambiguity, and stylistic density. Like all academic critics, critics of Cather have tried to justify their own tasks. Those who have not wished to admit an attraction to the fairy-tale qualities of Cather's novels have reached to other critical topics to explain the fiction's deep emotional resonance. In so doing, critics have uncovered a great variety of interesting and important aspects of Cather's fiction, but have largely left unexplained what is, in my view, the central organizing impulse and source of power in the novels.

Edward and Lillian Bloom protest that "the fact that Cather's buoyant spirit generally causes an optimistic note to prevail in her fiction by no means lessens the seriousness of her inner fears."[101] The Blooms concede the cheerful tenor of the fiction and yet, defensively, wish to hide this truth in the assumption that optimism is naive and simplistic, while sober reflections on life's difficult social and moral problems are mature and distinguished. Another critic who seems uncomfortable with the "happy ending" quality in Cather that she is nonetheless attracted by is Lois Feger. In an article in 1970, she expresses her dissatisfaction with the status of *My Àntonia* as a high school text: "It is ironic that this book which has become one widely read in high school should really be saying or implying such pessimistic things about life, but after reading *My Àntonia* in terms of its dark dimension, it is difficult to see it in the old innocent 'country-life' way. Even the so-called 'happy ending' has its limitations."[102] In her need to present the novel as serious and adult, Feger — in company with Robert Scholes, James Miller, and others — feels that she must deny the novel's simplicity, happy optimism, and celebration of innocence, and focus instead on its "dark," complex, and threatening realities.[103] More recently, Susan Rosowski has given this approach a new twist by discussing the dark undercurrent to romantic optimism, such as in Cather's use of the Gothic in *Sapphira and the Slave Girl*. Arguing that "in her mature writing Cather seldom resolves moral ambiguities and contradictions,"[104] Rosowski implies her own critical standard that serious art must be psychologically complex.

Similarly, David Stouck, in his 1975 book on Cather, tries to elevate Cather's literary status by deemphasizing the celebratory and positive in her novels and emphasizing, instead, thematic tensions and darkness. Approaching Cather with the belief that "in every work of art there exists a fundamental tension between two irreconcilable motives, for art has its source and momentum in conflict that cannot be resolved,"[105] he offers readings that see not personal fulfillment but loss and estrangement; not recovery but alienation; not success but struggle and failure; not wish fulfillment but tragedy in the face of life's "ugly realities."[106] Although Stouck acknowledges that Cather's writing elicits a "nostalgic, reflective response,"[107] he subordinates this response to his assumptions about great modern literature: "In literature, writers in the twentieth century, having exhausted the easy emotional appeal of romanticism and realism, have turned to more reflective and intellectually disciplined forms of writing. An appreciation of writers like James Joyce, Virginia Woolf, and Faulkner demands a disciplined participation in a form of writing which constantly puts the reader to the test intellectually."[108] For Stouck, "the easy emotional appeal of romanticism" is not to be taken seriously, while the intellectual demands of formal complexity command respect. Thus, although he uneasily concedes that "Cather's formal experimentation may seem very uncomplicated,"[109] he sets out to prove that Cather can hold her own when measured against great modern stylists like Woolf and Faulkner. As if protesting to his readers that he hasn't been taken in by the emotional power of Cather's fiction, Stouck writes of *Death Comes for the Archbishop,* "The emotion we do experience, rather than being the result of a personal identification with the protagonists, is of a higher order."[110] For Stouck, the attention to form in Cather seems not simply an aesthetic consideration but a psychological strategy to distance the reader from his emotional engagement with the text in an effort to support his discourse on a "higher" level of intellectual ground. As he says, "A constant awareness of form in art has the effect of making us emotionally detached in our esthetic response. To the degree that we are conscious of form, we become objective and involved on an intellectual or reflective plane."[111] Understandably, many Cather critics during the 1970s and 1980s seem to have struggled with a sense of inferiority in dealing not only with American literature, traditionally thought less rig-orously intellectual than British and European literature, but with litera-ture by a woman — one who might be considered provincial, simple, and sentimental, at that. This anxiety over one's own role as critic is perhaps best registered by James Woodress. In discussing *My Àntonia,* for exam-

ple, he distinguishes between the response of the unsophisticated freshman and the sophisticated professor:

> The freshman finds a simple, human story dealing with genuine people facing
> recognizable problems. He can relate to it; he is touched by the real feeling
> evoked; he can read it without a dictionary or recourse to someone else's
> notes or annotations. The professor finds in the novel, besides a moving story,
> a richness of allusions, myth, and symbol presented by one of the great
> stylists of this century.... It is the intellection coming from European culture
> that gives one room to swim in Cather's fiction. She did not write intellectual
> novels, but there is substance in them to nourish the mind."[112]

As critical readers of Cather, we all resemble the professor of literature
whom Woodress describes. Needing to justify our own critical tasks, we
find it necessary to distinguish our responses to the texts from that of the
naive freshman; we would like to believe that the notes that we supply to
Cather's texts are crucial to an understanding of them. In order to make a
case for Cather's novels as literary "classics," Woodress emphasizes the
surface eclecticism and intellectual content of the texts with their
classical allusions, myths, and symbols. I believe, however, that it is the
response of the freshman within us that provides a truer indication of the
source of Willa Cather's profundity, for her power is primarily emotional
rather than intellectual. Because critics have not let themselves be guided
by their emotional response to the novels, they have often not articulated
the real nature of her power.

I would like to question our criteria as literary critics of "great" art.
Why should we automatically privilege the art of real experience, characterized by pessimistic darkness, failure, moral complexity, intellectual
difficulty, and ambiguity, over the art of fairy tales, characterized by optimistic lightness, success, moral simplicity, emotional power, and idealized characters? I wish, finally, to make a defense of Cather's celebratory
art, not by denying, but by recognizing its escapist quality of wish fulfillment. Jane Tompkins has argued for the significance of nineteenth-
century American domestic and sentimental fiction on the grounds that it
performs an important "cultural work" for its audience;[113] from a different point of view, I would like to argue that Willa Cather's fiction is
significant because it performs a no less important "psychological work"
for its audience. As we can see by the devoted homage of her readers,
Cather's novels have always fulfilled essential needs.

Paradoxically, I find myself most in agreement with the arguments
made by the critics of the 1930s, but instead of wishing to disparage
Cather's art, I wish to explain it and its continuing power. Back in 1937,

Lionel Trilling shrewdly perceives what readers find in Willa Cather when he writes that *The Professor's House* "epitomizes as well as any novel of our time the disgust with life which so many sensitive Americans feel, which makes them dream of their preadolescent integration and innocent community with nature."[114] Yet, whereas he imagines that Cather's backwards-looking vision would make her "increasingly irrelevant and tangential — for any time,"[115] it has, in fact, contributed to her long-lived popularity. It is true, as Trilling says, that Cather's novels do not show us how to live in our own times, but they do powerfully show us how to dream. Cather's novels have continued to make her readers dream nostalgically of their own "preadolescent integration" and childhood. As a reviewer of *The Song of the Lark* writes in 1915, "Any account of the loyalty of young hearts to some exalted ideal, and the passion with which they strive, will always in some of us rekindle generous emotions.... Sorry indeed must be the condition of one in whom Thea Kronborg's struggle would not stir some answering pulse."[116] That answering pulse is stirred in Randolph Bourne when he confesses that the "youthful wistfulness" in Cather's stories "made at least one Dakotan youth quite weak with homesickness."[117] For him, as for many readers today, it is "the indestructible fragrance of youth"[118] that has proven to be Cather's most enduring legacy, as readers continue to recover a sense of their own childhood integration from the characters in the novels.

Throughout the decades, readers have described their experience of reading Willa Cather according to similar images and metaphors — images and metaphors drawn from the novels themselves. Although David Stouck and others have emphasized the darkness in Cather, readers typically discuss the effect of her fiction in terms of light imagery. H. L. Mencken, for instance, sees a "luminosity" — "a pathos that is genuinely moving" — as the central effect of *My Àntonia*.[119] George White describes the source of Cather's popularity in her "bright vision of perfection."[120] Maxwell Geismar identifies as most "Catheresque" the "glimpses of those bright moments in life 'which are few, after all, and so very easy to miss.'"[121] In a 1974 article entitled "Willa Cather: The Light Behind her Books," Margaret Howe Freydberg sees the light as the token of Cather's "entire correspondence with her original condition."[122] As these descriptions suggest, the radiant animus behind Cather's works invites readers to repair to an ideal visionary world illumined by their own shining, youthful egos.

In 1936, Margaret Lawrence writes, "Cather is concerned mostly with lives that are touched with romance, and have upon other lives a curious lifting effect."[123] The same thing could be said of the effect that Cather's characters have on her readers. Escaping from their own ordinary lives into a better fictional world, readers describe the power of the novels in terms of their "uplifting" quality. H. L. Mencken, writing about *My Àntonia*, was one of the first to observe that "there is something in it to lift depression";[124] he attributes this effect to Cather's ability to get "poetry into the commonplace."[125] Although W. C. Brownell, a contemporary of Cather's, finds the source of his pleasure in her books "essentially elusive," he describes his reaction to *My Àntonia* in terms reminiscent of Mencken's: "I feel somehow as if the proper epithets to characterize the book were something 'up,' almost physically floating above the material, as it were."[126] In describing the upward spiritual mobility experienced in reading Cather, readers pick up on Cather's own imagery in the novels. Dorothy Canfield Fisher recalls the image of the "noble upward flight of an eagle" in *The Song of the Lark*, and suggests that "to read Miss Cather's novel is to see an eagle soar up through all this pettiness, on broad sure wings, carrying us in spirit with her to the heights."[127] For Fisher, this upward flight is an especially welcome escape from "the stagnant air since the end of the war." Readers as diverse as a Supreme Court justice and one of Cather's childhood friends describe their experience of reading Cather in similar terms, suggesting that Cather's novels exert a universal effect, cutting across not only time and gender but professional and educational backgrounds. When Ferris Greenslet sent Supreme Court Justice Oliver Wendell Holmes a copy of *My Àntonia* in 1930, the eighty-nine-year-old jurist wrote to him that the book "lifts me to all my superlatives. I have not had such a sensation for a long time."[128] Cather's childhood friend Irene Miner Weisz describes a similar feeling of buoyancy in reading her novels. Recalling how she has only to "browse around in one of those books" to "sail away into another world," Weisz reads Cather's novels for the delicious sense of release — what she calls a warm "feeling of lightness and content" — that they afford her from her simple everyday duties. Encountering in the stories something of her "own thoughts and feelings," she is able to "come back to earth ... refreshed" and newly equipped with "something to help one through life."[129] Much like Weisz, Don Beckman, a reader in the early 1970s, turns to Cather's fiction for a refreshing sense of escape from the commonplace realities of his own life, to return to life renewed. When he read "A Wagner Matinée," which reminds him of his "own surroundings" and his "own life," he recalls that "words fell away from the page and I was mysteriously transported above fields and farms, straight into the world of good music. When the story reached its shattering end, dropping me back into a life of drab reality ... I promised myself that one day I too would leave the farm and go to the city ... and hurry away to the opera."[130] Either that, or pick up another Cather novel. Indeed, for

Margaret Howe Freydberg, reading Cather's novels is fully as inspiring as attending any concert. After reading *Death Comes for the Archbishop*, she "closed the book feeling simply exalted, and then suddenly recalled hearing Bach played one afternoon by André Marchal in the Church of Saint Sulpice in Paris — an experience of being borne up and wrapped around in clouds of powerfully sublime sound."[131]

Cather's novels have been hugely popular with the most "macho" male reader of all — the American soldier. During World War II, Cather received hundreds of letters from soldiers who were reading her books in pocket-sized Armed Services Editions.[132] Although she answered many of their letters, and even wrote to grieving parents, she soon found herself too overwhelmed by the volume of letters to respond. As she wrote to Ferris Greenslet during the Christmas season in 1944, she was so inundated with letters and gifts from soldiers from around the world that she found it impossible to write them all back; as she explained, the multitudes of homesick boys in the trenches had become an emotional burden.[133] But surely Cather's novels were themselves the best form of correspondence that she could have provided to the men in their lonely outposts. To the soldier who was weighed down by pain, sickness, isolation, hardship, and fear, Cather's novels offered the consolation that the soul could be made whole and invincible again.

Throughout her life, Cather received innumerable letters from appreciative readers. Edith Lewis recounts how, in her last years, Cather especially enjoyed her correspondence with readers from all over the world: "The flood of letters which poured in to her from half the countries of the world — letters that were truly from 'the people,' not from any particular class of people, bringing to her their gratitude, their homage, their affection, in the kind of language she most appreciated — the language art cannot invent — were a sort of giving back to her, a return in kind, of the qualities of feeling she had herself expended in her writing career" (WCL, 187). Although we do not have these letters, Lewis gives us examples and quotations. Cather received admiring letters from: "The boy who read her books in Braille, but never referred in his letter to his blindness; the old missionary in New Mexico, who after riding among his parishes all day, sat up until dawn to finish the *Archbishop*; the British officer in Borneo, who wrote: 'Your book has been my companion on many a long and weary trip in the jungle, and if I have read it once, I must have read it a hundred times'; the young priest dying in the Italian Dolomites, who wrote: 'I beseech you to abide by me in thought and prayer" (WCL, 187). From one reader, she received a letter saying, "You are a great lady, and we are only poor folk, but I would love to count myself your friend." From a boy in Wisconsin, she received a note testifying, "Your books have somehow helped me ... to take heart again in my effort to rebuild my health and life" (WCL, 187). Who are these people who wrote to Willa Cather? Judging from Lewis's catalogue, it seems that Cather has been especially successful in enlisting the sympathies of the needy: the blind, the old, the exiled and weary, the dying, the impoverished, the sick and devastated. Surprisingly, the young priest dying in the mountains of Italy turns not to God but to Willa Cather, as if she herself could offer him the comfort and intercession of a priest. Indeed, not only Catholics but all those in need of spiritual faith and reassurance have read Cather's novels as they would read the Bible. Lewis reports that one of Cather's readers writes, "There is no book, barring the word of God, that has taken so firm a hold on me" (WCL, 187). Professor St. Peter had said in his speech to his students that art and religion are the same thing, after all, and in Willa Cather's novels, it may be that art becomes a substitute for religion.

Willa Cather's novels are more popular today than they have ever been before. What can our attraction to her tell us about our own needs as readers in the 1990s? Although we may not necessarily be old, exiled, sick, or dying, like the readers whom Lewis cites, we may nonetheless have experienced many disabling losses: loss of faith in a benevolent God, in open frontiers, in responsible governments, in higher institutions, in clean and safe cities, in satisfying careers, in perfect families, in strong marriages. There are more single, divorced, and lonely people today than ever before. Whereas, in another time, people might have turned towards the church for spiritual consolation, in the secular modern age, readers can turn towards Willa Cather's novels to be confirmed in their faith in the possibilities of the human soul. As one reader resonantly describes the relationship between Cather and her readers:

> Her monumental characters are just that, monuments, like churches to which people go to be told about the potential of the human spirit, and about realizable goals of virtue and strength. We get the message. And its idealism is of the utmost value.... What she cared most about — the natural world and the natural spirit — are the essentials that we ourselves care most about, although we may know it only dimly.... She tells us about integrity directly, through the elaboration of integrity itself, in a way that penetrates to the core of whatever integrity we ourselves have. And tells us to prize it, that it is the only thing. This is, I believe, one of the reasons why we are so significantly moved by her work — it reaches down into some well of knowledge in us, and touches whatever integrity remains there.[134]

Individual integrity is at last, as this reader says, "the only thing" for Willa Cather. Edith Lewis tells the story of how, when Cather was a little girl, she used to refuse help from her parents, protesting "Self Alone! Self Alone!" (WCL, 175) It may be that the self alone is the only reliable thing that readers in the 1990s have left to worship.

In her poem, "My Declaration of Self-Esteem," Virginia Satir, a writer in the 1970s, expresses a secular creed of total self-acceptance and self-creation that has much in common with Cather's theology of the self. As she writes,

> I own everything about me — my body, including everything it does; my mind, including all its thoughts and ideas; my eyes, including the images of all they behold; my feelings, whatever they may be — anger, joy, frustration, love, disappointment, excitement; my mouth, and all the words that come out of it, polite, sweet or rough, correct or incorrect; my voice, loud or soft; and all my actions, whether they be to others or to myself.
>
> I own my fantasies, my dreams, my hopes, my fears.
>
> I own all my triumphs and successes, all my failures and mistakes.
>
> Because I own all of me, I can become intimately acquainted with me. By so doing I can love me and be friendly with me in all my parts. I can then make it possible for all of me to work in my best interests....
>
> I own me, and therefore I can engineer me.
>
> I am me, and I am okay.[135]

Disregarding the forces of heredity, environment, chance, or providence, the speaker of the poem imagines that she possesses and creates herself and all that she imagines, does, and sees. Resting on the metaphor of self-ownership, this poem expresses a deep psychological and cultural need that goes a long way to explain why readers have been attracted to the myth of self-possession in Willa Cather, not only in the 1970s, but today. In spite of feelings of vulnerability, alienation, or helplessness in the face of troubling circumstances beyond one's control, Cather, like the writer of the 1970s poem, reassures her readers that they can prevail and make sense out of a confusing world by focusing their attention and love on the construction of a self that is completely autonomous, illimitable, and self-sufficient, beholden to no other person or power for a sense of identity and self-worth. The reader of Cather, like the speaker of the poem, is assured that she can become her own best companion, even her own God; all she need do is appreciate her essential inner nature. For descendants of the "me generation" who have once again made individual happiness the utmost goal, Willa Cather has written the fairy tale of the modern age, proclaiming the timeless victory of the human spirit.

Willa Cather once defined the "fine reader" as a person who, like her own exceptional characters, is distinguished not only by an academic or wealthy background but by a "quickness and richness of mentality," a "fineness of spirituality" (WCP, 69). As she goes on to say, "It's the shape of the head that's of importance: it's the something that's in it that can bring an ardor and an honesty to a masterpiece and make it over until it becomes a personal possession." As Cather knew, writing was not merely the artist's "one really precious possession" (Pref. AB, vii); her novels were ultimately written for the reader's "possession" as well. In a remarkable letter written to Cather in 1932, we can see how one reader, John Curran, appropriating Cather's own vocabulary, took "possession" of her work. Seeing through Willa Cather's masquerade to recognize her behind the masks of her characters, Curran acknowledges that his love for characters like Thea Kronborg is more deeply a love for her. As he writes,

> I wonder if you ever stop to think of the thousands of "heart friends" you must have? Such a friend is one who possesses you so intimately and so surely that not even you could disturb his calm and wonderful possession of you.... He picks you up, bit by bit, from the lines and from between the lines of your work. At the end, he has you even more surely than you have yourself — he knows you as you do not know yourself, in those bits of yourself that you have expressed unconsciously, and of which you remain unconscious.... He has only the best you.[136]

This letter must have pleased Willa Cather, who wished to project a part of her soul in her art and have it impress the reader. In her fiction, her readers would never encounter her grating human weaknesses but only her most refined self. It is a tribute to Willa Cather's success that her readers can feel the energy and ardent passion of her own personality as it infuses her pages. Finally, however, Cather's readers find in her novels not simply a possession of her but of their own "best selves." A reader like John Curran can be so confident in his possession of Thea Kronborg and, in turn, of Willa Cather herself, trusting that they hold no secrets from him, only because he is able to identify with them completely as if they were extensions of himself. Like Willa Cather, perhaps her "heart friends," who sit in the twilight alone with their inarticulate longing for complete happiness, empathize with the characters in the novels who seem to share their dreams. Seeing the possibility for the reader's personal identification with Cather's characters, George White writes, "It makes no difference whether the individual [in Cather] is a painter, a farmer, a writer, a priest, a pianist, an unlabeled human: Thea, practicing out the break in her middle voice, or Alexandra, dispelling the spectre of land-failure, or you. Self-creation is to Willa Cather the first concern of man."[137] You, me, even the most "unlabeled" reader, no matter of how small importance, can claim kin with the divine characters in the fiction so as imaginatively to create herself and her destiny anew. For Margaret Howe Freydberg, reading Cather similarly involves a process of imaginative possession, or assimilation. After reading Cather's novels, she understands that "my entire self, my heart and senses as well as my mind, had been engaged in assimilating this art. But also, I, my entire self that is, instinctively recognized that the force, the animus behind Willa Cather's greatest work, was the very exceptional quality of *her* entire self."[138] By assimilating Willa Cather's essential "self" from the fiction, the reader more importantly recovers a sense of her own "entire self." Feeling their ravaged egos restored by the imaginative possession celebrated in the novels, readers have in turn possessed Willa Cather as their own.

As long as we don't call it by the wrong name, or take refuge in the idea that it is unnamable, then we too can appropriate Willa Cather's fantasy of imaginative possession and feel empowered by it. Cather consciously made her choice when she turned away from realism in her early work and embraced art as a form of "escape" from the real world. Similarly, we should understand that the emotionally captivating story in Cather's fiction tells not of real life but of a fantasy of escape from reality's compromises in a narcissistic quest for sovereignty. Although critics arguing for universal values in Cather's work have interpreted the selfishness in the novels as selflessness,[139] we should appreciate that it is the undisguised egoism at the heart of her fiction that makes her most universal in her appeal to her readers. We should recognize, above all, that if we love Willa Cather, that is most deeply because we love ourselves.

Notes

Chapter 1:
The Explicable Presence of "The Thing Not Named"

1. Sandra M. Gilbert and Susan Gubar, *The Madwoman in the Attic: The Woman Writer and the Nineteenth-Century Literary Imagination* (New Haven: Yale University Press, 1979), 50.

2. Ibid., 49.

3. Ibid., 50.

4. Sharon O'Brien, *Willa Cather: The Emerging Voice* (New York: Oxford University Press, 1987), 4.

5. Ibid.

6. O'Brien does, for example, acknowledge Whitman's influence in *O Pioneers!* In addition, O'Brien makes her most convincing argument when she discusses how Cather identified herself at the beginning of her career with a romantic male quest for autonomy and power. She rightly discusses how Cather, as a young woman, accepted a romantic aesthetic theory infused with the late nineteenth-century ideology of masculinity, exemplified by writers like Rudyard Kipling. Drawing on Cather's 1890s reviews, O'Brien shows how Cather imagined the artist as "a manly warrior, conqueror, or knight" (*Willa Cather: The Emerging Voice*, 150). She historicizes Cather's embracing of a "cult of manhood" as part of a national desire to combat a fear of overcivilization and fin-de-siècle decadence (ibid.).

As O'Brien acknowledges, Cather found the female literary tradition highly problematic. In her early career, she took pains to separate herself from a female line of influence and, by contrast to Virginia Woolf, sought not to recover a female lineage of her own, but to repudiate it. As she wrote in 1895, "Sometimes I wonder why God ever trusts talent in the hands of women, they usually make such an infernal mess of it. I think He must do it as a sort of ghastly joke" (WP, 275).

Cather's disparaging comments about other women artists have become notorious. For example, she asked of the actress Mary Anderson, upon her retirement from the stage, "Has any woman ever really had the art instinct, the art necessity?" (KA, 158). Cather saw a conflict between women's social roles as mothers and wives and their vocations as artists. She rejected all of the various "female" literary traditions available to her: the "contemptible feminine weakness" and "mawkish sentimentality" (KA, 408) of the sensationalist novel; the "hankering for hobbies and missions" (KA, 406) characteristic of the novel advocating social reforms like Stowe's *Uncle Tom's Cabin*; the "sex consciousness that is abominable" (KA, 409) of the domestic novel with the conventional marriage plot that reinforced the ideology of romantic love.

7. O'Brien, *Willa Cather: The Emerging Voice*, 189.

8. Ibid., 347.

9. Ibid., 388.

10. Sharon O'Brien, "Mothers, Daughters, and the 'Art Necessity': Willa Cather and the Creative Process," in *American Novelists Revisited: Essays in Feminist Criticism*, ed. Fritz Fleischmann (Boston: G. K. Hall, 1982), 282.

11. Sharon O'Brien, "The Unity of Willa Cather's 'Two-Part Pastoral': Passion in *O Pioneers!*" *Studies in American Fiction* 6 (1978): 158.

12. O'Brien, *Willa Cather: The Emerging Voice*, 423.

13. For a standard discussion of the social expectations of women in the nineteenth century, see Barbara Welter, *Dimity Convictions: The American Woman in the Nineteenth Century* (Athens: Ohio University Press, 1976). Welter sees four cardinal virtues that comprise "the cult of true womanhood": piety, purity, submissiveness, and domesticity.

14. See Elizabeth Stuart Phelps, *The Story of Avis*, ed. Carol Farley Kessler (New Brunswick, N.J.: Rutgers University Press, 1985) and Kate Chopin, *The Awakening and Selected Stories* (New York: Penguin, 1985).

15. See, for example, Virginia Woolf, *To the Lighthouse* (New York: Harcourt Brace Jovanovich, 1927; repr. 1955) and Carol Gilligan, *In a Different Voice: Psychological Theory and Woman's Development* (Cambridge: Harvard University Press, 1982).

16. Sarah Orne Jewett did exert an influence on Cather, but, as I shall discuss in my chapter on *Alexander's Bridge*, Jewett's influence on Cather was not primarily literary but social. As a daughter of the New England gentry, a "lady, in the old high sense" (NUF, 85), Jewett offered Cather a view of a genteel, upper-class existence. Cather was attracted by Jewett's social background and gracious home, with its "patina of the Chippendale and Hepplewhite, the old portraits and prints" (WC: AM, 58), and hoped that some of that "patina" would rub off on her. Jewett's advice to Cather in a letter concerning the proper conditions for writing is well known: "You must find a quiet place.... [Y]ou must find your own quiet centre of life, and write from that." See Sarah Orne Jewett to Willa Cather, 13 December 1908, in *Letters of Sarah Orne Jewett*, ed. Annie Fields (New York: Houghton Mifflin, 1911), 249. Jewett wrote this letter in December 1908, well before Cather had written her first novel, *Alexander's Bridge*.

O'Brien sees Jewett as exerting an influence on Cather only after she wrote *Alexander's Bridge*, a novel she reads as a "male" story that distorts Cather's true female creative impulses. To the degree that Jewett was an influence on Cather, however, she influenced the writing of *Alexander's Bridge* as much as *O Pioneers!* As I shall argue, it was in the process of writing *Alexander's Bridge* that Cather found her "own quiet centre of life" and made such an inner center the goal of her hero's quest as well. If Jewett gave Cather anything, it was an egoistic confidence in her own inner integrity. Jewett understood and confirmed Cather's belief in "force" as the artist's essential energy and creative spark. Jewett's famous advice to Cather in her letter of 13 December 1908, to "keep and guard and mature your force," merely echoes Cather's own artistic creed, expressed as early as 1896, when she wrote in a review that "the artist ... learns to cherish and guard his emotional force" (WP, 700).

Jewett's stories bear superficial similarities to Cather's novels. Their nostalgic elegiac tone, reminding us that, once upon a time, there was a heroic cast to New England, would have elicited Cather's sympathies. By writing about her native Maine, Jewett reassured Cather that she could turn back to her own native Nebraska in her second novel for her ostensible subject matter. Yet, as I shall argue in my chapter on *O Pioneers!*, Cather's romanticizing of the landscape has little in common with the realistic treatment of nature in regional fiction. Her early reviews reveal only contempt for the works by female regional writers such as Kate Chopin, Mary Wilkins Freeman, and Rose Terry Cooke; she not only lacks respect for their "limited powers and limited imagination" (WP, 278), but implicitly rejects Freeman's and Jewett's New England nuns as "melancholy freaks" (WP, 278). In fact, the worlds that Jewett and Cather create are strikingly different. In *The Country of the Pointed Firs*, for example, Jewett celebrates the female art of healing and nurturing through the herb gatherer and storyteller Mrs. Todd. Clearly, however, Cather does not identify herself with such quaint figures of local color. The character who most resembles Mrs. Todd in Cather's fiction is, perhaps, Old Mrs. Lee in *O Pioneers!*, a minor character whose incessant chatter and insatiable love of home-baked goodies provide humorous distraction for the central characters, Alexandra and Marie.

17. Sarah Orne Jewett, *The Country of the Pointed Firs and Other Stories*, ed. Mary Ellen Chase (New York: Norton, 1981), 46.

18. My reading of Cather is indebted to Quentin Anderson's view in *The Imperial Self: An Essay in American Literary and Cultural History* (New York: Knopf, 1971) of the self-absorbing consciousness of nineteenth-century American writers such as Emerson, Whitman, and James.

19. Richard Poirier, *A World Elsewhere; The Place of Style in American Literature* (New York: Oxford University Press, 1966), 50.

20. Edward A. and Lillian D. Bloom, *Willa Cather's Gift of Sympathy* (Carbondale: Southern Illinois University Press, 1962), 172.

21. Cather's preface to *The Song of the Lark*, written 16 July 1932, is repr. in the Houghton Mifflin edition of 1988, pp. xxxi–xxxii.

22. Letter from Reginald Cook, Director of the Bread Loaf School of English, to Willa Cather, 14 April 1949, as he recalls one of Cather's lectures on art that was given at Bread Loaf in July 1922. See WWC, 208.

23. Willa Cather to William Lyon Phelps, 29 May 1943, Yale University, New Haven.

24. David Stouck, "Willa Cather and the Impressionist Novel," in *Critical Essays on Willa Cather*, ed. John J. Murphy (Boston: G. K. Hall, 1984), 58.

25. O'Brien, *Willa Cather: The Emerging Voice*, 127.

26. O'Brien is the only critic to have tried to identify the implied presence in Cather's novels. In a more recent study — *Willa Cather's Modernism: A Study of Style and Technique* (Cranbury, N.J.: Associated University Presses, 1990) — Jo Ann Middleton borrows a term from science — "vacuole" (54) — to describe the indeterminate gap in Cather's fiction.

27. Gilbert and Gubar, *The Madwoman in the Attic*, 47.

28. Adrienne Rich, *On Lies, Secrets, and Silence: Selected Prose 1966–1978* (New York: Norton, 1979), 200–201.

29. O'Brien, *Willa Cather: The Emerging Voice*, 155.

30. Gilbert and Gubar, *The Madwoman in the Attic*, 49.

31. As the medical profession and a conservative right made women's love for other women seem unnatural at the turn of the century, the "Boston Marriage" that earlier writers like Sarah Orne Jewett had enjoyed with Annie Fields became less acceptable. See Carol Smith Rosenburg, "The Female World of Love and Ritual: Relations Between Women in Nineteenth Century America," in *Disorderly Conduct: Visions of Gender in Victorian America* (New York: Knopf, 1985). Extending this argument, C. Susan Wiesenthal argues that Cather would have been self-conscious about the public perception of her living with other women. See "Female Sexuality in Willa Cather's '*O Pioneers!*' and the Era of Scientific Sexology: A Dialogue Between Frontiers," *Ariel: A Review of International English Literature* 21(January 1990): 41–63.

32. Lionel Trilling, "Willa Cather," in *After the Genteel Tradition: American Writers 1910–1930*, ed. Malcolm Cowley (New York: W. W. Norton & Co., 1937), 148. Repr. in James Schroeter, ed., *Willa Cather and her Critics* (Ithaca: Cornell University Press, 1967).

33. I would like to qualify this statement by making a distinction between Cather's ideal "kingdom of art" in her imagination and the actual subject matter of her novels. Cather explores sexuality in a variety of ways in her fiction; indeed, sexuality is thematically central to most all of her works. Cather repeatedly stages compelling and passionate scenes of sexuality in her short stories and novels that seem simultaneously to fascinate and repel her. The pattern of voyeurism in Cather's fiction — seen in such characters as Don Hedger in "Coming Aphrodite," Frank Shabata in *O Pioneers!*, Jim Burden in *My Ántonia*, Niel Herbert in *A Lost Lady*, or Sapphira Colbert in *Sapphira and the Slave Girl* — suggests that Cather herself was self-consciously examining

sexuality from a variety of viewpoints. In scenes such as the moonlit reunion of Nils and Clara in "The Bohemian Girl," or Emil and Marie's furtive kiss in the gypsy tent during the French Carnival, Cather palpably infuses sexual encounters with a yearning pull that electrifies the pages with a tender and breath-taking passion. That Cather could create such vivid scenes suggests that she could sympathize with sexual experiences. But if Cather wished to imaginatively observe and participate in the life of sexuality from a distance, she did not wish to embrace sexuality as a reality in her own life as an artist. Her romantic notions of the artist's high calling, perhaps made necessary and confirmed by the needs of her own complex psychosexual identity, encouraged her to view sexuality as the antagonist of her soul. Ultimately, then, to preserve the integrity of her soul in art, Cather had to ban sexuality from the kingdom. While the majority of Cather's novels include sexuality, they are ultimately devoted to excluding that sexuality as a threatening presence from their imaginative borders, as if Willa Cather were, in the process of writing, trying to translate the commonplace and inescapable realities of life into the aestheticized world of the ideal to which she felt she owed her greatest imaginative allegiance.

34. See, for example, Cather's counsel to Kipling to renounce marriage and "go back" to the land of romance and poetry. Matrimony, she warns him, "has shorn the wings of your freedom and your freedom was your art.... If the climate is not good for Mrs. Kipling then remember that you were married to your works long before you ever met her" (KA, 316–18).

35. Willa Cather, "The Treasure of Far Island," in CSF, 275, 273.

36. In her book *Willa Cather and the Fairy Tale* (Ann Arbor, Mich.: UMI Research Press, 1989), Marilyn Berg Callander elaborates some of the allusions to fairy tales within Cather's novels.

37. Quentin Anderson, "Willa Cather: Her Masquerade," *New Republic* 153 (27 November 1965): 29.

38. See Willa Cather, "The Treasure of Far Island," in CSF, 275–76.

39. See, for example, Bernice Slote's essays in *The Kingdom of Art* (Lincoln: University of Nebraska Press, 1966) and Susan Rosowski, *The Voyage Perilous: Willa Cather's Romanticism* (Lincoln: University of Nebraska Press, 1986) for a view of Cather as a romantic who exalted the world of the imagination and invested reality with transcendent symbolic meaning.

40. Susan Rosowski, "Willa Cather — A Pioneer in Art: *O Pioneers!* and *My Àntonia*," *Prairie Schooner* 55 (Spring-Summer 1981): 144.

41. Rosowski, *The Voyage Perilous*, 8.

42. Ibid., 8–9.

43. For example, in the *Nebraska State Journal*, 10 March 1895, Cather writes that the authentic artist must infuse his art with real feeling: "Into his own art an actor should bring the spoils of every other art on earth, and above all the arts of living and loving. He should give his emotions an anchor that will reach down into the very depths of the very nature of things and hold him to the truth" (KA, 144). Advising that the artist "should know how it felt to be an Egyptian,

... how it feels to be a thirsty Bowery boy" (KA, 144–45), Cather adopts a Whitmanesque artistic persona. Although this statement has been read as proof of Cather's broad sympathies (Rosowski, *The Voyage Perilous*, 9–10), it really expresses a more self-centered impulse of appropriation, as Cather, like Whitman, expresses a desire to "reach down," or claim all other consciousnesses as her "own," as if they were merely "the spoils" of her imaginative conquests.

44. Offended by Whitman's frank embrace of all sensual and physical experience, Cather writes in her 1896 review of him, "The poet's task is usually to select the poetic. Whitman never bothers to do that, he takes everything in the universe from fly-specks to the fixed stars" (WP, 280). Herself wanting to take only the lofty stars of an ideal nature, Cather found Emerson's "high religious expression" and "exalted spiritual fervor" (WP, 582) more congenial to her tastes.

45. Willa Cather, "The Treasure of Far Island," in CSF, 276.

46. According to Elizabeth Shepley Sergeant, Cather told her that she "accumulated people and places" (WC: AM, 49).

47. Willa Cather to Elizabeth Shepley Sergeant, 7 December 1912, University of Virginia, Charlottesville.

48. Willa Cather to Dorothy Canfield Fisher, 7 April 1922, University of Vermont, Burlington.

49. Willa Cather to H. L. Mencken, 6 February 1922, photocopy in the Bernice Slote Collection, University of Nebraska, Lincoln.

50. Willa Cather to Will Owen Jones, 22 March 1927, University of Virginia, Charlottesville.

51. Willa Cather to Sarah Orne Jewett, 19 December 1908, Harvard University, Cambridge.

52. Dorothy Van Ghent, *Willa Cather*, University of Minnesota Pamphlets on American Writers, no. 36 (Minneapolis: University of Minnesota Press, 1964), 8.

53. Willa Cather to Dorothy Canfield Fisher, 8 April 1923, University of Vermont, Burlington.

54. Willa Cather to Irene Miner Weisz and Carrie Miner Sherwood, 16 May 1941, Willa Cather Pioneer Memorial, Red Cloud, Nebraska.

55. Leon Edel, "Willa Cather: The Paradox of Success," lecture delivered at the Library of Congress, 12 October 1959 (Washington, D. C.: Library of Congress, 1960), in James Schroeter, ed., *Willa Cather and her Critics* (Ithaca: Cornell University Press, 1967), 256–57.

56. Ibid., 257.

57. According to the convention established by other Cather scholars, I summarize and paraphrase Cather's letters.

58. In his pioneering structuralist study, *Willa Cather's Imagination* (Lincoln: University of Nebraska Press, 1975), David Stouck stresses "the broad range of modes, forms, and themes to be found in her fiction" (1). Similarly, John Murphy notes the "experimental nature" of Cather's books and the "variety of

fictional shapes" they assume. See *Critical Essays on Willa Cather*, ed. John J. Murphy (Boston: G. K. Hall, 1984), 1. Merrill Skaggs recently argues that Cather "had always tried a new experiment with every book she wrote" (*After the World Broke in Two: The Later Novels of Willa Cather* [Charlottesville: University Press of Virginia, 1990], 2). Jo Ann Middleton concurs that "Cather actively tried a new approach with each book, and each book dictated its own experiment" (*Willa Cather's Modernism*, 41).

59. Perhaps a notable exception to this "male" fantasy of power is Cather's *Shadows on the Rock*, a novel that Ann Romines has interestingly discussed in terms of female domestic ritual. Even in this novel, however, as Romines notes, much of the action occurs as storytelling of male plots lived out vicariously by the girl heroine. Ann Romines, *The Home Plot: Women, Writing and Domestic Ritual* (Amherst: The University of Massachusetts Press, 1992).

60. Critics have long recognized that the divided, or split, self is a central subject of Cather's fiction. Recently, critics have argued that Cather's creativity was fed by psychological conflicts of her own. For instance, Hermione Lee proposes the thesis that "Cather's work gets its energy from contraries" (*Willa Cather: Double Lives* [New York: Pantheon Books, 1989], 16). Similarly, Patrick Shaw writes that "conflicts — especially the homoerotic tensions — were the energy source for her creativity" (*Willa Cather & the Art of Conflict* [Troy, NY: Whitston Publishing Company, 1992], 3). In my view, however, this emphasis upon opposing impulses or themes in Cather's work mistakes its real motive, which is invariably to overcome a sense of fracture and dividedness, particularly between the self and its various antagonists in the world. Cather's work after *Alexander's Bridge* is characterized most deeply not by contraries but by unities, as Cather seeks to restore her characters to unbroken wholeness.

61. Laura Winters, *Willa Cather: Landscape and Exile* (Selinsgrove, Pa.: Susquehanna University Press, 1993), 38.

62. Ibid., 39–40.

63. Ibid., 49.

Chapter 2: *Alexander's Bridge*: Cather's Bridge to the Soul

In the text for this chapter, parenthetical references that include only page numbers refer to the Bison edition (Lincoln: University of Nebraska Press, 1977) of Willa Cather's *Alexander's Bridge*.

1. David Daiches, *Willa Cather: A Critical Introduction* (Ithaca: Cornell University Press, 1951), 15.

2. See the discussion by Bernice Slote in her introduction to *Alexander's Bridge* (Lincoln: University of Nebraska Press [Bison ed.], 1977), xiii–xv.

3. Ibid., xv– xvi.

4. James Woodress, *Willa Cather: Her Life and Art* (New York: Pegasus, 1970), 139.

5. Bartley's marriage to Winifred Pemberton may reveal something of Willa Cather's "marriage" to the equally distinguished and aristocratic Isabelle McClung, the daughter of a prominent family in Pittsburgh with whom Cather lived from 1901 to 1906. Though Cather's relationship with Isabelle McClung may well bear on the novel in important ways, I have chosen to discuss this relationship in more detail in my later chapter on *My Àntonia*. I would note, however, that if the comparison between Winifred and Isabelle holds, then it suggests that Cather, like Bartley, was uneasily trying to come to terms with her presence in Isabelle's socially and culturally polished circle; moreover, it suggests that she may have been unconsciously trying to come to terms with how well she was temperamentally, and even sexually, suited to Isabelle as a beloved friend. Though Sharon O'Brien makes much of Cather's psychosexual identity, she does not apply her theories of Cather's lesbianism to the novels she discusses. If Cather were projecting some of her passionate feelings for Isabelle McClung into the novel, then it seems clear that these feelings were complicated — they were not to be admitted or consummated in a physical relationship. Moreover, the self-love that Cather dramatizes in *Alexander's Bridge* and her other novels suggests that, for her, close relationships with other women were, like Bartley's love for Hilda, secondary attachments born out of a fundamental narcissism. Ultimately, the novel suggests that Cather, like her surrogate, embraced regressive fantasies over sexual ones; no more than Bartley, it seems, was Cather willing to make the transition from childhood innocence to adulthood sexuality. The novel finally rejects the "wifely" tie along with all of the other external acquisitions in Bartley's life as burdensome and threatening to the self. Through her surrogate, Bartley, Cather seems to give her strongest allegiance to her own primitive ego rather than to another. O'Brien has argued that Cather was forced to conceal an illicit, socially unacceptable love. One reason why Cather so idealized the romantic self may have been to escape from the guilt and anxiety of an impermissible homoerotic bond with a woman, or from the distastefulness of sexuality in general.

6. Willa Cather to H. L. Mencken, 6 February 1922, in the Bernice Slote Collection, University of Nebraska, Lincoln.

7. During 1907–8, Cather lived in an apartment on Chestnut Street just above Charles Street and the Charles River. See Bernice Slote in her introduction to *Alexander's Bridge* (Lincoln: University of Nebraska Press [Bison ed.], 1977), xii.

8. For a broader account of Annie Fields's home as a "privileged sanctuary and a center of power" (618) for Cather and other communities of women, see Judith Fryer, "What Goes on in the Ladies Room? Sarah Orne Jewett, Annie Fields, and Their Community of Women," *Massachusetts Review: A Quarterly of Literature, the Arts and Public Affairs* (Winter 1989): 610–28.

9. Willa Cather, "148 Charles Street," in NUF, 53, 54.

10. Willa Cather to Sarah Orne Jewett, 24 October 1908, Harvard University, Cambridge.

11. Ibid.

12. Willa Cather to Sarah Orne Jewett, 24 October 1908, Harvard University, Cambridge.

13. Willa Cather to Mariel Gere, 2 May 1896, Willa Cather Pioneer Memorial, Red Cloud Nebraska.

14. Willa Cather to her Aunt Franc, 23 February 1913, photocopy in the Bernice Slote Collection, University of Nebraska, Lincoln.

15. Ibid.

16. Willa Cather to Zoë Akins, 14 March 1912, Henry E. Huntington Library, San Marino, California.

17. Ibid.

18. Willa Cather to Sarah Orne Jewett, 17 December 1908, Harvard University, Cambridge. See also Willa Cather to Elizabeth Shepley Sergeant, 27 June 1911, University of Virginia, Charlottesville.

19. Cather celebrates her escape from office chains after leaving *McClure's* in the fall of 1911 in her letter to Elizabeth Shepley Sergeant of 12 September 1912 (University of Virginia, Charlottesville). In a letter to Sergeant dated 13 March 1912, also at the University of Virginia, Cather looks forward to her freedom from her enslavement at her job.

20. S. S. McClure was in Europe for the summer of 1911, leaving all of the editorial responsibility to fall on Cather's shoulders. See Woodress, *Willa Cather: Her Life and Art*, 139.

21. Willa Cather to Sarah Orne Jewett, 17 December 1908, Harvard University, Cambridge. Biographical references in this paragraph and the next are taken from this important letter.

22. Anderson, "Willa Cather: Her Masquerade," 29–30.

23. Willa Cather to Zoë Akins, 14 March 1912, Henry E. Huntington Library, San Marino, California.

24. In the serialized version of the novel, "Alexander's Masquerade," Cather writes of Bartley's experience in the office, as of her own, that "a million details swallow you" (Willa Cather, "Alexander's Masquerade," *McClure's* 38 (3) (February 1912): 388.

25. Willa Cather to Zoë Akins, 5 January 1945, Henry E. Huntington Library, San Marino, California.

26. Willa Cather to Will Owen Jones, 7 May 1903, University of Virginia, Charlottesville.

27. Willa Cather to Sarah Orne Jewett, 17 December 1908, Harvard University, Cambridge.

28. Projecting herself through her autobiographical heroine, Thea Kronborg, in *The Song of the Lark*, Cather has Thea reflect on the risks of leaving a secure

home to pursue a career as an artist: "But if she failed now, she would lose her soul. There was nowhere to fall, after one took that step, except into abysses of wretchedness" (SL, 381).

29. For Cather, the excitement of meeting new people in the office was both stimulating and exhausting. As Edith Lewis writes, "People had always excited Willa Cather; and the continual impact of new personalities, the necessity of talking to and being talked to by so many people, exhausted her nervously" (WCL, 70).

30. For example, Glen Love concludes, "For Cather, the essential American genius was scientific and progressive" (Glen A. Love, "The Cowboy in the Laboratory: Willa Cather's Hesitant Moderns," in *The Westerner and the Modern Experience in the American Novel* [Lewisburg, Pa.: Bucknell University Press, 1982], 115).

31. For fictional recreations of Cather's childhood memories of playing on an island in the Republican River with her brothers, see her "Dedication" to her first book of poems, *April Twilights*, and her two short stories "The Treasure of Far Island" (CSF, 265–82), and "The Enchanted Bluff" (CSF, 69–77). See also WWC, 43.

32. See the original serialized version of *Alexander's Bridge* as "Alexander's Masquerade" in *McClure's* 38 (5) (March 1912): 533.

33. Van Ghent, *Willa Cather*, 14.

34. Woodress, *Willa Cather: Her Life and Art*, 140.

35. Sharon O'Brien has rightly seen the destruction of Bartley Alexander's bridge at the end of the novel as proof of his limitations as an artist, but for the wrong reasons. Assuming that Cather's exemplary artist is "female" — one who selflessly gives herself up to her material in love — O'Brien argues that Bartley loses his artistic authority because of his "male" desire to conquer his material by willful "force." In conclusion, she writes, "As the bridge-builder, Bartley imposes his designs upon nature, asserting the self, rather than giving it up. Consequently, the 'crack' in his nature is his failure to integrate into the creative process the self-effacing qualities Cather eventually associated with the 'gift of sympathy'" (*Willa Cather: The Emerging Voice*, 390). In my view, O'Brien misunderstands the nature of Bartley's "force," which Cather conceives of not as a physical, external power of action but as an inner energy that has all the power of an electric current or intense blood flow. Though O'Brien faults Bartley for his virile "force" and inability to "give up" the self, Bartley's inner force, or vitality, is the salvation of his art; only because he has been forced to give up too much of himself to others does his bridge become weakened by a faulty design.

36. Willa Cather to Elizabeth Shepley Sergeant, January 1913, University of Virginia, Charlottesville.

37. Sharon O'Brien interestingly argues that Cather's decision to write her first novel, a "longer, more ambitious, and male-dominated genre" (*Willa Cather: The Emerging Voice*, 383) than the short story or sketch — the "female" preserve of writers like Jewett — filled her with authorial anxieties that surface

in the collapse of the bridge. See O'Brien, *Willa Cather: The Emerging Voice*, 382–93. I would argue, however, that it was not the idea of creating a longer work that intimidated Cather but the prospect that such ambition would be thwarted. Bartley betrays Cather's fear of having to squeeze her art within constricting molds that are too small for her personality.

38. For example, John Randall argues that "there is no reason given in the story why Alexander should be killed or have his bridge collapse because of his love affair with Hilda" (*The Landscape and the Looking Glass: Willa Cather's Search for Value* [Cambridge: The Riverside Press, 1960], 41). Most critics who have seen a connection between Bartley's destruction and his affair with Hilda have done so from a moral point of view, concluding that Cather punishes her hero for his adulterous affair. James Woodress, for example, sees Bartley's "dalliance with Hilda" as evidence of "the crack in his moral nature" (James Woodress, *Willa Cather: A Literary Life* [Lincoln: University of Nebraska Press, 1987], 219).

39. Speech given by Willa Cather in 1933 in New York at the dinner of the Friends of the Princeton University Library, Whitney Darrow Collection, Box 1, Folder 1, Manuscripts Division, Department of Rare Books and Special Collections, Princeton University Libraries.

Chapter 3: A Pioneer in Art: Staking Out the Claim to Consciousness in *O Pioneers!*

In the text for this chapter, parenthetical references that include only page numbers refer to Willa Cather, *O Pioneers!* (Boston: Houghton Mifflin, 1913).

1. Eva Mahoney, "How Willa Cather Found Herself," *Omaha World Herald*, 27 November 1921, p. 7.

2. See the copy of her poem "Prairie Spring" that Cather sent to Sergeant on 5 July 1912, University of Virginia, Charlottesville.

3. Frederick Taber Cooper's review, "Big Moments in Fiction and Some Recent Novels," appeared in *Bookman* 37 (August 1913): 666–67. Repr. in *Critical Essays on Willa Cather*, ed. John J. Murphy (Boston: G. K. Hall, 1984), 112–13.

4. See Quentin Anderson's *The Imperial Self* for a discussion of the appropriating consciousness of nineteenth-century American writers like Emerson, Whitman, and James.

5. See John Murphy, "A Comprehensive View of Cather's *O Pioneers!*," in *Critical Essays on Willa Cather*, ed. John Murphy, 124–27, for a good discussion of Whitmanesque aspects of the novel.

6. Ralph Waldo Emerson, "The Poet," in *Selections from Ralph Waldo Emerson*, ed. Stephen E. Whicher (Boston: Houghton Mifflin, 1960), 240–41.

7. Ralph Waldo Emerson, "Nature," in *Selections from Ralph Waldo Emerson*, ed. Stephen E. Whicher (Boston: Houghton Mifflin, 1960), 23.

8. Ibid.

9. Emerson, "Nature," 24.

10. See, for example, Cather's letter to Witter Bynner of 7 June 1905 (at Harvard University, Cambridge), in which she attributes the lack of beauty in her early stories like "A Wagner Matinée" to her own early years as a girl in the bleak and desolate Nebraska prairie. In the same letter, she recalls the disastrous state of the country during the 1890–94 drought, when many of her old immigrant neighbors, burdened by debts and mortgages, began to go insane and to commit suicide.

11. Willa Cather to Elizabeth Shepley Sergeant, 20 April 1912, University of Virginia, Charlottesville.

12. Willa Cather to Sarah Orne Jewett, 17 December 1908, Harvard University, Cambridge. In addition, see her letter to Dorothy Canfield Fisher of 7 April 1922, University of Vermont, Burlington, in which she discusses the greatest pleasure of writing as a heightened sense of inner life or self-possession.

13. Willa Cather to Mariel Gere, 1 August 1893, Willa Cather Pioneer Memorial, Red Cloud, Nebraska.

14. Willa Cather to Witter Bynner, 7 June 1905, Harvard University, Cambridge.

15. Emerson, "Nature," 24

16. Woodress, *Willa Cather: Her Life and Art*, 32.

17. Emerson, "Nature," 55.

18. Woodress, *Willa Cather: Her Life and Art*, 32.

19. Emerson, "Nature," 24.

20. Willa Cather to Mariel Gere, 12 March 1896, Willa Cather Pioneer Memorial, Red Cloud, Nebraska.

21. Emerson, "Nature," 53.

22. Ibid., 54.

23. Ralph Waldo Emerson, *The Journals and Miscellaneous Notebooks of Ralph Waldo Emerson*, ed. William H. Gilman, et. al. (Cambridge: Belknap Press of Harvard University Press, 1963), 3:303.

24. Emerson, "Nature," 27.

25. Willa Cather to Elizabeth Shepley Sergeant, 20 April 1912, University of Virginia, Charlottesville.

26. Emerson, "Nature," 44.

27. For example, John Randall sees Alexandra as "actively giving herself to something," which he likens to the land's "tutelary genius quite in keeping with the spirit of Greek and Roman mythology" (*The Landscape and the Looking Glass*, 67). Similarly, Sharon O'Brien argues that Alexandra's achievement arises "from losing the self in something larger, from self-abnegation" ("The

Unity of Willa Cather's 'Two-Part Pastoral,'" 158).

28. I argue that Alexandra moves ahead retentively towards unity with her self. By contrast, Susan Rosowski sees Alexandra's wagon ride into the stormy night as an expansive "movement out of the self to unity with an other" ("Willa Cather — A Pioneer in Art," 144).

29. Willa Cather to Elizabeth Shepley Sergeant, 20 April 1912, University of Virginia, Charlottesville.

30. Henry David Thoreau, *The Portable Thoreau*, rev. ed., ed. Carl Bode (New York: Penguin Books, 1979), 450.

31. Emerson, "Nature," 24.

32. Ibid., 26.

33. Ibid., 22.

34. Ibid., 44.

35. Ibid., 30.

36. For the typical reading, see Edward and Lillian Bloom, *Willa Cather's Gift of Sympathy*, 34–35.

37. Emerson, "Nature," 29.

38. Emerson, "The Poet," 230.

39. Emerson, "Nature," 55.

40. Rosowski, *The Voyage Perilous*, 49.

41. Emerson, "Nature," 38.

42. Ibid., 29.

43. Ibid., 38.

44. Ibid., 56.

45. Ibid., 38.

46. Willa Cather to Elizabeth Shepley Sergeant, 14 August 1912, University of Virginia, Charlottesville.

47. Willa Cather to Elizabeth Shepley Sergeant, 15 June 1912, University of Virginia, Charlottesville.

48. For an excellent discussion of some of the parallels between *O Pioneers!* and Genesis, see Murphy, "A Comprehensive View of Cather's *O Pioneers!*," 114–17.

49. Willa Cather to Elizabeth Shepley Sergeant, January 1913, University of Virginia, Charlottesville.

50. Emerson, "The Poet," 233.

51. Ibid., 234.

52. Willa Cather to Elizabeth Shepley Sergeant, 12 September 1912, University of Virginia, Charlottesville.

53. In her article, "The Music of Time: Henri Bergson and Willa Cather," *American Literature* (May 1985): 226–39, Loretta Wasserman discusses Bergson's ideas of memory and time as applied to *My Àntonia* and *The*

Professor's House. More recently in her book, *Willa Cather: A Study of the Short Fiction* (Boston: Twayne Publishers, 1991), she discusses Bergsonian intuition as a psychic force linking the individual to the flow of energy (élan vital) in the world of nature. See also Tom Quirk, *Bergson and American Culture: The Worlds of Willa Cather and Wallace Stevens* (Chapel Hill: The University of North Carolina Press, 1990).

54. Quirk, *Bergson and American Culture*, 128.

55. Willa Cather to Elizabeth Shepley Sergeant, 14 August 1912, University of Virginia, Charlottesville.

56. Henri Bergson, "Introduction à la Métaphysique," in *Revue de Métaphysique et de Morale* vol. 11 (1965) (Johnson Reprint Corporation): 3; originally published 1903, Librairie Armand Colin.

57. Ibid., 4.

58. Ibid.

59. Willa Cather to Elizabeth Shepley Sergeant, 22 April 1913, University of Virginia, Charlottesville.

60. Willa Cather to Elizabeth Shepley Sergeant, January 1913, University of Virginia, Charlottesville.

61. Sarah Orne Jewett to Cather, 13 December 1908, in Jewett, *Letters of Sarah Orne Jewett*, 248.

62. In Sharon O'Brien's view, the fact that Alexandra sympathetically lets the land shape itself illustrates the woman writer's "ability to abandon the ego rather than to impose it upon her subject" (*Willa Cather: The Emerging Voice*, 388). However, the fact that the land readily yields itself up to Alexandra without her physical effort or conscious control is only because Alexandra has assimilated the land as part of her own deepest consciousness, symbolically indistinguishable from her own ego. Moreover, although Alexandra may seem selfless by letting the land shape itself, she lets it shape itself in her own flattering self-image.

63. Willa Cather to Elizabeth Shepley Sergeant, 7 December 1912, University of Virginia, Charlottesville.

64. Willa Cather to Elizabeth Shepley Sergeant, 7 December 1912, University of Virginia, Charlottesville.

65. This and the following quotation are from Mahoney, "How Willa Cather Found Herself," 12.

66. This and the following quotation are from ibid., 7.

67. O'Brien, "The Unity of Willa Cather's 'Two-Part Pastoral,'" 168.

68. Ibid.

69. Ibid., 162.

70. For another discussion of Cather's characters' avoidance of sex, see Blanche Gelfant's article "The Forgotten Reaping-Hook: Sex in *My Àntonia*," *American Literature* 43 (March 1971), in which she insightfully comments,

"Whenever sex enters the real world (as for Emil and Marie in *O Pioneers!*), it becomes destructive, leading almost axiomatically to death" (61).

71. Mahoney, "How Willa Cather Found Herself," 7.

72. Sarah Orne Jewett (*Letters of Sarah Orne Jewett*, 245) seems to quote back to Willa Cather a phrase of her own in her letter to Cather of 27 November 1908.

73. Sarah Orne Jewett to Willa Cather, 13 December 1908, in ibid., 247.

74. Willa Cather, "Plays of Real Life," *McClure's* 40 (March 1913), 72.

75. Sarah Orne Jewett to Willa Cather, 13 December 1908, in Jewett, *Letters of Sarah Orne Jewett*, 248.

76. Willa Cather to Elizabeth Shepley Sergeant, March 1913, University of Virginia, Charlottesville.

77. Willa Cather to Sarah Orne Jewett, 17 December 1908, Harvard University, Cambridge.

78. Among the many interpretations of these antecedents, see, for example, Susan Rosowski's discussion of the lovers' deaths against the background of earlier myths like the biblical Garden of Eden, the tale of Pyramus and Thisbe in Ovid's *Metamorphoses*, and Keats's "The Eve of St. Agnes" (*The Voyage Perilous*, 54–56). Blanche Gelfant, in her introduction to the Penguin edition of *O Pioneers!* ([New York: Viking Penguin Inc., 1989], xxix–xxxi), discusses how the death of the lovers resonates back to the tale of Francesca and Paola in Dante's *Inferno*.

79. One possible explanation for the hyperbolic language of Cather's descriptions of heterosexual relationships can be found in Susan Wiesenthal's essay "Female Sexuality in Willa Cather's 'O Pioneers!'" Arguing that Cather set out to controvert current medical and cultural assumptions about the New Woman and homosocial relations between women, she shows how Cather reverses "her society's binary equation of deviant sexuality with disease and heterosexuality with health" (54). Through her portrait of the New Woman Alexandra, Cather reveals a deviant sexuality as vital and healthy, whereas in her portrait of Emil and Marie, she reveals a "normal" sexuality as unnatural and morbid, leading to pain, sickness, and decay.

O'Brien notes that Cather wrote "The Elopement of Allen Poole" (as we have seen, the prototype for the story of the lovers in *O Pioneers!*) "in the midst of her love affair with Louise Pound, and the story's mingling of sexual desire with disappointment, pain, and death may owe something to the conflicts aroused by that relationship" (*Willa Cather: The Emerging Voice*, 209).

80. Willa Cather to Elizabeth Shepley Sergeant, 22 April 1913, University of Virginia, Charlottesville.

81. Willa Cather to Elizabeth Shepley Sergeant, 7 December 1912, University of Virginia, Charlottesville.

82. Rosowski has assumed that when Carl tells Alexandra, "You belong to the land ... as you have always said. Now more than ever" (307), he is

confirming her selfless devotion to greater "universal" values (Rosowski, *The Voyage Perilous*, 60). Alexandra belongs to the land, however, as Emerson had belonged to the greater oversoul; Carl's lines echo Emerson's idea that, when man becomes "conscious of a universal soul within," he knows that "it is not mine, or thine, or his, but we are its; we are its property and men" (Emerson, "Nature," 32).

83. Mahoney, "How Willa Cather Found Herself," 7.

84. Woodress, *Willa Cather: Her Life and Art*, 154.

Chapter 4: Thea Kronborg's "Song of Myself": The Artist's Imaginative Inheritance in *The Song of the Lark*

In the text for this chapter, parenthetical references that include only page numbers refer to Willa Cather, *The Song of the Lark* (Boston: Houghton Mifflin, 1915; repr. 1926). References to the preface are cited in the text as "pref. SL" and refer to the 1932 edition.

1. Stouck, *Willa Cather's Imagination*, 183–84. Stouck was the first critic to call *The Song of The Lark* a *kunstlerroman*.

2. Anderson, "Willa Cather: Her Masquerade," 31. Many critics, of course, have noted the romantic dualism between the two selves in Cather's characters. Rosowski, for example, notes that "Cather wrote of two worlds — the spiritual world and the physical one, an ideal world and an ordinary one — and of two selves in each person — an immortal soul and a mortal body, an artistic self and a common one" (*The Voyage Perilous*, 5). In her view, "the most basic need of the 'soul' ... is to bring the two together" (5).

3. Anderson, "Willa Cather: Her Masquerade," 30.

4. Recently, a couple of critics have also considered the fairy tale element in *The Song of the Lark*. Susan Rosowski calls the novel "an apparently realistic fiction with the magical possibilities of a fairy tale" ("Writing Against Silences: Female Adolescent Development in the Novels of Willa Cather," *Studies in the Novel* 21 [Spring 1989]: 63). In her book *Willa Cather and the Fairy Tale*, Marilyn Callander devotes a chapter to *The Song of the Lark*. Extending a comparison that H. L. Mencken once made between the novel and the fable of Cinderella, Callander discusses the novel as a Cinderella story with Oedipal dimensions. In my view, Callander's argument that Thea "finds her identity when she finds her prince" (7) seems to give too much credence to Thea's marriage to Fred Ottenburg, an event which Cather deliberately subverts and postpones for most of the novel, including it — finally — only as an off-stage event mentioned in passing in the epilogue. Moreover, Callander's argument implies that Thea needs to complete her identity through a man, when Cather clearly puts the emphasis on Thea's personal self-fulfillment. Although

Callander argues that "the oedipal dilemma ... underlies the action in *Lark*" (8), I believe that the only real love affair in the story is between Thea and her self, and that the adoration she wins from her entourage of male admirers merely confirms this self-love.

5. Willa Cather to Dorothy Canfield Fisher, 15 March 1916, University of Vermont, Burlington.

6. See Bruno Bettelheim, *The Uses of Enchantment* (New York: Alfred A. Knopf, 1975), 36. Bettelheim discusses the difference between dreams and fairy tales, and the operation of fancy versus reality within fairy tales (35–41 and 83–86).

7. Rosowski, "Writing Against Silences," 63.

8. See Theodore Dreiser's autobiographical novel *The Genius* (Cleveland: The World Publishing Company, 1915, 1946), in which Eugene Witla continually strives to "get on," "get along," or "get up" in the world. That Dreiser makes his exemplary artist a painter who records an objective panorama, while Cather makes hers a singer who projects an inner life, suggests the crucial difference between their respective aesthetics of realism and romance.

9. Susan Rosowski comes closest to recognizing the extended metaphor of inheritance in the novel when she writes, "Throughout Cather describes Thea's growth in terms of claiming that which is for her, of 'possession' — the phrase runs like a motif through the book as Thea makes hers a bedroom, an ancient cave, and an idea of art" ("Writing Against Silences," 64).

10. Willa Cather to Mr. John S. Phillipson 15 March 1943, Willa Cather Pioneer Memorial, Red Cloud, Nebraska.

11. Willa Cather to Dorothy Canfield Fisher, 7 April 1922, University of Vermont, Burlington.

12. Willa Cather to Elizabeth Shepley Sergeant, 27 June 1911, University of Virginia, Charlottesville.

13. Mahoney, "How Willa Cather Found Herself," 7.

14. Even the supporting cast recognizes that Thea's most exalted mission is to find herself and that they must not stand in her way, despite their personal disappointments. Thea's would-be lover, Fred Ottenburg, sends her off to study in Germany with the parting advice, "Get all you can" (380). Though we would expect him to be thinking of the vast cultural and musical experiences awaiting her there, he anticipates for her a more personal gain: her second self. As he puts it, "I can't help feeling that you'll gain, somehow, by my losing so much. That you'll gain the very thing I lose. Take care of her, as Harsanyi said. She's wonderful!" (380) Thea takes Fred's advice with a vengeance.

15. Richard Giannone, *Music in Willa Cather's Fiction* (Lincoln: University of Nebraska Press, 1968), 90.

16. Willa Cather, "Three American Singers," *McClure's* 42 (December 1913): 42. The real prototype of Thea Kronborg in this, Cather's most overtly autobiographical novel, is Cather herself.

17. Writing that Thea's "highest moments involve the loss of self in art," Susan Rosowski insists that Cather's female artist is self-abnegating in her devotion to an impersonal and universal ideal ("Willa Cather's Women," *Studies in American Fiction* 9 [Autumn 1981]: 265). Arguing that Cather experienced writing as "self-abandonment to a powerful force and joyous loss of self," Sharon O'Brien similarly contends that Cather's exemplary artist, who is "female," commits herself to art out of selflessness ("Mothers, Daughters, and the 'Art Necessity,'" 282). Also stressing the artist's loss of self, but as a more painful self-sacrifice, Stouck contends that Cather "did not overlook the hard fact that success is purchased at a high price" (*Willa Cather's Imagination*, 184).

18. Willa Cather to Dorothy Canfield Fisher, n.d., University of Vermont, Burlington.

19. I paraphrase Cather's description, in her 1932 preface to the novel, of Thea's ordinary daily life. See SL, xxxi–xxxii.

20. Willa Cather, editorial column, *Red Cloud Republican* 18 July 1890. For another expression of Cather's artistic principle of complete physical assimilation, see her article on Stephen Crane: "The detail of a thing has to filter through my blood, and then it comes out like a native product, but it takes forever" (WP, 776–77).

21. I refer to Cather's famous line, "The world broke in two in 1922, or thereabouts" (NUF, v).

22. Randall, *The Landscape and the Looking Glass*, 43.

23. Walt Whitman, "There Was a Child Went Forth," in *Leaves of Grass, Comprehensive Reader's Edition*, ed. Harold W. Blodgett and Sculley Bradley (New York: New York University Press, 1965), 364–66.

24. For example, Edward and Lillian Bloom, in *Willa Cather's Gift of Sympathy*, argue that Thea profits from "the lesson of the past" and gains humility from appreciating a "historical ideal" (40). Similarly, David Stouck argues that Thea loses her sense of art as individual expression, and gains a sense of its "communal aspect" as part of a tradition of ongoing universal values (*Willa Cather's Imagination*, 195). For a more recent psychological reading of Thea's appropriation of "the rich communal and mythic roots of America" (23) see Lois Parkinson Zamora, "The Usable Past: The Idea of History in Modern U. S. and Latin American Fiction," in *Do the Americas Have a Common Literature?*, ed. Gustavo Pérez Firmat (Durham, N. C.: Duke University Press, 1990), 7–41.

25. Willa Cather, "The Birth of Personality: An Appreciation of Thomas Mann's Biblical Trilogy," *The Saturday Review of Literature* (6 June 1936): 3. In this chapter, all subsequent references to the essay are to this page.

26. In my interpretation, I disagree with the standard interpretation offered by David Stouck, that Thea bathes in the stream and discovers the Indian women's pottery as a revelation of "man's age-old desire for something beyond himself" (*Willa Cather's Imagination*, 195).

27. John Randall, for example, argues that "this passage embodies the idea of art as order, as a pattern which is imposed upon the chaos of human experience in an attempt to render it meaningful" (*The Landscape and the Looking Glass*, 49).

28. Willa Cather to Sarah Orne Jewett, 17 December 1908, Harvard University, Cambridge.

29. Willa Cather to Elizabeth Shepley Sergeant, 19 November 1920, University of Virginia, Charlottesville.

30. Willa Cather to Elizabeth Shepley Sergeant, 20 April 1912, University of Virginia, Charlottesville.

31. Willa Cather to Elizabeth Shepley Sergeant, 15 June 1912, University of Virginia, Charlottesville.

32. Willa Cather to Elizabeth Shepley Sergeant, 20 April 1912, University of Virginia, Charlottesville.

33. Willa Cather to Elizabeth Shepley Sergeant, 30 May 1912, University of Virginia, Charlottesville.

34. Willa Cather to Elizabeth Shepley Sergeant, 21 September 1915, University of Virginia, Charlottesville.

35. Willa Cather to Sarah Orne Jewett, 17 December 1908, Harvard University, Cambridge. The remaining biographical references in this paragraph are from this letter.

36. Willa Cather to Mary Miner, 8 August 1935, Newberry Library, Chicago.

37. Willa Cather to Mariel Gere, 18 August 1902, Willa Cather Pioneer Memorial, Red Cloud, Nebraska.

38. Willa Cather to Dorothy Canfield Fisher, 15 March 1916, University of Vermont, Burlington.

39. According to Elizabeth Shepley Sergeant (WC: AM, 49), Cather told her that she "accumulated people and places."

40. Willa Cather to Mrs. George Seibel, 31 January 1916, Willa Cather Pioneer Memorial, Red Cloud, Nebraska.

41. Ibid.

42. See Jean Schwind, "Fine and Folk Art in *The Song of the Lark*: Cather's Pictorial Sources," *Cather Studies* 1 (Lincoln: University of Nebraska Press, 1990), for a discussion of the significance of Mr. Kohler's piece-picture as a legacy of childhood that informs Thea's mature art (97–98). Though, as Schwind points out, the piece-picture is a work of extraordinary craftsmanship, it does not provide, in my view, a convincing model for Thea's, or Cather's, art. A "kind of mosaic" made from stitching together thousands of pieces of fabric, the piece-picture is an art composed of fragments of experience; a project of Fritz Kohler's apprenticeship as a tailor in Germany that required him "to copy in cloth some well-known German painting," it is a derivative work created secondhand; a copy of *Napoleon Retreating from Moscow*, it is a crowded canvas of a grand historical event; a hand-stitched quilt, it represents a domestic

tradition normally associated with the female arts. Fragmentary, derivative, historically representational, and yet domestic, the piece-picture represents a different tradition from Thea's art, which is unified, original, individual, and projected from her own soul.

43. Willa Cather to Sarah Orne Jewett, 17 December 1908, Harvard University, Cambridge.

44. Willa Cather to Mariel Gere, 4 August 1896, Willa Cather Pioneer Memorial, Red Cloud, Nebraska.

45. Willa Cather to Ferris Greenslet, 28 March 1915, Harvard University, Cambridge.

46. It is tempting to speculate that, at some level, Willa Cather herself used her art as a way of paying back her enemies and rewarding her friends for the degree of faith that they had put in her. In a letter to Mariel Gere of 10 January 1897 (Willa Cather Pioneer Memorial, Red Cloud, Nebraska), written from Pittsburgh, Cather rejoices that her newfound independence and work as a journalist will give her the opportunity to settle old scores. For a discussion of how Cather took revenge on Mrs. Canfield in *The Troll Garden*, see Mark Madigan, "Willa Cather and Dorothy Canfield Fisher: Rift, Reconciliation, and *One of Ours*," *Cather Studies* (Lincoln: University of Nebraska Press, 1990), 1:115–29.

47. David Stouck, for example, sees the end of the novel as Cather's "vision of art's service to life" (*Willa Cather's Imagination*, 198) whereby Thea's success fulfills the dreams of her childhood friends in repayment for the parts that they have played in her development. With a similar emphasis, Susan Rosowski contends that, at the end of the novel, "second-self reproduction and regeneration extends to others" ("The Pattern of Willa Cather's Novels," *Western American Literature* 15 [1981]: 255). In my view, Cather enlists life — the lives of others — in the service of the artist's own egoistic regeneration.

48. Like Thea, Cather liked to imagine that her early friends and mentors had vicariously lived out their dreams of success through her. As she wrote in a letter of 30 April 1909 to Mr. E. J. Overing, she took pleasure in trying to live up to the faith that others like her old teacher Miss King had put in her. (Willa Cather Pioneer Memorial, Red Cloud, Nebraska).

49. Rosowski, "Willa Cather's Women," 264–65.

50. Sigmund Freud, "On Narcissism: An Introduction," *Standard Edition of the Complete Psychological Works of Sigmund Freud*, ed. and trans. James Strachey (London: Hogarth Press, 1957), 14:91.

Chapter 5: *My Àntonia*: The Imaginative Possession of Childhood

In the text for this chapter, parenthetical references that include only page numbers refer to Willa Cather, *My Àntonia* (Boston: Houghton Mifflin, 1918, with original introduction; Boston: Houghton Mifflin, 1926; with revised introduction, Sentry ed., 1954). Unless otherwise specified, references are to the Sentry edition of the revised 1926 text. References to the first edition of the novel, which contains the longer original introduction, specify 1918 before the page number.

1. See, for example, O'Brien, "Mothers, Daughters, and the 'Art Necessity,'" 265–98, and Rosowski, "Willa Cather's Women," 261–75.

2. See, for example, Jean Schwind, "The Benda Illustrations to *My Àntonia*: Cather's 'Silent' Supplement to Jim Burden's Narrative," *PMLA* 100 (1) (January 1985): 51–67.

3. I give no page number since Cather's 1926 revised edition of *My Àntonia* does not paginate the introduction.

4. See Schwind, "The Benda Illustrations to *My Àntonia*." Schwind argues that the novel's "realistic" illustrations are meant to undermine Jim's "romantic" narrative. Yet her distinction between genres does not altogether hold, since the woodcuts often romanticize common and ordinary characters by portraying them against glorifying sunsets, etc., while Jim's own narrative is itself pictorial, as he continually tries to capture and idealize the past as pictures in his memory. Cather's letters to Ferris Greenslet, her publisher at Houghton Mifflin, reveal that she regarded the pictures not as a separate, subversive narrative but as an inextricable, complimentary part of the written text. She insisted that the pictures be matched precisely opposite the pages they were meant to illuminate. They were meant to be a part of the text, and not to stand alone. (Willa Cather to Ferris Greenslet, 17 July 1918, Harvard University, Cambridge).

5. Willa Cather to Dorothy Canfield Fisher, 15 March 1916, University of Vermont, Burlington. See also Willa Cather to Elizabeth Shepley Sergeant, 3 August 1916, University of Virginia, Charlottesville, on how hard Isabelle's marriage is and always will be.

6. Cather met Isabelle McClung in the dressing room of Lizzie Hudson Collier, the leading actress of the Pittsburgh Stock Company during the theater season of 1898–99. See Woodress, *Willa Cather: Her Life and Art*, 90–91, for an account of the meeting.

7. Willa Cather to Zoë Akins, 20 May 1939, Henry E. Huntington Library, San Marino, California.

8. Leon Edel, "A Cave of One's Own," in *Critical Essays on Willa Cather*, ed. John J. Murphy (Boston: G. K. Hall, 1984), 212.

9. Ibid.

10. Phyllis Robinson, *Willa: The Life of Willa Cather* (Garden City, N.Y.: Doubleday, 1983), 4.

11. Ibid.

12. Willa Cather to Will Owen Jones, 20 May 1919, University of Virginia, Charlottesville.

13. Willa Cather to Mr. Winter, 5 November 1919, Colby College Library, Waterville, Maine.

14. Willa Cather to Carrie Miner Sherwood, 7 September 1936, Willa Cather Pioneer Memorial, Red Cloud, Nebraska.

15. Willa Cather to Carrie Miner Sherwood, 10 November 1921, Willa Cather Pioneer Memorial, Red Cloud, Nebraska.

16. Rosowski, *The Voyage Perilous*, 81.

17. In her Bohemian childhood friend Annie Sadilek Pavelka, Cather chose a model for a heroine who could replace Isabelle in her affections. Àntonia's father, Mr. Shimerda, was based on the real Annie's father, who also committed suicide soon after Cather arrived in Nebraska. Similarly, Jim's grandparents are based on Cather's own, with whom she and her family first lived when she, like Jim, traveled from Virginia to Nebraska. Members of the entire Miner family play roles in the story as the Harlings, and Cather's teacher at the University of Nebraska, Herbert Bates, appears as Jim's teacher, Gaston Cleric. As James Woodress has noted, minor characters — such as the Negro pianist, Blind d'Arnault; the lecherous moneylender, Wick Cutter; and the hotelier, Mrs. Gardener — all have real life prototypes. See Woodress, *Willa Cather: Her Life and Art*, 177.

18. Willa Cather to Bishop George Beecher, 2 January 1935, Nebraska State Historical Society, Lincoln.

19. Willa Cather to Ferris Greenslet, 21 September 1940, Harvard University, Cambridge.

20. Willa Cather to Carrie Miner Sherwood, 20 January 1937, Willa Cather Pioneer Memorial, Red Cloud, Nebraska.

21. Willa Cather to Irene Miner Weisz, 6 January 1945, Newberry Library, Chicago.

22. Willa Cather to Dorothy Canfield Fisher, 8 April 1921, University of Vermont, Burlington.

23. Willa Cather to Dorothy Canfield Fisher, 21 June 1922, University of Vermont, Burlington.

24. Willa Cather to May Willard, 6 May 1941, University of Virginia, Charlottesville.

25. Willa Cather to Dorothy Canfield Fisher, 10 October 1899, University of Vermont, Burlington.

26. See O'Brien, *Willa Cather: The Emerging Voice*, 127–34, for her definition of "lesbian" and its basis in Cather's college friendships, particularly with Louise Pound.

27. That Cather should have lamented in a letter to Louise Pound that one Miss De Pue found female friendships unnatural (Willa Cather to Louise Pound, 15 June 1892, Duke University, Durham), suggests that she herself wished to accept female attachments as natural, socially acceptable, and free of any shameful or deviant associations. Perhaps the closest literary parallel to the

relationship between Willa Cather and Isabelle McClung (or to that between Cather and her best college friend, Louise Pound), is the intensely emotional preadolescent friendship between Anne Shirley and her "bosom friend," Diana Barry, in Lucy Maud Montgomery's *Anne of Green Gables* (1908). As the young Anne and Diana solemnly exchange vows of eternal "love" and devotion, give each other locks of hair to wear around their necks, send each other love notes to sleep with under their pillows, and swear to be "faithful" to each other unto death, they stage themselves as lovers in a romantic scene of parting that derives its florid, pathetic rhetoric from sentimental, romantic nineteenth-century novels. (Lucy Maud Montgomery, *Anne of Green Gables* [New York: Avenel Books, 1908; repr. 1986); 103-8). Similarly, Cather's "love" letters, such as those to Louise Pound or those about Isabelle McClung, are replete with self-consciously adopted romantic poses, stylized and stilted rhetoric, and histrionic literary artifice as if she too were enjoying playing an imaginative part in an exciting melodrama of her own scripting and directing. In her letters to Louise Pound over the summer of 1893, expressing disappointment at their separation, Cather, like Anne Shirley, seems to revel in her despair as if she were, in part, enacting the stock romantic role of the unrequited lover. (Willa Cather to Louise Pound, 15 June and 29 June 1893, Duke University, Durham.) Like the passionate but asexual relationship between Anne Shirley and Diana Barry, Cather's friendships with both Louise Pound and Isabelle McClung originated from a mutual love of literature and drama. Coediting the literary magazine and acting with Louise in the drama society at the University of Nebraska, and meeting Isabelle backstage in Pittsburgh, Cather continued to cultivate a "staged" quality in her female relationships that owes much to literary antecedents.

28. See Deborah Lambert, "The Defeat of a Hero: Autonomy and Sexuality in *My Àntonia*," *American Literature* 53 (1982), 676–90, and Judith Fetterley, "*My Àntonia*, Jim Burden, and the Dilemma of the Lesbian Writer," in *Lesbian Texts and Contexts: Radical Revisions*, ed. Karla Jay and Joanne Glasgow (New York: New York University Press, 1990), 145–63. Though Lambert and Fetterley have argued that Cather assumed her male persona in *My Àntonia* as a mask for her lesbian love for Annie Sadilek, there is no evidence in Cather's biography to suggest that she felt a sexual passion for her childhood friend. It seems likely that Cather chose Annie Sadilek as the model for her heroine not because she was in love with her but because she provided a more appropriable alternative to Isabelle McClung. A woman of humble origins and close to the earth, Annie was as different as possible from the well-bred and culturally literate woman from Pittsburgh. As a person from her past whom Cather did not know intimately, Annie could be easily grafted into Cather's consciousness as a precious figure who could inspire her art. Most importantly, Annie was a friend from childhood and so seemed relatively removed from the divisive world of sexuality that had robbed Cather of Isabelle.

29. David Stouck, "Perspective as Structure and Theme in *My Àntonia*," *Texas Studies in Literature and Language* 12 (Summer 1970): 287.

30. Willa Cather to Dorothy Canfield Fisher, n. d., University of Vermont, Burlington.

31. Sharon O'Brien reads this passage as evidence of the artist's urge towards self-dissolution and self-abandonment ("The Unity of Willa Cather's 'Two-Part Pastoral,'" 158).

32. Emerson, "Nature," 53.

33. This and the following quotation come from Emerson's famous passage in "Nature": "All mean egotism vanishes. I become a transparent eyeball; I am nothing; I see all; the currents of the Universal Being circulate through me; I am part or parcel of God" (24).

34. Sigmund Freud, "Beyond the Pleasure Principle," in *The Standard Edition of the Complete Psychological Works of Sigmund Freud*, ed. and trans. James Strachey (London: The Hogarth Press, 1955), 18:57.

35. O'Brien, *Willa Cather: The Emerging Voice*, 108.

36. Gelfant, "The Forgotten Reaping-Hook," 77.

37. Willa Cather to Dorothy Canfield Fisher, 22 June (no year), University of Vermont, Burlington.

38. Rosowski, *The Voyage Perilous*, 77.

39. Emerson, "Nature," 24.

40. Daiches, *Willa Cather: A Critical Introduction*, 39.

41. Michael Peterman, "Kindling the Imagination: The Inset Stories of *My Àntonia*," *Approaches to Teaching Cather's* My Àntonia, ed. Susan J. Rosowski (New York: The Modern Language Association of America, 1989), 160. Peterman, supporting Bettelheim's notion that young people learn through undidactic tales, disputes Gelfant's reading of the tale as a "grisly acting out of male aversion" to female sexuality, offering instead the possibility that its lesson is to "avoid ... betrayal of one's closest friends" (160). Both readings seem resonant in the context of Cather's resentment of Isabelle McClung's marriage. My interest, however, is less in the moral of the story than in the psychological impulse of the children's appropriation of it.

42. Callander, *Willa Cather and the Fairy Tale*, 28.

43. Willa Cather to Carrie Miner Sherwood, 27 January 1934, Willa Cather Pioneer Memorial, Red Cloud, Nebraska.

44. In my view that Cather gives priority to Jim's ideal imaginative creation of Àntonia, I disagree with Susan Rosowski and other feminist critics who argue that Cather "builds tension against [Jim's] account." See Rosowski, "Willa Cather's Women," 266.

45. For a discussion of "the conventional relations between the sexes" in this scene, see Susan Rosowski, "Willa Cather's Pioneer Women: A Feminist Interpretation," in *Where the West Begins: Essays on Middle Border and Siouxland Writing, in Honor of Herbert Krause*, ed. Arthur R. Heseboe & William Geyer (Sioux Falls, S. D.: 1978), 140.

46. Gelfant, "The Forgotten Reaping-Hook," 69–70.

47. Ibid., 70.

48. Romines, *The Home Plot*, 149.

49. Marilyn Callander has observed that "Snow White is yet another image of permanence" in Jim's story, "frozen as she is in perfection until the prince's kiss arouses her to love, to sex, and to death" (Callander, *Willa Cather and the Fairy Tale*, 22).

50. David Daiches, for example, finds the novel to be structurally "flawed" because "the story of Jim and Àntonia and their relations is not really borne out by the story" (*Willa Cather: A Critical Introduction*, 47).

51. Terence Martin, "The Drama of Memory in *My Àntonia*," *PMLA* 84 (March 1969): 308.

52. Gelfant, "The Forgotten Reaping-Hook," 69.

53. Ibid., 66.

54. E. K. Brown, *Willa Cather: A Critical Biography*, completed by Leon Edel (New York: Alfred A. Knopf, 1953), 202.

55. Rosowski, *The Voyage Perilous*, 86.

56. Emerson, "Nature," 41.

57. Willa Cather to Mr. John S. Phillipson, 15 March 1943, Willa Cather Pioneer Memorial, Red Cloud, Nebraska.

58. Willa Cather to Dorothy Canfield Fisher, 7 April 1922, University of Vermont, Burlington.

59. Willa Cather to H. L. Mencken, 6 February 1922, photocopy in the Bernice Slote Collection at the University of Nebraska, Lincoln.

60. Willa Cather to Dorothy Canfield Fisher, 21 March 1922, University of Vermont, in which she expresses gratitude that she had enough to feed her character until he was complete.

61. Willa Cather to Dorothy Canfield Fisher, 7 April 1922, University of Vermont, Burlington.

62. Cather almost always refers to her novels by name, as if they were living characters. Their vitality embodied her own personality. Regarding her characters as her closest companions, she could form a narcissistic imaginative bond with them that was more satisfying than real relationships could be. For Cather's reference to her Professor, see, for example, her letter to Irene Miner Weisz, 16 March 1925, Newberry Library, Chicago; for her declaration that she loves her Bishop, see her letter to Weisz, 11 January 1926, Newberry Library; for her possessive love of her Àntonia, see especially her letters to Ferris Greenslet, Harvard University, Cambridge, among them, 16 February 1942.

63. Willa Cather to Dorothy Canfield Fisher, 7 April 1922, University of Vermont, Burlington. For other discussions of the companionship that Cather found in her characters, see Willa Cather's letters to Elizabeth Sergeant of 7 December 1915, University of Virginia, Charlottesville; to Dorothy Canfield

Fisher of 8 May 1922, University of Vermont; to Carrie Miner Sherwood of 20 October 1937, Willa Cather Pioneer Memorial, Red Cloud, Nebraska.

64. James Miller argues that Jim's mature realization at the end of the novel is that "neither [he nor Àntonia] nor anyone else can possess the past, that the past is absolutely and irrevocably 'incommunicable' even to those who lived it" ("*My Àntonia*: A Frontier Drama of Time," *American Quarterly* 10 (4) [Winter 1958]: 477). Similarly, David Stouck argues that the novel moves Jim towards "the tragic realization that the past can never be recaptured" (*Willa Cather's Imagination*, 46). More recently, John Selzer argues that "*My Àntonia* is a comic novel recording its title character's triumph and its narrator's tardy but resolute enlightenment" that his past choices have been selfish and influenced by convention ("Jim Burden and the Structure of *My Àntonia*," *Western American Literature* 24 [1989]: 47). By contrast, I do not think that Jim Burden grows up to admit or regret the selfishness of his imaginative demands on others; in his belief that he can "possess" the past, regardless of change or other people, his childish innocence remains intact.

65. Willa Cather to Dorothy Canfield Fisher, 26 January 1922, University of Vermont, Burlington.

66. By contrast, Susan Rosowski argues that, in the final section of the novel, Jim "seems to have lost his personal identity" and that, conversely, Àntonia "emerges powerfully as herself" ("Willa Cather's Women," 267).

67. Evelyn Helmick and Josephine Donovan have emphasized that Jim becomes initiated through Àntonia into primordial matriarchal mysteries. See Evelyn Helmick, "The Mysteries of Àntonia," *The Midwest Quarterly* 17 (Winter 1976), 173–85, and Josephine Donovan, *After the Fall: The Demeter-Persephone Myth in Wharton, Cather, and Glasgow* (University Park, Pa.: The Pennsylvania State Press, 1988). Ann Fisher-Wirth also stresses the central importance of Àntonia as a female principle; for her, Àntonia represents the female body that Cather wanted to reclaim as a part of herself ("Womanhood and Art in *My Àntonia*," in *Willa Cather: Family, Community, and History*, ed. John J. Murphy et. al. [Provo, Utah: Brigham Young University, Humanities Publishing Center, 1990], 221–27).

68. Rosowski, *The Voyage Perilous*, 87.

69. By contrast, Susan Rosowski argues that Àntonia's storytelling allows her to reverse roles with Jim as the creative authority ("Willa Cather's Women," 267).

70. Susan Sontag, *On Photography* (New York: Farrar, Straus and Giroux, 1977), 3–4.

71. Marilyn Callander has noted that Jim's story functions as a fairy tale with a perfect mother and a happy resolution. See *Willa Cather and the Fairy Tale*, 28.

72. Willa Cather to Mr. George Seibel, 1932, Willa Cather Pioneer Memorial, Red Cloud, Nebraska.

73. Willa Cather to Mr. Milton Graff, 19 July 1925, Willa Cather Pioneer Memorial, Red Cloud, Nebraska.

74. Willa Cather to Dorothy Canfield Fisher, 26 January 1922, University of Vermont, Burlington.

Chapter 6: "Strong in Attack but Weak in Defence": Defending the Usurped Territory in *A Lost Lady*

In the text for this chapter, parenthetical references that include only page numbers refer to Willa Cather, *A Lost Lady* (New York: Alfred A. Knopf, 1923; repr. Vintage, 1972).

1. Willa Cather, "Nebraska: The End of the First Cycle," in *These United States*, ed. Ernest Gruening (New York: Boni and Liveright, 1924), 151.

2. Ibid., 141–53.

3. John Randall, for example, calls the novel Cather's "blanket condemnation of the present" (*The Landscape and the Looking Glass*, 196). Similarly, James Woodress writes that it reflects "the author's ever-increasing disenchantment over the moral climate of the twenties" (*Willa Cather: Her Life and Art*, 203).

4. Cather, "Nebraska," 151.

5. Ibid., 143.

6. Willa Cather to Elizabeth Shepley Sergeant, 28 September 1914, University of Virginia, Charlottesville.

7. Skaggs, *After the World Broke in Two*, 6. For another good discussion of the causes of Cather's 1922 depression, see Woodress, *Willa Cather: A Literary Life*, 335–36.

8. Woodress, *Willa Cather: A Literary Life*, 333; Skaggs, *After the World Broke in Two*, 6–10.

9. Skaggs, *After the World Broke in Two*, 10.

10. Willa Cather to Dorothy Canfield Fisher, 29 September 1922, University of Vermont, Burlington.

11. Willa Cather to Elizabeth Shepley Sergeant, 19 November 1913, University of Virginia, Charlottesville.

12. Harold Bloom, Introduction to *Modern Critical Interpretations; Willa Cather's* My Ántonia (New York: Chelsea House Publishers, 1987), 3–4.

13. David Stouck, for example, reads *The Professor's House* as a conflict between those characters who exhibit a selfish desire for power and possessions, and those like the Professor, who are guided by a selfless transcendence of individual ambition. See *Willa Cather's Imagination*, 96–109.

14. Willa Cather to Zoë Akins, 19 April 1937, Henry E. Huntington Library, San Marino, California.

15. F. Scott Fitzgerald, *The Great Gatsby* (New York: Charles Scribner's Sons, 1925), 99.

16. James Fenimore Cooper, *The Pioneers or The Sources of the Susquehanna* (New York: Penguin, 1823; repr. 1964). Natty Bumppo's friend, Chingachgook, the last of two of the Mohican tribe, spends most of his time reminiscing about the glorious heroic days of the past.

17. For a different view of Cather's use of history, see Joseph Urgo, "How Context Determines Fact: Historicism in Willa Cather's *A Lost Lady*," *Studies in American Fiction* 17 (1989), 183–92. Urgo argues that the novel ironically critiques Niel Herbert's "curious and dangerous sense of history" (191) and is consciously critical about the way that history can be falsified, or "dehistoricized," by memories or nostalgia.

18. Willa Cather to Carrie Miner Sherwood, 12 February 1934, Willa Cather Pioneer Memorial, Red Cloud, Nebraska.

19. Dalma Brunauer was one of the first to assert that "Niel Herbert is not a mouth piece of the author.... Marian Forrester is a 'lost lady' in the eyes of Niel, and not of Miss Cather." See Dalma Brunauer, "The Problem of Point of View in *A Lost Lady*," *Renascence* 28 (Autumn 1974): 47–48. See also Kathleen Nichols, "The Celibate Male in *A Lost Lady*: The Unreliable Center of Consciousness," *Regionalism and the Female Imagination* 4 (1978), 13–23, and Diane Cousineau, "Division and Difference in *A Lost Lady*," *Women's Studies* 11 (1984), 305–22. Though Kathleen Nichols argues that Cather's third-person narration separates her angle of vision from Niel's, Cather first composed the novel as Niel's first-person narrative (see WCL, 125). In the novel itself, her third-person account indistinguishably merges with his point of view, so that, finally, his consciousness is the only one we enter. Moreover, his consciousness so controls the novel that all of the exemplary secondary characters — like Mr. Ogden or Niel's uncle, Judge Pommeroy — speak to confirm his views. Cather abandoned the first-person point of view not because she suddenly found herself lacking in sympathy for Niel — she had, in fact, identified herself too closely with him — but because she hoped that the third-person narration would give her bitter and emotional text the semblance of objectivity and aesthetic distance.

Finally, I should note that skepticism of Niel Herbert has not been limited to female feminist critics. Recently, for example, Lawrence Berkove argued that Niel's nostalgic love of the past at Marian's expense forces us to recognize that he "is not a reliable narrator; his opinions cannot be trusted" ("*A Lost Lady*: The Portrait of a Survivor," *The Willa Cather Yearbook* [Lewiston, N.Y.: Edwin Mellen Press, 1991], 1:61).

20. Willa Cather to Irene Miner Weisz, 6 January 1945, Newberry Library, Chicago.

21. For an interesting different reading of the significance of Mrs. Forrester's rings, see Skaggs, *After the World Broke in Two*, 52–53.

22. Sigmund Freud, "Family Romances," in *Standard Edition of the Complete Psychological Works of Sigmund Freud*, ed. and trans. James Strachey

(London: Hogarth Press, 1958), 14:237–41. See Cousineau, "Division and Difference in *A Lost Lady*," 305–22. I am also indebted to John Swift for drawing my attention to the connection between Cather's "family romance" and Freud's in his excellent paper "The Family Romance of *A Lost Lady*," presented at the National Willa Cather Symposium, Brigham Young University, September 1988.

23. Freud, "Family Romances," 241.

24. Woodress, *Willa Cather: Her Life and Art*, 22.

25. Cather's recollection — "I was little and homesick and lonely and my mother was homesick and nobody paid any attention to us. So the country and I had it out together" — suggests that Cather felt that she had to confront the "naked" desolation of the prairie alone (WWC, 140). For other accounts of Mrs. Cather's aloofness and estrangement from Willa, see WWC, 29–31.

26. Woodress, *Willa Cather: Her Life and Art*, 22.

27. Ibid., 36.

28. Ibid., 23.

29. Edel, "A Cave of One's Own," 211.

30. See O'Brien, "Mothers, Daughters, and the 'Art Necessity,'" 288. Also see Nichols, "The Celibate Male in *A Lost Lady*," 13–23. John Swift has also discussed the dynamic of the sexual drive in the child's passion for the mother in his paper "The Family Romance of *A Lost Lady*."

31. O'Brien, "Mothers, Daughters, and the 'Art Necessity,'" 288.

32. Willa Cather to Zoë Akins, 15 December 1934, Henry E. Huntington Library, San Marino, California.

33. Willa Cather to May Willard, 6 May 1941, University of Virginia, Charlottesville.

34. Willa Cather to Zoë Akins, 19 April 1937, Henry E. Huntington Library, San Marino, California.

35. I paraphrase here from *Alexander's Bridge* (Lincoln: University of Nebraska Press [Bison ed.], 1977), 39: "That consciousness was Life itself. Whatever took its place, action, reflection, the power of concentrated thought, were only functions of a mechanism useful to society; things that could be bought in the market."

36. Niel's service to the Captain in the final chapters leads David Stouck to argue that "*A Lost Lady* is a pastoral of experience because it brings its hero from childhood innocence to adult awareness and acceptance of life" (Stouck, *Willa Cather's Imagination*, 59).

37. See, for example, Woodress, *Willa Cather: A Literary Life*, 350, or Skaggs, *After the World Broke in Two*, 59.

38. Cather wrote the book during the winter and spring of 1922, between her return from Nebraska and her one teaching stint at Bread Loaf. See Willa Cather's letter to Irene Miner Weisz, 6 January 1945, Newberry Library, Chicago.

39. Merrill Skaggs (*After the World Broke in Two,* 50) has also noted such a connection between Jan Hambourg and the novel.

40. Woodress, *Willa Cather: Her Life and Art,* 173.

Chapter 7: "Letting Something Go": The Costs of Self-Possession in *The Professor's House*

In the text for this chapter, parenthetical references that include only page numbers refer to Willa Cather, *The Professor's House* (New York: Alfred A. Knopf, 1925; repr. Vintage, 1973).

1. Winters, *Willa Cather: Landscape and Exile,* 40.

2. Willa Cather to Irene Miner Weisz, 31 December 1943, Newberry Library, Chicago.

3. Willa Cather to Dorothy Canfield Fisher, 26 May 1944, University of Vermont, Burlington.

4. Edel, "A Cave of One's Own," 200–217.

5. To Edel's biographical account I would add that Cather made her trip to Aix-les-Bains for the curative mineral baths; though stricken during her visit with the Hambourgs by neuritis in her right arm and shoulder (see Woodress, *Willa Cather: A Literary Life,* 338–39), she was as desperately suffering from a strained emotional condition, which may well have been the underlying cause of her physical ailment. While Cather may have found her therapy for her arm in the warm springs of France, she found a more satisfying cure for her anxieties by writing the novel, which she began with intensity upon her return to the States in November.

6. Edel, "A Cave of One's Own," 214.

7. Willa Cather to Irene Miner Weisz, 11 January 1926, Newberry Library, Chicago. Cather asks Mr. Weisz to insure her luxurious mink coat because it is the first valuable possession she has ever owned.

8. Frank Novak, "Crisis and Discovery in *The Professor's House,*" *Colby Library Quarterly* (1986): 119.

9. Doris Grumbach, "A study of the small room in *The Professor's House,*" *Women's Studies* 11 (1984): 330.

10. For a good discussion of the symbolic meaning of the Professor's garden as "a form of escape," see Thomas Strychacz, "The Ambiguities of Escape in Willa Cather's *The Professor's House,*" *Studies in American Fiction* 14 (1986), 50–51.

11. I would revise the emphasis of the traditional interpretation expressed by David Stouck that "the Professor comes to recognize that the family's desire for wealth and status is being fulfilled at the expense of all the civilized values he

has lived and fought for" (David Stouck, "Willa Cather and *The Professor's House*: 'Letting Go With the Heart,'" *Western American Literature* 7 [1972]: 18).

12. In reality, St. Peter's childhood was not so free, for when he was eight years old, he "nearly died" when his family "dragged" him away from the lake to the plains of Kansas. The resemblance between his story and Willa Cather's suggests that in this Blue Lake there is something of the Blue Ridge Mountains. This biographical parallel is further supported by the similarity between the Professor's family and Willa Cather's: he has a strong-willed Protestant mother, a gentle father, and a patriarchal grandfather, as had she.

13. See Cather's essay entitled "Escapism," in which she defends the proposition, "What has art ever been but escape?" (OW, 18).

14. Woodress, *Willa Cather: A Literary Life*, 369.

15. Strychacz, "The Ambiguities of Escape," 52.

16. Clive Hart discusses how such interruptions become a "leitmotiv" in book 1. See Clive Hart, "'The Professor's House': A Shapely Story," *Modern Language Review* 67 (April 1972): 274.

17. Edel, "A Cave of One's Own," 213.

18. As magnanimous as the Professor's apology to Louie is, however, it is interesting to note that he apologizes not for his own treatment of Louie but for the selfish behavior of Rosamond and Scott, on to whom the Professor's bitterness towards Louie seems displaced. By having the Professor apologize in this indirect way on behalf of others, Cather seems to mitigate his guilt for his uncharitable feelings towards his son-in-law.

19. Critics have recognized that the forms are symbolically associated with the women of the household. See, for example, Hart, "'The Professor's House,'" 278.

20. Richard Dillman notes the pun on Outland's name ("Tom Outland: Emerson's American Scholar in *The Professor's House*," *The Midwest Quarterly* 25 [Summer 1984]: 376).

21. Maynard Fox, "Two Primitives: Huck Finn and Tom Outland," *Western American Literature* 1 (Spring 1966): 26–33.

22. Dillman, "Tom Outland: Emerson's American Scholar in *The Professor's House*," 375–85.

23. Alfred A. Knopf, "Random Recollections of a Publisher," *Massachusetts Historical Society Proceedings* 73 (1961): 99. Knopf reemphasized the point in 1974. See Knopf, "Miss Cather," in *The Art of Willa Cather*, ed. Bernice Slote and Virginia Faulkner (Lincoln: University of Nebraska Press, 1974), 205.

24. Woodress, *Willa Cather: Her Life and Art*, 186.

25. Willa Cather, "Portrait of the Publisher as a Young Man," in *Alfred A. Knopf Quarter Century* (Norwood, Mass.: Plimpton Press, 1940), 9–26.

26. Willa Cather to Mary Austin, 9 November 1927, Henry E. Huntington Library, San Marino, California.

27. Willa Cather to Zoë Akins, 28 October 1937, Henry E. Huntington Library, San Marino, California.

28. For a different interpretation of Jan Hambourg's influence over Willa Cather, see John B. Gleason, "The 'Case' of Willa Cather," *Western American Literature* 20 (1986), 275–99. Gleason argues that Cather was influenced by Hambourg in positive ways and valued his friendship.

29. Willa Cather to Ferris Greenslet, 16 February 1942, Harvard University, Cambridge. Again, in a letter to Greenslet, protesting the reprinting of one of the novel's chapters in an omnibus, Cather reveals her desire to guard her fiction as personal property: she was fearful of allowing even a knothole to be cut in the fence within which she had hoped to protect Àntonia (Willa Cather to Ferris Greenslet, 3 May 1943, Harvard University, Cambridge). She remained stubbornly opposed to all commercialized adaptations of her works in films, radio, anthologies, excerpts, or cheap or illustrated editions on the grounds that they prevented readers from knowing her writing personality (Willa Cather to Ferris Greenslet, n. d., Harvard University, Cambridge). She viewed unwanted alterations to her texts as figurative dismemberments of her characters and her own soul (Willa Cather to Ferris Greenslet, 29 January 1937, Harvard University, Cambridge).

30. Willa Cather to Zoë Akins, 15 December 1936, Henry E. Huntington Library, San Marino, California.

31. Willa Cather, "Mesa Verde," *The Denver Times* (31 January 1916); repr. in Susan Rosowski and Bernice Slote, "Willa Cather's 1916 Mesa Verde Essay: The Genesis of *The Professor's House*," *Prairie Schooner* 58 (Winter 1984): 86.

32. Willa Cather to Carrie Miner Sherwood, 26 July 1935, Willa Cather Pioneer Memorial, Red Cloud, Nebraska.

33. Willa Cather to Mr. Stanfield, 19 October 1926, University of Virginia, Charlottesville. In another letter to Dorothy Canfield Fisher, Cather again suggests that whereas she feels a fullness of life at her island retreat at Grand Manan, New Brunswick, she returns to New York only to exhaust her vitality (20 December 1929, University of Vermont, Burlington).

34. Edel, "A Cave of One's Own," 215.

35. Ibid., 216.

36. For an interesting psychoanalytic reading of "Tom Outland's Story" as an "archeological dig" in search of family origins, see John Swift, "Memory, Myth, and *The Professor's House*," *American Literature* 20 (1986): 301-14.

37. About the compositional history of "Tom Outland's Story," James Woodress notes that Cather probably finished it in the late summer of 1922 at Grand Manan (*Willa Cather: A Literary Life*, 323). To my knowledge, however, none of Cather's biographers or critics has discussed the significance of her beginning the story in 1916.

38. Willa Cather to Ferris Greenslet, 22 August 1916, Harvard University, Cambridge.

39. Cather quotes Louie Marsellus on the unnumbered title page of the novel.

40. Edel, "A Cave of One's Own," 216.

41. See, for example, James F. Maxfield, "Strategies of Self-Deception in Willa Cather's *Professor's House*," *Studies in the Novel* 16 (Spring 1984), in which he argues that the Professor's identification with his presexual self is "a supreme act of hubris," a rebellion "against all forms of 'external' coercion, not just sexuality" (81).

42. For another reading of the name "Godfrey," as well as the names in the novel in general, see Rhoda F. Orme-Johnson, "The Uses of Names in *The Professor's House*," *The Willa Cather Yearbook* (Lewiston, N.Y.: The Edwin Mellen Press, 1991). She suggests that "Godfrey" is an allusion to Godfrey of Bouillon, the perfect Christian knight who defended the Holy Sepulcher in Jerusalem in 1099 during the First Crusade (131); further glossing "Godfrey" as meaning "peace of God," she interestingly suggests that at the end of the novel the Professor as "'crusader' is at last catching a glimpse of the Holy Land, the Kingdom of Heaven within" (140).

43. I here agree with the emphasis that Thomas Strychacz puts on the ambiguities of the ending of the novel when he says that the Professor's "survival is not necessarily an affirmation" ("The Ambiguities of Escape," 58).

44. Grumbach, "A study of the small room in *The Professor's House*," 343.

45. John Swift has written that in *The Professor's House*, the "images of original identity and strength ... betray themselves as only that, images, wishfully constructed signs of the primary but not the primary itself" ("Memory, Myth, and *The Professor's House*," *Western American Literature* 20 [1986], 311).

46. The dilemma that Robert Frost poses in his poem "The Oven Bird" — "what to make of a diminished thing" — could well be the epigraph for the subsequent unwritten chapter in St. Peter's life, as he learns to live with a sense of diminished possibilities and joy. Robert Frost, "The Oven Bird," in *The Poetry of Robert Frost*, ed. Edward Connery Lathem (New York: Holt, Rinehart and Winston, 1969), 120. I share my sense of the subdued note of the ending with Michael Leddy, who also quotes Frost's line in his article "*The Professor's House*: The Sense of an Ending" (*Studies in the Novel* 23 [Winter 1991], 448).

47. Randall, *The Landscape and the Looking Glass*, 234.

48. The Berengaria was the name of the actual ship on which Cather sailed home from Cherbourg in October 1923 after visiting the Hambourgs in France (Woodress, *Willa Cather: A Literary Life*, 339). Most likely, Isabelle and Jan would have made the crossing on the same ship; at any rate, Cather would have thought of the ship as the connecting link between herself and her friends on the other side of the Atlantic.

Chapter 8: "How to Recover a Bishopric": Cather's Recovery of the Imaginative Territory in *Death Comes for the Archbishop*

In the text for this chapter, parenthetical references that include only page numbers refer to Willa Cather, *Death Comes for the Archbishop* (New York: Alfred A. Knopf, 1927; repr. Vintage, 1971).

1. Willa Cather to Ida Tarbell, n.d., photocopy from Reis Library, Allegheny College, in the Bernice Slote Collection, University of Nebraska, Lincoln.

2. Randall, *The Landscape and the Looking Glass*, 284.

3. Woodress, *Willa Cather: Her Life and Art*, 221.

4. In her letter to *The Commonweal*, Cather describes how she drew upon *The Life of the Right Reverend Joseph P. Machebeuf*, by William Joseph Howlett, for the story of Father Machebeuf (the prototype of Father Vaillant) and Father Lamy (the prototype of Father Latour). See OW, 7–8. Ultimately, however, Cather drew more upon her own life than upon history in writing the novel; as she said in a 1928 interview, "I spent a large part of fifteen years in the southwest, living the life of the southwestern people. I have ridden thousands of miles on ranch ponies, and the experiences I have related in the stories ... are not based upon fancies or upon reading of that territory and those people, but upon my own life and experiences there" (WCP, 103).

5. After Vernon Loggins, on the "I Hear America" radio show, stated as fact that Cather had become a Catholic, Cather began receiving letters from Catholics asking about her conversion. See, for example, the two letters from John J. Walsh to Willa Cather at the University of Virginia (undated, ca. 1940?) and her exasperated response to the head of his English Department, 7 February 1940. See also Woodress, *Willa Cather: A Literary Life*, 410–11, for a discussion of the confusion over Cather's religion. Edith Lewis reports that among the hundreds of letters that Cather received about *Death Comes for the Archbishop*, "there were a great many interesting ones from nuns and priests" (WCL, 147).

6. For an early article, see Michael Williams, "Willa Cather's Masterpiece," *The Commonweal* 6 (28 September 1927): 490–92, quoted in OW, 13: "Her book is a wonderful proof of the power of the true artist to penetrate and understand and to express things not part of the equipment of the artist as a person. Miss Cather is not a Catholic, yet certainly no Catholic American writer that I know of has ever written so many pages so steeped in spiritual knowledge and understanding of Catholic motives and so sympathetically illustrative of the wonder and beauty of Catholic mysteries, as she has done in this book." For a more recent article, see, for example, John Murphy, "Willa Cather and Catholic Themes," *Western American Literature* 17 (1982), 53–60. In 1988, an entire volume, *Literature and Belief*, published by Brigham Young University College

of Humanities, was devoted to "the religious dimension" (foreword) in Cather's novels, within which essays by Marilyn Arnold and John Murphy are devoted to religion in *Death Comes for the Archbishop*.

7. John J. Murphy, "Cather's New World Divine Comedy: The Dante Connection," *Cather Studies*, ed. Susan J. Rosowski (Lincoln: University of Nebraska Press, 1990), 1: 21–35.

8. Ibid., 33.

9. John Randall discusses how *Death Comes for the Archbishop* is not really Catholic in its outlook. Showing how Cather's priests use their religious authority for selfish and worldly gain, he suggests that Cather's main interest is not in Catholicism but "rather civilized living" (298). See Randall, *The Landscape and the Looking Glass*, 295–303, for an examination of the deceptively religious tone of the novel.

10. Such an anagogical approach has, for instance, framed David Stouck's reading of the book as a modern saint's life, structured as a series of discontinuous, spiritually exemplary emblems. See Stouck, *Willa Cather's Imagination*, 131–32.

11. Rosowski, *The Voyage Perilous*, 5.

12. Stouck, "Willa Cather and *The Professor's House*," 23.

13. Rosowski, *The Voyage Perilous*, 162.

14. In "Avignon," the fragment of her last unpublished novel, *Hard Punishments*, written between 1944 and 1946, Cather defines "miracle" in imaginative rather than religious terms. Again focusing on a priest, this time in a cathedral in Avignon, she writes, "All about him he could feel something more beautiful than light or music: the kindling of emotion, faith, belief, imagination — which is itself a miracle.... Was there, he asked himself, anything in all the Universe, anything so wonderful as wonder — wonderment?" Though a religious miracle arouses faith in the transcendent, Cather here defines "miracle" as the individual's amazement at his own capacity to appreciate the illusions of beauty created by his imagination. See "Avignon," University of Virginia, Charlottesville.

15. John Randall discusses "the almost complete elimination of conflict from the book" (*The Landscape and the Looking Glass,* 281). Whereas Randall sees the lack of dramatic conflict as an aesthetic flaw and an abnegation of moral authorial responsibility, I seek to explain it as a necessary narrative strategy.

16. For the most detailed psychoanalytic reading of the cave, see Patrick W. Shaw, "Women and the Father: Psychosexual Ambiguity in *Death Comes for the Archbishop*," *American Imago* 46 (Spring 1989), 69–72. Viewing the cave as "a synecdochic representation of Cather's own fragmented sexuality" (72), Shaw discusses images of oral sex, menstruation, birthing, and maternity to posit that Cather was divided between embracing and denying homoerotic impulses. As Shaw tactfully observes, however, if Cather were "a lesbian writer who had come to terms with her nontraditional sexuality," she "would probably not be so squeamish" (72) about the cave's female symbolism.

17. David Stouck expresses the traditional view that the cathedral "is an art object which is not only communal in origin and function, but which is also created in the service of an ideal of which the basis is the negation of self in God" (Stouck, *Willa Cather's Imagination*, 149).

18. Emerson, "The American Scholar," *Selections from Ralph Waldo Emerson*, ed. Stephen E. Whicher (Boston: Houghton Mifflin, 1960), 74.

19. Patrick Shaw argues that Willa Cather displaced her lesbianism in the priestly "marriage." As he says, "The priests' relationship affords [Cather] a safe method by which the preferred homoeroticism can be depicted without incurring the ire of a shocked public: removed to the long ago and far away and blessed by the authoritative if not infallible church, "Jean Marie" and "Joseph" can sleep together, eat together, argue and discuss without having to apologize for the lack of heterosexual contact and the absence of progeny" (Shaw, "Women and the Father," 67). Whether or not Cather was actively lesbian, she may well have been dramatizing an acceptable form of friendship between women such as she herself had known.

20. Shaw has remarked that the friendship between Latour and Vaillant "is the ideal relationship Cather envisioned, free from intersexual conflicts and maternal obligations" (Shaw, "Women and the Father," 67). Moreover, it may, at some level, represent the ideal relationship that Cather herself lived with Edith Lewis. For a good discussion of the enabling relationship between Cather and her "wifely partner" Lewis, see Patricia Lee Yongue, "Willa Cather and Edith Lewis: Two Stories, Two Friends," in *The Willa Cather Yearbook* (Lewiston: The Edwin Mellen Press, 1991), vol. 1. As Yongue states, Lewis "performed invaluable domestic and technical services for Cather and posed no threat to Cather's dominant ego and assertiveness. Quite the contrary, although she had her own work outside the home, she seemed voluntarily to find her greatest glory in Cather's, her next greatest glory in freeing Cather to write" (187). Yongue briefly notes that "the Latour-Vaillant coupling seems to explain something of her relationship with Edith Lewis" (201). Certainly, insofar as Vaillant keeps the household affairs in order, sees to the practical running of the parish, worships the Bishop, and frees him to live the life of the mind in his study, he plays the "wifely" role that Lewis filled for Cather.

21. Randall, *The Landscape and the Looking Glass*, 307.

22. For David Stouck, these conventional religious expectations are fulfilled in this scene, as the Bishop's "spiritual crisis is resolved through ... a renewed renunciation of temporal power" (*Willa Cather's Imagination*, 145).

23. Randall, *The Landscape and the Looking Glass*, 301–2.

24. Willa Cather to Fanny Butcher, quoted in Woodress, *Willa Cather: A Literary Life*, 396.

25. Randall, *The Landscape and the Looking Glass*, 302.

26. Willa Cather to Carrie Miner Sherwood, 22 March 1941, Willa Cather Pioneer Memorial, Red Cloud, Nebraska.

27. As Ann Fisher-Wirth discusses, the Bishop has another compensatory fantasy at the end of his life when he recalls the restoration of the Canyon de Chelly to the Navajos. As a story of displaced people allowed to return from exile, this seemingly irrelevant digression adumbrates the Bishop's own longings for a return to the Garden of Eden. See Ann Fisher-Wirth, "Dispossession and Redemption in the Novels of Willa Cather," *Cather Studies*, ed. Susan J. Rosowski (Lincoln: University of Nebraska Press, 1990), 1:36. Fisher-Wirth discusses the novel's "attempts to transform a sense of loss into a sense of possession" (51), a term that she equates with a religious sense of "redemption." Whereas she believes that this pattern begins with *Death Comes for the Archbishop*, I argue that this is the central strategy that informs Cather's works from the beginning.

28. For an interesting reading of the narrative's temporal movements, one leading forward in time and space, taking Latour to his death, and one leading backward in history and memory, see John Swift, "Cather's Archbishop and the 'Backward Path,'" *Cather Studies* 1:55–67. Swift aptly notes that the novel's regressive impulse may be meant "to undo or repudiate time and its primary effect, death, and that the novel's 'plot,' read through its temporal conflicts, may be the attempt to delay death by circling back to birth" (59–60).

Interestingly, Cather's letters on her own father's death, which occurred on 3 March 1928, suggest how she means us to regard death as a beautiful thing in *Death Comes for the Archbishop*. As she describes seeing her father's face suffused by the light of the rosy dawn, she implies that he has returned home to the beginning of things when he was happy and complete. See Willa Cather's letter to Zoë Akins of 7 June 1941, Henry E. Huntington Library, San Marino, California. Reflecting that the appearance of her father had replenished her soul, she vicariously experienced his apparent self-restoration in death. See Willa Cather's letter to Dorothy Canfield Fisher of 3 April 1928, University of Vermont, Burlington. We have seen that Willa Cather took imaginative possession of all things "other" and alien — landscapes, people, and history — but surely her greatest imaginative leap of faith was to appropriate even death itself.

Chapter 9: "The Ownership that was Right": Imaginative Bonds of Slavery in *Sapphira and the Slave Girl*

In the text for this chapter, parenthetical references that include only page numbers refer to Willa Cather, *Sapphira and the Slave Girl* (New York: Alfred A. Knopf, 1940).

1. For a more extended discussion of the Gothic elements in *Sapphira and the Slave Girl*, see Woodress, *Willa Cather: A Literary Life*, 483–84, and Rosowski, *The Voyage Perilous*, 235–345.

2. Woodress, *Willa Cather: A Literary Life,* 483.

3. Skaggs, *After the World Broke in Two,* 181.

4. Ibid., 177.

5. Elizabeth Ammons, *Conflicting Stories: American Women Writers at the Turn into the Twentieth Century* (New York: Oxford University Press, 1991), 134.

6. Toni Morrison, *Playing in the Dark: Whiteness and the Literary Imagination* (Cambridge: Harvard University Press, 1992), 25.

7. Ibid., 25.

8. Morrison writes that Cather "employs [the black characters] in behalf of her own desire for a safe participation in loss, in love, in chaos, in justice" (*Playing in the Dark*, 28). In my view, Cather does not create her black characters in order to experience vicariously their thrilling stories or dangerous journeys, which are largely omitted from the plot. Cather creates her black characters not to identify with them, but to have them identify with and confirm the identity of her surrogate.

9. Edith Lewis recalls that *Sapphira and the Slave Girl* "was a novel written against circumstance. One catastrophe after another blocked its path; the sudden death of her brother Douglass — the most bitter, I think, of all her losses; the death of Isabelle Hambourg; the second World War.... Against all these things, she worked at *Sapphira* with a resoluteness, a sort of fixed determination which I think was different from her ordinary working mood; as if she were bringing all her powers into play to save this, whatever else was lost" (WCL, 184).

10. Morrison, *Playing in the Dark*, 18.

11. Nancy Till is referred to throughout the text as the "gold-coloured" (SSG, 284) girl.

12. Ammons, Conflicting Stories, 135.

13. Woodress, *Willa Cather: A Literary Life*, 482–83.

14. Willa Cather to Miss Janet Masterton, 15 March 1943, Willa Cather Pioneer Memorial, Red Cloud, Nebraska.

15. Ibid.

16. O'Brien, *Willa Cather: The Emerging Voice*, 45, 44.

17. Ibid., 44. O'Brien's interpretation of maternal bonds as examples of "compassion" for others seems particularly untenable when we consider the actual mother-daughter bond that is acted out in this scene between Till and her daughter Nancy. As Toni Morrison has recognized, this relationship is sadly deficient. Because of Till's complete allegiance to her white mistress, Nancy must conceal her fears and plans from her mother throughout the novel. Disturbed by Till's lack of sympathy for her daughter, Toni Morrison sees in the relationship the assumption that "slave women are not mothers; they are 'natally dead,' with no obligations to their offspring or their own parents" (Morrison, *Playing in the Dark*, 21).

Chapter 10: "Making it Over Until it Becomes a Personal Possession": Willa Cather and the Reader

1. Sinclair Lewis, "The Greatest American Novelist," *Newsweek* 11 (3 January 1938): 29.

2. George L. White, Jr. "Willa Cather," (Summaries of Eminent Living Novelists), *Sewanee Review* 50 (January-March 1942): 18.

3. Brown, *Willa Cather: A Critical Biography,* 179.

4. Ferris Greenslet to Willa Cather, 30 April 1914, Harvard University, Cambridge.

5. Ferris Greenslet to Willa Cather, 8 March 1916, Harvard University, Cambridge.

6. Woodress, *Willa Cather: A Literary Life,* 274.

7. Ferris Greenslet to Willa Cather, 29 April 1916, Harvard University, Cambridge.

8. Ferris Greenslet to Willa Cather, 3 December 1918, Harvard University, Cambridge.

9. Ibid.

10. Ferris Greenslet to Willa Cather, 27 October 1921, Harvard University, Cambridge.

11. I wish to thank Alan Andrés of Houghton Mifflin for this insight and for the preceding information about the recent sales of *My Àntonia,* which he kindly gave me during a phone conversation in September of 1992.

12. Woodress, *Willa Cather: A Literary Life,* 334.

13. Ibid., 352.

14. I wish to thank Lu Ann Walther, the Executive Editor of Vintage Classics, a division of Random House, published by Knopf, for this statistic, which she gave me in a phone call in September 1992. Although she could not divulge the figures for the number of paperback editions of Cather's books sold, she stressed that it was an honor for Cather to be selected for the Vintage Classics series, since that line is held in high esteem.

15. Woodress, *Willa Cather: A Literary Life,* 433.

16. Ibid., 555.

17. In 1917, Cather was awarded an honorary degree from the University of Nebraska, and in subsequent years was awarded degrees from Michigan, Columbia, Yale, New York University, Berkeley, Creighton, and Smith. In 1931, she was the first woman to receive an honorary degree from Princeton University, receiving more applause than Charles Lindbergh, Newton Baker (Wilson's Secretary of War), or Frank Kellogg (the former Secretary of State), who also received degrees (Brown, *Willa Cather: A Critical Biography,* 326.) In 1930, Cather was awarded the Howells Medal by the American Academy of Arts and Letters for *Death Comes for the Archbishop.* In 1931, she was named

by the readers of *Good Housekeeping* magazine as one of "the twelve greatest living American women" (*Good Housekeeping* 93 [September 1931], 34–35). In 1944, she was granted the gold medal for fiction by the National Institute of Arts and Letters, given once a decade for an author's total accomplishment, and second in prestige only to the Nobel Prize (Brown, *Willa Cather: A Critical Biography,* 325).

18. See, for example, Willa Cather to Ferris Greenslet, 23 August 1945, Harvard University, Cambridge, for an account of the different translations that she owns of *Death Comes for the Archbishop*.

19. Brown, *Willa Cather: A Critical Biography,* 230.

20. Willa Cather to Ferris Greenslet, February 1942, Harvard University, Cambridge.

21. Anonymous Review of *O Pioneers!* in *Nation* (4 September 1913): 210–11.

22. Robert Morss Lovett, *The New Republic* (26 October 1927): 267.

23. Zona Gale, "My Favorite Character in Fiction," *Bookman* 63 (May 1926): 323.

24. James Ford, "Willa Cather Visits the Cliff-Dwellers," *The Literary Digest International Book Review* (November 1925): 775.

25. H. W. Boyton, *Nation* (14 October 1915): 462.

26. René Rapin, *Willa Cather,* ed. Ernest Boyd, Modern American Writers Series (New York: Robert M. McBride and Company, 1930), 45–46.

27. John Curran to Willa Cather, 1932?, from Indianapolis, Indiana, Willa Cather Pioneer Memorial, Red Cloud, Nebraska.

28. Willa Cather to Dorothy Canfield Fisher, 7 April 1922, University of Vermont, Burlington.

29. Brown, *Willa Cather: A Critical Biography,* 194.

30. Floyd Dell, "A Good Novel," *Chicago Evening Post Friday Literary Review* (25 July 1913), repr. in *Dictionary of Literary Biography,* Documentary Series (Detroit: Gale Research Company, 1982), 1:67.

31. Francis X. Connolly, "Willa Cather: Memory as Muse," in *Fifty Years of the American Novel: A Christian Appraisal,* ed. Harold C. Gardiner (New York: Charles Scribner's Sons, 1952), 69.

32. See Maxwell Geismar, "Willa Cather: Lady in the Wilderness," in *The Last of the Provincials: The American Novel, 1915–1925* (Boston: Houghton Mifflin, 1947), repr. in Schroeter, ed., *Willa Cather and Her Critics,* 179. H. L. Mencken, in his review of *My Àntonia* ("Sunrise on the Prairie," *Smart Set* 58 [February 1919]; repr. in Schroeter, ed., *Willa Cather and Her Critics,* 9), believes that *My Àntonia* is remarkable for its "extraordinary reality." Carl Van Doren similarly suggests that Àntonia imparts the "glory of reality" to all she touches ("Willa Cather," in *Contemporary American Novelists: 1900–1920* [New York: Macmillan, 1922], repr. in Schroeter, ed., *Willa Cather and Her Critics,* 18).

33. Latrobe Carroll, "Willa Sibert Cather," *Bookman* 52 (3 May 1921); repr. in WCP, 22.

34. Don Beckman, "The Song of the Lark," *Opera News* 35 (27 February 1971), 6–7.

35. Brown, *Willa Cather: A Critical Biography*, 340.

36. Williams, "Willa Cather's Masterpiece," 492.

37. Today, the Christian critics John Murphy and Marilyn Arnold, who teach literature at Brigham Young University, similarly argue that Cather's main interests were not secular but religious; Murphy has devoted an entire volume of criticism, *Literature and Belief*, to religious themes in Cather's fiction. *Literature and Belief: Willa Cather Issue*, ed. John J. Murphy (Provo: Brigham Young University, 1988).

38. David Harrell, "Willa Cather's Mesa Verde Myth," *Cather Studies* (Lincoln: University of Nebraska Press, 1990), 1:130–43. See also Louis Auchincloss, "Willa Cather," in *Pioneers and Caretakers: A Study of Nine American Women Novelists* (Minneapolis: University of Minnesota Press, 1965), 92–122.

39. J. W. Donohue, "Two Women: A Centennial," *America* 128 (31 March 1973): 277.

40. See WWC, in which Bennett traces the characters and events in the novels to local prototypes. See also Bernice Slote, "Willa Cather as a Regional Writer," *Kansas Quarterly* 2 (Spring 1970): 7–15, and Bruce Baker, "Nebraska Regionalism in Selected Works of Willa Cather," *Western American Literature* 3 (Spring 1968): 19–35.

41. James Keough, "Willa Cather's Pastoral Vision: Going Home to Rural America," *Sierra* 64 (January-February 1979): 62.

42. Ibid., 64–65.

43. See, for example, Fetterley, "*My Àntonia*, Jim Burden, and the Dilemma of the Lesbian Writer," 145–63. In addition, Fetterley and other lesbian feminist critics present at the Fourth National Cather Seminar in Santa Fe, New Mexico, June 1990, strongly implied that one had to be a lesbian critic to properly understand Cather's work.

44. John J. Murphy, "The Respectable Romantic and the Unwed Mother: Class Consciousness in 'My Àntonia,'" *Colby Library Quarterly* 10 (September 1973): 149–56.

45. Jane Tompkins, *Sensational Designs: The Cultural Work of American Fiction: 1790–1860* (New York: Oxford University Press, 1985), 192.

46. In my discussions of the general historical trends in Cather criticism from the 1920s through the 1950s, I am indebted to the work of James Schroeter in his historical anthology of criticism, *Willa Cather and Her Critics*.

47. T. K. Whipple, "Willa Cather," *New York Evening Post* 4 (8 December 1923), repr. in Schroeter, ed., *Willa Cather and Her Critics*, 35.

48. Ibid., 50.

49. Van Doren, "Willa Cather," 13.

50. Edmund Wilson, review of *A Lost Lady, Dial* 76 (January 1924), repr. in Schroeter, ed., *Willa Cather and Her Critics*, 28–29.

51. Lloyd Morris, "Willa Cather," *The North American Review* 219 (May 1924): 652.

52. Ibid., 642.

53. Review of *O Pioneers!*, *Nation* 97 (4 September 1913): 210.

54. Louis Kronenberger, "Willa Cather," *Bookman* 74 (October 1931): 140.

55. Clifton Fadiman, "Willa Cather: The Past Recaptured," *Nation* 135 (7 December 1932): 563.

56. Lionel Trilling, "Willa Cather," in *After the Genteel Tradition: American Writers 1910–1930*, ed. Malcolm Cowley (Carbondale: Southern Illinois University Press, 1936), 48.

57. Granville Hicks, "The Case Against Willa Cather," *English Journal* 22 (November 1933), repr. in Schroeter, ed., *Willa Cather and Her Critics*, 144.

58. Geismar, "Willa Cather: Lady in the Wilderness."

59. Alfred Kazin, *On Native Grounds* (New York: Reynal & Hitchcock, 1942), xi.

60. Alfred Kazin, *Twentieth-Century Literary Criticism* (Detroit: Gale Research Company, 1978), 11:98.

61. In addition to Kazin's *On Native Grounds* and Brown's biography, see David Daiches, *Willa Cather: A Critical Introduction* (New York: Collier Books, 1962), and Van Wyck Brooks, *The Confident Years: 1885–1915* (New York: EP Dutton, 1952).

62. Francis Connolly is typical in seeing Cather defending positive values; her writing is the "progress from one level of meaning and value to another; from the level of nature to the level of mind, and from the level of mind to the level of spirit" (74). His Christian perspective on her characters as "valiant spirits who live and die for ideals" (70) and whose "immense, epic vitality ... derives from intrinsic virtues of mind and heart" (70), says a lot about why Cather would have been popular in the 1950s, with its emphasis on traditional, conservative, clean-cut, and wholesome domestic virtues. Connolly's impression of Àntonia, for example, as the fulfilled and happy wife and mother who incarnates kindness and moral goodness could as well be a description of the cheerful, socially proper, and morally pure housewife popularized by Donna Reed and others. Connolly, "Willa Cather: Memory as Muse."

63. Kazin, *On Native Grounds*, 170.

64. Ibid., 164.

65. Ibid., 169.

66. Geismar, "Willa Cather: Lady in the Wilderness," 174 and 200.

67. Henry Steele Commager, "Traditionalism in American Literature," *Nineteenth Century and After* 146 (November 1949): 311–26. Brooks, *The Confident Years*.

68. Frederick Hoffman, *The Twenties: American Writing in the Postwar Decade* (New York: Viking Press, 1955), 161.

69. Schroeter, ed., *Willa Cather and Her Critics*, 229–33.

70. Robert Scholes, "Hope and Memory in *My Àntonia*," *Shenandoah* 14 (Autumn 1962): 24–29.

71. Leon Edel, "Willa Cather: The Paradox of Success," 251.

72. Edward and Lillian Bloom, *Willa Cather's Gift of Sympathy*, x.

73. Ibid., 139.

74. Ibid., 250.

75. Sharon O'Brien, "Becoming Noncanonical: The Case Against Willa Cather," *American Quarterly* 40 (1) (March 1988): 110–26.

76. Ibid., 116. According to O'Brien, language such as "feminine," "romantic," "sentimental," "soft," and "small" and a circle of associations led to a demotion in Cather's status from "woman" to "minor writer."

77. Kronenberger, "Willa Cather," 134.

78. Ibid., 140.

79. Ibid., 135.

80. Ibid.

81. Ibid., 136.

82. This and the following quotations are from Fadiman, "Willa Cather: The Past Recaptured," 565.

83. For all his criticism of Cather, Granville Hicks recognizes the source of her appeal to her audience when he writes, "Miss Cather's dreams have beauty and are not without nobility, and it has brought consolation to many readers" (Hicks, "The Case Against Willa Cather," 146).

84. Implicit in O'Brien's argument is the assumption that Cather has failed to please male critics because she is not telling a "male" story in her novels. She notes, for example, that "critics could view [*Shadows on the Rock*] as peripheral because, although it addresses the central American story of immigration, transplanting, and resettlement, it does not tell the male version of that story." In O'Brien's view, Cather "was challenging the gender-coded myth of America" in all of her novels, beginning with *O Pioneers!* See O'Brien, "Becoming Noncanonical," 125.

85. Louise Bogan, "American-Classic," *The New Yorker* (8 August 1931), repr. in Schroeter, ed., *Willa Cather and Her Critics*, 126.

86. Whipple, "Willa Cather," 50.

87. Kronenberger, "Willa Cather," 135. Mr. Justice Oliver Wendell Holmes wrote to Cather that she had the "gift of the transfiguring touch" (Brown, *Willa Cather: A Critical Biography*, 336).

88. Kazin, *On Native Grounds*, 165.

89. Review of *O Pioneers! Nation* 97 (4 September 1913): 210.

90. Van Doren, "Willa Cather," 14.

91. Ibid., 14

92. Henry Seidel Canby, "A Novel of the Soul," a review of *The Professor's House*, *Saturday Review of Literature* 2 (26 September 1925), 151; repr. in *Critical Essays on Willa Cather*, ed. John J. Murphy (Boston: G. K. Hall, 1984), 200.

93. Whipple, "Willa Cather," 50 and 49.

94. Ibid., 48–49.

95. Percy Boynton, "Willa Cather," *English Journal* 13 (June 1924): 379–80.

96. Randolphe Bourne, "Diminuendo," a review of *The Song of the Lark*, *The New Republic* 5 (11 December 1915): 153.

97. White, Jr. "Willa Cather," 21.

98. Ibid.

99. Willa Cather to Carrie Miner Sherwood, 28 June 1939, Willa Cather Pioneer Memorial, Red Cloud, Nebraska.

100. Margaret Lawrence, *The School of Femininity: A Book for and about Women as They Are Interpreted Through Feminine Writers of Yesterday and Today* (New York: Frederick A. Stokes Co., 1936), 359.

101. Edward and Lillian Bloom, *Willa Cather's Gift of Sympathy*, 250.

102. Lois Feger, "The Dark Dimension of Willa Cather's *My Àntonia*," *English Journal* 59 (September 1970): 774–79.

103. See also Scholes, "Hope and Memory in *My Àntonia*," 24–29, in which he argues that Cather uses the Adamic myth to stress the tragedy of the fall rather than the recovery of innocence: "Àntonia's life is a triumph of innocence and vitality over hardship and evil. But Willa Cather does not celebrate this triumph; rather, she intones an elegy over the dying myth of the heroic Innocent, over the days that are no more" (29). Similarly, James Miller argues that *My Àntonia* explores "the dark recesses of the American psyche" (113), as the vanishing frontier and American dream register the country's "anguished sense of loss" (115). James Miller, "*My Àntonia* and the American Dream," *Prairie Schooner* 48 (Summer 1974): 112–23.

104. Rosowski, *The Voyage Perilous*, 215.

105. Stouck, *Willa Cather's Imagination*, 46.

106. Ibid., 187. For instance, in his efforts to define *The Song of the Lark* as "a psychologically complex art form," Stouck must argue that the "artist's dedication is at once a creative and potentially tragic commitment" (ibid., 184).

107. Ibid., 135.

108. Ibid, 134–35.

109. Ibid, 135.

110. Ibid.

111. Ibid., 134.

112. Woodress, *Willa Cather: A Literary Life*, 294.

113. Tompkins, *Sensational Designs*, xi–xix.

114. Trilling, "Willa Cather," 52.

115. Ibid., 153.

116. F. A. G., "A Woman's Climb from Nebraska to the Stage," a review of *The Song of the Lark*, *Boston Evening Transcript* 13 October 1915, p. 22.

117. Bourne, "Diminuendo," 153.

118. Randolphe Bourne, "Morals and Art from the West," a review of *My Àntonia*, *The Dial* 65 (14 December 1918): 557. See also Rapin, *Willa Cather*, who discusses the power of *The Song of the Lark*: "There is youth in the book, its delight in itself, its adventures, its bitterness and its doubt" (44). Similarly, Philip Gerber, in discussing Àntonia, says, "Her secret is enthusiasm — to retain a child's delight in existence. Her effervescence contrasts with the aridity of lives around her" (Philip Gerber, *Willa Cather* [Boston: G. K. Hall (Twayne United States Authors Series), 1975], 90).

119. Mencken, "Sunrise on the Prairie," 9.

120. White, Jr. "Willa Cather," 19.

121. Geismar, "Willa Cather: Lady in the Wilderness," 184.

122. Margaret Freydberg, "Willa Cather: The Light Behind her Books," *American Scholar* 43 (Spring 1974): 282.

123. Lawrence, *The School of Femininity*, 359.

124. Mencken, "Sunrise on the Prairie," 9.

125. Ibid., 12.

126. W. C. Brownell to Viola Roseboro, quoted in Brown, *Willa Cather: A Critical Biography*, 204–5.

127. Dorothy Canfield Fisher, *New York Times Book Review* (10 September 1922): 14.

128. Supreme Court Justice Oliver Wendell Holmes to Ferris Greenslet, quoted in WC: AM, 244.

129. Irene Miner Weisz to Willa Cather, 4 January 1945, Newberry Library, Chicago.

130. Beckman, "The Song of the Lark," 7.

131. Freydberg, "Willa Cather," 286.

132. Brown, *Willa Cather: A Critical Biography*, 321.

133. Willa Cather to Ferris Greenslet, 24 January 1945, Harvard University, Cambridge.

134. Freydberg, "Willa Cather," 287.

135. Virginia Satir, "My Declaration of Self-Esteem," in *Peoplemaking* (Palo Alto, Calif.: Science and Behavior Books, Inc., 1972), 27–29.

136. John Curran to Willa Cather, 1932, from Indianapolis, Indiana, Willa Cather Pioneer Memorial, Red Cloud, Nebraska.

137. White, Jr. "Willa Cather," 21.

138. Freydberg, "Willa Cather," 282.

139. This is one of the major premises of Susan Rosowski's argument in her *The Voyage Perilous*.

Bibliography

Ammons, Elizabeth. *Conflicting Stories: American Women Writers at the Turn into the Twentieth Century.* New York: Oxford University Press, 1991.

Anderson, Quentin. *The Imperial Self: An Essay in American Literary and Cultural History.* New York: Knopf, 1971.

———. "Willa Cather: Her Masquerade." *New Republic* 153 (27 November 1965): 28–31.

Arnold, Marilyn. *Willa Cather: A Reference Guide.* Boston: G.K. Hall & Co., 1986.

Auchincloss, Louis. "Willa Cather." In *Pioneers and Caretakers: A Study of Nine American Women Novelists.* Minneapolis: University of Minnesota Press, 1961.

Baker, Bruce Paul. "Nebraska Regionalism in Selected Works of Willa Cather." *Western American Literature* 3 (Spring 1968): 19–35.

Beckman, Don. "The Song of the Lark." *Opera News* 35 (27 February 1971): 6–7.

Bergson, Henri. "Introduction à la Métaphysique." In *Revue de Métaphysique et de Morale,* vol. 11 (1903) (Librairie Armand Colin). Repr. 1965, Johnson Reprint Corporation.

Berkove, Lawrence. "*A Lost Lady*: The Portrait of a Survivor." In vol. 1 of *The Willa Cather Yearbook,* edited by Debbie A. Hanson. Lewiston, N.Y.: Edwin Mellen Press, 1991.

Bettelheim, Bruno. *The Uses of Enchantment.* New York: Alfred A. Knopf, 1975.

Bloom, Edward A., and Lillian D. Bloom. *Willa Cather's Gift of Sympathy.* Carbondale: Southern Illinois University Press, 1962.

Bloom, Harold. Introduction. *Modern Critical Interpretations; Willa Cather's My Àntonia.* New York: Chelsea House Publishers, 1987.

Bogan, Louise. "American-Classic." *The New Yorker* (8 August 1931): 19–22. Repr. in James Schroeter, ed., *Willa Cather and her Critics.* Ithaca: Cornell University Press, 1967.

Booth, Alice. "Willa Cather." *Good Housekeeping* 93 (September 1931): 34–35, 196–98.

Bourne, Randolphe. "Diminuendo." Unsigned review of *The Song of the Lark*, almost certainly by Randolphe Bourne. *The New Republic* 5 (11 December 1915): 153–54.

———. "Morals and Art from the West." Review of *My Àntonia*. *Dial* 65 (14 December 1918): 557.

Boynton, Percy H. "Willa Cather." *English Journal* 13 (June 1924): 373–80.

Boyton, H. W. "Varieties of Realism." *Nation* 101(14 October 1915): 461–62.

Brooks, Van Wyck. *The Confident Years: 1885–1915*. New York: EP Dutton, 1952.

Brown, E. K. *Willa Cather: A Critical Biography*. Completed by Leon Edel. New York: Alfred A. Knopf, 1953.

Brunauer, Dalma. "The Problem of Point of View in *A Lost Lady*." *Renascence* 28 (Autumn 1974): 47–48.

Callander, Marilyn Berg. *Willa Cather and the Fairy Tale*. Ann Arbor, Mich.: UMI Research Press, 1989.

Canby, Henry Seidel. "A Novel of the Soul" (a review of *The Professor's House*). *Saturday Review of Literature* 2 (26 September 1925): 151. Repr. in *Critical Essays on Willa Cather*, edited by John J. Murphy. Boston: G. K. Hall, 1984.

Carroll, Latrobe. "Willa Sibert Cather." *Bookman* 52 (3 May 1921): 212–16.

Cather, Willa. "Alexander's Masquerade." *McClure's* 38 (February 1912): 385–95; (March 1912): 523–36; (April 1912): 659–68.

———. "Nebraska: The End of the First Cycle." In *These United States*, edited by Ernest Gruening. New York: Boni and Liveright, 1924.

———. "Plays of Real Life." *McClure's* 40 (5) (March 1913): 63–72.

———. "Portrait of the Publisher as a Young Man." In *Alfred A. Knopf Quarter Century*. Norwood, Mass.: Plimpton Press, 1940.

———. "The Birth of Personality: An Appreciation of Thomas Mann's Biblical Trilogy." *The Saturday Review of Literature* (6 June 1936): 3–4, 20–21.

———. "Three American Singers." *McClure's* 42 (2) (December 1913): 33–48.

Commager, Henry Steele. "Traditionalism in American Literature." *Nineteenth Century and After* 146 (November 1949): 311–26.

Connolly, Francis X. "Willa Cather: Memory as Muse." In *Fifty Years of the American Novel: A Christian Appraisal*, edited by Harold C. Gardiner. New York: Charles Scribner's Sons, 1952.

Cooper, Frederick Taber. "Big Moments in Fiction and Some Recent Novels." *Bookman* 37 (August 1913): 666–67.

Cooper, James Fenimore. *The Pioneers or The Sources of the Susquehanna*. New York: Penguin, 1823, repr. 1964.

Cousineau, Diane. "Division and Difference in *A Lost Lady*." *Women's Studies* 11(December 1984): 305–22.

Daiches, David. *Willa Cather: A Critical Introduction*. Ithaca: Cornell University Press, 1951; repr. New York: Collier Books, 1962.

Dell, Floyd. "A Good Novel." *Chicago Evening Post Literary Review*, 25 July 1913.

Dillman, Richard. "Tom Outland: Emerson's American Scholar in *The Professor's House*." *The Midwest Quarterly* 25 (Summer 1984): 375–85.

Donohue, John W. "Two Women: A Centennial." *America* 128 (31 March 1973): 276–79.

Donovan, Josephine. *After the Fall: The Demeter-Persephone Myth in Wharton, Cather, and Glasgow*. University Park, Pa.: The Pennsylvania State Press, 1988.

Edel, Leon. "A Cave of One's Own." In *Critical Essays on Willa Cather*, edited by John J. Murphy. Boston: G. K. Hall, 1984.

———. "Willa Cather: The Paradox of Success." Lecture delivered at the Library of Congress, 12 October 1959, Washington, D. C.: Library of Congress, 1960. In James Schroeter, ed., *Willa Cather and her Critics*. Ithaca: Cornell University Press, 1967.

Emerson, Ralph Waldo. "The American Scholar." *Selections from Ralph Waldo Emerson*, edited by Stephen E. Whicher. Boston: Houghton Mifflin, 1960.

———. *The Journals and Miscellaneous Notebooks of Ralph Waldo Emerson*. Vol. 3. Edited by William H. Gilman, et. al. Cambridge: Belknap Press of Harvard University Press, 1963.

———. "Nature." In *Selections from Ralph Waldo Emerson*, edited by Stephen E. Whicher. Boston: Houghton Mifflin, 1960.

———. "The Poet." In *Selections from Ralph Waldo Emerson*, edited by Stephen E. Whicher. Boston: Houghton Mifflin, 1960.

Fadiman, Clifton. "Willa Cather: The Past Recaptured." *Nation* 135 (7 December 1932): 563–65.

Feger, Lois, "The Dark Dimension of Willa Cather's *My Àntonia*." *English Journal* 59 (September 1970): 774–79.

Fetterley, Judith. "*My Àntonia*, Jim Burden, and the Dilemma of the Lesbian Writer." In *Lesbian Texts and Contexts: Radical Revisions*, edited by Karla Jay and Joanne Glasgow. New York: New York University Press, 1990.

Fisher, Dorothy Canfield. *New York Times Book Review* 10 September 1922.

Fisher-Wirth, Ann. "Dispossession and Redemption in the Novels of Willa Cather." In *Cather Studies*, edited by Susan J. Rosowski (Lincoln: University of Nebraska Press, 1990), 1:36–54.

———. "Womanhood and Art in *My Àntonia*." In *Willa Cather: Family, Community, and History*, edited by John J. Murphy et. al. Provo, Utah: Brigham Young University, Humanities Publishing Center, 1990.

Fitzgerald, F. Scott. *The Great Gatsby*. New York: Charles Scribner's Sons, 1925.

Ford, James L. "Willa Cather Visits the Cliff-Dwellers." *The Literary Digest International Book Review* 3 (November 1925): 775.

Fox, Maynard. "Two Primitives: Huck Finn and Tom Outland." *Western American Literature* 1 (Spring 1966): 26–33.

Freud, Sigmund. "Beyond the Pleasure Principle." In vol. 28 of *The Standard Edition of the Complete Psychological Works of Sigmund Freud*, edited and translated by James Strachey. London: Hogarth Press, 1955.

———. "Family Romances." Vol. 14 of *Standard Edition of the Complete Psychological Works of Sigmund Freud*, edited and translated by James Strachey. London: Hogarth Press, 1958.

———. "On Narcissism: An Introduction." In vol. 14 of *Standard Edition of the Complete Psychological Works of Sigmund Freud*, edited and translated by James Strachey. London: Hogarth Press, 1957.

Frost, Robert. "The Oven Bird." In *The Poetry of Robert Frost*, edited by Edward Connery Lathem. New York: Holt, Rinehart and Winston, 1969.

Freydberg, Margaret. "Willa Cather: The Light Behind her Books." *American Scholar* 43 (Spring 1974): 282–87.

Fryer, Judith. "What Goes on in the Ladies Room? Sarah Orne Jewett, Annie Fields, and Their Community of Women." *Massachusetts Review: A Quarterly of Literature, the Arts and Public Affairs* (Winter 1989): 610–28.

G., F. A. "A Woman's Climb from Nebraska to the Stage." Review of *The Song of the Lark. Boston Evening Transcript* 13 (October 1915): 22.

Gale, Zona. "My Favorite Character in Fiction." *Bookman* 63 (May 1926): 322–23.

Geismar, Maxwell. "Willa Cather: Lady in the Wilderness." In *The Last of the Provincials: The American Novel, 1915–1925*. Boston: Houghton Mifflin, 1947. Repr. in James Schroeter, ed., *Willa Cather and her Critics*. Ithaca: Cornell University Press, 1967.

Gelfant, Blanche H. "The Forgotten Reaping-Hook: Sex in *My Àntonia*." *American Literature* 43 (March 1971): 60–82.

———. Introduction. *O Pioneers!*, by Willa Cather. New York: Viking Penguin, 1989.

Gerber, Philip. *Willa Cather*. Twayne United States Authors Series. Boston: G. K. Hall, 1975.

Giannone, Richard. *Music in Willa Cather's Fiction*. Lincoln: University of Nebraska Press, 1968.

Gilbert, Sandra M., and Susan Gubar. *The Madwoman in the Attic: The Woman Writer and the Nineteenth-Century Literary Imagination*. New Haven: Yale University Press, 1979.

Gleason, John B. "The 'Case' of Willa Cather." *Western American Literature* 20 (1986): 275–99.

Grumbach, Doris. "A study of the small room in *The Professor's House*." *Women's Studies* 11 (1984): 327–45.

Harrell, David. "Willa Cather's Mesa Verde Myth." *Cather Studies* (Lincoln: University of Nebraska Press, 1990), 1:130–43.

Hart, Clive. "'The Professor's House': A Shapely Story." *Modern Language Review* 67 (April 1972): 271–81.

Helmick, Evelyn. "The Mysteries of Àntonia." *The Midwest Quarterly* 17 (Winter 1976): 173–85.

Hicks, Granville. "The Case Against Willa Cather." *English Journal* 22 (November 1933): 703–10. Repr. in James Schroeter, ed., *Willa Cather and her Critics*. Ithaca: Cornell University Press, 1967.

Hoffman, Frederick J. *The Twenties: American Writing in the Postwar Decade*. New York: Viking Press, 1955.

Jewett, Sarah Orne. *The Country of the Pointed Firs and Other Stories*. Edited by Mary Ellen Chase. New York: Norton, 1981.

———. *Letters of Sarah Orne Jewett*, edited by Annie Fields. Boston: Houghton Mifflin, 1911.

Kazin, Alfred. *On Native Grounds: An Interpretation of Modern American Prose Literature*. New York: Reynal & Hitchcock, 1942.

———. *Twentieth-Century Literary Criticism*. Vol. 11. Detroit: Gale Research Company, 1978.

Keough, James. "Willa Cather's Pastoral Vision: Going Home to Rural America." *Sierra* 64 (January-February 1979): 62–66.

Knopf, Alfred A. "Random Recollections of a Publisher." *Massachusetts Historical Society Proceedings* 73 (1961): 92–103.

———. "Miss Cather." In *The Art of Willa Cather*, edited by Bernice Slote and Virginia Faulkner. Lincoln: University of Nebraska Press, 1974.

Kronenberger, Louis. "Willa Cather." *Bookman* 74 (October 1931): 134–40.

Lambert, Deborah. "The Defeat of a Hero: Autonomy and Sexuality in *My Àntonia*." *American Literature* 53 (1982): 676–90.

Lawrence, Margaret. *The School of Femininity: A Book for and about Women as They Are Interpreted Through Feminine Writers of Yesterday and Today*. New York: Frederick A. Stokes Co., 1936.

Leddy, Michael. "*The Professor's House*: The Sense of an Ending." *Studies in the Novel* 23 (Winter 1991): 443–50.

Lee, Hermione. *Willa Cather: Double Lives*. New York: Pantheon Books, 1989.

Lewis, Sinclair. "The Greatest American Novelist." *Newsweek* 11 (3 January 1938): 29.

Love, Glen A. "The Cowboy in the Laboratory: Willa Cather's Hesitant Moderns." In *The Westerner and the Modern Experience in the American Novel*. Lewisburg, Pa.: Bucknell University Press, 1982.

Lovett, Robert Morss. " A Death in the Desert." *New Republic* 52 (26 October 1927): 266–67.

Madigan, Mark. "Willa Cather and Dorothy Canfield Fisher: Rift, Reconciliation, and *One of Ours*." *Cather Studies* (Lincoln: University of Nebraska Press, 1990), 1:115–29.

Mahoney, Eva. "How Willa Cather Found Herself." *Omaha World Herald*, 27 November 1921, pp. 7–12.

Martin, Terence. "The Drama of Memory in *My Àntonia*." *PMLA* 84 (March 1969): 304–11.

Maxfield, James F. "Strategies of Self-Deception in Willa Cather's *Professor's House*." *Studies in the Novel* 16 (Spring 1984): 72–84.

Mencken, H. L. "Sunrise on the Prairie." *Smart Set* 58 (February 1919): 143–44. Repr. in James Schroeter, ed., *Willa Cather and her Critics*. Ithaca: Cornell University Press, 1967.

Middleton, Jo Ann. *Willa Cather's Modernism: A Study of Style and Technique*. Cranbury, N.J.: Associated University Presses, 1990.

Miller, James E., Jr. "*My Àntonia*: A Frontier Drama of Time." *American Quarterly* 10 (4) (Winter 1958): 476–84.

———. "My Àntonia and the American Dream." *Prairie Schooner* 48 (Summer 1974): 112–23.

Morris, Lloyd. "Willa Cather." *North American Review* 219 (May 1924): 641–52.

Morrison, Toni. *Playing in the Dark: Whiteness and the Literary Imagination*. Cambridge: Harvard University Press, 1992.

Murphy, John J. "A Comprehensive View of Cather's *O Pioneers!*" In *Critical Essays on Willa Cather*, edited by John J. Murphy. Boston: G. K. Hall, 1984.

———. "Cather's New World Divine Comedy: The Dante Connection." In *Cather Studies*, edited by Susan J. Rosowski (Lincoln: University of Nebraska Press, 1990), 1:21–35.

———. "The Respectable Romantic and the Unwed Mother: Class Consciousness in 'My Àntonia.'" *Colby Library Quarterly* 10 (September 1973): 149–56.

———. "Willa Cather and Catholic Themes." *Western American Literature* 17 (1982): 53–60.

Murphy, John J., ed. *Critical Essays on Willa Cather*. Boston: G. K. Hall, 1984.

———. *Literature and Belief: Willa Cather Issue*. Provo, Utah: Brigham Young University, 1988.

Nichols, Kathleen. "The Celibate Male in *A Lost Lady*: The Unreliable Center of Consciousness." *Regionalism and the Female Imagination* 4 (1978): 13–23.

Novak, Frank. "Crisis and Discovery in *The Professor's House*." *Colby Library Quarterly* (1986): 119–32.

O'Brien, Sharon. "Becoming Noncanonical: The Case Against Willa Cather." *American Quarterly* 40 (1) (March 1988): 110–26.

———. "Mothers, Daughters, and the 'Art Necessity': Willa Cather and the Creative Process." In *American Novelists Revisited: Essays in Feminist Criticism*, edited by Fritz Fleischmann, pp. 265–98. Boston: G. K. Hall, 1982.

———. "'The Thing Not Named': Willa Cather as a Lesbian Writer." *Signs* 9, no. 4 (Summer, 1984): 576–601.

———. "The Unity of Willa Cather's 'Two-Part Pastoral': Passion in *O Pioneers!*" *Studies in American Fiction* 6 (1978): 157–71.

———. *Willa Cather: The Emerging Voice*. New York: Oxford University Press, 1987.

O'Connor, Margaret Anne. "A Guide to the Letters of Willa Cather." *Resources for American Literary Study* 4 (Autumn 1974): 145–72.

Orme-Johnson, Rhoda F. "The Uses of Names in *The Professor's House*." In *The Willa Cather Yearbook*, vol. 1, edited by Debbie A. Hanson. Lewiston, N.Y.: The Edwin Mellen Press, 1991.

Peterman, Michael. "Kindling the Imagination: The Inset Stories of *My Àntonia*." In *Approaches to Teaching Cather's* My Àntonia, edited by Susan J. Rosowski. New York: The Modern Language Association of America, 1989.

Poirier, Richard. *A World Elsewhere; The Place of Style in American Literature*. New York: Oxford University Press, 1966.

Quirk, Tom. *Bergson and American Culture: The Worlds of Willa Cather and Wallace Stevens*. Chapel Hill: The University of North Carolina Press, 1990.

Randall, John. *The Landscape and the Looking Glass: Willa Cather's Search for Value*. Cambridge: The Riverside Press, 1960.

Rapin, René. *Willa Cather*. Modern American Writers Series, edited by Ernest Boyd. New York: Robert M. McBride & Co., 1930.

Review of *O Pioneers! Nation* 97 (4 September 1913): 210–11.

Rich, Adrienne. *On Lies, Secrets, and Silence: Selected Prose 1966-1978*. New York: Norton, 1979.

Robinson, Phyllis. *Willa: The Life of Willa Cather*. Garden City, N. Y.: Doubleday, 1983.

Romines, Ann. *The Home Plot: Women, Writing and Domestic Ritual*. Amherst: University of Massachusetts Press, 1992.

Rosenburg, Carol Smith. "The Female World of Love and Ritual: Relations Between Women in Nineteenth Century America." In *Disorderly Conduct: Visions of Gender in Victorian America*. New York: Knopf, 1985.

Rosowski, Susan J. "The Pattern of Willa Cather's Novels." *Western American Literature* 15 (1981): 243–63.

———. *The Voyage Perilous: Willa Cather's Romanticism*. Lincoln: University of Nebraska Press, 1986.

———. "Willa Cather — A Pioneer in Art: *O Pioneers!* and *My Àntonia*." *Prairie Schooner* 55 (Spring-Summer 1981): 141–44.

———. "Willa Cather's Pioneer Women: A Feminist Interpretation." In *Where the West Begins: Essays on Middle Border and Siouxland Writing, in Honor of Herbert Krause*, edited by Arthur R. Heseboe and William Geyer. Sioux Falls, S. D.: Center for Western Studies, 1978.

———. "Willa Cather's Women." *Studies in American Fiction* 9 (Autumn 1981): 261–75.

———. "Writing Against Silences: Female Adolescent Development in the Novels of Willa Cather." *Studies in the Novel* 21 (Spring 1989): 60–77.

——— and Bernice Slote. "Willa Cather's 1916 Mesa Verde Essay: The Genesis of *The Professor's House*." *Prairie Schooner* 58 (Winter 1984): 81–92.

Satir, Virginia. *Peoplemaking*. Palo Alto, CA: Science and Behavior Books, Inc., 1972.

Scholes, Robert. "Hope and Memory in *My Àntonia*." *Shenandoah* 14 (Autumn 1962): 24–29.

Schroeter, James, ed. *Willa Cather and Her Critics*. Ithaca, N. Y.: Cornell University Press, 1967.

Schwind, Jean. "The Benda Illustrations to *My Àntonia*: Cather's 'Silent' Supplement to Jim Burden's Narrative." *PMLA* 100 (1) (January 1985): 51–67.

———. "Fine and Folk Art in *The Song of the Lark*: Cather's Pictorial Sources." *Cather Studies* 1 (Lincoln: University of Nebraska Press, 1990): 89–102.

Selzer, John. "Jim Burden and the Structure of *My Àntonia*." *Western American Literature* 24 (1989): 45–61.

Shaw, Patrick. *Willa Cather & the Art of Conflict*. Troy, NY.: Whitston Publishing Company, 1992.

———. "Women and the Father: Psychosexual Ambiguity in *Death Comes for the Archbishop*." *American Imago* 46 (Spring 1989): 61–76.

Skaggs, Merrill Maguire. *After the World Broke in Two: The Later Novels of Willa Cather*. Charlottesville: University Press of Virginia, 1990.

Slote, Bernice. Introduction. *Alexander's Bridge,* by Willa Cather. Lincoln: University of Nebraska Press, 1977.

———. "Willa Cather as a Regional Writer." *Kansas Quarterly* 2 (Spring 1970): 7–15.

——— and Virginia Faulkner, eds. *The Art of Willa Cather*. Lincoln: University of Nebraska Press, 1974.

Sontag, Susan. *On Photography*. New York: Farrar, Straus and Giroux, 1977.

Stouck, David. "Perspective as Structure and Theme in *My Àntonia*." *Texas Studies in Literature and Language* 12 (Summer 1970): 285–94.

———. "Willa Cather and the Impressionist Novel." In *Critical Essays on Willa Cather*, edited by John J. Murphy. Boston: G. K. Hall, 1984.

———. "Willa Cather and *The Professor's House*: 'Letting Go With the Heart.'" *Western American Literature* 7 (1972): 13–24.

———. *Willa Cather's Imagination*. Lincoln: University of Nebraska Press, 1975.

Strychacz, Thomas. "The Ambiguities of Escape in Willa Cather's *The Professor's House*." *Studies in American Fiction* 14 (1986): 50–51.

Swift, John. "Cather's Archbishop and the 'Backward Path.'" *Cather Studies* (Lincoln: University of Nebraska Press, 1990), 1:55–67.

———. "The Family Romance of *A Lost Lady*." Paper presented at the National Willa Cather Symposium, Brigham Young University, September 1988.

———. "Memory, Myth, and *The Professor's House*." *Western American Literature* 20 (1986): 301–14.

Thoreau, Henry David. *The Portable Thoreau*. Revised edition. Edited by Carl Bode. New York: Penguin Books, 1979.

Tompkins, Jane. *Sensational Designs: The Cultural Work of American Fiction: 1790–1860*. New York: Oxford University Press, 1985.

Trilling, Lionel. "Willa Cather." In *After the Genteel Tradition: American Writers 1910–1930*, edited by Malcolm Cowley. New York: W. W. Norton & Co., 1937. Repr. in James Schroeter, ed., *Willa Cather and her Critics*. Ithaca: Cornell University Press, 1967.

Urgo, Joseph. "How Context Determines Fact: Historicism in Willa Cather's *A Lost Lady.*" *Studies in American Fiction* 17 (1989): 183–92.

Van Doren, Carl. "Willa Cather." In *Contemporary American Novelists: 1900–1920.* New York: Macmillan, 1922. Repr. in James Schroeter, ed., *Willa Cather and her Critics.* Ithaca: Cornell University Press, 1967.

Van Ghent, Dorothy. *Willa Cather.* University of Minnesota Pamphlets on American Writers. No. 36. Minneapolis: University of Minnesota Press, 1964.

Wasserman, Loretta. "The Music of Time: Henri Bergson and Willa Cather." *American Literature* (May 1985): 226–39.

———. *Willa Cather: A Study of the Short Fiction.* Boston: Twayne Publishers, 1991.

Whipple, T. K. "Willa Cather." *New York Evening Post* 4 (8 December 1923): 331–32. Repr. in James Schroeter, ed., *Willa Cather and Her Critics.* Ithaca: Cornell University Press, 1967.

White, George L., Jr. "Willa Cather." Summaries of Eminent Living Novelists. *Sewanee Review* 50 (January-March 1942): 18–25.

Wiesenthal, Susan C. "Female Sexuality in Willa Cather's 'O Pioneers!' and the Era of Scientific Sexology: A Dialogue Between Frontiers." *Ariel: A Review of International English Literature* 21(January 1990): 41–63.

Williams, Michael. "Willa Cather's Masterpiece." *The Commonweal* 6 (28 September 1927): 490–92.

Wilson, Edmund. Review of *A Lost Lady.* *Dial* 76 (January 1924): 79–80. Repr. in James Schroeter, ed., *Willa Cather and her Critics.* Ithaca: Cornell University Press, 1967.

Winters, Laura. *Willa Cather: Landscape and Exile.* Selinsgrove, Pa.: Susquehanna University Press, 1993.

Woodress, James. *Willa Cather: A Literary Life.* Lincoln: University of Nebraska Press, 1987.

———. *Willa Cather: Her Life and Art.* New York: Pegasus, 1970.

Yongue, Patricia Lee. "Willa Cather and Edith Lewis: Two Stories, Two Friends." In *The Willa Cather Yearbook,* vol. 1, edited by Debbie A. Hanson. Lewiston: The Edwin Mellen Press, 1991.

Zamora, Lois Parkinson. "The Usable Past: The Idea of History in Modern U. S. and Latin American Fiction." In *Do the Americas Have a Common Literature?,* edited by Gustavo Pérez Firmat. Durham: Duke University Press, 1990.

General Index